D1103860

Semiotic Perspectives

Semiotic Perspectives

Sándor Hervey
Reader in Linguistics, University of St Andrews

London
GEORGE ALLEN & UNWIN
Boston   Sydney

George Allen & Unwin (Publishers) Ltd,
40 Museum Street, London WC1A 1LU, UK

George Allen & Unwin (Publishers) Ltd,
Park Lane, Hemel Hempstead, Herts HP2 4TE, UK

Allen & Unwin, Inc.,
9 Winchester Terrace, Winchester, Mass. 01890, USA

George Allen & Unwin Australia Pty Ltd,
8 Napier Street, North Sydney, NSW 2060, Australia

First published in 1982

British Library Cataloguing in Publication Data

Hervey, Sándor
    Semiotic perspectives.
1. Semiotics
I. Title
001.51   P99
ISBN 0-04-400026-X

Library of Congress Cataloging in Publication Data

Hervey, Sándor G. J.
    Semiotic perspectives.
Bibliography: p.
Includes index.
1. Semiotics.   I. Title.
P99.H45 1982   001.51   82-8761
ISBN 0-04-400026-X   AACR2

Set in 10 on 11 point Times by
Rowland Phototypesetting Ltd, Bury St Edmunds, Suffolk
and printed in Great Britain
by Mackays of Chatham

Contents

Semiotic Perspectives

Introduction

My main purpose in these opening pages will be to call attention to – and, hopefully, to encourage the reader to ponder for himself – a number of basic and general issues concerning that vast field of study currently designated by the term 'semiotics'.

Naturally, the most fundamental point to ponder is this: what are the *typical questions semiotics poses for itself*? Whether we can put our finger on one single factor that provides widely divergent semiotic approaches with a homogeneous *raison d'être* depends on our ability to give a fairly satisfactory answer to this question.

There are, both in human behaviour and in the behaviour of other species, certain striking phenomena that, once they have been observed, show themselves in need of special explanation. Here are some random examples, formulated in a deliberately 'naïve' way:

(1) drivers, in general, do not enter streets displaying a device consisting of a red circle enclosing a horizontal white bar;
(2) the arm movements of a policeman on traffic duty 'control' the flow of traffic at an intersection;
(3) the play of coloured lights at certain street intersections 'controls' the flow of traffic;
(4) the vocal utterances of customers in a shop or restaurant 'determine' the products they are given by the staff;
(5) certain gestures seem invariably to evoke an angry response;
(6) a man wearing open sandals, frayed jeans, loose top, beads round his neck, long hair and an untrimmed beard will almost certainly be refused admittance to a smart hotel;
(7) a product glamorously presented in television advertising enjoys a rise in sales;
(8) a poem, play, novel or film may have the effect of making people laugh or cry;
(9) certain 'ritualised' movements seem to be a prerequisite to mating in animal species;
(10) certain 'ritualised' movements made by a 'scout' bee on returning to the hive appear to stimulate foragers to proceed directly to a nectar source.

In all these rather disparate examples, there is, however, a common factor: in all cases, we observe manifestations that tend – on the face of it somewhat unaccountably – to influence behaviour in more or less specific ways. These 'manifestations' are normally referred to as 'signals': the explanation for their tendencies to influence behaviour is that they do so by way of conveying 'messages'. The conveying of 'messages' by 'signals' constitutes the prototype of the phenomenon of 'communication'. Whether one conceives of *communication* as a dynamic process or as a static potential possessed by 'signals', whether one considers it in the context of the roles of 'sender' and 'receiver', or by making abstraction of these participants in a communicative act, the fact remains that communication draws its being from a *correlation* between 'signal' and 'message'.

The typical questions semiotics poses are all connected with the phenomenon of communication, conceived of as a correlation between 'signal' and 'message':

(*a*) Is there a correlation between *x* and *y* in such a way as to make *x* a 'signal' and *y* its corresponding 'message'?
(*b*) What form(s) does the 'signal' *x* take?
(*c*) What is the nature of the 'message' *y*?
(*d*) What motivates the correlation between 'signal' *x* and 'message' *y*?

In the light of the discussion so far, we may safely contend that, in all its varying forms, semiotics is the study of a phenomenon that manifests itself as a particular type of correlation: that between 'signals' and 'messages'. The individual items under scrutiny – occurrences of this type of correlative phenomenon – are 'communication acts/events'. Semiotics concerns itself, *par excellence*, with 'communication acts/events'.

Within this principle that offers an underlying homogeneity and unity to semiotics as a branch of 'learning', we must also accommodate the rather obvious disparity between an indefinite number of approaches that go under the name of 'semiotics'. To anyone who attempts to read widely in the subject (exhaustive reading is humanly impossible) it will soon become apparent that, rather than being a single, unified discipline, semiotics is an agglomeration of approaches with varying points of focus, varying points of view and varying scopes.

It is, perhaps, at this juncture that the reader can most conveniently be alerted concerning certain expectations that he might have formed on the basis of the title of this volume. In writing the volume, I have singled out a number of prominent semiotic approaches, approaches that are individually presented as various 'guises' in which semiotics appears on the current academic scene. The sum total of these approaches still fails by far to do justice to the real plethora of works that claim, or deserve (the two are not necessarily co-extensive) the title of 'semiotics'. While the expert on semiotics will doubtless discover many regrettable omissions, the total non-initiate may still find more than enough variety with which to cope. My coverage, in other words, falls somewhat short of an exhaustive sampling of all major areas of semiotics, yet is cast in wide enough terms to qualify as a general 'overview' of the subject. There is, I suppose, a basic 'minimum' (though one that would be hard to define) of prominent approaches in semiotics that ought not to go unmentioned in a work of this kind. On the whole, however, I have given preference to a more in-depth discussion of a smaller sample of approaches over a more bibliographically complete (but also more superficial) treatment of a larger sample. Whether in doing so, I have succeeded in capturing a 'representative sample' is for the reader to judge.

Where an agglomeration of ideas cannot be listed, it becomes necessary, even at the risk of a resulting distortion and over-simplification, to generalise and to classify them. These risks notwithstanding, I shall offer certain salient ways in which semiotic approaches may be classified.

The crudest, though still relevant, categorisation is a purely 'geographical' one, according to which it is common to distinguish between (*a*) American trends in semiotics (for example, Peirce, Morris, Searle) and (*b*) European trends in semiotics (for example, Saussure, Prieto, functionalism, Barthes).

Many scholars have seen an almost unbridgeable gulf between the two traditions of American and European semiotics. As 'traditions', the two do, indeed, seem to be remarkably isolated from each other. This is not to say, however, that we should continue to conceive of semiotics as being divided into two 'camps' permanently sealed off one from the other. Though genuine attempts at a synthesis between the two traditions are few and far between (for example, Eco, 1976), there are approaches that have exercised an equal influence on both sides of the Atlantic (for example, Austin's theory of 'speech acts', or the semiology of Barthes).

A more intellectually satisfying way of classifying semiotic approaches is in terms of their scope and focus of interest. In blunt terms, there are semiotic points of view that lay claim to almost every area of behaviour as belonging (at least in principle) to their scope, as well as semiotic theses that focus exclusively on some highly specialised area (for example, semiotics of poetry, semiotics of the cinema, zoo-semiotic research).

Setting aside those approaches that, rather than attempting to offer a 'general' theory, concentrate on the elaboration of descriptive methodologies focusing on specialised topics, we are left, in essence, with the following categories of 'general' semiotics:

(1)   semiotic theories with a wide scope: theories whose scope of interest extends to *communication* as a whole (that is, everything that 'signifies' is semiotic); Peirce and Morris fall into this category;

(2)   semiotic theories with a medium scope:

    (*a*)   theories whose scope covers only cases of deliberate, conventional forms of communication (Austin, Searle and Prieto fall into this category);

    (*b*)   theories whose scope covers only systematic forms of communication (that is, everything that forms a system of 'signification' is semiotic); Barthesian semiology exemplifies this category;

(3)   semiotic theories with a narrow scope: theories whose scope is, in principle at least, restricted to systems of conventions for communication (that is, only 'signals' from conventional systems in-

tended for communication are semiotic); Saussure, functionalism and axiomatic semiotics belong to this category.

Adopting a semiotic theory with a wide scope is not necessarily an advantage – a theory designed to cover 'signification' in general is a relatively blunt instrument when interest is focused specifically on the difference between conventional 'signals' and 'natural signification' (for example, the interpreting of symptoms), or between systematic 'signals' and randomly significative phenomena. By being wide in scope, a theory tends to blur and distort important distinctions.

Theories with a medium scope experience some of the same problems of focus: those designed to cover deliberate and conventional forms of communication find it difficult to build up a picture of semiotic systems, and tend to treat all conventional 'signals' in an 'anecdotal' fashion; those designed to cover systems of communication underestimate the fundamental differences between conventional and causal or instinctual behaviour, and tend to be over-enthusiastic in 'discovering' systems of 'signification' in all forms of behaviour. Theories with a medium scope also have a tendency to transcend their rather fluid limits, thus assuming, to all practical purposes, a wide scope.

Semiotic theories with a narrow scope have a less catholic view of 'semiotic events' in general, but, by being restricted, they have the advantage of focusing on a more homogeneous set of phenomena. Applying a homogeneous set of principles within a relatively more homogeneous scope, they are, therefore, less liable to distort what they describe. A rigorous application of a narrowly defined scope is also less prone to producing a fluid scope with a wide band of 'marginal' borderline cases.

Semiotic theories can be placed into three broad categories of 'inductive', 'deductive' and 'speculative' types. Without attempting to go into too sophisticated details, this categorisation is made with respect to the type of 'theory-building strategy' employed by various theories:

(1) an 'inductive' theory is built up by observing and collating observed instances of communication, and drawing subsequent generalisations from these phenomena (for example, Morris, Austin);
(2) a 'deductive' theory is constructed from abstract and general principles (for which experience with observed data provides only an informal background), and its adequacy is tested by subsequent descriptive applications to semiotic phenomena (for example, Saussure, functionalism, axiomatic semiotics);
(3) a 'speculative' theory builds up its conjectural tenets (whether under the guise of 'observations', or as general and abstract principles) as a convenient 'fiction', but endows them with reality in the light of their plausibility (for example, Barthes).

We shall refrain here from attempting to evaluate the relative merits of 'inductive', 'deductive' and 'speculative' theorising, and offer these categories merely as a useful way of registering and rationalising certain salient differences of attitude that give a different 'flavour' to the semiotic approaches discussed in this volume.

It should be noted that the volume does not in any way attempt to give a historical treatment of the agglomeration of semiotic disciplines. One result of this lack of 'historicity' is that it leaves little room for the discussion of semiotic controversies. There is, however, one continuing controversy, of a highly divisive nature, which deserves separate and general consideration here: namely, the controversial relationship between linguistics and semiotics.

The two extremes of this controversy can be formulated as follows:

(*a*) *linguistics* is the 'parent' discipline of semiotics; it has the more 'inclusive' theory – semiotics is the application of notions borrowed (or, at most, adapted) from linguistics to communication outside of natural language;
(*b*) *semiotics* is the meta-discipline of which linguistics is a sub-discipline; the scope of semiotics is inclusive of the scope of linguistics; linguistic notions are merely specialised semiotic notions developed particularly for describing natural languages.

A third, intermediate, position can be distinguished: namely, that linguistics and semiotics are separate, independent disciplines with mutually exclusive scopes (languages and non-linguistic semiotic systems respectively) and with a minimum of interchange of ideas and methods.

The position according to which linguistics is the 'parent' discipline of semiotics enjoys considerable popularity. The major points marshalled in favour of this position are aimed at demonstrating that natural language 'includes' all other systematic means of communication and that, therefore, *to know human natural language guarantees the understanding of the functioning of any other form of communication*. If this is the case, semiotics boils down simply to looking in other areas of communication for the properties first encountered in natural languages. This attitude makes semiotics into the application and extension of the descriptive methodology of linguistics to 'languages' other than human natural languages – typified by descriptions of 'the vocabulary of Braque' (in semiotics of painting) or 'the syntax of Rimsky-Korsakov' (in semiotics of music).

The inclusiveness of human natural language is in part bolstered by the observation that, whereas any message couched in non-linguistic terms can be expressed also in linguistic terms, linguistic messages cannot in general be expressed by non-linguistic means. This 'argument', however, is easily shown to be based on a *non sequitur*. The scope of linguistics and the scope of semiotics do not consist of 'messages', but of correlations between 'signals' and 'messages' – the 'inclusion' of non-linguistic 'messages' in linguistic ones does not, therefore, have anything to do with the relative scopes of linguistics and semiotics. What is involved is simply a matter of 'translatability'; 'messages' in non-linguistic systems are said, in general, to be translatable into natural languages, but not vice versa. This demonstrates the relative 'richness' of natural languages as compared to non-linguistic systems, but it is no argument for the inclusion of other systems in natural languages. If inclusion of one system in another could be deduced from 'inter-translatability', we should have to conclude, nonsensically, that English is included in French, and French in English.

As for the 'argument' that human language includes all the properties that one might encounter in other semiotic systems, this gets its support from two directions. In one direction, the argument might be said to be effective in that it satisfies the intuitions of the layman who is all too ready to place human language at the top of the 'evolutionary tree', with all other communication systems being satisfactorily reduced to the status of 'rudimentary languages' imperfectly foreshadowing, or imperfectly modelled on, natural language. In fact, however, as Mounin forcefully argues (Mounin, 1968), the designation of non-linguistic systems as 'languages' is merely metaphorical and question-begging. Justifying the assimilation of these systems to languages proper is a matter of structural similarities that should not be assumed, but should be independently established by comparison of the systems involved. Valid comparison, is however, out of the question once a 'language-like' nature has been imposed *a priori* on non-linguistic systems. The assumption that, by way of the inclusion of semiotics in linguistics, all communication systems are more or less rudimentary 'languages' is, therefore, to be rejected as being a mere prejudice detrimental to scientific investigation.

In another direction, the inclusion of all communication in human languages satisfies the descriptive needs of certain types of semiotics. While semiotics remains in practice the 'poor relation' of linguistics – inevitable if we consider the incalculable amount of research done in linguistics over the last two centuries – it would be unrealistic to expect linguistics to borrow its concepts and methods from semiotics, but extremely tempting and convenient for semiotics to draw on the conceptual armoury of linguistics. Under the circumstances – with linguistics being in fact the far more 'mature' discipline – it would seem to follow that any kind of 'fostering' relationship between the two disciplines must make linguistics into the 'parent' discipline. Such a line of 'argument' appears, however, to have fallen into the trap of giving a literal interpretation to the metaphorical term 'parent' discipline. The historical 'accident' whereby a part of a discipline constitutes a focal growth point prior to and far in advance of developments in other parts of the discipline does not make the developed part a 'parent' discipline of the under-developed part – we are not dealing with genuine genetic relationships here. At best, linguistics may be called a 'pilot' discipline of semiotics. The logical relationship remains unaffected by historical 'accident', and, as such, has to be decided on logical grounds.

As a matter of fact, unless the scope of semiotics is defined by explicit reference to the term 'non-linguistic', this scope will automatically include in its core the *genus* of natural languages, alongside an indefinite number of other communication systems. The only way to prevent the inclusion of the field of phenomena proper to linguistics in the field of phenomena proper to semiotics is by arbitrarily cutting off all links between linguistics and (non-linguistic) semiotics.

Principles designed for a narrow linguistic scope cannot reasonably be expected to apply in a satisfactory manner to a wider semiotic scope. On the other hand, principles designed for a wider scope of semiotic phenomena can only be declared irrelevant to natural languages if one is prepared to deny that *languages constitute a type of semiotic system*. It seems that even proponents of the 'linguistics includes semiotics' point of view are not prepared to go that far.

As long as natural languages fall automatically in the general category of semiotic systems, the most logical, as well as the methodologically soundest, strategy is to develop semiotics (and within it a semiotic linguistics) on the basis of a comparison between different structural types of semiotic system. Natural languages may still turn out to hold pride of place among these systems (by being the 'richest' and most structurally sophisticated), but only if they prove to deserve this position from a semiotic point of view. Nor will 'borrowing' of concepts from linguistics be totally precluded – though it will be restrained from running wild – as long as specifically linguistic terms are first traced back to the general semiotic principles from which they can be derived, and are only subsequently applied, *mutatis mutandis*, to semiotic systems at large.

As for the actual practice of an adaptation of descriptive linguistics for analysing such objects as paintings, music, sculpture, etc., it must be remembered that the mere possibility of such analyses does not establish the presumption that the resulting descriptions are worthwhile. After all, it is possible to base a description (in anthropology) of nuclear families on the model of inorganic chemistry: the 'chemical formula' H_2WC_4 could be used for representing a family as an 'inorganic compound' whose 'atoms' are two husbands, one wife and four children. (It is obvious that the borrowed terms of chemistry can only be taken metaphorically. It is, however, not clear just how literally one should interpret such terms as 'the vocabulary of Braque' or 'the syntax of Rimsky-Korsakov'.)

The analogy that makes an 'inorganic compound' out of H_2WC_4 does not, of course, entail the view that the structure of the nuclear family can be successfully affiliated to inorganic chemistry. For similar reasons, those who affiliate semiotics to linguistics are begging the question of the appropriateness of applying linguistic terms in semiotic analyses. The prevalent attitude seems to be: if it can be done at all, this proves that it was successfully done. However, as our everyday experience teaches, 'to do' is not a synonym of 'to do well'. The analogy, for instance, between inorganic compounds and the nuclear family is a possible one, but not a particularly good one, and certainly not one that is strong enough to support the inclusion of anthropology in inorganic chemistry (a ludicrous suggestion). Likewise, the analogy claimed between natural language and various 'rudimentary languages' may be a possible analogy, but not necessarily a good one – and certainly not one that is strong enough to justify the inclusion of semiotics in linguistics. On the whole, therefore, the wholesale application of linguistics to systems that are claimed *a priori* to be 'languages' is a practice whose value is suspect.

As a final note to this introductory discussion, we must add the explicit reminder that – even compared to linguistics – semiotics is a relatively new field of study. Although it presents rather a 'scattered' appearance – both in terms of its diverse schools of thought and in terms of the disparate areas it covers – it is a subject endowed with a considerable dynamism that makes it a force to be reckoned with in all branches of the humanities and social sciences. Without subscribing to the 'imperialistic' tendencies whereby some semiotic theories threaten to engulf all areas of human knowledge – an exaggerated pretension, to say the least – we should recognise semiotics as one of the most vital disciplines of our time.

1

A Background to Semiotics: Saussure and Peirce

1.1 Introduction

This chapter is intended to serve a twofold purpose. It sets the scene for later chapters in two ways.

First, it pinpoints the beginnings of modern semiotics in the works of the two pioneering figures of the discipline to whose respective points of view most of subsequent theorising in semiotics can be traced. These two major figures are Ferdinand de Saussure (1857–1913), the acclaimed founder of European-type *sémiologie*, and Charles S. Peirce (1839–1914), the originator of the American tradition in 'semiotic(s)'. The mutual autonomy of the European tradition of *sémiologie* and the American tradition of 'semiotic(s)' which, in general, has remained largely intact to date, finds its natural exposition as part of this dual background. (See for instance the remarks of Jeanne Martinet, in a paper presented at the University of St Andrews in spring 1980, who argues that the two traditions are so far apart as to make even a fruitful comparison impossible.)

Secondly, and equally importantly, this chapter presents an excellent opportunity for discussing, under the headings of salient Saussurean and Peircean ideas, a number of influential assumptions that semiologists or semioticians continue to make or to modify. A discussion of these rather fundamental assumptions, notions and distinctions would, if left till a later stage, seriously impede and interrupt the exposition of more recent developments in the field. These developments are, however, often not easy to explain, understand or appreciate without reference to the appropriate background of Saussurean or Peircean ideas. Without pretending to offer anything like a comprehensive account of the theories of Saussure and Peirce – such accounts can be found elsewhere (some are mentioned in the References) – this section aims to cover enough of the background of Saussurean and Peircean assumptions to make it possible for these assumptions to be taken for granted in the main body of the text.

1.2 Saussurean Fundamentals

1.2.1 *Form* versus *Substance*

In any scientific discourse worthy of the name, it is necessary to be able to make the shift from a purely observational consideration of single, concrete phenomena (which are individual variables) to a presentation of abstract entities which (by virtue of the very abstractions made) capture aspects of constancy and regularity in function or behaviour. In Saussurean theory, the distinction between the aspect of concrete, variable objects or events on the one hand, and the aspect of abstract constants (said to underlie the variables) on the other, is captured by the dichotomy of *substance versus form*.

One way of expressing this (essentially *concrete versus abstract*) dichotomy is by noting that, whereas 'reality' (the world of phenomena) consists of substances, systems and structures (the world of regularities, patterns, rules, and so on) contain forms. The forms of systems provide the 'rationale' behind, and thereby give a patterned appearance to, the essentially variable substances of 'reality' – forms are 'imposed on' substances; conversely, substances give concrete 'realisations' to forms. Without forms, substances would be amorphous, a hopeless jumble of senseless events; without substances, forms would be vacuous, and lacking in any kind of real, practical applicability.

A number of examples with a Saussurean flavour can be used to clarify both the distinction and the inter-relation between form and substance.

Example 1

> two 50p coins
> one £1 note
> £1's worth of assorted change
> £1's worth of assorted chocolates

all have the same monetary value (£1) and can be exchanged for one another

The monetary value   £1.00   (belonging to a system of monetary values) is a form – it is regular and constant over an imponderably large range of variable objects of all sorts of shapes and sizes; that is, everything that, at a given point 'is worth £1.00'. In fact, as anyone with a bank account is (sometimes painfully) aware, the monetary value £1.00 is a 'notional figure'. One can even have – £1.00 in one's account; whereas attaching a minus value to two actual 50p coins, or to an actual bundle of assorted change, is nonsensical. In other words, actual 50p pieces, bundles of assorted change, goods worth a certain sum, and so on, are concrete objects: they exemplify substance. Values attached to substances (making them equivalent to other substances having the same value) are 'imposed on' them by means of the forms (for example, £1.00, £5.00, and so on) of a monetary system. It is in this sense that the forms of a monetary system give structure to a range of substances to which monetary values are attached. Without monetary values, that is, forms, banknotes revert to being bits of paper, coins are just pieces of shaped metal, and goods are prized purely by immediate demand and supply.

Example 2

The Edinburgh–London night-train leaves every night at 10.30 p.m., provides sleeping accommodation and a restaurant-car, etc.

This way of speaking of *the* Edinburgh–London night-train (generically) creates the impression that we are dealing with one constant entity with regularly specifiable properties. Yet there is no guarantee that a single carriage, a single member of the crew, in fact any single concrete detail, will be the same on two different occasions of the departure of what we call 'the same train'. How are we to reconcile the obvious lack of sameness in terms of physical trappings with the equally obvious fact that, if I always travel to London from Edinburgh on a train leaving at 10.30 p.m., then I am fully entitled to say: 'I always go to London by *the same* train'?

The *form–substance* dichotomy makes immediate and complete sense of this apparent paradox. The 'sameness' of the 10.30 p.m. night-train is an 'abstract' sameness (it would be wiser to call it 'equivalence'), whereas the physical differences are a matter of 'concrete' detail. In other words, the concept of 'the 10.30 p.m. night-train from Edinburgh to London' is a form; the physical composition of particular trains leaving on particular occasions is a variable on the level of substance. While each night-train leaving Edinburgh for London at 10.30 p.m. is identical in form to every other such train, every single one of these trains is different in substance from the rest.

Example 3
Chess is a favourite example of semioticians and of philosophers of language (as we shall see later, Chapter 4, Section 4.5.5, p. 108). The distinction between form and substance is just one of the illustrations for which this example has been used.

In understanding, for instance, what a knight is in a game of chess, one needs reference to the system of rules in which it is determined how a knight functions in a game of chess. Its placing on the board, its characteristic L-shaped move – these are the things that set it apart from other chess-pieces, and 'make it what it is' (that is, these are the considerations that determine the identity of the piece). The knight considered in this light is a value in a system of other values, identified in abstraction from particular games of chess played with particular chess-sets; it is, in other words, a form in the system of chess. There are, of course, individual chess-pieces that one can hold in one's hand – they may be made of more or less any solid material, they can be shaped more or less at will, as long as they are recognisable as distinct from all other pieces with different values in the same chess set (this point will occupy us further on, Section 1:2.2, p. 12); if lost, they can even be temporarily replaced with some convenient object at hand. In short, the physical make-up of a particular chess-piece is a matter of substance. As long as the appropriate form is imposed on a given object, it can, irrespective of differences in substance, be perfectly viable in playing the role of a 'knight' in a game of chess. Form and substance are not only clearly different in the example of chess, but, of the two, form has a degree of priority over substance.

1.2.2   Opposition and Value – Identity Defined by Differences

From the foregoing example of chess we have gathered that the crucial factor in the identity of, say, the 'knight' (that which makes a 'knight' what it is) lies in the difference between what a 'knight' can do (according to the rules) and what other pieces can do. The sum total of the characteristics that make up the potentials of a 'knight', and which set this piece apart from other pieces, can be thought of as the *value* of a 'knight'. Since the value of a 'knight' is an abstraction of all that characterises 'knight'-hood (in chess), there is, to all intents and purposes, no difference between ' "knight" as a form in the system of chess' and 'the value of the "knight" in the system of chess'. That is to say, to all intents and purposes, it is just as correct to say that forms '*have* values' as it is to say that forms '*are* values'.

This point can be made with even more force through the example of monetary systems. While £1.00 is set apart from all other monetary non-equivalents through the difference between what one can do with £1.00 and what one can do with smaller or greater sums, the form £1.00 both *has* a definite and a determinate value, and *is* a definite and determinate value. Furthermore, to oppose (that is, differentiate or set apart) £1.00 to other alternative monetary values amounts to a practical demonstration of the definite and determinate nature of the value £1.00 (as one of the possible forms encountered in a monetary system). *Opposition*, which boils down to demonstrating the co-existence of different alternative forms that can be set off against each other in a given system, is both the criterion and the yardstick by which the value of any given form – and, therefore, its very being – is measured. As opposition entails difference, and the very being of a form (its value) is that which makes it different from all other forms, the identity of a form is neither more nor less than its differences from other forms. A form is what it is simply by virtue of not being any of the other (functionally non-equivalent) forms that co-exist with it in a given system.

The original Saussurean dictum: '*dans la langue il n'y a que des différences*' can be rephrased 'in systems, it is the *differences* that count'. This has important repercussions on one's whole way of thinking. Instead of starting with a positive conception of entities, the entities of a system (forms, not substances) are to emerge from a network of oppositions that are 'negatively' conceived. This attitude can be referred to as 'identity determined by differences'.

1.2.3   The Notion 'System'

While substances constitute amorphous and heterogeneous masses, systems consist of homogeneous and organised networks of forms. A system is an organised whole in which, in the words of Saussure, '*tout se tient*' (everything hangs together). In part this has already been said in connection with the way forms emerge out of networks of oppositions. What has not been mentioned is the abstraction made, in Saussurean thought, of the axis of time and change through time as part and parcel of the abstracting out of forms and systems of forms. Given that a system is a network of co-existing and mutually opposed alternatives, and that, by definition, everything must hang together in such a system, it is not possible, at one and the same time, to take account also of alternatives that used to exist, let alone of alternatives that may exist at some future stage. A system can only be conceived, or laid out, as it happens to be at some arbitrarily fixed point in time – with all the co-existing, opposed alternatives being seen as 'simultaneous'. This assumption can be crystallised in the statement that Saussure conceives of systems as being, by definition, *synchronic*.

It would be a complete misunderstanding to construe the above as a denial on the part of Saussure of the reality or relevance of continual processes of change that affect systems. On the contrary, it should be remembered that Saussure made his *début* in the field of *diachronic* (historical) linguistics, and counts among the advantages of his synchronic conception of systems (in particular, language-systems) the fact that it will facilitate and improve the whole methodology of diachronic linguistics. As a matter of fact, the definition of systems as being in essence synchronic in no way alters one's recognition of the fact that systems are subject to change. It merely puts this fact in a different light; instead of viewing change as a continuous line of development in what remains all the time 'the same system', changes show up as the substitution of one system for another, each time the network of opposed forms is significantly altered.

Saussure's concern with systems is directed particularly at semiological systems, that is, systems with the purpose of establishing communication by means of arbitrary signs (see below, Section 1.2.4, p. 14). These systems of forms have the function of mediating between two domains of substance which are in themselves amorphous. The two domains, according to Saussure, are *the amorphous mass of thought* from which are drawn thoughts to be expressed in the form of messages, and *the amorphous mass of physical manifestations* (in the case of languages: sounds) from which are drawn the means of expression.

1.2.4   Sign and Symbol – Arbitrariness and Motivation

In the previous paragraph allusion was made to the fact that semiological systems are those systems that have the purpose of enabling their users to communicate by means of arbitrary signs. That is to say, it is part of the definition of semiological systems to contain a network of forms of a particular type, a type Saussure calls *signs*. Signs are the particular forms by means of which semiological systems achieve their characteristic function of mediating between the substance of thought and the substance of physical expression (in the case of languages: sounds). We may say, therefore, that, in essence, signs are mediators between messages and signals.

Not all forms that mediate between what one might call 'physical signals' and what one might call 'messages' qualify for the status of being signs (just as, therefore, not all systems of/for communication are semiological systems in the Saussurean sense). This term is reserved for forms that mediate specifically *by virtue of* arbitrarily established links (associations) that are traditionally transmitted and have to be learned before one can make use of the systems (for example, languages) to which they belong. In the usual interpretation of Saussurean thought, a link or association is arbitrary if and only if there is no trace of evidence that it may be motivated by a natural connection between substances, that is, when it is fashioned by convention alone. Thus, the condition of arbitrariness is fulfilled by linguistic signs such as 'dog', 'book', 'walk', 'black', and so on, where there is no conceivable trace of evidence that some natural link may exist between the physical means of expression (in this case: the sounds) and that which is expressed. As a way of emphasising the arbitrary nature of such signs, Saussure calls attention to the fact that 'the same' concepts are expressed by different physical means in other languages (for example, *'chien'*, *'livre'*, *'se promener'*, *'noir'*).

The condition of arbitrariness – if it is interpreted as total lack of motivation – is not fulfilled by a form such as 'cuckoo', for, although it can be pointed out that its equivalents in other languages are sometimes unrecognisably different (e.g. French *'coucou'*, German *'Kuckuck'*, Hungarian *'kakukk'*, Swahili *'tama la bibi'*, Chinese *'dù jūan'*, and so on), there is a traceable connection between the sounds used as means of expression and the sounds made by the bird referred to. In other words, the association is said to be motivated by a naturally perceived similarity between the physical means of expression and some property of the object that constitutes the substance of the message expressed. Such forms that perform their mediating function at least partly by virtue of some form of motivation (for instance, the motivation provided by onomatopoeia in the case of 'cuckoo') are, accordingly, not to be classified as signs, but as symbols. Although I fully admit the trace of onomatopoeic motivation that is detectable in the case of 'cuckoo', I would deny that this form is understood by virtue of that motivation. At best, the onomatopoeia might allow one to hazard an intelligent guess at what 'cuckoo' might mean – it certainly does not constitute a sufficient basis for understanding that word; only a knowledge of the conventions of English does that. Therefore, I would unhesitatingly classify 'cuckoo' as a sign, albeit a motivated one.

1.2.5   Signs as Janus-like Forms – A Dyadic Analysis

Since signs are mediators between two substances, they are readily conceived of as forms that face at once in two opposite directions (like the two faces of the Roman god Janus). One aspect of a sign faces in the direction of the amorphous mass of thoughts, the mass in which is located the concept which that sign expresses; the other aspect faces in the direction of the mass of physical manifestations, the mass from which is drawn the means by which the sign in question is expressed. (It is worth noting, in passing, that a sign considered as a form in its two-faced totality is 'realised' (cf. Section 1.2.1, p. 10) in two substances at one and the same time.)

The conceptual aspect of a sign is called, after Saussure, the *signified* (*signifié*); the aspect of physical manifestation is referred to as the *signifier* (*signifiant*). Saussure insists on a strictly two-way association between signified and signifier, and places these two faces of the sign in a *one–to–one relation of mutual implication* that is analogous with the relationship between two sides of a coin.

In short, Saussure proposes a *dyadic* analysis of the internal structure of a sign, which he represents diagrammatically (see Figure 1.1).

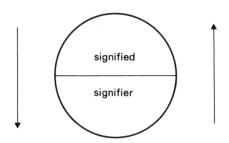

Figure 1.1

1.2.6 The Projected Scope of Semiology

At the time of Saussure's lectures on which the posthumous publication of *Cours de linguistique générale* (Saussure, 1916) was based, semiology did not exist as a discipline. In his discussion of semiology, Saussure was, therefore, both attempting to lay down guidelines for a future discipline and attempting to predict the direction in which that discipline would develop.

In the first place, Saussure foresaw and recommended the autonomy of semiology as a discipline – its separation from other disciplines such as philosophy, anthropology and the physical sciences. This autonomy was to be achieved by means of semiology adopting its own exclusive and unique point of view, a point of view at once determining the range of phenomena with which the discipline is to concern itself (that is, its 'object') and the particular aspect of these phenomena which are to be abstracted out for semiological description (that is, the 'subject matter'). Semiology, by virtue of its proper point of view not shared by other disciplines, was envisaged as *the* discipline for the study of all that is *social*, *conventional* and *systematic* in *communication* (probably, but not necessarily, between humans).

At the same time as liberating semiology from a number of hetero-geneous disciplines with which the study of communication was tra-ditionally linked, Saussure made an attempt to attach it to the then newly conceived and fashionable discipline of *social psychology* (most com-monly associated with the theories of Durkheim). The allocation of semiology to social psychology (that is, semiology as a sub-discipline properly included in social psychology) seemed particularly appropriate from the point of view of Saussure's conception of language ('*langue*') as a phenomenon at once social in nature and a psychic reality in the minds of a community of speakers. Other semiotic phenomena, dependent (by definition) on the use of signs (in fact: systems of signs), were analogously conceived as psychic realities shared by particular social groups.

Presumably, the attaching of semiology to social psychology would have had the effect of making that discipline dependent, after all, on a pair of heterogeneous disciplines: *sociology* and *psychology* (a somewhat wasted effort after Saussure's attempts to remove such heterogeneous forces from an autonomous semiology). This, however, would not have been apparent to Saussure who would have perceived the new discipline of social psychology as being, itself, autonomous, rather than a synthesis between an independent sociology and an independent psychology.

As it happens, followers of Saussure were least keen to latch on to the psychic-mental aspects of his ideas and were, therefore, wont to ignore the emphasis he placed on semiology as a branch of social psychology. Furthermore, the discipline of social psychology itself did not enjoy the continued success and advancement that Saussure apparently predicted for it. This is not to say that the discipline became totally extinct – it has even enjoyed a form of revival most recently in the work of Roland Barthes (Chapter 5, p. 126) – but that it failed to join the ranks of established disciplines, and that semiology was able to develop independently of it, and to achieve far more success in its own right than can be claimed for social psychology.

While Saussure's directives to make of semiology an autonomous discipline have, by and large, had a beneficial effect on the development of the discipline, the most frequently cited 'definition' of the scope of semiology attributed to Saussure (one cannot be sure that he intended to give such a loose definition of scope) did not fare quite so well. In this 'definition', Saussure is reported to have projected a semiology that 'studies the life of signs nurtured in the womb of social life'. (I do not think the translation, which is my own, is too extremely 'literary' as a rendering of 'la vie des signes au sein de la vie sociale'). The very style in which this statement is couched (though it might sound less like a 'purple passage' in French than in my English rendering) is more suggestive of an utterance with emotive content than of a technical definition.

Where the emotive content of a 'definition' has a preponderance over the literal interpretation of the terms used, this creates an open invitation to follow 'the spirit of' the proposed 'definition' in various directions according to the taste of its subsequent interpreters. To this we owe various elastic interpretations of the Saussurean scope of semiology and, in more general terms, the surprising heterogeneity of semiological approaches that claim to be Saussurean in spirit (compare, for instance, the semiology of Mounin, or of Prieto, with that of Barthes). In particular, 'strict' interpreters of Saussure have tended to regard semiology as being narrower in scope (limited in effect to fully conventional and fully systematic means of intentional communication) than others who, like Barthes, have chosen to see a semiological pattern in virtually the whole of human social behaviour.

1.3 Peircean Fundamentals

1.3.1 Natural Classes

Although 'a great many logicians say there is no such thing' as a *natural class* (Peirce, 1960), for the reason that all classes are equally arbitrary creations, Peirce offers an original and persuasive defence of a notion of *natural classes*.

This defence rests upon drawing a comparison between 'trivial' and 'significant' (the terms are mine, not Peirce's) ways of classifying objects. A typical example of a trivial classification would be the grouping together of all organisms with the property of 'having legs' – a hetero-geneous class (for all that its members have a common defining prop-erty) whose establishment sheds no light whatsoever on the biological or zoological world.

As against such unhelpful classification, we may set classes that are significant, in that they shed light on the very existence, and reflect the *raison d'être*, of the objects that belong to them. Classes of this type deserve a special status. Their significance derives from that 'aim com-mon and peculiar to' all their members (Peirce, 1960) which is used in their definition. The definition of such a class is given in terms of the 'common final cause' which is the very purpose to which members owe their existence. Thus, for instance, such everyday objects as bathroom taps may be severally classified in a multiplicity of classes according to their various physical properties – but they are assigned to a significant class only when classified, with a view to their purpose, among *objects that dispense water at the turn of a knob*.

Classes defined in terms of purpose (Peirce calls such a purpose 'an operative desire') are designated by Peirce as natural (or real) classes in token of their special status over other possible classes.

Every class can be said to be defined by an idea – that of certain defining properties abstracted from potential members of the given class. It is, however, only in the case of natural classes that the defining idea fixes on the 'causal' factor (Peirce's 'final causation') whereby a whole marshals its parts into the task of fulfilling a purpose that pertains to the whole. Thus, for instance, the ultimate 'causing' factor, the idea that defines a clock as a whole, is that of accurate time-keeping, which is to be distinguished from the direct mechanical causation (Peirce's 'efficient causation') whereby parts of a clock move as a result of such 'blind' physical factors as the tension of the spring, the driving of one cog by another interlocking cog, etc. As indicated by this example, the general idea of accurate time-keeping would be ineffective without the minutiae of mechanical tasks and movements performed by the various parts of a clock. But, far more importantly, these mechanical details could never have arisen without the overriding purposive idea of accurate time-keeping. Mechanical causes and effects are the servants of a so-called 'final cause' (that is, the purpose of a whole entity); a 'final cause' dominates and organises mechanical causation towards some 'ultimate' function. That is to say, without mechanical causation, there would only be inert ideas without the power to act, whereas without dominating ideas of 'final causation' even the faultless working of mechanical causation would be senseless, no more than 'mere chaos'.

This persuasive and compelling way of distinguishing between mechanical details of causation and an overriding idea of purpose ('final cause') lays a foundation for Peirce's belief that definitions made in terms of mechanical details create relatively trivial classes, whereas definitions in terms of some overriding purposive idea create really significant classes. The distinction opens the way to Peirce's definition of a *natural class* as a 'family whose members are the sole offspring of and vehicles of one idea from which they derive their peculiar faculty' (Peirce, 1960).

Accordingly, one can arrive at the definition of a natural class only 'when one can lay one's finger upon the purpose to which a class of things owes its origin' (Peirce, 1960).

Reflecting, on Peirce's behalf, the conclusions from the foregoing paragraphs back on the subject of semiotics itself, we should find that the field of 'semiotic phenomena' offers itself as a natural class. There is in the totality of semiotic events (in particular, that is, events that owe their existence to systems of conventions; see Introduction, p. 3) a purpose (Peirce's term 'operative desire' would seem to be particularly apt here), a single idea from which all such events 'derive their peculiar faculty' and to which the class of such events 'owes its origin'. In general terms, that idea or purpose is the 'final cause' of communication.

1.3.2   Science, Scientific Method and a Typology of Sciences

In a manner typical of his philosophy, Peirce points to the desirability of starting with a general, but definite, idea of what one means by 'science', before going on to discuss, or to engage in, particular sciences. (This is yet another instance of how, in Peirce's thought, 'general' and 'abstract' ideas dominate 'particular' and 'concrete' ones. We have already encountered another instance of this in the domination of particular details of mechanical causation by a general idea of 'final cause'.) Furthermore, the class of sciences (as a general category) should itself be defined as a natural class. This poses an obligation for putting one's finger on the purpose, the idea, behind sciences as a whole, identifying the 'operative desire' in all science. Peirce follows up the posing of this extremely ambitious task by settling on the view that 'the life of science is in the desire to learn'; that is to say, the overriding purpose of all science is *to learn whatever can be learned, by whatever means that are available and appropriate.* (This conception has, incidentally, an important message to those who imagine sciences to be essentially 'experimental', essentially connected with the use of instruments, measurements and laboratory techniques; in other words, those whose idea of 'science' is strictly opposed to the 'humanities', restricted as it is to those physical sciences that appear under the label of 'science subjects' in school curricula. Peirce's conception of 'science' is very much wider than this, and rightly so, since he manages to bring his natural class of sciences under the same dominating idea of the desire to learn.)

Under the heading of learning *by whatever means that are appropriate*, Peirce distinguishes between four major types of method for arriving at conclusions; that is to say, four kinds of reasoning (cf. Aristotle):

(1) *Deduction:* the mode of reasoning which examines the state of things implicitly asserted by the bringing together of certain explicit premisses, perceiving in that state of things relations that are not explicit in the premisses as such. (This is the kind of reasoning used in mathematics, geometry and logical systems, where certain premisses are accepted 'on faith', and the theoretician's major concern is to learn what conclusions can be derived *given* these premisses.)

(2) *Induction:* the mode of reasoning that adopts a general conclusion on the basis of examining representative samples. Such reasoning is limited to the calculation of averages, or ratios, from which we may conclude that Peirce's view of Induction is essentially probabilistic and/or statistical. The conclusions reached are no more than approximations. (Peirce gives the example of assessing the quality of a shipment of coffee-beans by taking samples from various parts of the hold. The example shows up all too clearly the dangers of being cheated by the evidence of samples; treating samples as *representative* is, in itself, an 'act of faith'.)

(3) *Retroduction* (cf. Aristotle's term often translated as 'abduction'): the mode of reasoning in which a hypothesis is adopted provisionally, on the condition that its possible consequences are capable of experimental verification. In this mode of reasoning it is never possible to conclude the truth of the provisionally adopted hypothesis, but experimental evidence can be expected to reveal the *falsity* of the hypothesis, if it does, indeed, disagree with facts. On the other hand, if falsification does not in fact take place, in spite of a genuine and continued search for factual counter-evidence, the provisional hypothesis continues to be maintained (albeit still always provisionally). (The description of this method given by Peirce is more than strongly reminiscent of the mode of reasoning nowadays chiefly associated with Karl Popper's 'conjectures and refutations' (Popper, 1963, 1965 and 1972). Paradigm examples of this mode of reasoning are provided by astronomical theory where, frequently, the existence of planets can be predicted, as consequences of certain provisional hypotheses, long before these consequences can be tested by the actual observation of the planets whose existence has been predicted.)

(4) *Argument by Analogy:* the weakest mode of reasoning, whereby it is inferred that a limited set of objects similar in certain important respects are likely to be similar also in other respects that are, for some reason, 'hidden from view'. (Peirce cites as an example the inference according to which, if Earth and Mars are similar in a number of hitherto observed respects, then it is likely that Mars, too, is inhabited by living organisms. In this example, one can recognise the hallmark of 'speculative' argumentation: having *some* reason to believe that Mars is inhabited is a dubious form of having

'learnt' something. The 'speculative' nature of this mode of reasoning is further highlighted by the consideration that theological arguments frequently fall into this mode. For instance, we may say that the 'Prime Mover' argument for the existence of God consists in the inference that, since all known artificial structures that are in motion have to be set in motion by a pre-existing force, then the universe, which is in many respects similar to artificial structures with moving parts, must also have been set in motion by a pre-existing force (that is, God). In some fields, as we see from this example, 'learning' as a result of pure faith can only be supplemented – one could hardly even say 'supplanted' – by a 'speculative' reasoning which is little better than no reasoning at all, though it is far more insidious.)

Peirce's typology (or classification) of the whole field of human science is, as one may well expect, highly elaborate and intricate. Nor can the whole of this typology be the concern of a book on semiotics. However, since the question of what kind of science semiotics is remains a topical question – and since the Peircean answer, one of the most influential answers, can only be understood in terms of his overall scheme of sciences – a brief sketch of this overall scheme will have to be attempted here. (The reader is referred, for further details, to Peirce's *Collected Papers*; Peirce, 1960.)

The scheme I shall present, in a diagrammatic form, is an amalgam of slightly different versions outlined in Vol. 1 of Peirce's *Collected Papers* (Peirce, 1960) and explores the subdivisions only down to a certain depth. My strategy will be to set out the scheme in Figure 1.2 and discuss its categories below:

Theoretical sciences: sciences pursued for the sake of gaining knowledge alone (one would be tempted to call this first branch, the branch of 'pure' sciences).

Practical sciences: sciences pursued for their utility in daily life (the list of practical, 'applied' sciences given by Peirce includes a range of skills and crafts from navigation to gold-beating; the technical side, at least, of what most of us think of as 'arts' would, apparently, constitute 'practical science' in Peirce's conception).

Sciences of discovery: sciences dedicated to advancing theoretical knowledge, that is, to the gaining of *new* knowledge.

Sciences of review: sciences dedicated to the arranging of results obtained in the course of sciences of discovery. (Such sciences do not attempt to gain *new* knowledge, but, rather, to collate existing knowledge, ultimately into one coherent 'body of knowledge'. The highest form of the sciences of review is the *philosophy of science* itself, which, accordingly, is not considered to be a branch of philosophy, but a different and, in a sense, higher order of scientific activity.)

Mathematics: sciences dedicated to the study of purely deductive systems (algebra, geometry, mathematical logic, and so on), and which, therefore, have no concern with the external existential truth (or falsity) of

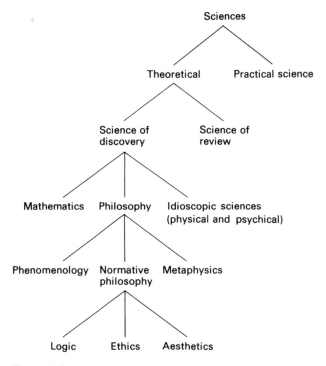

Figure 1.2

propositions (for example, a+b = b+a regardless of any 'real' facts external to algebra itself). Mathematics is unique in its exclusive use of Deduction (see p. 19); furthermore, mathematical sciences are not in need of any separate science of reasoning (logic), as, by definition, they *have* – one might almost say: they *are* – their own rules of reasoning.

Philosophy: sciences dedicated to the in-depth analysis of observed things within the range of ordinary, everyday experience and, therefore, to the gaining of knowledge about facts that escape the untrained eye precisely because of the degree to which they permeate one's daily life. (Such sciences, also termed 'cenoscopic' after Jeremy Bentham's usage (Bentham, 1843), require an ability to ponder things deeply, rather than to explore the outside world more widely, more extensively, or with more precise instruments and measurements. In fact, the use of special observational devices or instruments – microscopes, telescopes, X-ray machines, and so on – is totally inappropriate to philosophical/ cenoscopic sciences. In such sciences, the only 'instrument' is the trained, perceptive and precise mentality of the analyst himself. According to such a description of cenoscopic science, a large section of those disciplines that are currently referred to as 'social sciences' (including sociology, semiotics and linguistics) should belong essentially to cenoscopy. Incidentally, those who consider statistical methods, using special instruments, inappropriate to such 'social sciences', would find a justification for their opinion in the views propounded by Peirce.)

Idioscopic sciences: sciences dedicated to discovering *new* knowledge about aspects of the world outside and beyond the range of everyday experience; accordingly, these are sciences that concentrate on special techniques of observation (exploration, travel, the use of instruments that 'assist' and magnify the normal use of the senses or that measure and record in ways that are beyond the normal means of the senses, etc.).

Idioscopic sciences further subdivide into the physical sciences and the psychical sciences. (Unfortunately, it is only the physical sciences that seem to fully satisfy that aspect of the definition of idioscopy according to which the ideal mode of reasoning is Retroduction. While the confronting of predicted observables with actually observed facts is the cornerstone of idioscopic sciences as represented by physical sciences, it is clear from Peirce's discussion that psychic (or human) sciences concern themselves, by definition, with 'facts of mind' that cannot be directly perceived: they are either intuited or inferred. This makes Retroduction invalid in psychic sciences.)

Phenomenology: science dedicated to the unravelling of the evidence of the senses, and the philosophical problems presented by the interpretation of such evidence. (As such, phenomenology sets itself the task of exploring the nature and types of experientially knowable objects and the factors by virtue of which such objects become known. We shall have some occasion in the following section (3.3, p. 23) to review those salient points of Peirce's phenomenology without which his notion of 'semiotic' cannot be expounded.)

Metaphysics: science dedicated to giving an account of the universe of mind and matter in an abstract, philosophical way, as opposed to empirically (that is, the cenoscopic/philosophical counterpart of physical and psychical sciences).

Normative philosophy: science dedicated to giving an account of how things ought to be (or how they should be done) from a certain ideal point of view. (There are essentially three types of normative value-judgement that concern normative philosophy: value-judgements that lay down an ideal standard for reasoning, value-judgements that lay down a standard for morality, and value-judgements that lay down a standard for beauty. These three types of what, for Peirce, is in essence the same concern with ideal standards directed at three different objectives, lead to the three-way subdivision of normative philosophy.)

Logic: science dedicated to analysing the nature of truth (and of its obverse: falsity) and to laying down standards of clarity and rationality in the expression of propositions.

Ethics: science dedicated to analysing the nature of good (and its obverse: evil) and to laying down standards of fairness and morality in behaviour.

Aesthetics: science dedicated to analysing the nature of beauty (and of its obverse: ugliness) and to laying down standards for the creation and judgement of what is 'artistically' pleasing.

1.3.3 Phenomenology: the Three Categories of Phenomena

Peirce characterises three degrees of existence, each typically comprised of entities whose nature and apprehension are of a higher order than that of the degree below (that is to say, he gives a hierarchy of 'levels of existential entity'). The three degrees or levels are designated by the terms: 'Firstness', 'Secondness' and 'Thirdness'.

'Firstness' is defined as 'the mode of being of that which is such as it is, positively and without reference to anything else' (Peirce, 1977). Accordingly, those things that are real, and can be apprehended as such without regard for other things – that exist, as it were, in isolation, as things unto themselves – have 'Firstness' as their mode of existence. Peirce designates such things as 'firsts'. Typical 'firsts' are such ideas as pure *qualities of feeling* (experienced merely, not reflected upon) and mere outward appearances (sensed only, not analysed or rationalised). Thus, the *quality of red* taken in isolation and in abstraction from any particular object that might have that quality would constitute a paradigm example of a 'first'. In this interpretation, qualities are potential and *sui generis*.

It goes almost without saying that the mode of presentation (or should one say 'representation'?) of things that are by nature 'firsts' is as single terms: that is to say, as *monads*.

'Secondness' finds its simplest definition as 'the mode of being of that which is such as it is, with respect to a second but regardless of any third' (Peirce, 1977). Less superficially, any 'thing' which could not exist, or be apprehended for what it is, without its intrinsic relation to some second 'thing' is by its nature a 'second'. Accordingly, 'Secondness' generally consists in one thing acting upon another, in such a way that, by virtue of the inter-action itself, both things acquire a status (and are apprehended as having that status) beyond their mere qualities or appearances. With respect to each other, these things are not what they would be if they existed in isolation (*sui generis*). We may say that 'seconds' are characterised by the fact that they act (upon a single other thing) in a particular capacity. Using this terminology makes Peirce's example of a *married couple*, cited as the typical example of a pair involving 'seconds', particularly clear and convincing. Here is Peirce's own exposition of the example (Peirce, 1960):

> A married couple is not a man. Neither is it a woman, and *a fortiori* it is not, at once, a man and a woman. Nor is it disjunctively either a man or a woman. It is a third object, to whose constitution, which is its nature, and therefore to its existence, too, a man is requisite and a woman is requisite. A pair is an object to whose constitution a subject and another subject are necessary and sufficient.

Taking matters further along the same lines, we may add that it is the idea of a 'husband', and that of a 'wife', that are actually the paradigm examples of 'Secondness', since each of them necessarily implies a pair (namely, a married couple). They do so in the sense that a 'husband' is, indeed, not (just) a man, but 'a–man–in–the–capacity–of–being–married–to–a–woman'. Conversely, a 'wife' is not (just) a woman, but rather, 'a–woman–in–the–capacity–of–being–married–to–a–man'. A symbolic representation of the nature of 'husbandhood', and of 'wifehood' shows up these ideas even more clearly as being typical of 'Secondness':

'husband' = man x (in his capacity of being married to) woman y
'wife' = woman y (in her capacity of being married to) man x

The ideas of 'husband' and 'wife' are converse pairs constituted by the fact that in each of them a person is seen intrinsically as *acting in a particular capacity*. Without the notion of *acting in some capacity* there is no such thing as a 'husband' or as a 'wife'. We may conclude in general that 'Secondness' derives its essence from the notion of 'acting in a capacity with regard to a *single* other thing'.

The appropriate mode of representation for 'Secondness', and for things that belong to the category of 'seconds', is as pairs: that is to say as *dyads*. (The representation and analysis of the ideas of 'husband' and 'wife' in the preceding paragraph illustrate the Peircean notion of a *dyad*.)

The condensed definition of 'Thirdness' can be given as 'the mode of being of that which is such as it is, in bringing a second and a third into relation with one another' (Peirce, 1977). We may say, therefore, that the keyword of this hierarchically highest level of existence is *mediation*. A given thing is a 'third' if its nature (in fact its overriding purpose, see Section 1.3.1, p. 17) is to *mediate* a particular, otherwise non-existent, relationship between two further things. It is, in other words, not sufficient to say that, where 'seconds' involve two participants, 'thirds' involve three participants. It is also necessary to add that the participants are so arranged that just one of the three has the role of mediating some relation between the other two, a relation that these two cannot contract of themselves.

1.3.4 Trichotomies and 'Triadomany'

Binarism is the passion of those who tend to see everything as divided into two categories, or antithetical, opposing extremes, that is to say, who insist on conceiving the universe in terms of a multitude of polarities: good–evil, black–white, true–false, and so on.

In Peirce's thought, there is plenty of room for the use of binary distinctions, that is to say, dichotomies, where he considers these to be appropriate. The whole idea of 'Secondness', and of 'seconds', bears witness to the place attributed to notions that are based on dichotomies.

On the other hand, many have been struck with the overwhelming use Peirce makes of triads, especially where it comes to the hierarchically higher notions of 'Thirdness' and of 'thirds'. Ideas based on a three-way division or classification abound in Peircean theory, to such an extent that Peirce himself felt the need to answer and anticipate possible charges of an 'obsession' with trichotomies (three-way distinctions). Though his coinage of the term 'triadomany' for designating a craze or mania for trichotomies carries jocular overtones, the joke has an edge of seriousness to it. In disclaiming an affliction by 'triadomany', Peirce affirms that wherever he has felt the need to use trichotomies – often in places where other thinkers have been satisfied with dichotomies, as, for instance, in defining the nature of 'signs' (compare Sections 1.2.5, p. 14 and 1.3.5, p. 26) – he has done so for reasons that are fully rational, and not out of a pathological concern with the magical number three.

The importance of trichotomies follows from Peirce's conception of 'Thirdness' and, far from opening him to charges of 'triadomany', is a logical and necessary consequence of the definition of 'thirds' as ideas that are essentially trichotomous, since they require the participation of three mutually distinct *relata*. Furthermore, the undoubted use Peirce makes of divisions that are not into three (divisions into two or into more than three), together with his frequent reluctance to introduce yet another triadic division, are ample evidence for his wholly reasonable attitude to trichotomies. In short, trichotomies are important for valid and intrinsic reasons inherent in Peircean thought, not (as one sometimes feels in the case of binary theories) as a result of a Procrustean preoccupation with fitting all ideas into the same mould.

With apologies to the memory of C. S. Peirce (who might well have disapproved of the example), it strikes me that a particularly clear illustration of 'Thirdness' might be seen in the role of a divorce court in mediating the dissolving of a marriage. The partners involved – husband and wife – are powerless to bring about the legal termination of their (*dyadic*) marriage-relation, and the defining purpose of a divorce court is precisely that of *mediating* between *husband* and *wife* (the other two participants) in such a way as to make legal divorce possible.

A symbolic representation of this example (in the form of a *triad*, the appropriate mode of presentation for 'Thirdness') brings the mediatory nature of 'thirds' sharply into focus (see Figure 1.3).

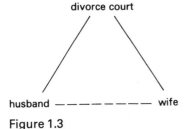

divorce court

Broken line represents a
relationship present only
by virtue of *mediation*
through a 'third'

husband — — — — — — — wife

Figure 1.3

The relationship mediated between *husband* and *wife* is that of '*being divorced*' – of themselves, that is, without the *divorce court* as a mediator, husband and wife cannot make this relationship come about. It is to be especially noted from the symbolic representation, that only one of the participants in a triad (the participant placed at the apex of the triangle) has a mediating role; it is only this participant that has the status of a 'third'. In anticipation, and to allay the reader's possible impatience with background ideas apparently unconnected with semiotic matters, I should point out that signs are, in Peirce's conception, triadic mediators that exemplify 'Thirdness' *par excellence*.

In view of Peirce's contention that any idea requiring four or more participating objects in its definition can be reduced to triads, whereas triads are not reducible to dyads any more than dyads are to monads, the three categories of 'Firstness', 'Secondness' and 'Thirdness' are all that one requires for analysing the nature of any element found to be manifested in the phenomena science can apprehend.

1.3.5   Signs as 'Thirds'; a Triadic Conception

A 'sign' (also called by the more technical-sounding term, *representamen*) is defined by Peirce in accordance with the foregoing idea of 'Thirdness'. That is to say, just as 'thirds' *in general* mediate in a triadic relationship between two other relata, so 'signs' *in particular* are mediators between two other entities that they determine and dominate by virtue of their very power to mediate between them. Consequently, in order to understand the Peircean concept of 'sign', we need to fill in, in the general definition characterising all 'thirds', the details that make of 'signs' a particular sub-type of 'Thirdness'. When we have, in the general formula shown in Figure 1.4, specified and particularised the requisite pair of

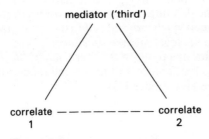

mediator ('third')

Broken line indicates a specific *mediated* relation; solid lines indicate the *domination* of the lower correlates by the mediating entity at the apex of the triangle

correlate — — — — — — correlate
1   2

Figure 1.4

'correlates' (between which the 'sign' typically mediates), and specified and particularised the nature of the mediating function, itself, we shall have gathered all that is central to the Peircean definition of 'sign'.

We should start, perhaps, by noting that, while outside of an actual, or at least fully potential (that is, potential with the power of being realised), triad of the requisite sort nothing is, or can be, a sign, there are no external restrictions on the kind of entity that may function as a sign once it is made to appear inside such a triad. Putting it more simply (though there does not appear to be any really simple way of expressing this with sufficient precision): anything may be suitable as a sign, but not unless and until it determines and dominates the two other correlates required for 'Thirdness'. (By way of an – unfortunately rather weak – analogy, we may say that any one may become a writer, but not unless and until he has put pen to paper.) At any rate, 'being a sign' is not a matter of having certain physical trappings, but rather of being appointed to a particular role, or capacity.

In so far as even Peirce himself finds it difficult to avoid discussing signs in their purely physical aspect (in which case one is talking about physical entities, not signs, just as one might talk about the 'toenails of a judge', as though it were the office and not the physical man to which the toenails pertain), some ambiguities arise around the terms 'sign' and its synonym, 'representamen'. The ambiguities have to do with the extent to which the whole triadic triangle is subsumed within a sign (or representamen), and the extent to which one can continue to call an entity a 'sign' once it has been completely abstracted from the triadic relationship that defines it. The terminological, and conceptual, malaise created by this ambiguity has led followers of Peirce (for example, Morris, cf. Chapter 2, p. 38) to distinguish, more or less precisely and more or less consistently, between 'sign' and 'sign-vehicle', the former being the fully integrated term in a sign-relation (with all of its necessary correlates being specified), while the latter is rather the physical entity in which the function of a sign is embodied. Unfortunately, in this usage, 'sign-vehicle' becomes at once a potential sign as divorced from its potential as a sign, and a purely physical entity that, none the less, takes its character from the purely non-physical, and purely potential, function of 'being the vehicle of a sign'. Each way we look at it, 'sign-vehicle' only succeeds in being a contradiction in terms.

The key to the Peircean notion 'sign' is not in the extrinsic nature of the term standing at the apex of the triangle but in the overall intrinsic nature

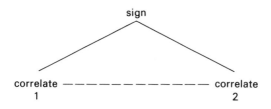

Figure 1.5

of the triadic correlation as a whole (see Figure 1.5). Thus, a sign is the mediator of a relationship of 'representation', or 'standing for', and this is its sole defining property. This relationship, in turn, cannot be fully grasped until one can explain what specific types of correlate constitute the parties between which the sign mediates, and what the outcome of the mediation is. (It might be helpful to refer back at this point to the analogy of a divorce court mediating legal dissolution of a marriage between a plaintiff and a defendant; see Section 1.3.4, p. 25.)

The two other correlates between which a sign mediates are called by Peirce 'Object' and 'Interpretant', so that the fully specified triad can be represented as in Figure 1.6. 'A sign mediates between the *interpretant . . .* and its object' (Peirce, 1977).

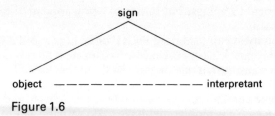

Figure 1.6

In this triadic correlation, the role of a sign is to establish a habit or general rule determining both the way the sign is to be 'understood' on the occasions of its use, and the kind of perceptible, or at least 'imaginable', features of experience to which the sign may be applied. Thus we may take it that the way a sign is to be 'understood' implies some kind of mental activity or state, whereas the features to which a sign can be applied presuppose something perceptual or experiential.

Let us say, for the sake of example, that we need to analyse, in a Peircean manner, the sign-function of a letter 'H' labelling one of a pair of bathroom taps. The way this sign is to be understood is, of course, by taking cognizance (a mental event/state) of the fact that the tap thus labelled is a hot-water tap; this, we may take it, is the *interpretant* of the sign. The kind of perceptible feature of experience to which the sign 'H' can be applied is part of some situation in which hot water is actually pouring out of a given tap (proving experientially that one's understanding of it as a hot-water tap was correct). The perceptual feature of a thing actually capable of dispensing hot water is what is referred to by the sign, namely, its object (some might say 'referent').

In a 'sign'-less context (which is, of course, hard to imagine, since we are in the habit of always operating with signs), there would, normally, be no connection between taking mental note of the fact that a given tap is a hot-water tap, and experiencing the sight, sound and feel of hot water pouring out of a tap. In fact, one could take cognizance that a given tap is a hot-water tap without ever having had the good fortune to use one – in which case one would be merely lacking in practical 'experience'. Equally, one could keep on watching hot water pouring out of all sorts of taps without forming a general mental conception of hot-water taps – in which case one would be 'sub-human'. For that matter, one could, on the one hand, have a perfectly good theoretical grasp of hot-water taps, and, on the other, a wealth of experience with hot water pouring out of particular taps, and yet fail, somehow, to make any connection between the two – in which case one would be 'stupid', 'educationally subnormal', or in some way 'mentally defective' (for example, 'aphasic').

A sign in the form of a letter 'H' is, by its functioning as a sign, sufficient to ensure, for all its users, that a connection between the mental recognition of hot-water taps (in general) and the experience of objects visibly dispensing hot water (in particular) is never overlooked, but becomes, on the contrary, a habit and a general rule. Thus, two things that without any sign would be unconnected become, by virtue of a sign, almost indistinguishable from one another – so much so that, to a normal intelligence, it may even appear counter-intuitive to suggest a separation between the 'concept' of hot-water taps, and the experience or perception of objects that give concrete realisation to such a 'concept'.

It is much less counter-intuitive, however, to note that, ordinarily, there is no connection between a letter 'H' and the way it is to be understood (as 'meaning' what it means in the bathroom example), nor between a letter 'H' and the sight, sound and feel of hot water pouring from a tap. The connection between sign and interpretant, and between sign and object are specially created links. If, by habit and as a general rule, we find it almost unavoidable to make such connections, this is due only to the 'representative' nature of the sign 'H'. This sign 'stands for', as well as (at the same time) mediates between, the two correlates which it dominates: object and interpretant. Once this intricate interplay between sign, object and interpretant is grasped – together with the rather special sense attributed to the expression 'stand for', which is usually conceived in a binary, and not in a mediatory, way – we are in possession of the essentials of Peirce's powerful and sophisticated triadic conception of 'signs'.

1.3.6 Classification of Signs; the Three Main Trichotomies

The triadic nature of signs implies that they can be looked upon, and subclassified, from three angles: (1) from the point of view of the mediating sign itself; (2) from the point of view of the object of the sign; (3) from the point of view of the interpretant of the sign.

Each of these three ways of viewing and classifying signs gives rise, in turn, to a dimension in which three distinct possibilities are in mutual contrast; that is to say, they lead to the positing of three separate trichotomies. Before examining these trichotomies, and the categories of sign resulting from their cross-classification, it is as well to point out that Peirce's classification does not stop at this point, but continues, by way of further intricate trichotomies whose complexities place them beyond the scope of the present discussion, to a cross-classification yielding sixty-six different kinds of sign. (The reader is referred to Irwin C. Lieb's summary of Peirce's classification of signs. This condensed, and extremely useful account is to be found in both Lieb's edition of the Peirce–Welby correspondence (Peirce, 1953) and Hardwick's more recent edition of this correspondence (Peirce, 1977), in each case as an appendix.)

1.3.7 The Trichotomy from the Point of View of the Mediating Sign: Qualisign, Sinsign, Legisign

According to their material nature signs fall into three categories, categories that follow, in their turn, from the three basic levels in Peircean phenomenology: 'Firstness', 'Secondness' and 'Thirdness'. That is:

(1)   if the sign, or rather the material substance of the sign, has the nature of a 'first' (that is, a quality or appearance sensed *sui generis*), Peirce speaks of a *qualisign*;

(2)   if the sign, or rather its material substance, has the nature of a 'second' (that is, an actual and active thing or event, unique by virtue of its one-time occurrence), Peirce speaks of a *sinsign*;

(3)   if the (material substance of the) sign has the nature of a 'third' (that is, a general rule or habit operating as a law, not as a single, once-off happening), Peirce speaks of a *legisign*.

Three points should be noted by way of comment. First, the actual effective operation of occurrences of signs (as opposed to their abstract classification) places *legisign*, *sinsign* and *qualisign* in a hierarchy, rather than a mere trichotomy. A legisign can occur concretely only when embodied in (realised by) a one-time event which is actually a sinsign; a sinsign, in turn, can only be recognised on the occasion of its occurrence by its perceived appearance which is actually a qualisign.

Secondly, both the above-noted hierarchy, and the statement that signs always establish a habit or general rule, would seem to suggest – and rather forcefully, at that – the conclusion that, strictly speaking, only legisigns reach the requisite level of generality and level of abstractness that is, by definition, required of signs.

Thirdly, and this is a point to which we shall have occasion to return briefly, Peirce regards a sinsign that embodies (or gives concrete realis-ation, on a given occasion to) a legisign – and all legisigns always occur in this way, if they are to occur at all – as a 'replica' or 'token' of that legisign. Consequently, a legisign subsumes – or perhaps even *is* – a class of virtual sinsigns. This member-to-class relationship does not accord happily with the idea that legisign and sinsign are different subcategories of the *same* category 'sign'. As for the term 'replica', which Peirce seems to use interchangeably with 'token' (for this notion, see also Section 1.3.11, p. 34), it is easier to see some force in the view that two or more sinsigns embodying the same legisign (for example, two separate occurrences of a 'no entry' sign, in two different places) are 'replicas' of one another, with respect to the (general) legisign 'no entry', than to take the view that these sinsigns are 'replicas' of the (abstract) legisign that they embody.

1.3.8   The Trichotomy from the Point of View of the Object; Icon, Index, Symbol

Taking account of the relationship of signs to their respective objects leads to a second trichotomy, yielding the following three alternatives:

(1)   if the sign denotes its object *by virtue of* a real similarity that holds between physical properties (cf. 'Firstness') of the sign and physical properties of its object, Peirce designates that sign as an *icon*;

(2)   if the sign denotes its object *by virtue of* a real cause–and–effect link (cf. 'Secondness') that holds between sign and object, Peirce desig-nates that sign as an *index*;

(3)   if the sign denotes its object *by virtue of* a general association of
       ideas that is in the nature of a habit or convention (cf. 'Thirdness'),
       Peirce designates that sign as a *symbol*.

As examples of *icons* (or *iconic signs*) we may cite such familiar cases as
diagrams that, albeit schematically, represent real properties of, among
other things, electrical circuits, buildings, geographical areas, and so on.
To this same category, one would assign also stylised figures used to
denote 'men' and 'women', respectively. Onomatopoeic words in languages would also be classified as iconic; for instance, the English word
'cuckoo' is said to denote its object (the bird) by virtue of a real similarity
between the sound of the word and the sound made by the bird. (As this
last example indicates, there are icons in the case of which it is actually
rather hard to maintain that the 'representation' is strictly *by virtue of* a
similarity. Though a similarity no doubt exists in such cases, and though
this similarity can be held partly responsible for motivating the choice of a
given material substance for the sign in question, it would be too much to
claim that that similarity alone is responsible for the link between sign and
object. Yet this is what is implied by the expression 'denotes *by virtue
of*'.)
   Those cases where a sign genuinely denotes its object by virtue of some
real physical connection belong to the category of indices. The paradigm
example that comes to mind is that of photographs, where a two-
dimensional representation resembling the photographed object in close
visual detail is created by mechanical/causal means. Photographs represent their objects with regard to visual similarity, but they do so by
virtue of the photographic process itself, a process in which (to cut a long
story short), light-waves reflected from the photographed object cause an
image to appear on light-sensitive paper. I would be strongly inclined
to designate photographs (and other similar recordings) as 'iconic
indices'.
   Other examples of indices – cases where iconicity seems to play no role
– are signs by which we interpret the natural world: lightning as a sign of
impending thunder, thunder as a sign of an impending storm, various
symptoms denoting that an organism is suffering from a particular disease
(that is, diagnosing an illness is a matter of interpreting indexical signs),
and so forth. Presumably, the transmitting of 'genetic information'
(programming the growth of an organism by 'instructions' that are
'encoded' in the genes in the course of reproduction) is also to be
classified as 'indexical'.
   Culturally determined, conventional signs provide the most clear-cut
examples of the Peircean category of symbols. (Note, by the way, the
terminological discrepancy whereby, for Saussure, the term 'symbol'
designates the presence of some 'natural' or 'iconic' element, whereas for
Peirce, on the contrary, 'symbolic signs' are those in which 'natural' or
'iconic' features are absent.) Signs from artificial man-made codes,
signalling systems, systems of classificatory labelling (library shelf-marks,
for example), logical and algebraic systems and, of course, both spoken
and written languages are all symbols *par excellence*.

1.3.9   The Trichotomy from the Point of View of the Interpretant: Rheme, Proposition, Argument

In this third trichotomy, signs are classified according to the nature of the *interpretant* that each of them represents. Once again, the alternative types – in this case, the types of interpretant – are provided by the phenomenological levels of 'Firstness', 'Secondness' and 'Thirdness'.

A sign that is to be 'understood' as representing a particular kind of object perceived through its appearance (cf. 'Firstness') is designated by Peirce as a *rheme* (the current term would probably be 'referring expression'). A rheme merely 'names', indicates, or calls attention to a particular kind of object. Names of classes, as well as proper names fall into this category. Another instance of a rheme is our earlier example of a letter 'H' labelling a bathroom tap, which is to be 'understood' as indicating that the tap is of a particular kind (that is, a hot-water tap).

A sign that is to be 'understood' as asserting the existence of some situation (concerning some thing, of course) is designated by Peirce as a *proposition* or *dicent* (sign). Such an interpretant requires the participation of that about which something is asserted and that situation whose existence is asserted of that something. Such an interpretant is notably dyadic in nature, and falls into the category of 'Secondness'.

A sign that is to be 'understood' as asserting the truth of something, by dominating and mediating between a premiss and a conclusion (these latter are propositions) is designated by Peirce as an *argument*. Such an interpretant needs, by definition, the participation of certain propositions to constitute the correlates between which an assertion of truth is mediated by the argument (see Figure 1.7). (The argument mediates the

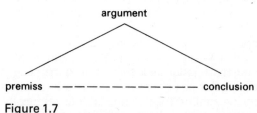

Figure 1.7

assertion of truth from premiss to conclusion; a relation indicated by a broken line in token of the fact that it is a relationship that premiss and conclusion cannot contract without the mediation of the argument.)

From this representation, it is clear that the type of interpretant involved in the case of an argument is of the nature of a 'third'. It emerges from this, also, that *asserting the truth* of the existence of something is of a higher order than *asserting the existence* of something. The latter involves us merely in the active capacities of 'Secondness', the former in the mediating function of truth operating over and above 'seconds', in the higher dimension of 'Thirdness'.

1.3.10 Ten Classes of Sign

The ten major classes of sign distinguished by Peirce result from cross-classification of the three foregoing trichotomies: (1) *qualisign – sinsign – legisign*, (2) *icon – index – symbol*, (3) *rheme – proposition/dicent – argument*.

The presentation of this cross-classification in the form of a matrix requires, first, the recognition of the fact that the property of 'Firstness' in qualisigns precludes the possibility of qualisigns having interpretants that are not mere rhemes (that is, interpretants that are, themselves, limited to 'Firstness'), and of qualisigns being other than iconically related to their objects.

For analogous reasons, sinsigns can only admit of 'Firstness' or 'Secondness' in their interpretants, and in the relations they bear to their objects – their own 'Secondness' precludes them from functioning as arguments, and from being symbols.

It is, then, in effect, only legisigns that can function in each of the capacities of rheme, dicent and argument, and be either iconic, or indexical, or symbolic with regard to their objects.

With these considerations in mind, the matrix in which we locate the ten possible classes of sign will not, in first instance, allow of *twenty-seven* (three times three times three – that is, the multiplication of three trichotomies) categories, but only of eighteen. Furthermore, as we see from the matrix, another eight of the apparently possible categories are empty. This is because

(1) *qualisigns* are automatically (and exclusively) *iconic*;
(2) *sinsigns* do not have the property of generality that would allow them to be *symbolic*;
(3) *iconic signs* are automatically (and exclusively) *rhematic*;
(4) *indexical signs* cannot transcend the 'Secondness' of the causal links by virtue of which they operate, and, therefore, cannot be used as *arguments*.

The result of these considerations can be tabulated in the form of the matrix shown in Figure 1.8 in which Peirce's ten major categories of sign are accommodated. (Further subdivisions – Peirce's sixty-six subcategories of sign – fall beyond the scope of this exposition.)

Examples
Qualisign: the perception of a particular colour.
Iconic sinsign: an individual copy of a map.
Rhematic indexical sinsign: an involuntary cry of pain.
Dicent sinsign: a windsock indicating (on a particular occasion) the direction of the wind.
Iconic legisign: the traffic-sign giving warning of falling rocks, onomatopoeic words ('bang', 'buzz', 'cuckoo', etc.).
Rhematic indexical legisign: lightning in its (general and habitual) capacity of serving notice of impending thunder.

		icon	index	symbol
qualisign		Qualisign		
sinsign	rheme	Iconic sinsign	Rhematic indexical sinsign	
	dicent		Dicent sinsign	
legisign	rheme	Iconic legisign	Rhematic indexical legisign	Rhematic symbol
	dicent		Dicent indexical legisign	Dicent symbol
	argument			Argument

Figure 1.8

Dicent indexical legisign: the classical symptoms indicative of the fact that a person is suffering from measles, the red dashboard light indicating that the engine is overheating.

Rhematic symbol: the sign of the Red Cross, common nouns ('cow', 'vache', 'Kuh', etc.); proper names ('John', 'Jeanne', 'Johann', etc.).

Dicent symbol: propositions in logical systems ($x \ni Y$; i.e. x is a member of class Y); propositions in algebraic systems ($a + b = z$); declarative sentences in languages ('two and two make four').

Argument: syllogisms, whether in logical or in linguistic form: $x \ni Y, z \& q = x, \therefore (z \& q) \ni Y$. This married couple belongs to the tennis club. The union of Peter and Sally constitutes this married couple. $\therefore$ Peter and Sally are joint members of the tennis club.

1.3.11 The 'Type'–'Token' Dichotomy

In Peirce's explanation, as we saw above (Section 1.3.7, p. 30), the term 'token' appears as a synonym of 'replica' and the latter is explained as a sinsign occurring on a particular occasion, and representing on that occasion a particular legisign. A legisign is necessarily abstract, and virtual, embodying in itself a general, conventional rule or habit – whereas the corresponding sinsign(s) only illustrate, without being comprised of, something general and habitual.

Thus, laying aside the categorial difference between sinsign and legisign (which, according to Peirce, are subtypes of the same type of entity called 'sign'), we are left with a significant abstractional difference whereby a legisign is a general type, and its representative sinsigns (not all sinsigns, of course, conform to a general type or legisign) are concrete instances or tokens of the use of that legisign.

What post-Peircean thinkers (philosophers, linguists, semioticians) have extracted from the resulting *type–token* distinction, that is to say, the way this distinction is currently applied, relates exclusively to the abstractional difference between types and tokens.

The application of the distinction in a linguistic context goes a long way to illustrating, by way of example, the nature of that distinction. For instance, a word as listed in a dictionary constitutes the abstraction of a general rule or habit of usage (it captures whatever is considered to be constant about the pronunciation and the meaning), and as such is a type. On the other hand, any actual utterance of that word, made by a particular speaker on a particular occasion, is, while conforming in a suitable way with the word defined as a type, a mere one-time occurrence, or token of the word in question. (This is reminiscent in a way of what Saussure had to say about distinguishing a word as a form – his example is the word 'Messieurs' – from each use of that word, uses in which the substance is constantly renewed, and which constitute each a separate and individual physical and psychic event.)

Some analogies that may illuminate the type–token dichotomy might be: equating 'type' with a concept of species and 'token' with particular specimens (for example, if I speak of 'The Horse'. I mean the whole species as a type, but if I speak of Red Rum, I mean a particular specimen/token); or equating 'type' with a particular abstract currency-value, say $1.00, and 'token' with a particular bank-note having that value. As we see from the two analogies, the type–token dichotomy is partly supported by a distinction between classes and members, and partly by a distinction between what is abstract and what is (relatively) concrete.

1.3.12 The Scope of 'Semiotic'

Peirce makes use of the term 'semiotic' – not '*a* semiotic' (which in some usages is short for 'a semiotic *system*'), nor 'semiotics' (which is its near-synonym in current Anglo-Saxon usage) – to designate an autonomous branch of science (just as Saussure used the term '*sémiologie*' to designate an autonomous science).

A comparison, in very general terms, between Saussure's '*sémiologie*' and Peirce's 'semiotic' serves as a useful starting-point in explaining the scope of the latter. The two major differences that emerge from such a comparison are (1) a considerable discrepancy in breadth of scope; (2) a significant discrepancy in emphasis.

Ironically, the terminological discrepancy between Peirce's use of 'sign' and Saussure's use of '*signe*' serves to conceal at first sight the immense difference in breadth of scope between 'semiotic' and '*sémiolo-*

gie'. As far as scope (of phenomena included) is concerned, Peirce's 'semiotic' – which he defines as 'the general theory of signs' – covers a vastly larger range, to which Saussure's 'sémiologie' stands roughly as the map of a country does to the map of the whole world. The analogy is not quite fair, however, since it is not necessarily a good thing to try to encompass a wider scope (with more chances of distortion in the description), rather than to narrow one's vision to a less wide field (within which the chances of precision are greater). Be that as it may, the comparison of relative scopes is put into proper perspective if we remember that what for Saussure is a 'signe' corresponds (fairly closely) to what for Peirce is a 'symbol', and that, while for Saussure the field of 'signes' constitutes the total scope of 'sémiologie', for Peirce 'symbols' are just a subcategory of entities within his field of interest. Peirce's field of interest extends beyond that of symbols to icons and indices. As a result, his general theory of signs presumably embraces every field where the 'signification' of something can in some way or other be 'interpreted'. This aspect of the difference between Saussure and Peirce can be summed up by the generalisation that Peirce's 'semiotic' is a theory of 'signification', while Saussure's 'sémiologie' is a theory of 'systems of conventions for communication' (cf. Introduction, p. 3).

Differences of emphasis, beyond those of scope, are, of course, largely attributable to the matter of direction of approach. At the risk of over-generalisation, we may say that Peirce looks upon the subject-matter of 'the general theory of signs' as a philosopher seeking to apply his philosophy to an area that he is most particularly interested in, believing it to hold the keys to such notions as 'understanding', 'inference', 'interpretation', 'knowledge', 'thought', 'truth', and so on. Accordingly, for Peirce 'semiotic' is a part, and a very vital part at that, of his conception of philosophical/cenoscopic science. As part and parcel of the direction in which Peirce approaches 'semiotic', it is understandable that his essentially philosophical concern with the question of 'how signification works (in principle)' leads him to concentrate most of the emphasis on a *natural* (Section 1.3.1, p. 17) classification of signs in terms of purpose and function.

Saussure, on the other hand, is interested in a theoretical typology of entities with significative function only (or virtually only) for the purpose of isolating the class of 'signe', so that the rest of his theory can be restricted to this class. Approaching, as he does, 'sémiologie' from the direction of 'linguistics', he is looking to 'sémiologie' for general principles (of systems of conventions for communication) that can be applied subsequently to the study of languages. As a 'linguist' he seeks in 'sémiologie' for notions other than those that chiefly concerned Peirce: 'convention', 'social norm', 'associative relations', 'systemic means of expression', 'systems of values within a code', 'syntagmatic/constructional systems within a code', etc.

The overall impression from this part of the comparison is that Peirce's emphasis is almost exclusively on the nature of communicative and significative entities, with relatively little attention paid to systems of such entities, and the constructional means by which systems may form complex symbols. (This impression is not wholly fair, with a view to Peirce's interest in 'syntax' and in the construction of logical systems with syntactic rules; however, this aspect of Peirce's work is of more concern to 'pure logic' than to 'descriptive semiotics'. As such, I do not feel that what Peirce means by 'syntax' falls within the scope of this discussion.) Peirce's relative lack of interest in actual systems or codes, as opposed to the devising of artificial logical codes, does not in any way belittle the importance of his work, which is no less great than that of Saussure, merely different.

Just as Saussure is belittled sometimes by what certain of his followers have made of his ideas, so Peirce's 'general theory of signs' may appear in a caricature version in the work of those who were influenced by him. This is particularly noticeable in behaviouristic adaptations of Peircean theory, where his fundamental question of 'how signification works (*in principle*)' is transformed into the altogether different question of 'how signification works (*in practice*)'. For certain, Peirce would have been the last to approve of attempts to answer the latter, practical question except by way of first answering the former, theoretical one.

2
Semiotics as a Behavioural Theory: Charles Morris

2.1 The Purpose of Morris' 'Semiotic'

2.1.1 Introductory Remarks

Designating the discipline that studies communication by the term 'semiotic' (as opposed to 'semiology' or 'semiotics') is a characteristic American usage. As such, it is symptomatic in the work of Morris, and of others, of the influence exercised by the ideas of Peirce on the general study of communication in the United States.

As we have seen, Peirce's original formulation of the term 'semiotic' designates 'the comprehensive doctrine of signs' or, in other words, 'the systematic study of signs'. The term 'sign' itself appears in the work of Peirce as an all-embracing term for the entire category of entities with the generic function of 'signification' (see Chapter 1, Section 1.3.12, p. 36).

Peirce's interest lay in the analysis and classification of all those abstract entities that, by virtue of their generic function and purpose, have the theoretical and logical status of 'signs'. The processes by which such (essentially statically conceived) constants become effective on the actual occasions of their use are only of indirect and secondary interest to Peirce – he is primarily concerned with *principles* and *constants*, not with *processes* and *variables*. Accordingly, we shall find that – in spite of Morris' obvious indebtedness to Peirce (virtually the only direct forerunner of Morris in the general study of communication) – the work of Peirce and the work of Morris fall into different perspectives.

2.1.2 Fundamental Departures from the Peircean Tradition

The term 'semiotic' fixes, both for Peirce and for Morris, the entire scope of study – and fixes it at the same wide extension covering all 'signs'. In both cases, anything that 'signifies' is an object of intrinsic interest for 'semiotic'.

However – and this is where a fundamental difference between Peirce and Morris begins to emerge – in Morris' formulation, the purpose of 'semiotic' is first and foremost the examination of actual and real processes concrete in time and space (that is, at best, what Peirce would have referred to as 'tokens' or 'replicas' of signs, rather than signs as 'types', see Chapter 1, Section 1.3.11, p. 34). These processes, which Morris calls processes of 'semiosis', are examined without a prior reflection on the types of sign they involve, and whatever eventually emerges in the way of general, theoretical principles is the result of inductive inference and inductive generalisation (cf. Section 2.3.2, p. 54). This makes Morris' 'semiotic' a science with a wholly different flavour from Peirce's non-inductive, philosophical 'semiotic'. Furthermore, in Morris' conception, each process of 'semiosis' is to be understood as a chain of events, with each complete chain constituting a complete communication *act*. What we are presented with in Morris' work, then, is an attempt to analyse communication *acts* into linked sequences of processes or events. The *process* of 'semiosis' is Morris' real object of study.

2.1.3 'Semiotic' and Behaviourism

There is an obvious connection between such a conception of 'semiotic', in which communication acts are seen as chains of events, one following automatically from another, and behaviouristic-mechanistic models of communication. Much of Morris' inspiration lies, therefore, in behavioural psychology, and especially in experimental work on 'conditioned reflexes' and 'substitutive behaviour' (Pavlov's famous experiments, for example). In this connection, Morris' 'semiotic' invites direct comparison with Bloomfield's earlier development of a behaviouristic-mechanistic model of the 'act of speech' (Bloomfield, 1935). In a sense, we may say that Bloomfield's model is a primitive version designed for 'acts of *speech*' of the model of 'semiosis' developed by Morris for the wider range of *all* communication acts.

In Bloomfield's model

$$S \rightarrow r \ldots s \rightarrow R$$

the component processes are initiated by a *practical stimulus* (S) that operates on the speaker and triggers off a *linguistic substitute response* (r) in the speaker. This response consists in the production of sound-waves, and the process linking the organisms of speaker and hearer is conceived of simply as the travelling of these sound-waves through the air (represented in the model by '. . .'). When these sound-waves reach the auditory organs of the hearer, they act upon them in their capacity as a *linguistic substitute stimulus* (s). The sequence is terminated by calling forth in the hearer an appropriate practical response to the linguistic substitute stimulus.

Such a segmentation of the speech act into successive component processes, linked together by mechanical/causal connections, is clearly far too simplistic. Its inadequacies are not difficult to uncover – for instance, it fails to elucidate the constancy of linguistic expressions and their meanings by smothering them in the infinite and imponderable variety of practical stimuli and corresponding practical responses (that is, the unpredictability of R from S, or of S from R) – (cf. Alston, 1964). This, however, is not the subject of our discussion at present. Suffice it to say, that the purpose of Morris' account of 'semiosis' is similar to that of Bloomfield's account of the 'act of speech' – in both cases an event or process initially regarded as an integral whole (*a* communication act, or *an* act of speech) is to be analysed as a sequence of mechanically/causally linked subprocesses. It is in this sense that Morris' 'semiotic' is an analytical study of 'specific action in a specific situation' (Morris, 1964).

Morris, while equating his aims with the development of 'semiotic' as a comprehensive doctrine of signs, equates 'sign' with 'sign-process' or 'semiosis'. Thus, since the sign is interpreted as a process – or, to be more precise, as an act – the contention that 'semiotic' can 'most profitably be developed on a biological basis and specifically within the framework of the science of behaviour' (Morris, 1964) becomes virtually a tautology. This points the way for Morris to take as his natural starting-point 'some distinctive kind of behaviour which agrees fairly well with frequent usage of the term "sign" ', and to develop 'semiotic' from this starting-point under the guidance of certain general principles of behaviour.

2.2   The Ingredients of 'Semiosis'

2.2.1   Paradigm Cases of 'Semiosis'

As a focal point of Morris' discussion of 'sign-behaviour', he isolates certain types of behaviour as being clear-cut, paradigm cases of 'semiosis'. Much of the argument centres round, and is developed from, the analysis of two paradigm examples.

The first of these, involving the *conditioned response* of a dog trained to seek food at a certain place on hearing a buzzer, represents a typical behavioural ('stimulus–response') process exemplifying the category of 'natural sign'. As such, this case marks one of the extremes of 'sign-behaviour', that is 'sign-behaviour' of the least 'intellectual' or 'conventional' type.

The opposite extreme of 'sign-behaviour' is pinpointed by the example of a driver who, on being verbally informed that a landslide has blocked the road ahead, responds by avoiding the obstacle. In this example, Morris sees the operation of a 'language sign' – presumably representing (in polar contrast to conditioned response) the human, intelligent and conventional use of signs.

The common factor to the two polar extremes – and therefore taken by Morris to constitute the defining core of 'semiosis' in all its manifestations – is the fact that in both paradigm examples, the organism responding to the production of a stimulus, dog and driver respectively, 'behave in a way that satisfies a need'. From this, Morris concludes that the type of behaviour to which 'sign-behaviour' belongs is 'goal-seeking behaviour', and that, therefore, signs should be identified and discussed within the general framework of 'goal-seeking behaviour'.

As Morris explains, although the *buzzer* and the *spoken message* are not reacted to in the way that an organism would react, respectively, to *food* and the *presence of a landslide*, 'yet in some sense, both the buzzer and the words control or direct the course of behaviour toward a goal in a way similar' to the presence of the actual stimuli (of food and landslide, respectively). This would suggest that Morris considers signs as 'substitute stimuli', having in mind the idea of some behavioural 'equivalence' between the concrete stimulus of some object (for example, food) and certain other stimuli that are reacted to 'as though' they were that object (for example, buzzer). Yet Morris is careful enough to point out that 'the response to food is to food itself, while the response to the buzzer is not to *it* (italics mine) as if it were food'. This makes it rather difficult to avoid a certain amount of indecision as to whether there is, in fact, 'some sense' in which signs are 'substitutes' for other stimuli and, if so, what that sense is. On the face of it, it would seem more plausible to maintain that, rather than 'substituting for' the stimulus of food, the stimulus of the buzzer directs attention to (or raises the expectation of) obtaining food.

Be that as it may, Morris' preliminary formulation of the notion 'sign' does not help to remove the source of this indecision:

> If A controls behaviour towards a goal in a way similar to (but not necessarily identical with) the way something else, B, would control behaviour with respect to that goal in a situation in which it were observed, then A is a sign. (Morris, 1946)

There are many serious objections to this, even as a preliminary formulation. In the first place, it is not at all clear that 'sign behaviour' must, in general, be 'goal-seeking' on the part of the sign-producing organism (if any), or 'goal-orientated' on the part of the responding organism. In much of everyday linguistic behaviour, the necessity to identify an appropriate, or plausible 'goal' towards which the use of particular signs (say, 'I've just seen a zebra') is directed would provide considerable embarrassment.

In the second place, there are serious difficulties with the notion of 'similarity'. Not only have we no real inkling of what it means for A and B to control behaviour similarly towards a given goal (would a hammer and a wooden clog control behaviour similarly with respect to fixing a nail?), but there are also embarrassing questions with regard to the similarity of A and B in Morris' formulation. Supposing B to be a bowl of food, and A to be a perfect replica (producing all the appropriate stimuli of sight and even smell) of a bowl of food made out of some non-edible substance, would one still want to regard A as a sign? Certainly, if one did so, the mechanisms of the 'sign-process' would be significantly different from those of a 'similar'(?) process in which the sound of the buzzer acted as a sign.

Thirdly, it seems unfortunate, though fairly typical of Morris' style of argumentation, that in what is meant to be a solidly down-to-earth behavioural study of 'specific action in a specific situation', he resorts to imagined situations. His definition of 'sign' as a 'substitute stimulus' falls back on what *would* happen in a situation whose details are controlled by his imagination (and not what *does* happen), thereby putting his 'observations' into the 'subjunctive' mood.

2.2.2   Preliminary Notions of 'Sign-Behaviour'

Preliminary formulations point the way to more precise, and hopefully more successful formulation, and it is Morris' intention to develop a more tenable and sophisticated formulation of 'sign-behaviour' than the one discussed above. For this he requires to clarify the concept of 'similarity of behaviour', as well as that of 'goal-seeking behaviour', a task which he attempts through the four basic notions: (1) preparatory stimulus, (2) disposition to respond, (3) response-sequence, (4) behaviour family.

In the notion of 'preparatory stimulus', Morris hopes to find a candidate for replacing the inauspicious notion of 'substitute stimulus'. To lay the foundations for the concept of 'preparatory stimulus', he provides the following definitions: (a) 'stimulus' for 'any physical energy which acts upon a receptor of a living organism'; (b) 'stimulus object' for 'the source of this energy'; (c) 'response' for 'any action of a muscle or gland'.

These definitions create the impression that the terms 'stimulus' and 'response' have been freed from any mutual dependence upon one another – the necessary presence of an accompanying response is not built into the definition of 'stimulus', nor the necessary presence of a triggering stimulus into the definition of 'response'. This would be odd in principle, since an energy not responded to (if this is at all possible) would not normally be called a stimulus, and an action not triggered off by a stimulus (if there may be such an action) would not normally be called a response. In practice, however, neither any other behaviourist, nor Morris himself, would conceive of a 'responseless stimulus' or of a 'response not in reaction to a stimulus'. Thus nothing positive is gained by pretending that 'stimulus' can be defined independently of 'response' and 'response' defined independently of 'stimulus'.

Morris' purpose in developing the notion of 'behaviour-family' seems 'stimulus' and 'response' from their mutual dependence. By this device he attempts to make room for the crucial notion of 'preparatory stimulus': a stimulus that *does not cause* a response, but merely influences a subsequent response to some other stimulus. Thus, the effects of a 'preparatory stimulus' are not direct, but are manifested only in the modification of the response to some other overt stimulus. This does not mean that preparatory stimuli themselves are covert – the buzzer in Morris' example is overt enough, to be sure – but rather that no direct response to the stimulus object ensues from a 'preparatory stimulus'. Thus the stimulus of the buzzer does not trigger off a direct response to the buzzer itself, but is rather instrumental in a response leading up to and culminating (ideally) in the consuming of food. Since, however, all behavioural links are fundamentally causal, a stimulus that does not actually cause a response by direct means seems to be somewhat in the nature of a contradiction in terms. Perhaps the best way to understand the notion of 'preparatory stimulus', under the circumstances, is by analogy with 'catalysts' in chemical reactions. (I am indebted to Dr D. Roberts, Department of Linguistics, University of St Andrews, for suggesting this analogy.) A 'preparatory stimulus' might, in other words, be seen as a kind of

---

ERRATUM

Page 42, paragraph 4, first line, *should read*

Morris does, however, have a positive purpose in apparently freeing

behavioural 'catalyst' whose role is the indirect control of reactions – a contributory (or 'disposing') factor, not a direct cause.

Behavioural accounts of communication, in general, face the difficulty that 'semiosis' (for example, the act of linguistic utterance) does not need to involve any overt response to the production of a sign. The notion of 'preparatory stimulus' is part of Morris' solution to this problem. The other half of the solution resides in the concept of a 'disposition to respond'.

While a response is to be understood as an action performed in reply to a stimulus, a 'disposition to respond' must be seen as a state brought about through the agency of a 'preparatory stimulus'. In fact, a 'disposition to respond' is to be understood as some, presumably specific, state of an organism such that, when certain additional circumstances obtain, a specific response will be released. That is to say, a 'disposition to respond' occasioned by the operation of a 'preparatory stimulus' is not, as such, an overt response, but a latent potential for a future, conditional response (that is, Morris is, here again, speaking about concrete facts in a 'subjunctive' mood). 'Dispositions to respond' are knowable in concrete terms only through the ultimate overt responses that might be released under favourable conditions. The set of appropriate conditions are (circularly) those which favour the release of suitable overt responses. Therefore the notion of 'disposition to respond' must be interpreted as an 'operational fiction' designed to fill the gap left by the lack of observable response in a substantial number of cases of 'semiosis'.

In order to locate 'sign-behaviour' fair and square within 'goal-seeking' behaviour, Morris develops the notion of 'response-sequences' in a very specialised sense. A 'normal' response-sequence in his conception is not only a causally linked sequence of responses, but a sequence that is completed by having the character of a full circle:

| stimulus object A | . . . | set of responses | . . . | terminal response *directed at goal-object A* |

That is to say, one and the same object A appears both as the initial stimulus object and as the final goal-object to which a terminal response is directed.

The prototype of a complete 'response-sequence' is illustrated by practical, non-communicative behaviour, for instance, in the chain of responses that the stimulus, emanating from a rabbit (stimulus object) may set up in a dog, and that finds its satisfactory (for the dog, that is) culmination in the terminal response of the dog eating the rabbit (goal object).

While all sequences involving responses must be initiated by a stimulus object – a stimulus is a physical energy, and physical energy must emanate from some specific physical source – it is not necessarily the case that every sequence will come round full circle, and culminate in an overt response directed at the initial source of stimulus. That is to say, the terminal goal-object is not necessarily identical with the initial stimulus object. It is, however, only when stimulus object and goal-object are identical that Morris is prepared to speak of a (complete) 'response-sequence'.

The completion of a 'response-sequence' is said to provide (indirect) evidence of a specific 'disposition to respond'. It is argued that satisfactory termination of a 'response-sequence' is the fulfilment of a latent 'disposition' that pre-dates the actual terminal response, and yet is a 'disposition' towards the ultimate goal-object. In terms of the *dog eats rabbit* example, this argument seems to have some force. It is quite plausible to say that the very sight (stimulus) of the rabbit creates, in the dog, the anticipation (disposition) of eating the self-same rabbit (goal-object). Morris annexes incomplete 'response-sequences' to complete ones, in order to be in the position to maintain that the former, too, provide evidence of a specific 'disposition to respond'. Thus, if the sounding of a buzzer only causes the habituated dog to respond by salivation, we are to interpret this event as part of a food-orientated 'response-sequence' (even though the dog cannot eat the buzzer, and may not be able to fulfil its anticipation of food in any way whatsoever). On this basis, the 'disposition' set up by the sound of the buzzer is taken to be exactly akin to the 'disposition' that would figure in a complete 'response-sequence' that is initiated by the stimulus of food and that terminates in the successful obtaining of food.

The treatment of 'response-sequences' presupposes that there are clear-cut natural boundaries between the three categories (1) complete response-sequences; (2) incomplete response-sequences that are, nevertheless, analogous with *parts* of complete response-sequences; and (3) sequences of events that fall altogether outside the realm of 'goal-seeking' behaviour. If there are no such natural boundaries, the identification of incomplete 'response-sequences' as parts of the appropriate complete 'response-sequences' cannot even be attempted. But without this identification we lack the fundamental evidence for talking about specific 'dispositions to respond' in cases of incomplete 'response-sequences'. The specification of 'preparatory stimuli' in terms of indirect evidence, must suffer accordingly.

It does not help, at this point, to be assured by Morris that sufficient evidence for the 'dispositions' set up by 'signs' would be provided if one could measure the effects of 'preparatory stimuli' in terms of 'the state of the organism – say its brain waves'. The fact remains that, while such measurements are in the realms of practical impossibility, 'dispositions to respond' can only be posited on the insufficient evidence provided by highly suspect analogies between what happens when there is an overt response to an overt stimulus, and what can be imagined to happen when there is no overt response, or the overt response is not directed at the overt stimulus object.

Morris' purpose in developing the notion of behaviour-family' seems to be clear. If there were 'behaviour-families' (natural classes of goal-seeking behaviour), and if certain incomplete 'response-sequences' (those involving 'preparatory stimuli' and oblique responses) belonged in the same 'behaviour-family' as do certain complete 'response-sequences', it would be valid to transpose the 'dispositions' made overt in complete sequences to incomplete sequences belonging to the same 'behaviour-family'. The intention, in other words, is to use the similarity between members of the same 'behaviour-family' as a basis for treating those situations in which overt response is lacking analogously with those situations in which there is an overt response.

To one and the same 'behaviour-family', Morris intends to assign members that are (1) disparate in the nature of initial stimulus; (2) disparate in the nature of ultimate response; (3) disparate in both initial stimulus and ultimate response; (4) not response-sequences at all, because there is no response directed at a goal-object. Thus 'behaviour-families' are close-knit only in their nucleus – they are extended and elastic groups as to actual membership.

The nucleus of a 'behaviour-family' is a group of 'response-sequences' initiated by similar stimulus objects and terminating in these objects as similar goal objects. Thus, to take a simple example, all rabbits are similar as stimulus objects. They are also similar objects as goal objects in satisfying hunger (that is, as food). Therefore, one can assign to the same 'behaviour-family' all response-sequences that start with a stimulus emanating from any given rabbit, and terminate with the self-same rabbit being eaten. This grouping creates the nucleus of the rabbit–food 'behaviour-family'. So far, the situation is relatively straightforward. One only needs to assume that, whatever differences there may be between any two members of the rabbit–food 'behaviour-family', these differences can be ignored in a typology of behaviour. In fact, whether the response-sequence involves a black dog seeing, hearing and smelling a white rabbit, and finally eating that same rabbit, or whether it involves a grey wolf seeing, hearing and smelling a black rabbit, and finally getting to eat that rabbit, is indifferent to the membership of these response-sequences in one and the same 'behaviour-family'.

By ignoring minor differences between food-seeking organisms (dog, wolf, and so on) and between rabbits-as-food-objects (white, black, etc., rabbits) a relatively close-knit group of response-sequences has been formed. This group, however, only constitutes the nucleus of a 'behaviour-family' of the extended kind that Morris requires for his purposes. To the same 'behaviour-family' he hopes to assign also, for instance, events initiated by the sounding of a buzzer, or the uttering of certain words, and terminating in the eating of a rabbit. Here it must be remembered that the explanatory potential of Morris' theory depends on being able to say that the same 'disposition to eat a rabbit' *may* be set up by the sounding of a buzzer, or by the uttering of certain words, as *is* triggered off by the stimulus of a rabbit. This sameness of 'disposition to respond' hinges on the membership of the *buzzer–food*, or *words–food*, behaviour-sequence in the *rabbit–food* 'behaviour-family', in spite of the obvious disparity of the respective stimulus objects.

In the above situation, the presence of a rabbit as goal-object served as a link between behaviour initiated by the stimulus of a rabbit and behaviour initiated by some other 'preparatory stimulus'. The notion of 'behaviour-family' is, however, wider than this, and embraces behaviour sequences in which even this link is absent. For instance, the rabbit–food 'behaviour-family' must be extended so as to accommodate situations in which there is no overt response to a rabbit (or, for that matter, to any actual food). Thus, the sounding of the buzzer, or the uttering of certain words, need to be only potentially linked to the eating of a rabbit – in the sense that this might be an appropriate response released in the right circumstances. This is, of course, an integral part of the idea that the 'disposition' set up by buzzer or words can be identified as the same 'disposition–to–eat–a–rabbit', whether that disposition remains latent, or whether it is released in an overt response.

Common 'behaviour-family' membership could be claimed, under the extended notion of 'behaviour-families', for the following behavioural sequences.

rabbit stimulus	→	disposition–to–eat–a–rabbit	. . .	eating of rabbit
buzzer stimulus	→	disposition–to–eat–a–rabbit	. . .	eating of rabbit
verbal stimulus	→	disposition–to–eat–a–rabbit	. . .	eating of rabbit
buzzer stimulus	→	disposition–to–eat–a–rabbit	. . .	
verbal stimulus	→	disposition–to–eat–a–rabbit	. . .	

Discussion of the notions 'preparatory stimulus', 'response-sequence', 'disposition to respond' and 'behaviour-family' leads on to Morris' formulation of the sufficient conditions for something to be a 'sign' (Morris 1946):

If anything, A, is a preparatory stimulus which in the absence of stimulus objects intitiating response-sequences of a certain behaviour-family causes a disposition in some organism to respond under certain conditions by response-sequences of this behaviour-family, then A is a sign.

The import of this formulation is that A is recognised as being a sign if (though not necessarily only if) it produces a 'disposition' that one would normally expect to be produced by some other stimulus object. The normal stimulus object is typically *absent* from sign-behaviour. Thus, an object A operates as a sign on condition that it does *not* initiate a 'normal' response-sequence terminating in a response to A as a goal object – otherwise A is not a sign, but merely an ordinary stimulus object. If there is a terminal response in the behaviour-sequence initiated by A, and A is a sign, then that response must be directed at a goal-object other than A. This response must, therefore, be of a type that would normally complete a response-sequence initiated by an object other than A. The only guarantee that the response is not merely to a normal stimulus object doubling as goal-object is the absence of such an object. Thus, if the response evoked by A is of a type normally terminating a response-sequence whose goal-object is B, then, in order for A to be a sign, A must substitute for, and exclude the presence of, B. Furthermore, a terminal response itself may be absent when A operates as a sign, as long as it seems possible to maintain that the response to A, had there been any, would have been of the type normally associated with the stimulus of B.

When the buzzer acts as a sign, and there is, of course, no food as a stimulus object, so that there cannot be any terminal response to food as goal-object either, we have a behaviour sequence whose only 'constant' link with the behaviour-family of 'food-directed' response-sequences is the 'disposition' produced by the buzzer. It is the alleged sameness of this 'disposition' with the 'disposition' mediating in response-sequence of the type

$$\text{food-stimulus} \rightarrow \text{disposition X} \rightarrow \text{eating of food}$$

which constitutes the sole common property between sign-behaviour and normal response-sequences.

The powerful notion of 'disposition to respond' is absolutely central to Morris' semiotic, and provides, as we shall see below, a stepping-stone between his formulation of 'semiosis' in the context of the notions 'preparatory stimulus', 'response-sequence' and 'behaviour-family' on the one hand, and his analysis of sign-behaviour as being constituted by a set of inter-related factors on the other.

2.2.3 Analytic Models of 'Semiosis'

Semiosis, as a process, is analysed by Morris in terms of the interplay between five basic factors – though the list of factors is not constant throughout his works. If we were to conflate the two major versions (Morris, 1946 and 1964 – see below), a set of six factors would be yielded. I propose to discuss mainly the 1946 version, but, for reference, the following table comparing this version to the later one may be consulted:

1946 version	*1964 version*
(1) Sign = preparatory stimulus	(1) Sign = stimulus
(2) Interpreter = organism for which something is a sign	(2) Interpreter = organism responding to stimulus
(3) Interpretant = disposition caused by a sign in the interpreter to respond by response-sequences of some behaviour-family	(3) Interpretant = disposition to react in a certain way as a result of the sign
(4) Denotatum = anything that would permit the completion of the response-sequence to which the interpreter is disposed by the sign	
(5) Significatum = sufficient and necessary conditions for something to be a denotatum of the sign	(4) Signification = kind of object towards which the interpreter's disposition to respond is directed by the sign
	(5) Context = whole situation in which the sign occurs

The notable differences between the two formulations are in the deletion of the term 'denotatum' from, and the addition of the term 'context' to, the later version. The fact that the latter is relatively unimportant as compared to the deleted 'denotatum' (in that Morris makes very little use of 'context') is my main reason for centring discussion round the 1946 version. For the rest, the notions are more or less equivalent in both versions, even where the change of terminology from 'significatum' to 'signification' seems to suggest the contrary.

Of the five terms in the 1946 version, 'sign' has already been extensively discussed, and 'interpreter' is sufficiently obvious not to require discussion. This leaves the notions 'interpretant', 'denotatum' and 'significatum', and the interplay between them, for further analysis.

By the 'interpretant' of a sign, Morris means that 'disposition' which is produced (in the interpreter) by the sign, and which is specifically directed at a response characteristic of some identifiable behaviour-family. Such a 'disposition' is, presumably, the common factor that classifies together those signs (or sign-vehicles) that are of the same sign-type. In other words, what Bloomfield would have called the 'constant and specific' features of 'meaning' – for instance, what we would think of as the 'lexical' meaning of a 'word' – would, according to Morris, reside in features of the 'interpretant'. The notion 'interpretant' – stateable in terms of some specific 'disposition to respond' – is, therefore, a crucial theoretical and descriptive notion.

The notion of 'denotatum', defined as an object that would enable the interpreter to complete a particular type of response-sequence, clearly hinges on the 'interpretant' of the sign, that is, the 'disposition' produced by the sign. The type of response-sequence which the 'denotatum' is potentially able to fulfil is the type of response-sequence to which the sign disposes the interpreter. Thus, deciding the nature of the 'denotatum' of a sign requires prior knowledge of the nature of the 'disposition' ('interpretant') produced by the sign. Given this knowledge, one may pick on any particular object that would be suitable as a goal-object in a response-sequence where the latent 'disposition' created by the sign is released in an appropriate terminal response.

If it is the case that one can discover the definition of a class (that is, the sufficient and necessary properties of its members) from observation of members of that class, then finding the 'signification' (Morris, 1964) or 'significatum' (Morris, 1946) of a sign will follow automatically from the identification of objects that qualify as 'denotata' of the sign. On the other hand, it may be the case that we need to know what 'kind' of object may qualify as a 'denotatum' in advance of deciding whether a particular object does or does not qualify as such. Alternatively, 'denotatum' and 'significatum' may be interdependent in the sense that to know one is to know the other. This would be quite acceptable, as, in any case, specification of the 'interpretant' includes reference to both the 'kind' of object to which the sign disposes the interpretant to respond ('significatum'), and actual objects ('denotata') at which this disposition is aimed in specific instances. At any rate, 'denotatum' is implied by 'significatum', and the removal of the notion 'denotatum' from Morris' 1964 version merely deletes from explicit mention a factor that is, in any case, implicit in the notion of 'signification'.

In order to illustrate the application of the five-term analysis of semiosis, we shall analyse Morris' classic examples of (a) a *dog* conditioned to seek food at a certain place on hearing a *buzzer*, and (b) a *driver* alerted by word of mouth that there is a landslide blocking the road ahead.

In the example of the dog, semiosis involves the following factors

Sign = Sound of the buzzer

Interpreter = the dog   Interpretant = disposition
                         (set up by the buzzer in
                         the dog) to seek food at
                         place *x*

Denotatum = a piece of   Significatum = the condition
     food found at   of there being food at
     place *x*   place *x*

In this instance of semiosis, the sound of the buzzer acts as a preparatory stimulus setting up a 'disposition' in the dog (which has been conditioned in the Pavlovian manner) to seek food in a certain place. To put it bluntly, the effect of the buzzer is to produce a certain specific expectancy. This expectancy, in its purely latent form, constitutes the 'interpretant' of the sign. This 'interpretant' has no necessary correlates in externalised behaviour, since it suffices for it to exist in latent form, yet its character is wholly conceived in terms of the specific form of overt behaviour to which the buzzer disposes the dog: namely the seeking of food in place *x*. Of course, in the case of a controlled experiment in which the dog has been conditioned to expect the presence of food in place *x* each time the buzzer sounds, one may claim to know, *a priori*, the exact character of the dog's expectation. Since the dog has been conditioned towards a specific kind of behaviour, it is not implausible to assume that, each time the buzzer sounds, this is the kind of behaviour that the dog is disposed to perform, and that it is so disposed independently of whether there is actually any food at place *x*.

Once knowledge of the 'interpretant' is claimed or assumed, the rest of the terms of semiosis are known by implication. What enables the dog to fulfil its expectations of finding food at place *x* on any given occasion, can, of course, only be some edible object at place *x* on that particular occasion. Thus it is obvious (tautologically) that the particular piece of food at a place *x* on a given occasion must be the 'denotatum' of the sound of the buzzer. If, on a given occasion, there happens to be no food at place *x*, one merely remarks that in this case, there is absence of a 'denotatum'. The sound of the buzzer may or may not actually denote in given instances.

While the sound of the buzzer may lack a 'denotatum', it can never lack a 'significatum'. But this it cannot fail to have in any case, because the 'significatum' of the sound of the buzzer is a tautological implicate of its 'interpretant'. Having said that the 'interpretant' is a disposition to seek food at place x, we have already stipulated that the general condition for there being a 'denotatum' (or, for that matter, the 'kind' of object towards which the dog's disposition is directed by the sign) is food present at place x. Thus we may say that 'interpretant', 'denotatum' and 'significatum' are not three independent factors engaged in semiosis; rather, both 'denotatum' and 'significatum' are dependent on, and follow from 'interpretant'. Therefore, although Morris starts with the view that semiosis is intrinsically a five-term relation, and qualifies this by pointing out that only four of the terms (with the exception of 'denotatum' which may be absent) are *sine qua non* conditions for a sign-process, in final analysis only three of the terms represent separately relevant, independent and necessary factors.

Further revealing points concerning Morris' analysis of semiosis can be uncovered by examining his example of the sign-process that takes place when a driver is verbally informed of the presence of a landslide blocking the road ahead. The example as contrived by Morris is analysed as follows:

$$Sign = Spoken\ words\ (sic!)$$

Interpreter = the driver
                                     Interpretant = disposition (set up by the spoken words in the driver) to avoid the landslide at place x

Denotatum = the landslide at place x
                                  Significatum = the condition of there being a landslide at place x

It may seem unfair to refer to this example as being 'contrived'. However, the fact of the matter is that – except for Morris' stipulation of this as a 'fact' – we have no guarantee that the 'sign' will dispose the driver to avoid the landslide (rather than, say, to go and help clear it out of the way). As we are not even informed of the particular words that act on the driver as preparatory stimulus, we simply have to accept Morris' word that these words, and the driver's external and internal situation, are indeed such that he becomes disposed to avoid the landslide by taking a side-road. However, in accepting this, we are no longer dealing with a real empirical situation whose factors are to be determined by observation. Instead, we are faced with an idealised situation whose factors are predetermined – in fact 'contrived' – by Morris himself. The infinite variability of linguistic stimuli, and of the responses evoked by them, is totally ignored by this idealisation. Instead, the situation is dealt with as though it were a controlled experiment similar to controlled experiments with conditioned response.

Given that in a particular instance the spoken words produce in the driver a disposition to avoid the landslide, we also automatically infer that the goal-object of the disposition must be the landslide at place x. On this basis, therefore, an actual landslide at place x will, in each case where there is a 'denotatum', constitute the 'denotatum' of the sign in question. Of course, there may not be any landslide at that place – the driver's informant may be telling a lie, or be merely mistaken. This is provided for in that (as we have already seen) signs may or may not denote. However, the sign will necessarily have a 'significatum', since the nature of the 'significatum' is automatically determined by the 'interpretant' of the sign. Here, unfortunately, we are faced with a possibility of obtaining two different results in reconstructing the 'significatum' and 'denotatum', according to how we interpret Morris' intention, as we shall see below.

If we approach the 'significatum' via the 'denotatum', we must conclude (in agreement with Morris' own conclusions) that, since particular landslides at the place x are the objects of the driver's expectation ('disposition'), these are the 'denotata' of the sign in question. Accordingly, the 'significatum', which is constituted by the defining properties of the 'denotata', must be the general condition of there being a landslide at the designated place.

On the other hand, if we approach the 'significatum' via the 'interpretant', and – taking Morris at his word – look for the 'kind' of object that might enable the driver to perform the behaviour to which the sign has disposed him, we will have to conclude that the landslide itself is the last thing that could fulfil the driver's disposition to *avoid the landslide at place* x. In fact, if the driver has been disposed (by the words uttered) to avoid the landslide, the 'kind' of object that might enable him to satisfy his disposition to evasive action would be something like a side-road down which he can turn before he comes to the landslide at place x. In this sense, then, on a purely dispositional account, the 'significatum' of the sign turns out to be the *condition of there being a side-road before place x.*

If the 'significatum' is the 'kind' of object towards which the interpreter's disposition is directed by the sign, it is at least possible to maintain that this must be the 'kind' of object that might permit the completion of the behaviour to which the interpreter is disposed by the sign. In that case, the 'kind' of object that can serve could well be a *side-road before place x*, and the 'denotatum' becomes, in any given instance, a particular side-road that fulfils the driver's need.

On the other hand, if the driver's disposition is to be equated with his expectation of finding a landslide at place x, then the 'significatum' is, indeed, the *condition of there being a landslide at place x*, and the denotatum is, in each instance, a particular landslide at place x.

The latter is consistent with the idea that, through the use of certain spoken words, the driver has been informed of the presence of a landslide at place x. This is, of course, extremely plausible on the face of it, but its connection with the driver's disposition to respond by choosing an alternative route is, to say the least, tenuous. Counter-intuitive though it may be, the analysis of the *driver–landslide* example would, if interpreted in the light of Morris' view of semiosis in the context of goal-directed behaviour, have the following form:

Sign = Spoken words

Interpreter = the driver

Interpretant = disposition (set up by the spoken words in the driver) to avoid the landslide at place x.

Denotatum = a particular side-road (permitting the driver to avoid the landslide, as he has been disposed to do by the sign).

Significatum = the condition of there being a side-road before place x.

2.3   Derived Notions of 'Semiotic'

2.3.1   Dimensions of Signification

The analysis of 'semiosis' provides Morris with a basis for developing a theory of 'modes of signification'. Contrary to first impressions (which are actually corrected by Morris himself) these 'modes of signification' are not designed as mutually exclusive properties that lead to the classification of signs. Rather, they are 'dimensions' on which the signification of particular instances of 'semiosis' is to be assessed. Thus, as Morris points out, individual sign-processes may function simultaneously in several 'modes of signification' to varying degrees.

Once again – as in the case of the terms involved in 'semiosis' – there is no definitive list of the 'modes of signification'. Instead, we may conveniently distinguish the set of modes given in Morris, 1946 from that given in Morris, 1964:

1946 version		*1964 version*	
(1)	Designative mode	(1)	Designative mode
(2)	Appraisive mode	(2)	Appraisive mode
(3)	Identificative mode		
(4)	Prescriptive mode	(3)	Prescriptive mode
(5)	Formative mode	(4)	Formative mode

As a first step in the explanation of 'modes of signification', it must be pointed out that, although Morris conceives of these modes as being matters of the 'significatum' (or 'signification'), and asserts that the dimensions in question involve looking at sign-processes from 'the angle of the significatum', they can only be meaningfully discussed in terms of the 'interpretants' of signs. Thus, Morris maintains that the modes are characterised by 'different types of significata', but follows this up with the statement that a 'significatum' necessarily involves an interpretant, and 'hence the major kinds of significata must be distinguished in terms of distinctions between interpretants'. There is, of course, no objection to this – given that we have already noted how 'significata' are entirely determined by the behavioural dispositions that signs produce in 'interpreters' towards certain kinds of object. We may, however, feel that the term 'mode of signification' is a slight misnomer, in that relevant discussion of these modes involves the dimension of 'interpretant', rather than that of 'significatum'.

When explained in terms of a categorisation of types of 'disposition to respond', the major 'modes of signification' (excluding the 'formative mode') can be given the following characterisations:

(1) *Designative mode:* the sign directs attention to a certain object with certain salient characteristics: that is, the disposition is directed at a *property* (discriminatum) of objects, rather than at the objects themselves; a sign that operates in this dimension is called a 'designator'.

(2) *Appraisive mode:* the sign directs attention to the preferential treatment of certain objects; that is, the disposition produced by the sign is constituted by a *value judgement* with regard to certain objects (valuata); a sign that operates in this dimension is called an 'appraisor'.

(3) *Identificative mode:* the sign directs attention to a certain spatial-temporal region; that is, the disposition is directed towards some spatio-temporally located *entity* (locatum); a sign that operates in this dimension is called an 'identifier'.

(4) *Prescriptive mode:* the sign directs attention to performance of certain required responses, as opposed to others; that is, the disposition is a disposition to a required *action* (obligatum); a sign that operates in this dimension is called a 'prescriptor'.

The *formative mode*, and signs operating as 'formators', will require separate treatment. These do not unfold from considerations of the nature of the disposition produced by the sign, and are, as such, probably not capable of a 'dispositional' explanation. The first four modes are, however, differentiated in terms of the type of 'disposition to respond' that they involve. These four dimensions may be illustrated by the following examples that shed light on Morris' purpose in classifying 'modes of signification':

(1) the sign 'red' operates as a *designator* in producing a 'disposition to respond' to a certain kind of *colour property* (regardless of whatever object may manifest that property);

(2) the sign 'good' operates as an *appraisor* in producing a 'disposition to respond' by *preferring* certain objects (as being more beneficial to the interpreter than others);

(3) the sign 'that book' operates as an *identifier* in producing a 'disposition to respond' constituted by the interpreter's attention being drawn to the spatio-temporal *location* where the book in question is to be found;

(4) the sign 'go away' operates as a *prescriptor* in producing a 'disposition to respond' by performing a certain kind of *action* (one that involves the interpreter's departure from a certain location).

The modes of signification outlined above leave out of consideration a further important class of signs: the so-called 'logical signs' (such as 'not', 'and', 'or', etc.). These signs Morris designates as 'formators' – signs operating in the 'formative mode'. This further mode cannot be dispensed with, for without it, a significant type of 'meaning' (variously described as 'logical', 'grammatical', or 'structural' throughout the literature) would be left unaccounted for. Morris is committed, in one respect, to taking the view that in, say, 'book *and* pen', the sign 'and' is not a mere connective between other signs, but that it also signifies, in its own right, something about the situation in which it is uttered. In another respect, however, Morris is even more strongly committed to treating the 'formative mode' on a par with other modes of signification. This commitment forces him to interpret the signification of 'and' as some kind of 'disposition to respond' produced in an interpreter by the sign 'and'. Unfortunately, in the case of 'formators', Morris is unable to specify a characteristic type of 'disposition to respond' by which they can be identified and explained. He falls back, therefore, on explaining 'formators' in terms of the operations they perform on the *signs* that they inter-connect – rather than on dispositions that they might, in their own right, produce in an interpreter.

2.3.2 Types of Sign

Morris makes use of the intellectual framework provided by his five-term analysis of 'semiosis' to develop a number of important categories into which signs may fall (apart from the earlier-discussed categories established in the dimension of 'modes of signification').

(1) *Unisituational sign: a sign-vehicle that does not belong to any sign-family.*

Morris remarks that such signs rarely, if ever, occur. It is probable that, by this remark, he understates the case – for it would seem that such signs could not exist *in principle*. Once a given sign-vehicle has been shown capable of setting up a particular disposition in an interpreter (without which there can be no talk of 'sign-vehicle' at all), it is no longer possible to preclude the occurrence of a similar sign-vehicle producing a similar disposition in the same interpreter on another occasion. In other words, unless it is maintained that there are physical events that are not similar to any other physical events (and therefore cannot, in that sense, be reproduced), every sign-vehicle automatically implies a sign-family to which belong other, similar sign-vehicles producing, on different occasions, a similar 'disposition to respond' in at least one interpreter.

(2) *Plurisituational sign: a sign-vehicle which belongs, as do most (sic!) sign-vehicles, to some particular sign-family.*

(3) *Interpersonal sign: a sign which has the same signification for a number of interpreters.*

In Morris' formulation, sign-vehicles belonging to the same sign-family have 'the same' significatum *for a given interpreter*. 'Interpersonal signs' require the 'sameness' of significatum to hold between different interpreters. In order to cross the boundary between different organisms acting as interpreters, the notion of a 'sign-family' must be broadened beyond the context of a given interpreter. The notion of 'interpersonal sign' points the way to Morris' formulation of 'language sign' as a type of sign that, characteristically, has the same signification for communicator and interpreter alike.

(4) *Interpreter-family: a group of interpreters for whom a sign has the same signification.*

The recognition of 'sameness' of signification between numbers of interpreters automatically entails that every 'interpersonal sign' determines a group of organisms for whom that sign has 'the same signification'. The notion of 'interpreter-family' would, presumably, constitute a factor in determining 'speech-communities'.

(5) *Comsign: a subspecies of interpersonal sign, having the same signification for the organism that produces it as it has for its interpreter.*

In the category of 'comsigns' Morris attempts to capture the notion of certain signs being produced deliberately for creating a specific disposition in an interpreter. The communicator using a 'comsign' knows the exact nature of the disposition he intends to produce in the interpreter, because the sign in question would create just such a disposition in him (that is, the communicator) if he were in the role of interpreter. Thus, 'comsign' hinges on the putative interchangeability (Hockett, 1958) of roles between communicator and interpreter.

(6) *Vague sign: a sign whose signification does not permit the determination of whether a given x is or is not a denotatum of that sign.*

Doubtless, Morris is motivated by the observation of the use of proper names (John, Smith, John Smith, and so on) to set up his category of 'vague signs'. From the fact that, say, *John Smith* has a signification in terms of the condition that only male humans can qualify as denotata of the sign, it is impossible to determine whether a given individual male human is or is not a denotatum of *John Smith*.

(7) *Unambiguous sign-vehicle: a sign-vehicle that has only one significatum, and, consequently, belongs to only one sign-family.*

(8) *Ambiguous sign-vehicle: a sign-vehicle that has several significata, and, consequently, belongs to several sign-families.*

Morris is motivated to make the distinction between 'ambiguous' and 'unambiguous' signs by the observation that, while certain signs (for example, typewriter) can only have one kind of object as their denotata, other signs (for example, table) must be multiply classified according to the different kinds of object that may qualify as their denotata (for example, a dining-table and a mathematical table do not constitute *one* kind of object).

(9) *Singular sign: sign whose significatum permits only one denotatum, the conditions for denotatum-hood being so restricted as to admit of only one object in reality.*

When Morris exemplifies 'singular sign' by citing the expression (sign) 'the President of the United States in 1944', it is clear that he has in mind the time-honoured philosophical problem of 'uniqueness of reference'. It is possible that there may indeed be sign-families such that each of their members can only be used to denote a unique physical object – as opposed to, say, the sound of the buzzer which, in a conditioned response experiment, can have any piece of food as its denotatum on a given occasion. It should, however, be noted that 'the President of the United States in 1944' is a 'singular sign' *by accident*, and not by nature. It is a mere contingent historical fact that in 1944, there did not happen to be more than one President of the United States. The significatum of this sign is not, in fact, so limited as to permit only one denotatum.

Another example of 'singular sign' cited by Morris is that of the personal pronoun 'I'. The basis on which this statement rests is that the sign 'I' permits only the speaker, one speaker at a time, to qualify as a denotatum. The sign 'I' has, in fact, a significatum which permits the denotatum to be, in each case, *the person who is speaking* – but since this person varies from occasion to occasion, the sign 'I' has as many possible denotata as there are speakers to utter it.

(10) *General sign: a sign whose significatum permits any number of possible denotata, the conditions for denotatum-hood being so fixed as to admit a whole range of objects that may answer the specifications.*

Unless successful examples are found to illustrate the category of 'singular signs', the suspicion may remain that *all signs* are 'general signs'. We may, however, supply Morris with the example of the expression 'the Matterhorn' as a sign that may well qualify for uniqueness of reference, given which, the notion 'general sign' is no longer trivial.

Morris alludes to the possibility of putting signs on a scale (*hierarchy* might be a better term) according to degree of generality. Presumably this would involve the idea that a sign *x* whose significatum permits as possible denotata all the objects that are permitted to be denotata of another sign *y*, plus a number of further objects, is *more general* than the sign *y*.

From the example of Figure 2.1 it is clear that more and less general signs are what, nowadays, are most commonly known under the terms 'superordinate' and 'hyponym', respectively (Lyons, 1963, cf. also 'hyperonym' and 'hyponym' in Hervey, 1970 and 1979). A sign *x* which is

class of objects
permitted to serve
as denotata by the
significatum of
sign *x*

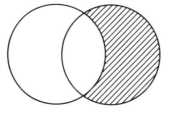

class of objects
permitted to serve
as denotata by the
significatum of
sign *y*

Figure 2.1

more general than, or equally as general as, another sign *y* is said by Morris to be an *analytic implicate* of the sign *y*. Lyons' example (Lyons, 1968) of 'flower' as *superordinate* to 'tulip' – if a given object is a *tulip* then it is a *flower* – would serve to illustrate Morris' idea of a more general sign being an analytic implicate of a less general one. Mutual superordination (Lyons, 1968) – in the case of equally general signs, such as, say, 'oculist' and 'eye-doctor' – illustrates what Morris means by equally general signs being analytic implicates of one another: if someone is an oculist, then he is an eye-doctor, and vice versa.

(11)   *Reliable sign: a sign is reliable to the degree to which members of its sign-family are found to denote (actual existing objects) in actual instances.*

It was noted earlier that, while a sign must, by requirement, have a significatum that is always present on all the occasions on which the sign is involved in semiosis (sign-process), it is not actually necessary that there be a real physically concrete denotatum on each occasion. It is not too difficult to see what this means in the case of the dog conditioned to seek food at place *x*. Each time the buzzer sounds but no food is found, there is absence of denotatum, though not of significatum. The more frequently this happens, the more the buzzer will lose its reliability (not to say: credibility) as a sure indication to the dog that there will be food at place *x*.

The degree of frequency with which an interpreter has encountered the use of a sign to mislead, or to tell a lie – or at least to produce an expectation unfulfilled by the circumstances – is what Morris has in mind as the criterion of the 'reliability' of the sign. It might seem, however, that measurement of degree of reliability – even if it is not seen as a general property of the sign *in abstracto*, but as its 'reliability' for *a particular interpreter* – would require a kind of statistical operation for which it would be impossible, in all but the most artificial cases, to provide numerical data. It is not, in general, feasible to calculate the number of times an interpreter has encountered a particular sign.

(12)   *Synonymy: the relation between different sign-families with the same signification.*

This notion of *synonymy* throws doubt on the degree to which 'sameness' of signification guarantees membership of the same sign-family. If earlier we may have thought that having the 'same' significatum automatically classified sign-vehicles into the same sign-family, we seem now to have to change our views; sign-vehicles with the 'same' signification belong either to one sign-family, or to several different, but synonymous, sign-families.

(13) *Language or lansign system: a set of plurisituational comsigns restricted in the ways in which they may be combined, that is, a system of Comsign-families with restricted combinations.*

In accordance with these equivalent definitions, 'language' is characterised by the possession of five properties:

(*a*) it is composed of a plurality of signs;
(*b*) each sign is *interpersonal*; that is, has the same signification for the whole of an interpreter-family (for example, speech community);
(*c*) each sign is a *comsign*; that is, has the same signification for communicator and interpreter alike;
(*d*) each sign is *plurisituational*; that is, it belongs to a sign-family, and is not limited to a single occurrence in one unique situation;
(*e*) the signs are combinable in certain restricted ways.

This gives us a wide sense of 'language' according to which not only human natural languages, or other human systems of communication, qualify for being called 'languages', but the term is equally applicable to signs used in, say, communication by social bees.

The property of combinability turns out to be one of the most significant properties of 'lansign systems'. The nature of this property is not explored by Morris. Presumably he would require a behavioural account of what communicators and interpreters are doing when they combine signs, rather than merely use them in juxtaposition to one another. No such account is to be found in the work of Morris. This lack imposes severe limitations on his conception of 'languages' in particular and 'sign-systems' in general.

3

Semiotics as a Theory of 'l'Acte Sémique': Luis Prieto

3.1 The Mechanism of Indication

3.1.1 Introductory Remarks

When taken in its entirety, Prieto's approach to semiotics has a unique character. In a way that is superficially similar to Morris' 'semiotic', a major part of Prieto's semiotic theory is concerned with presenting an analytic model of what happens when a particular message is conveyed by the occurrence of an 'index'. However, two major considerations make Prieto's approach fundamentally different from the type of approach exemplified by that of Morris: (*a*) an equal concern for a general typology of 'indices' and of 'codes', alongside the development of a model for individual communication acts; (*b*) *independent* development of a theory of 'indices' and of 'codes', as opposed to such theories being *induced* from a model of communication acts (these theories are merely expected to be congruent with factors in the analysis of '*l'acte sémique*', and vice versa).

In spirit, Prieto's approach is typically Saussurean. In the ideas of Saussure, also, three separate, though convergent, strands may be distinguished: 'sign theory' (viz. *l'arbitraire du signe*), implying the germ of a typology of indices), 'language as a system' (viz. '*langue*', implying the germ of a typology of semiological systems) and 'model of speech acts' (viz. '*circuit de la parole*', implying an analysis of the mechanisms of concrete communication acts).

While Morris' conceptual progression from particular cases of 'semiosis' to a generalisation of certain categories of 'sign' (and to some general idea of 'systems of signs') can be called typically inductive, this is not the case with Prieto, in spite of his direct concern with particular communication acts. For one thing, in the case of Prieto, the abstract notions of his theory of 'indices' and of 'codes' exercise at least as strong an influence on his view of individual communication acts, as that exercised, conversely, by the analysis of '*l'acte sémique*' on his view of 'indices' and 'codes'. Any priority that might be attached to explicating individual communication acts by a model of their mechanism is almost entirely a matter of presentational strategy. The model of '*l'acte sémique*' is dealt with first (in Prieto's three-pronged attack on semiological problems), because it is deemed to be strategically the best way to introduce the reader, through consideration of particular acts, to the three separate, though convergent aspects of Prieto's semiological theory. This gives the reader a foothold in concrete reality, and thereby sets a scene of 'realism' for the abstractions that are to follow. The difference between Prieto's 'realism' and that of Morris is still a very marked one: Prieto's theory could have been presented in reverse order (and it would still have made sense, though it might have been more difficult to comprehend); Morris' could not.

3.1.2 Preliminary Notions of 'L'Acte Sémique'

The preliminary explanation providing the starting-point of Prieto's analysis of '*l'acte sémique*' is an extremely general one concerning the conditions under which any particular phenomenon can be said to 'indicate' something. The two necessary conditions involved are: (*a*) recognition that the *indicating entity* (object, event or circumstance, in short, any phenomenon that can be sensed) *belongs to a specific class*, and (*b*) ability to infer – from membership of the indicating entity in the given class – the fact that some *other* (indicated) entity *belongs to a specific class*.

It should be noted from the outset that the above formulation precludes the possibility of an entity being trivially interpreted as an 'indicator' of its own identity. That is to say, the simple fact of perceiving and recognising an entity for what it is (that is, as belonging to a certain specific class) should not be confused with the process of *indication*.

According to the formulation of the conditions under which indication takes place, its mechanism must involve the association of a member of one class (the *indicator*) with a member of another class (the *indicated* entity); the relationship between *an indicator* and *an indicated* entity is mediated by a relationship between the class to which the former belongs and the class to which the latter is assigned. In other words, at the basis of the one-time association of 'indicator' and 'indicated' lies a more general and regular association between the class of which the 'indicator' is a member and the class to which the 'indicated' entity is assigned by inference. Such classes cannot, of course, exist in a vacuum; each must belong to its own Universe of Discourse. In genuine cases of indication there are, by definition, two separate – but regularly associable – Universes of Discourse involved: (1) The Universe of Discourse of the 'indicator', together with all the other phenomena that might have appeared in the place of that 'indicator' had the situation been different, namely, the INDICATIVE UNIVERSE OF DISCOURSE; (2) The Universe of Discourse of the 'indicated' entity, together with all the facts that might have appeared in its place had the 'indicator' been different, namely the INDICATED UNIVERSE OF DISCOURSE.

In the context of indications inferred from 'natural' events, both the Universe of Discourse of which an 'indicator' is a member, and the Universe of Discourse to which the 'indicated' entity belongs, present the problem of potentially involving every item of human experience, and being no more restricted than the whole of the universe of all perceivable and conceivable entities. There is, in the way Prieto construes 'indication', a definite understanding that 'indicators' select and restrict their Universe of Discourse, and also select and restrict the corresponding Indicated Universe of Discourse. We are given to understand that the extent of this selection and restriction can be known from considering what other entities 'could stand in the place of' a given 'indicator', and, by implication, the range of entities that 'could stand in the place of' a given 'indicated' entity. This, however, is no straightforward matter, as will be seen in the examples given below, and the vagueness of what is meant by 'could stand in the place of' makes for certain lacunae in the 'mechanism of indication'.

Certain paradigm examples can be cited for a more concrete understanding of indications inferred from 'natural' events. One typical example comes from interpreting indications of bad weather. The situation we need to imagine is one in which, from the *colour of the evening sky*, it is inferred on a particular occasion that there will be a *storm at sea* the next day. Figure 3.1 represents Prieto's view of how the mechanism of indication operates in such a case.

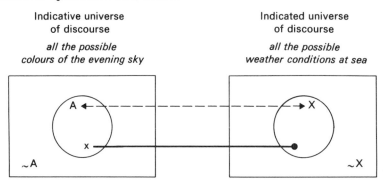

Indicative universe of discourse

Indicated universe of discourse

all the possible colours of the evening sky

all the possible weather conditions at sea

A = all the possible colours of the sky that may indicate an impending storm at sea.
X = all the possible cases of storms at sea.
x = the colour of the evening sky on the particular occasion in question.
• = storm at sea the day after the particular occasion in question.

Figure 3.1

The particular appearance of the evening sky (represented as x) automatically establishes its context, an Indicative Universe of Discourse, as being constituted by the (actually unlimited) range of possible appearances the evening sky may present. In this, we have to consider the example as particularly favourable to Prieto's exposition – not in all cases does the extension of the Indicative Universe of Discourse (that is, all the 'indicators' that 'could stand in the place of' a given 'indicator') seem to be so clearly determined by common sense. Even here, however, if one were inclined to split hairs, one might ask why the Indicative Universe of Discourse is restricted to only the colour of the evening sky, to the exclusion of other weather-portents.

Within the Universe of Discourse of all possible colours of the evening sky, we must imagine the existence of different types, or broad categories (red sky, overcast sky, orange sky, etc.). The class brought into play by the 'indicator' is one of these categories, namely one that is 'regularly' associated with the probability of a storm at sea on the following day (see class A and its association with class X, represented by a broken arrow in Figure 3.1). This 'regular' association should pre-exist, it would seem, the particular occasion on which indication takes place. (Prieto's theory is rather brief on explaining what the mechanism of such 'regularities' might be. The issue, which is rather a matter of a 'theory of indices', is, as far as Prieto's model of communication acts is concerned, dismissed with the remark that the association in question is one of (material) implication: *if* the colour of the evening sky is such and such, *then* there will be a storm at sea the next day.)

Appearance of one member of the class designated as A on the diagram (Figure 3.1) has the effect of partitioning the Indicative Universe of Discourse into the class in question and its *complement*, represented by $\sim A$ in Figure 3.1 As a result, and a 'reflection', of this partition taking place on the Indicative plane, a corresponding partition occurs in the Indicated Universe of Discourse, also into a class (class X in Figure 3.1) and its *complement*, represented by $\sim X$ in Figure 3.1. Understanding the indication in this instance has therefore the form of recognising that the weather on the following day is likely to be of the type belonging to class X, namely a case of storm at sea.

3.1.3   'Indication' and Understanding

In further explication of what it means to understand the indication furnished by a particular 'indicator', Prieto refers to the existence of a latent uncertainty which the interpretation of an 'indicator' diminishes or dispels. In terms of the present example, we may say that, initially, there is a total uncertainty as to what the weather conditions are likely to be on the following day. It is by resolving this uncertainty, in terms of the inference that the weather will be of the type classified as 'storm-at-sea', that the colour of the evening sky functions as an 'indicator'. Understanding the indication is, in other words, not a form of sensing a particular phenomenon (in this case, a future storm), but of recognising a determinate class of which that phenomenon is a member. As Prieto points out, the uncertainty disappears as soon as one class is identified as being that class to which the 'indicated' entity belongs. Precisely what member, with what concrete properties, of that class is involved does not need to be known in order to understand the indication, or resolve the uncertainty in question.

The same uncertainty remains unresolved, but is diminished, as soon as the 'indicator' is instrumental in identifying two or more rival classes, of a mutually exclusive nature, as being the classes to which, with the exclusion of any other class, the 'indicated' entity belongs. Indication, whether it involves resolving or diminution of uncertainty, functions by a 'leap' from a known and sensed particular (the 'indicator') to the consciousness of another particular (the 'indicated') whose only known property is its membership in a given class. In the present example, the known and sensed particular is, of course, the appearance of the evening sky on some particular occasion. The 'indicated' entity, 'stormy conditions at sea on a specific occasion', while still presumably a particular event, due to take place at a particular point in time and space, is only known in terms of its membership in the class of all possible cases of stormy conditions at sea. Indication does not enable one, of course, to experience the particular manifestation of the expected storm – all that is indicated is the expectation of some sort of weather conditions that would fall into the class of storms.

The mechanism of indication works only on the basis of an existing 'regular' correlation between a given class (type) of 'indicators' and a given class (type) of 'indicated' entities. In Figure 3.1, the dotted line between A and X represents this vital correlation, a correlation which must be known before indication can take place, and whose nature is explained by Prieto in logical terms as being that of *material implication*, that is, if A then X. One may perhaps wonder if material implication is not too strong a correlation to expect in all cases where indication takes place, for it seems that, regardless of the unreliability of logically inferring an impending storm from the appearance of the evening sky, that interpretation can be attached to the 'indicator' in question, provided that, for the moment, one is prepared to accept some degree of 'regularity' (by no means necessarily 'inevitability') in the appropriate correlation. Unless one is to recognise degrees within material implication, the correlation in question bears only a superficial resemblance to material implication. Though a necessary 'postulate' for the mechanism of indication, a correlation between type of 'indicator' and type of 'indicated' entity may, unlike cases of material implication, have no basis in objective fact: for example, the correlation of four-leaved clover with good luck, whose basis is pure superstition.

3.1.4 Set-Theoretical Ramifications of 'Indication'

The correlation of a *single* class in the Indicative Universe of Discourse with a *single* class in the Indicated Universe of Discourse is required for the total dispelling of an existing uncertainty, but only in so far as the classes in either Universe are mutually exclusive.

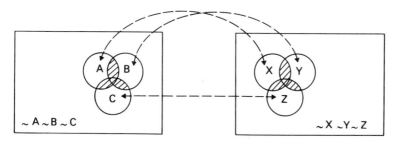

Figure 3.2

All the classes that properly include a given class in the Indicated Universe of Discourse are, according to Prieto, also in correlation with the class of 'indicators' associated with that given class. That is to say, a situation diagrammatically represented as in Figure 3.3 is said to imply that *A* is in correlation not only with *X* but also with *Y* and *Z*. If this were the case, however, the indication furnished by an 'indicator' from class *A* would be that the 'indicated' entity belonged to class *Z*, and there would be no basis to its interpretation as a member of class *Y* or class *X*. It seems, in fact, that here Prieto is confusing what can be directly 'inferred' from an 'indicator' with what can, logically speaking, be deduced from the fact that a given 'indicated' entity is a member of a given class. When we consider Figure 3.4, the difference between the 'inference-like' correlation between the classes *A* and *X* and the actual material implication between *X* and *Y* or *X* and *Z* appears all the more marked.

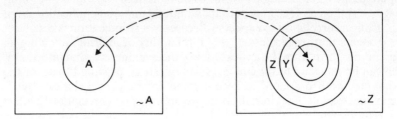

Figure 3.3

All the classes that are properly included in a class *A* of 'indicators' correlated with a class *X* of 'indicated' entities are, as Prieto points out, automatically correlated with the class *X* of 'indicated' entities. But it is precisely because such a correlation is quite automatic that it is also trivial, as Figure 3.4 shows. In this figure, the implication that *B* and *C* are correlated with *X* is seen as the obvious consequence of the fact that, if an 'indicator' does not belong to the *complement* of *A* (that is, to ~ *A*) then it must belong to some *subset* of *A*.

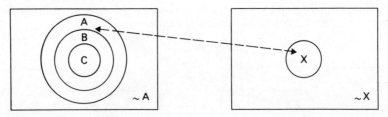

Figure 3.4

Because of what can be noted from Figures 3.3 and 3.4, Prieto stipulates that, given the occurrence of a particular 'indicator', that 'indicator' is to be taken to belong to the '*widest*' class from which regular 'inferences' can be made with regard to 'indicated' entities, while the 'indicated' entity in any given case must be taken to belong to the '*narrowest*' class that can be put into regular correlation with the appropriate class of 'indicators'. Figure 3.5 sums up this stipulation (in this figure, x represents a particular 'indicator').

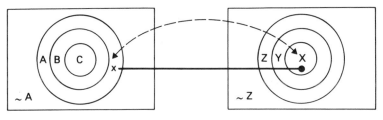

Indicative universe of discourse   Indicated universe of discourse

Figure 3.5

The rather abstract, formulaic presentation in Figures 3.2, 3.3, 3.4 and 3.5 can be supplemented by a discussion of yet another of Prieto's favourite examples, involving the 'interpreting' of certain types of hoof-prints. (I have slightly modified the example for the purposes of this discussion.)

Where mutually exclusive types (classes) of footprints are involved, say, the types

(*i*) ❚   (*ii*) ◖◗   and (*iii*) ∩   respectively,

the correlations that enable indication to take place on given occasions are as represented in Figure 3.6.

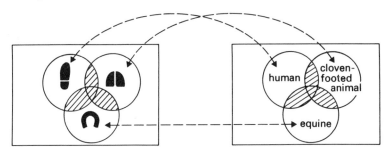

Figure 3.6

When confronted with hoofprints of type   ∩   , such prints may automatically be classed into one of two mutually exclusive classes of 'indicators': (*a*) relatively large prints of type   ∩   and (*b*) relatively small prints of type   ∩   of which the former can be put into corre-lation with (the class of) 'horses', and the latter with (the class of) 'donkeys', as shown in Figure 3.7.

Taking the class 'relatively large hoofprints of type   ∩   ', it is easy to see that any subset of this class is automatically, and trivially, corre-lated with the class of 'horses'. This trivial fact may, then, be ignored, and the 'widest' class alone considered to be correlation with the class of 'horses'. At the same time, the 'narrowest' class that can be put into regular correlation with 'relatively large hoofprints of type   ∩   ' is

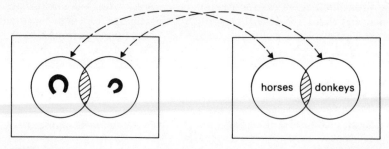

Figure 3.7

the class of 'horses', and other, more inclusive classes can be ignored as being trivial.

Thus, a given 'indicator' which is classified as a member of 'relatively large hoofprints of type ∩ ' would, on any given occasion, be interpreted in the most specific and 'narrowest' way possible, in fact, by 'inferring' that the animal which had left the tracks was a *horse* – although by implication, it is equally valid to conclude that this animal was an equine, a large mammal, etc.

The 'indicated' entity is considered, in first instance, as a member of the 'narrowest' class, in this case, that of 'horses', and only very indirectly as a member of 'equines', 'large mammals', etc. Dispelling whatever initial uncertainty exists in the observer of a relatively large hoofprint of type ∩ consists in making the link indicated by a solid line in Figure 3.8.

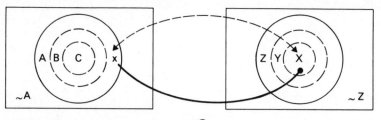

A = relatively large hoofprints of type ∩

X = horses

Y = equines

Z = large mammals

x = one particular relatively large hoofprint

● = one particular horse whose presence is indicated by the print

Figure 3.8

In terms of this example, one can conveniently explain also how it comes about – through the role of 'context of situation' – that the actual 'indicated' entity may on occasion be far more specific than just 'some unknown member of the class of horses'. Suppose that the person observing a relatively large hoofprint of type ∩ is in possession of the situational clues (*a*) the field he is walking through is enclosed by a fence; (*b*) there are only three donkeys belonging to Farmer Smith and one old grey gelding belonging to Farmer Giles that are allowed to graze in the field. Given such strong clues from the 'context of situation', the observer of the 'indicator' will not only 'infer' that the tracks he is following are those of a member of the class of 'horses', but, actually, that they were left by the old grey gelding belonging to Farmer Giles.

While a very important factor in the actual interpretation of 'indicators' in concrete situations, the supporting role of 'context' is supplementary to, rather than a part of, Prieto's model of the mechanism of indication. It is only that information which comes to the interpreter of a particular 'indicator' purely *by virtue of that 'indicator'* itself which can form part of the actual mechanism of indication. Bits of knowledge about the circumstances in which the ∩ 'indicator' is observed, while they may, in a highly significant way, decrease or dispel initial uncertainty as to what animal is being tracked, have to be seen as external to the mechanism of indication. They are, however, not external to Prieto's account of how actual 'indicators' are understood on concrete occasions, as we shall see below.

3.1.5   Success and Failure of Comprehension

For a discussion of how 'comprehension' takes place, as well as how it can malfunction, we must, while retaining the example of hoofprints, make reference also to the person involved in interpreting a given 'indicator', the *receptor*. As soon as the receptor takes cognisance of the presence of a potential 'indicator', this very fact produces in him a state of uncertainty that he seeks to resolve by interpreting the 'indicator'. Comprehension takes place when the receptor succeeds, by interpreting the 'indicator' (rightly or wrongly), in diminishing that uncertainty, and locating the 'indicated' entity in any class that is less inclusive ('narrower') than the Indicated Universe of Discourse. Incomprehension, on the other hand, is the receptor's failure to identify any class 'narrower' than the Indicated Universe of Discourse, or, perhaps, his failure even to identify a particular Indicated Universe of Discourse. Thus, for instance, if a particular receptor perceives what objectively is a relatively large hoofprint of type ∩ , but concludes from it only that some creature had passed that way, that receptor will have failed to diminish his initial uncertainty. Since the Indicative Universe of footprints is in correlation with the Indicated Universe of Discourse including all creatures that could conceivably leave footprints, a receptor who makes no more specific an interpretation than that the observed print was left by some creature, has not narrowed the possibilities to any class more restricted than the Indicated Universe of Discourse itself. Another way of expressing the same incomprehension is to emphasise that the *class of possible 'indicated' entities* identified by the receptor is significant only by contrast with a class of entities that are excluded from being potentially indicated by a given 'indicator'. Interpreting a hoofprint as indication that some creature has passed that way does not eliminate any members of the Indicated

Universe of Discourse, all members of that Universe being admitted as possible 'interpreted' entities. The hoofprint is, in effect, interpreted as 'this footprint was left by something that leaves footprints' (that is, in a wholly trivial way). In the absence of a class of excluded entities, there is no contrast to render significant the class to which the 'indicated' entity has been assigned.

It is also possible that a given receptor, on seeing a hoofprint, responds by failing to register it as an 'indicator' at all, observing the object in front of him merely for what it is, not for any potential indicative value. Yet again, the receptor may register that the hoofprint has some indicative potential, but may not associate it with the Indicated Universe of Discourse of 'creatures that leave footprints', or for that matter, with any specific Indicated Universe of Discourse, remarking merely that he has 'no idea what this object means'. In either case there would be total failure to relate the hoofprint to 'creatures that make footprints' (that is, to the appropriate Indicated Universe of Discourse), and comprehension would be totally precluded.

There is, however, a problem with the stipulation of the appropriate Indicated Universe of Discourse which, in Prieto, remains somewhat of a mystery. Arguably, a receptor who merely registers the connection of a hoofprint with 'some creature that makes footprints' has reached some degree of comprehension, having eliminated all sorts of entities from being potential 'indicated' entities (for example, inanimate objects, plants, and so on). If he is said to have failed totally in comprehension, as Prieto would have it, this is only on the understanding that he has failed to eliminate any entities from the appropriate Indicated Universe of Discourse, and that Universe of Discourse is comprised of 'all creatures that leave footprints'. It would seem, however, that identifying a particular Indicated Universe of Discourse (narrower than the whole Universe of experiences) constitutes, in itself, a form of comprehension. It is a comprehension that gives concrete shape to the receptor's initial uncertainty, rather than resolving that uncertainty.

Comprehension requires not only that the receptor identify the Indicated Universe of Discourse associated with a given 'indicator', but that he eliminate part of that Universe of Discourse as being *excluded* by the 'indicator' in question. Thus the receptor who, on observing a hoofprint, remarks that 'either a horse, or a donkey, or a mule must have passed that way' is, by eliminating all other classes of animals, reaching a considerable degree of partial comprehension. His uncertainty as to what creature left the tracks is narrowed down to (the logical sum of) three classes, as shown in Figure 3.9. A case such as the one represented by Figure 3.9 would, for Prieto, constitute an instance of 'partial comprehension'.

For total comprehension, the receptor needs to identify just *one* class in the appropriate Indicated Universe of Discourse as being the only class that is not excluded from consideration. It is understood, of course, in the light of the foregoing sections (see Figure 3.3), that the class thus identified is the 'narrowest' one regularly associated with 'indicators' of the type encountered. In other words, if the observer of a hoofprint of a relatively large size only concludes that the tracks were left by some

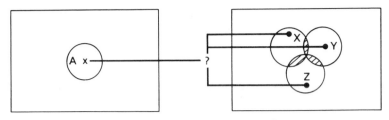

A = hoofprints of a relatively large size and of type ∩

X = horses

Y = donkeys

Z = mules

Figure 3.9

equine, then he is failing to exploit the full potential of the 'indicator', since relatively large hoofprints can, by regular association, be taken to exclude the possibility of the print having been made by a donkey or a small pony. On the other hand, an inference like 'if this hoofprint is large, then *only* a horse can have made it' has some claim to being considered as being rooted in some form of 'regularity', whereas this would not be so with 'inferences' correlating hoofprints to more restricted classes of 'indicated' entities. For instance, one would not feel justified in making inferences like 'if this hoofprint is large, then only a grey horse can have made it', or 'if this hoofprint is large, then only Farmer Giles' horse can have made it'. Of course, on given occasions, provided that the situational context provides further restrictive clues, such 'inferences' can actually seem valid – but the very mention of 'given occasions', and 'situational clues', underlines the fact that such correlations are not of a 'regular' nature. Accordingly, the receptor observing a relatively large hoofprint of type ∩ comes to total comprehension as soon as he eliminates all possibilities other than that the tracks were made by a horse. Naturally, if the circumstances allow it (by 'favouring' a more specific interpretation) the receptor may in fact come to a more specific conclusion as to which horse made the tracks. This, however, involves comprehension of a kind entirely different from comprehension of the 'indicator' (hoofprint) as such.

3.1.6 'Miscomprehension' of 'Natural' Indicators

Both within total and partial comprehension, Prieto allows for the possibility of 'miscomprehension'. The nature of miscomprehension sheds further light on Prieto's view of comprehension itself. It is, therefore, worthwhile to devote some space – as indeed Prieto himself does – to types of 'failure in communication'. The possible types of 'failure' are, however, more numerous and intricate in the case of semiotic acts proper ('*actes sémiques*') than in the interpretation of 'natural' phenomena as 'indicators'. Therefore, a more appropriate place for a fuller discussion of the failure of semiotic acts (*l'échec de l'acte sémique*) would be after we have examined Prieto's notion of 'semiotic acts'. As far as 'miscomprehension' of the colour of the evening sky, or of a footprint, is concerned, this can only have two sources: either in that the receptor has completely missed the appropriate Indicated Universe of Discourse (say, by associating the colour of the sky with the question of what country lies beyond the horizon, or associating a hoofprint with the plants that grow in the surrounding countryside); or in that the receptor, while identifying the appropriate Indicated Universe of Discourse, isolates a class of 'indicated' entities that cannot justifiably stand in 'regular' correlation with the 'indicator' (for example, taking the red colour of the sky to indicate that there will be snow on the next day, or taking a hoofprint as evidence that the tracks were made by an elephant). These are the only two ways in which communication that does not involve the deliberate production of a message by one organism for comprehension by another organism can go wrong.

3.2 Semiotic Acts

3.2.1   From Communication Events to Semiotic Acts

Semiotic acts are a special type of communication event. Thus, what goes for communication events in general holds good (*mutatis mutandis*) for semiotic acts in particular, though with the proviso, of course, that semiotic acts must have certain special properties by which they are distinguished from such cases as interpreting weather portents or footprints. The main differences that set off semiotic acts from other types of communication event spring from the necessary involvement of an additional participant in the mechanism of semiotic acts, namely, the producer of the 'indicator', referred to as the *sender* (*'émetteur'*).

It is a defining characteristic of semiotic acts that they are expressly produced by the sender for providing information, and can only be successfully interpreted if the receptor recognises them to have been expressly produced for that purpose. The 'indicator' is, in such a case, the realisation of a 'signal' necessarily involving the intention of the sender to communicate with the receptor, and also the receptor's consciousness of this intention in the sender. Prieto is well aware of the problems posed by dealing in intentions – whose nature remains to a large extent a mystery – but sees no alternative to operating with this factor which he, after Buyssens, considers indispensible to an account of the mechanism of semiotic acts.

3.2.2   'Notificative Indication' and 'Significative Indication'

As a result of the fact that the receptor must recognise that the sender intends to impart a message to him before he can understand what that message is, Prieto distinguishes between two types of information transmitted in semiotic acts (Prieto, 1966): 'notificative indication' and 'significative indication'.

'Notificative indication' is entailed as soon as a signal is produced, since it consists in the fact that the very production of a signal indicates to the receptor the sender's intention to communicate something. That is to say, 'notificative indication' serves notice of a communicative intent on the part of the sender, and is, as it were, the 'attention-seeking' aspect of a semiotic act. Throughout all semiotic acts 'notificative indication' has always the same constant value, which can be roughly rendered by the paraphrase: 'attention! this is intended to convey a message'. Though an essential aspect of semiotic acts, and an aspect that cannot be ignored in understanding Prieto's model of the mechanism of semiotic acts, we can dismiss 'notificative indication' from further discussion (but see its role in semiological systems, Chapter 6, Section 6.2.3, p. 168).

3.2.3 'Sematic Fields' and 'Noetic Fields'

It is the 'significative indication' of semiotic acts that varies according to the signal realised, and that parallels the indicative aspect of the communication events examined in the first part of this section. Though Prieto vacillates between 'type' and 'token' – in fact between distinguishing 'signal' from 'realisation of signal' and using 'signal' indiscriminately for both – I shall here adopt the convention of using 'signal' only for 'tokens', that is, in the sense of the 'indicator' produced by a specific sender on a specific occasion for the specific purpose of conveying information. With this in mind, the following parallels can be established between factors in the mechanism of indication in general and the mechanism of semiotic acts in particular.

Communication Events	*Semiotic Acts*
Ø	sender
'indicator'	'signal'
Indicative Universe of Discourse	Sematic field
'indicated' entity	message or sense
Indicated Universe of Discourse	Noetic field
'indicator' type	'expression' (*signifiant*)
Ø	notificative indication
class of 'indicated' entities in 'regular' correlation with given 'indicator' type	significative indication or 'content' (*signifié*)
receptor	receptor

Just as any communication event is said to bring into correlation two Universes of Discourse – Indicative and Indicated, respectively: so a semiotic act is explained as bringing into correlation the two Universes of Discourse referred to as the Sematic field and the Noetic field. The Sematic field is defined as the Universe of Discourse containing the 'signal' produced by the sender, together with all the alternative signals that could have appeared in its place, that is, with which it significantly contrasts. The extent of this Universe of Discourse is less problematic where we are dealing with a definite 'code', since such a 'code' would determine the outer limits of what signals significantly contrast with one another in terms of that code. Where a residual problem still remains is in 'signals' such as the hoisting of the jolly roger – for here one can either take a narrower view of the alternatives, considering the Sematic field to be constituted by all and only the flags that can be hoisted on the mast of a ship, or a wider view that admits, at the very least, any signal that can be used for identifying a vessel. The difference in extension of the Sematic field under these two views is already immense, even without admitting the possibility that all self-identifying insignia (including military insignia, heraldic signs, and so on) might constitute the same Sematic field. Without appeal to the definite limits of a 'code' the decision with regard to the extent of the Sematic field of a given 'signal' depends on what is meant by 'alternatives that could have appeared in the place of' the given 'signal', a notion which remains somewhat elastic, as Prieto himself admits (Prieto, 1977).

Given that the extent of the Sematic field created round a particular 'signal' can be determined, the Noetic field is simply that of all the indications that can be furnished by 'signals' within the Sematic field. Once again, the issue is clearest of all where there is a definite 'code' involved. For instance, the Noetic field of the highway code is restricted to all and only the messages that relate to regulations and indications intended for drivers of vehicles. Even more evident an example of a restricted Noetic field is that of traffic lights, where, by the limitations of the 'code', the Sematic field admits of only four types of 'signal', and the corresponding Noetic field is restricted to indicating four types of message: *stop*, *go*, *prepare to stop* and *prepare to go*.

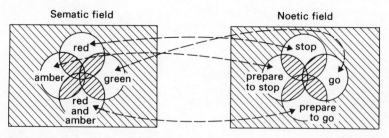

Figure 3.10

3.3 The Interpretation of a Signal

3.3.1 The Functioning of Signals

In order to explain the functioning of a signal, it is necessary to break down that functioning into a number of apparently successive 'steps'. However, the notion of an actual time-sequence of events within the operation of a semiotic act should not be taken too literally. We may take it that the mechanism functions largely unconsciously, and that what is described *in the model* as a process takes place in fact more or less simultaneously. With these reservations in mind, there is little harm in saying that a signal is 'initiated' by the conveying of notificative indication. Taking cognisance of the fact that the sender intends to convey a message, and perceiving the signal as identifying the particular Sematic field to which it belongs, lead to a state of uncertainty in the receptor. This uncertainty is given specificity by the fact that, on recognising the appropriate Sematic field, the receptor is, by automatic association, made aware also of the corresponding Noetic field. (As in the case of recognising the appropriate Sematic field, so also the identification of the appropriate Noetic field is relatively straightforward only where there is a clearly established 'code' involved in the process. Where the limits of a 'code' are given, one may be reasonably sure of the range of messages that can be expressed in that 'code' – that is, semiotic system. From this we may note that a theory of 'codes' is essential to Prieto's account of the mechanism of semiotic acts.)

Within the Noetic field which the receptor of a signal identifies (by way, as we have seen, of linking it with the Sematic field in which he locates the signal), the receptor's uncertainty has the precise form of an indecision as to which of a (perhaps indefinite) number of mutually exclusive classes in the Noetic field he should fix on as the class to which the sender's message belongs. Comprehension, therefore, can be seen as the dispelling (in part or totally) of the particular uncertainty in question, ideally by identifying the 'narrowest' Noetic class that corresponds to the signal in question. The members of this class are those messages ('indicated' entities) that are definitely not excluded from consideration through being inconsistent with the sender's production of the signal in question.

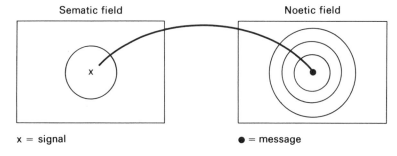

Sematic field   Noetic field

x = signal   ● = message

Figure 3.11

3.3.2   'Expression' and 'Content'

In the case of signals, the Noetic class to which the receptor attributes the message – this being the class which is associated with the sematic class represented by the signal – is called a *content* (*signifié*).

The underlying, presumably systematic, correspondence that enables a receptor to link a particular signal on a particular occasion with the content to which the sender's message belongs (as member of that content), is a correspondence not merely between the content (as a class in the Noetic field) and the signal produced, but rather between the content and a specific *class of signals*. This class of signals, referred to as an '*expression*' (*signifiant*), is at one and the same time the sematic class to which the signal is assigned and the sematic class in 'regular' correspondence with the given content. Here, unless we make reference to systematic conventions that transcend individual semiotic acts, some circularity is involved in identifying content in terms of the expression of which the signal is a member, and expression in terms of the content it corresponds with. Certainly, *signal*, *expression*, *content* and *message* can only be explained and defined in terms of one another.

The message or sense (Prieto appears to use both these terms, compare Prieto, 1966 with Prieto, 1977) comes to the receptor's consciousness through the recognition that it is one of the possibilities included in the content linked with the signal produced by the sender. In other words, taken apart from the role of circumstances in favouring a more specific interpretation (a role mentioned earlier, Section 3.1.4, p. 67, and to which we shall return later), signals are intrinsically indeterminate; what they convey is not the message, but some message of which all that is known is *that it is one member of a given noetic class* (that is, content). This is entirely in keeping with the way a signal itself is perceived and conceived: not as an individual, but rather as the representative of a specific sematic class (that is, expression).

3.3.3   Messages

In some publications (viz. Prieto, 1966), the impression is created that 'indicated' entities are, in some sense, the actual 'things' referred to by 'indicators' (or 'inferred' from them), and that signals involve analogous 'things' as the messages they convey. In more recent works (viz. Prieto, 1977), we find a clear statement of a different view of messages – one that makes them far from analogous with 'things' inferred from 'indicators' that are not deliberate signals.

Prieto's argument is that, in the case of signals produced with a deliberate intention of inviting a receptor to 'infer' messages from them, what is 'inferred' is not a 'thing' at all, but an *intention*, something in the nature of *what the sender wants to achieve* through emitting the signal. Consequently, if a sender utters the words 'It is raining', the 'indicated' entity should not be paraphrased as *the fact that it is raining*, but rather as *the intention of the sender to suggest to the receptor that it is raining*. Two apparent advantages of such a tortuous conception of the substance of messages are (*a*) that statements, questions and commands can be given a homogeneous treatment with regard to the messages they convey; (*b*) that lies (and false statements, in general) can be easily accounted for.

In connection with the first point, taking the sender's intention to be part of the message means that in each of

'It is raining'
'Is it raining?'
'Go away!'

the message is essentially of the same nature (that is, the influence the sender wants to exert on the receptor) with only the details remaining to be filled in according to the signal concerned, that is: the sender's intention that the receptor should *think that it is raining*; the sender's intention that the receptor should *say whether it is raining*; the sender's intention that the receptor should *move from the sender's vicinity*. In each case, the message is in the same mode, though with a different import, thus minimising the appearance that statements, questions and commands are intrinsically different categories of signal and of message.

As for the problem of lies, Prieto feels that the relationship between *signal* and *message* must be unaffected by truth or falsity – this being a matter of a further relationship between *message* and *reality*. If, on a given occasion, *it is not raining*, this should not be allowed to destroy the possibility of a normal link between 'It is raining' (signal) and *the fact that it is raining* (message). The question of whether it is raining or not (objectively speaking), cannot affect the relationship between signal and message if the former is 'It is raining' and the latter is *the sender's intention that the receptor should think that it is raining*.

It is hard to resist a couple of riders at this point. First, lies can be explained without recourse to making the sender's intention part of the actual message, say, in the following way.

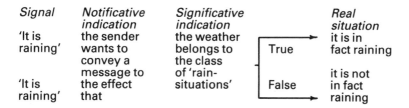

Signal	Notificative indication	Significative indication		Real situation
'It is raining'	the sender wants to convey a message to the effect that	the weather belongs to the class of 'rain-situations'	True	it is in fact raining
'It is raining'			False	it is not in fact raining

The discrepancy between truthful statements and false ones can be conveniently captured as a branching between two alternative relations by which the significative indication of a signal may be linked to the circumstances obtaining in the real situation. The nature of the relation between signal and significative indication (that is, message) is not affected by these alternatives.

Secondly, it seems anomalous that the sender's communicative intention should be incorporated twice over in the indication furnished by the signal: once as the notificative indication that all signals have in common, and once again as part of the particular significative indication of each signal. It seems in fact redundant to mention the sender's intention in formulating the actual message, since all signals have, by definition, a notificative indication signalling the fact that, whatever message follows, the sender intends to convey that message with the express purpose of influencing the receptor in some way.

3.4 Success or Failure of Semiotic Acts

3.4.1 The Sender's Role in Semiotic Acts

In the case of indicators that are not deliberately produced signals, comprehension and its disorders could be explained in terms of relatively few factors. Once we come to intentionally emitted signals, however, the additional factor of the sender (and the influence he wants to exercise over the receptor) makes the situation more complex. In fact, it is the sender who determines the 'target' relative to which comprehension may be judged. The sender intends to exercise an influence which is determinate in that it belongs to a particular class. Such a class – in fact, a *content* – forms part of the particular system of noetic classes in terms of which the sender decides what he does, and what he does not, want to say (that is, the possible interpretations he wants to include, and those he wants to exclude from consideration by the receptor).

3.4.2 Correct Comprehension

Correct comprehension of a signal, therefore, presupposes that there is an exact correspondence between the class (content) to which the sender attributes the message and the class (content) to which the message received is attributed by the receptor.

3.4.3 Complete Success of Comprehension

Complete success of a semiotic act requires comprehension to be both correct (in the way explained in Figure 3.12) and total (that is, the receptor has identified the message as being located in one class, rather than in the sum of a number of alternative mutually exclusive classes).

3.4.4 Partial Failure of Comprehension

Partial failure of a semiotic act results from the receptor's inability to dispel his initial uncertainty by locating the intended message unequivocally in a given class. This is manifested by a continued awareness of insufficient comprehension on the part of the receptor who is in the position of having decided that the class to which the sender attributes his own intention is one of two or more mutually exclusive classes (between which a choice has to be made), but who feels unable to further decide which of the rival classes is the correct one.

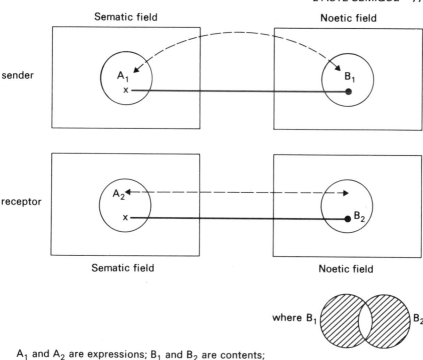

A₁ and A₂ are expressions; B₁ and B₂ are contents;
x indicates a signal and ● a message

Figure 3.12

There is a further possibility to be considered. It may be the case that the receptor is not aware of any discrepancy between the class to which he attributes the intended message and the class to which the sender attributes that message. If the discrepancy consists in the fact that the receptor has settled for a class wider than (that is, properly inclusive of) the class intended by the sender, then the situation is, logically speaking, similar to cases of partial failure. The similarity lies in the receptor's identification – in both types of case – of a class of intended messages of which the class of messages actually intended by the sender is a subset. The sole difference lies in the fact that in a case of partial failure, the receptor is aware of the need for further choice between rival subsets of the class to which he attributes the sender's intention, whereas in the other type of case, the receptor feels satisfied that his comprehension of the sender's intention is complete. That this feeling of satisfaction is, objectively speaking, a misapprehension on the part of the receptor would tend to suggest some sort of failure of the semiotic act. It could be argued that, in such a situation, the receptor has actually misunderstood the sender's intention by failing to grasp fully the specificity of the intended message. Prieto, however, considers communication to be successful in such an instance (Prieto, 1977).

3.4.5   A Paradigm Case of Correct Comprehension

Correct comprehension, interpreted as exact correspondence between the class to which the sender and receptor respectively allocate the intended message, can be illustrated by Figure 3.13.

Example I
The sender utters a signal, 'Give me a black pencil' and the receptor interprets this as a request for a black pencil, regardless of which one.

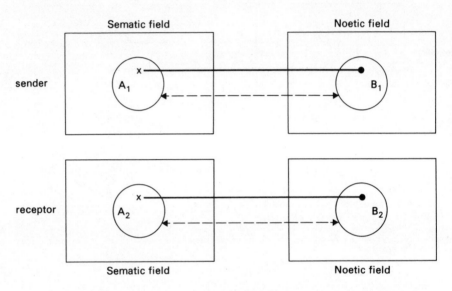

A₁ = class of signals constituting the *expression* of 'Give me a black pencil' for the sender.

A_1 = class of signals constituting the *expression* of 'Give me a black pencil' for the sender.

A_2 = class of signals constituting the *expression* of 'Give me a black pencil' for the receptor.

x represents the allocation of the signal in A_1 by the sender and A_2 by the receptor.

•   represents the allocation of the intended message in B_1 by the sender and B_2 by the receptor.

B_1 = class of sender's intentions consisting in *requests for single black pencils.*

B_2 = class of intentions interpreted by the receptor as *requests for single black pencils.*

Figure 3.13

As it will be readily noted, in this example, there is exact correspondence between B_1 and B_2. Complete comprehension resides in this exact correspondence.

3.4.6   Correct Comprehension under Conditions of Indecision

A similarly formulated example illustrates correct comprehension under different conditions (see Figure 3.14).

Example II
The sender utters a signal 'Give me your black pencil' and the receptor
interprets it as a request for one or other of the two black pencils he owns.

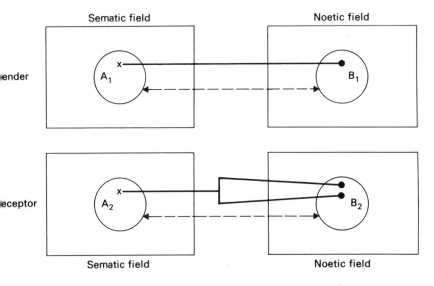

A₁ and A₂ represent the classes of signals to which sender and receptor respectively attribute the signal 'Give me your black pencil'.
x represents the allocation of the signal to A₁ by the sender and to A₂ by the
receptor.
⟶ represents the sender's unawareness of the fact that the receptor possesses
two black pencils.
⊐⟶ represents the receptor's awareness of the fact that the sender might be
asking for either one of his two black pencils.
B₁ = class of sender's intentions consisting in *requests for one single black
pencil belonging to the receptor.*
B₂ = class of intentions interpreted by the receptor as *requests for one single
black pencil belonging to the receptor.*

Figure 3.14

As will be readily seen, there is, here also, exact correspondence
between B_1 and B_2. Thus, although the sender's unawareness of the fact
that the receptor is in possession of two black pencils may create
indecision in the receptor as to which one the sender is asking for, the
semiotic act is totally successful.

3.4.7 Correct Comprehension under Conditions of Imperfect Overlap

A third type of case in which Prieto sees – rightly or wrongly – communication to be successful can be illustrated by a further example (see
Figure 3.15).

Example III
The sender utters the signal, 'Give me a pen', which the receptor interprets as a request for any kind of writing implement that writes in ink (including biros, felt-tipped pens, and so on), whereas the sender's intention is to ask specifically for a fountain-pen.

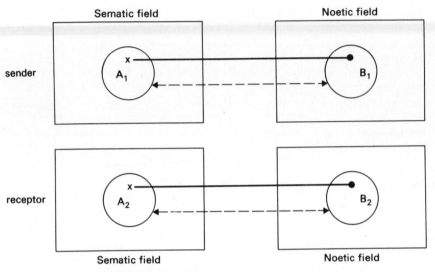

A₁, A₂, x and • are to be interpreted as in Examples I and II.
B_1 = class of sender's intentions consisting in *requests for one single fountain-pen.*
B_2 = class of intentions interpreted by the receptor as *requests for a single writing implement that writes in ink.*

Figure 3.15

It will be readily seen from the explanations of B_1 and B_2 that the two classes are in a relation of proper inclusion (see Figure 3.16). Although the receptor has failed to grasp the fact that the sender wants specifically a fountain-pen, a request for a fountain-pen falls within the class of intentions the receptor attributes to the sender. Furthermore, the receptor is satisfied with having settled on the appropriate class of messages, and feels no need to consider a choice as to whether the sender had intended to ask for a biro, or for a felt-tipped pen, or for a fountain-pen. Prieto considers such a semiotic act to be successful.

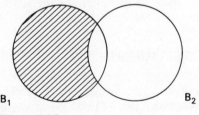

Figure 3.16

3.4.8 A Paradigm Case of Partial Failure of Comprehension

Example III can be usefully compared to a case which, although similar, illustrates partial comprehension.

Example IV
The sender utters the signal, 'Give me a pen', with the intention of asking specifically for a fountain-pen. The receptor interprets this as a signal of the sender's intention to ask for either a biro, or a felt-tipped pen, or a fountain-pen, but is not sure to which of these mutually exclusive classes the sender's intention should be attributed. In other words, these classes represent rival alternatives between which the receptor feels obliged to choose before he is satisfied that he has understood the sender's intention. (The normal response of the receptor in this case would be to ask for further information: for example, 'Do you mean a biro, a felt-tipped pen, or a fountain-pen?')

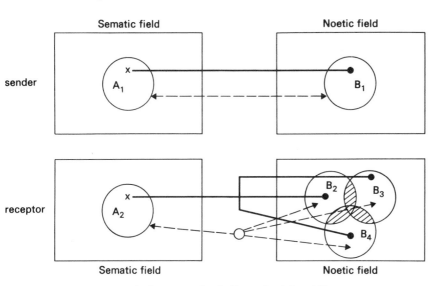

A_1, A_2, x and • are to be interpreted as in Examples I, II and III.
B_1 = class of sender's intentions consisting in *requests for one single fountain-pen.*
B_2 = class of intentions interpreted by the receptor as *requests for one single biro.*
B_3 = class of intentions interpreted by the receptor as *requests for one single felt-tipped pen.*
B_4 = class of intentions interpreted by the receptor as *requests for one single fountain-pen.*

Figure 3.17

As Figure 3.17 indicates, the receptor is undecided between the three classes B_2, B_3 and B_4. In this consists the lack of success of the semiotic act in question. As, however, one of these three alternative classes is actually in exact correspondence with B_1 (the class to which the sender himself attributes his own intention) we can say that the receptor is on the way towards complete comprehension and just does not quite get there. He has taken some correct steps towards identifying a class corresponding exactly with B_1, having narrowed down the possibilities to just three classes of which the appropriate class B_4 is one. Failure of the semiotic act is therefore suitably described as 'partial' failure.

3.4.9   Total Failure of Comprehension

Against partial failure, we may set off cases of total failure, which Figure 3.18 can be used to illustrate.

Example V
The sender utters the signal, 'Give me a black pencil' with the intention of asking for a pencil that *writes in black*. The receptor interprets this as a signal of the intention of the sender to ask for a pencil with a black stem, but which does not contain a black lead.

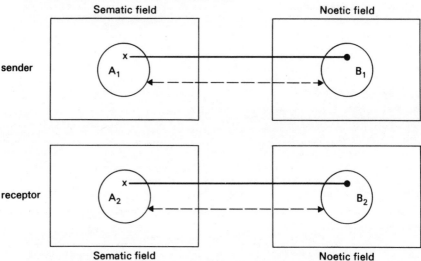

A_1, A_2, x and • are to be interpreted as in the foregoing examples.
B_1 = class of sender's intentions consisting in *requests for one single pencil that writes in black.*
B_2 = class of intentions interpreted by the receptor as *requests for one single pencil that has a black stem but does not write in black.*

Figure 3.18

The relationship between B_1 and B_2 is clearly one of mutual exclusion, diagrammatically representable as in Figure 3.19. The receptor has misunderstood the intended message in that he attributes to the sender a type of intention completely different from what the sender had in mind. (A normal response from the sender on being handed the 'wrong kind of pencil' would be to explain that he did not want a pencil with a black stem, but a pencil that writes black.)

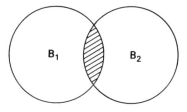

Figure 3.19

3.5   The Role of Situational Factors in Success or Failure of Semiotic Acts

3.5.1   Alternative Accounts of the Nature of Messages

In an earlier version, Prieto (1966) gives an account of the way situational factors may affect the success or failure of semiotic acts. In this account, however, more emphasis is laid on comprehension seen as the identification by the receptor of the exact message intended by the sender, as distinct from all other messages, rather than comprehension in the (later) sense of identification of a message merely through the class of intentions to which it belongs. In the earlier version, the requirements for comprehension are stronger and more exigent; communication is successful only if the receptor comes to appreciate exactly what the sender's intended message is. In the later version, it is sufficient for the receptor to realise that the sender is trying to convey some message belonging to a determinate class, given, of course, that sender and receptor have the same determinate class in mind.

An example might help to point up the difference between the two accounts. Suppose that the sender utters the signal 'Give me your pen', intending thereby to ask for that specific pen which he sees protruding from the receptor's pocket. In terms of the 1966 version, communication could only be considered successful, if the receptor unequivocally identifies the pen asked for as being the one protruding from his pocket. If the receptor happens to have another pen in his possession, and is, therefore, not absolutely clear as to which one the sender might want – or, for that matter, if the receptor is under the impression that either of the pens could equally well answer the sender's needs – communication would not be deemed successful according to Prieto's 1966 account. Looking at the same situation from the point of view of the later version (Prieto, 1977) communication would in fact be considered successful as soon as the receptor attributed the sender's intention to the appropriate class constituted by *requests for one single* (but *any* one single) *pen belonging to the receptor* (see Example II, Section 3.4.6, p. 79).

While to some extent the two accounts complement one another – it is to the earlier version that one must look for clarification of the role of situational factors – it is evident from the foregoing example that they also conflict drastically in the requirements they place on correct comprehension of a semiotic act. It is also evident why the 1977 version is to be preferred, the 1966 version being far too exigent in requiring that the receptor identify the precise message intended by the sender. The following discussion of the effect situational factors may have on comprehension is, however, drawn from the 1966 version.

3.5.2 Failure of Communication Caused by Situational Factors

Failure of communication caused by situational factors is of two types, designated by Prieto as 'miscomprehension' and 'ambiguity' respectively.

The simplest form of failure by miscomprehension can be illustrated by the example given in Figure 3.20.

Example VI: Miscomprehension
The sender utters the signal, 'Give me that pen', under the impression that the interpretation most favoured by the situation is that the pen asked for is the expensive Parker he has just seen the receptor put in his inside pocket. In other words, the sender is under the impression that he must be understood as having asked for the Parker. As it happens, however, the receptor has already put the Parker out of his mind, since it does not belong to him anyway, and is just in the process of reaching for another pen on his desk. That is to say, the circumstances, as regards the receptor, favour the interpretation that the pen asked for is the one on the desk.

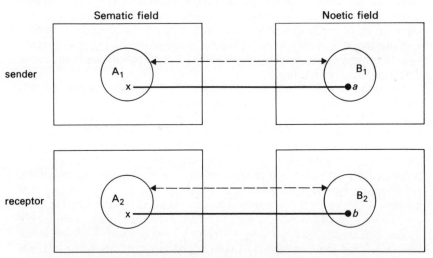

A_1, A_2 and x are to be understood as in Examples I–V.
B_1 and B_2 = class of messages consisting in *requests for a specific pen*.
• *a* = message construed as request for the *Parker pen* in the receptor's pocket.
• *b* = message construed as request for *another pen* on the receptor's desk.

Figure 3.20

Although there is total overlap between the classes B_1 and B_2, the fact that the circumstances are thought by the sender to favour the message *a*, but they actually favour message *b* as far as the receptor is concerned, leads to miscomprehension (see Figure 3.21).

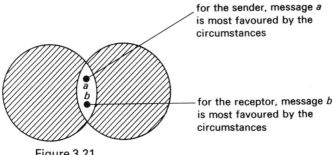

for the sender, message *a* is most favoured by the circumstances

for the receptor, message *b* is most favoured by the circumstances

Figure 3.21

The second type of miscomprehension brought about by the force of circumstantial factors involves a discrepancy between the actual classes of messages identified by sender and receptor respectively. This can be illustrated by Examples VII and VIII (Figures 3.22 and 3.23).

Example VII: Miscomprehension
The sender utters the signal, 'Give me something to write with', in the full expectation that, seeing a pen protruding from the receptor's pocket, the situation will favour the interpretation that the writing implement requested is the pen in question. The receptor, however, takes the request in its wide sense, and, since he has a pencil on the desk, sees the situation as favouring the interpretation that the pencil will fulfil the sender's expectations.

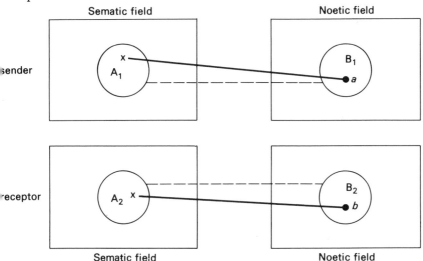

A_1, A_2 and x are to be understood as in Examples I–VI.
B_1 = class of messages constituted by *requests for a pen*.
B_2 = class of messages constituted by *requests for a writing implement*.
• *a* = sender's intended request for a given *pen* belonging to receptor.
• *b* = receptor's interpretation of message as request for a given *pencil*.

Figure 3.22

The class of messages to which the sender attributes the message which he considers to be most favoured by the circumstances is a narrower class than the class of messages among which the receptor locates the message that he considers to be most favoured by the circumstances.

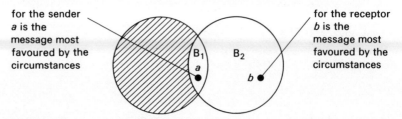

for the sender
a is the
message most
favoured by the
circumstances

for the receptor
b is the
message most
favoured by the
circumstances

Figure 3.23

Example VIII: Miscomprehension
The sender utters the signal, 'Give me a pen', expecting that, since the receptor has a biro in his hand, the situation will favour the interpretation of this signal as a request for the biro in question. The receptor, however, takes this request in a narrow sense, and, since he has a fountain-pen in his pocket, this circumstance influences him to interpret the sender's request as a request for his fountain-pen.

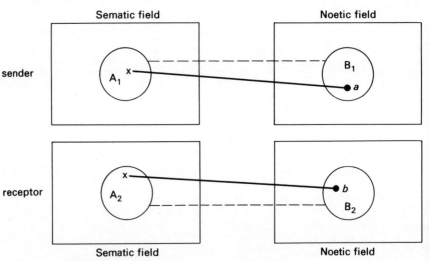

A_1, A_2 and x are to be understood as in Examples I–VII.
B_1 = class of messages constituted by *requests for a pen* (including biros).
B_2 = class of messages constituted by *requests for a fountain-pen*.
• *a* = sender's intended request for a given *biro*.
• *b* = receptor's interpretation of message as request for a given *fountain-pen*.

Figure 3.24

In Example VIII, the sender's idea of the class of messages admitted as potential interpretations of the signal in the given situation is wider than the class of messages to which, under the influence of the situation, the receptor attributes the message. In particular, the fact that the receptor has a fountain-pen makes him misunderstand the request (see Figure 3.25).

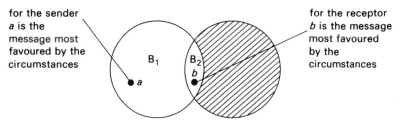

for the sender
a is the
message most
favoured by the
circumstances

for the receptor
b is the message
most favoured
by the
circumstances

Figure 3.25

Examples IX and X illustrate the two types of 'ambiguity' distinguished in Prieto.

Example IX: Ambiguity
The sender utters the signal, 'Give me the pen in your pocket', thinking thereby to ask for the one and only pen that answers this specification in a given set of circumstances. As it happens, however, there are two pens in the receptor's pocket, either of which could be the one intended by the sender.

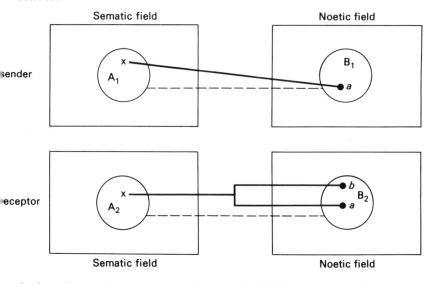

A_1, A_2 and x are to be understood as in Examples I–VIII.
B_1 and B_2 = class of messages constituted by *requests for a single pen in the receptor's pocket.*
• *a* = sender's intended request for a given pen in receptor's pocket.
• *b* = receptor's alternative interpretation as a request for another pen in his pocket.

Figure 3.26

Although sender and receptor agree on the class of messages admitted by utterances of signals of the type 'Give me the pen in your pocket', the fact that in the situation in question, the circumstances equally favour two alternative pens in the receptor's pocket, leads to ambiguity (see Figure 3.27).

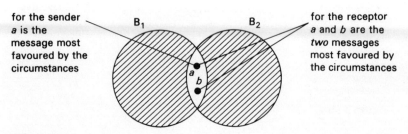

for the sender *a* is the message most favoured by the circumstances

B_1

B_2

for the receptor *a* and *b* are the *two* messages most favoured by the circumstances

Figure 3.27

Example X: Ambiguity
The sender utters the signal, 'Give me your pen', intending thereby to ask for the fountain-pen in the receptor's right hand. The receptor does, however, have a biro in his left hand as well. Thus, while the sender sees the circumstances as favouring an unambiguous request for the fountain-pen in the receptor's right hand, the receptor sees them as favouring two alternative interpretations to an equal degree.

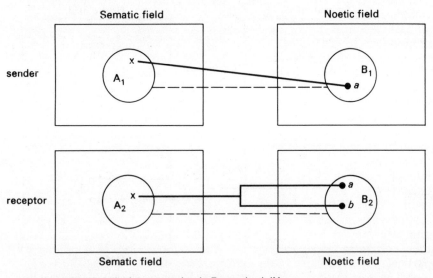

Sematic field

Noetic field

sender

A_1 x

B_1 a

receptor

A_2 x

a
b B_2

Sematic field

Noetic field

A_1, A_2 and x are to be interpreted as in Examples I–IX.
B_1 = class of messages constituted by *requests for a fountain-pen.*
B_2 = class of messages constituted by *requests for a writing implement that writes in ink.*
• *a* = sender's intended request for the *fountain-pen in the receptor's right hand.*
• *b* = receptor's alternative interpretation as a request for *the biro in his left hand.*

Figure 3.28

In the case of Example X, the sender and receptor do not agree on the exact extension of the class of potential messages admitted by the signal in the given circumstances. As the receptor is influenced by the situation to take a wider view of the possibilities, and as among these there are two interpretations equally favoured by the circumstances, the semiotic act fails by virtue of ambiguity (see Figure 3.29).

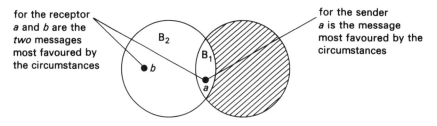

for the receptor
a and *b* are the
two messages
most favoured by
the circumstances

B_2

B_1

for the sender
a is the message
most favoured by the
circumstances

Figure 3.29

3.6 The Mechanism of Indication in the Context of Prieto's Semiotics

3.6.1 The Structure of Prieto's Theory

The present section is not a suitable place for examining Prieto's classification of indices and of communication systems (codes). Nevertheless, a global assessment of his model of communication events in general, and semiotic acts in particular, cannot be made out of context with these other two main areas of Prieto's approach to semiotics.

A global view of the overall semiotic theory can be summed up in the scheme shown in Figure 3.30. The solid arcs ⌒ indicate complementarity between what are developed as largely independent sub-theories, none of which is derived from the others. The broken arrows ----> indicate a degree of two-way traffic between the subtheories whereby notions in one subtheory may affect notions in another, e.g. (*a*) the notions of 'index' and 'sign' belong, strictly speaking, to 'theory of indices', yet they exercise a significant effect on interpreting the difference between 'natural' indicators and 'signals'; (*b*) the notion of 'code', itself, exercises a significant effect on interpreting, in the model of semiotic acts, 'sematic' and 'noetic' fields; (*c*) the notions 'signal' and 'message' are developed in the context of a model of semiotic acts, yet they exercise a significant effect on the interpretation of 'seme' as a particular type of index. (The constant interplay of notions is itself a global characteristic of Prieto's approach.) The solid arrows → indicate the use of the subtheories, either separately, or in conjunction with one another, for interpreting or explicating – that is to say 'describing' – actual cases of communication. (The fact that concrete events are viewed in the light of the whole or a part of semiotic theory – but semiotic theory is not viewed in the light of these concrete events – is itself a global characteristic of Prieto's approach.)

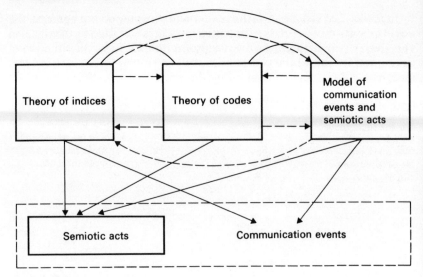

Figure 3.30

3.6.2   Integration of Semiotic Sub-Theories

Characteristically, the three 'components' that I have referred to as 'subtheories' are intended as parts of a three-pronged attack on the description of semiotic phenomena (see Figure 3.31).

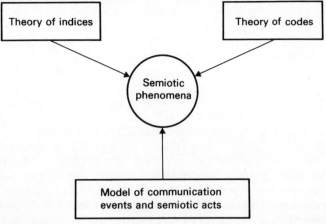

Figure 3.31

Since the intention is to produce a coherent and integrated description from these three points of attack, the three 'prongs' are clearly meant to converge on a common point. But for the fact that three, rather than two 'starting points' are involved, the analogy that springs to mind is that of constructing a bridge by starting from two sides of the river and meeting in the middle. The success of such a construction depends very much on the degree of dovetailing at the central meeting-point. This suggests that a very important consideration in assessing the overall semiotic theory developed by Prieto is whether his three main subtheories 'meet in the middle'.

It would appear that the convergence of the three subtheories is not entirely perfect, as we shall see from considering his example of 'a white stick carried by a blind man'. In this example, as in all other examples of semiotic acts, one would expect three homogeneous accounts that dove-tail into one another. Instead, approaching this example from the three angles seems to produce three heterogeneous, even conflicting, accounts.

(1) Viewed from the angle of *theory of indices*, there is no doubt but that a *white stick* carried by a blind man constitutes an index as deliberate and artificial/conventional as any sign that may be encountered in one of the codes in common usage in our culture (for example, Highway Code). This creates, from the point of view of the conventionality of the *white stick*, the expectation that there is a 'code' involved in its use.

(2) Viewed from the angle of *theory of codes*, it is understood that a 'sentence' in a code acquires its value and meaning by opposition to alternative 'sentences' in the same code. However, the *white stick* does not co-exist in a code with other 'sentences' (even mere absence of the white stick is excluded from belonging to any code). Thus, there is no justification for identifying 'white stick' as a 'sentence' in a code – or, for that matter, for attributing to it any value or meaning derived from its position in a system. This is in direct conflict with the expectation (reached from the angle of theory of indices), that *white stick* is a codified index. At the same time, this suggests that the mechanism of indication could not possibly operate since the pseudo-code to which *white stick* belongs admits no possibilities other than *white sticks carried by individuals* to its Sematic Field, nor possibilities other than messages to the effect that the *bearer has defective sight* to its Noetic Field.

(3) Viewed from the angle of the model for semiotic acts, the fact that carrying a white stick can obviously function as a signal forces one to give such instances the normal interpretation due to successful semiotic acts (see Figure 3.32).

This model, however, cannot correctly apply to the case in point if we consider, as we have seen above, the *white stick* from the point of view of theory of codes. The model indicates that (a) the Sematic Field (within which the class of *white sticks* is located) contains alternative signals belonging to the class $\sim A_1$, (b) the Noetic Field (within which the class of messages conveyed by white sticks is located) contains alternative messages belonging to $\sim B_1$. Since both Sematic Field and Noetic Field are always restricted to the signals and messages that belong to a code, respectively, and since only one class of signals and one class of messages can be said to belong to the pseudo-code in question, there can be no alternative signals in A_1 nor alternative messages in B_1.

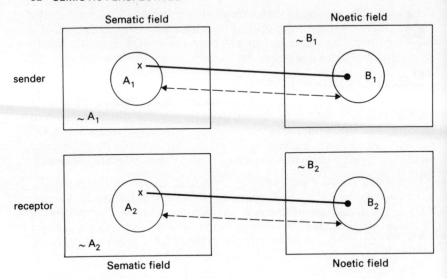

where A_1 and A_2 (being co-extensive) = white sticks carried by individuals;
B_1 and B_2 (being co-extensive) = class of messages constituted by the information
that the bearer has defective sight;
x   indicates a particular white stick carried on a given occasion;
•   indicates a message (intended and interpreted) to the effect that the
particular bearer of the white stick in question has defective sight.

Figure 3.32

3.6.3   Prieto's Semiotics in the Context of Functionalism

While Prieto's 'three-pronged' attack on semiotics constitutes the 'projection' of three abstract points of view, only two of these are conducive to structural description dealing in semiotic constants (types). The model of semiotic acts does not contribute to setting up such constants, but is designed for describing individual particulars, each a separate semiotic act in time and space. This fact makes Prieto's theory of '*l'acte sémique*' a theory suitable for the separate treatment it has been given here. The other two 'prongs' of Prieto's semiology are a version of Functional semiology, and are treated, accordingly, in the appropriate chapter (Chapter 6).

4

Semiotics as a Theory of 'Speech Acts': Austin and Searle

4.1 The Scope of the 'Theory of Speech Acts'

4.1.1 Introductory Remarks

Known as 'theory of speech acts', the realm of philosophical inquiry initiated by the philosopher J. L. Austin, elaborated upon by J. R. Searle, and currently peopled by many others (viz. Cole and Morgan, 1975) is, in effect, much wider in scope than the terminology of its adherents suggests. There is a conspicuous lack of the term 'semiotic', or its derivatives such as 'semiotics', 'semiotic act', and so on, from the terminology of Austin, Searle, *et alia*. Nevertheless, the correct context for consideration of the ideas of this group of scholars is that of communication in general, and semiotics in particular (see Bierwisch, 1980). In fact, but for its speech-oriented terminology, and its concentration on linguistic examples, the approach would be more aptly named 'theory of communication acts'.

For purposes of a global presentation of the 'theory of speech acts', Austin (the initiator of the theory) and Searle (probably its best-known current exponent) will be taken as representative of the approach. Both Austin and Searle studiously refer to the object of their interest as being 'language acts', 'speech acts', 'linguistic acts' or 'utterances', and draw their examples almost exclusively from the uses of English utterances. Yet the ideas they develop should not be seen as 'linguistics', but as a particular marriage of 'pragmatics' and 'semiotics' (the former can be roughly characterised as the 'study of the specific meanings of utterances in use by actual speakers in concrete contexts'; Searle *et al.*, 1980). It seems clear that the notions of the 'theory of speech acts' are just as applicable (*mutatis mutandis*) to non-linguistic communication acts of a conventional nature as they are to 'speech acts' in particular. A more realistic assessment of the scope of this theory would result from a simple substitution of the term 'semiotic' for the term 'speech' in virtually every case. In the actual discussion of the ideas of Austin and Searle, I shall, therefore, take the liberty of making this substitution wherever possible, in order to emphasise the broad semiotic import of the ideas presented.

In order to justify taking such terminological liberties, let us take the following illustration of the way Austin's 'speech-limited' terminology obscures the obviously wider semiotic import of his ideas. Austin establishes the category of *performative utterances* (to be discussed in more detail below) by referring to such speech acts as the uttering of 'I undertake to . . .' as binding ways of contracting to do something. However, given the right circumstances, the conventional act of shaking hands, or that of putting one's seal to a document, may be considered to be equally binding ways of contracting to do something. Thus, it is not only speech acts that have a right to belong to the category of *performatives* (though, of course, only speech acts can be called performative *utterances*). That is to say everything that can be said about performative *speech acts* – a particular subcategory of *semiotic acts* – can be said about all semiotic acts that have an analogous performative function. To give the impression, under these circumstances, that the category of performatives is limited to (and synonymous with) that of performative utterances would be little short of perverse. Performatives are a semiotic category, not a linguistic one, but to refer to them as 'performative utterances' serves to obscure this fact.

4.2   Austin's Initial Insight and its Implications

4.2.1   Austin's Preliminary Theory

The extremely promising idea with which Austin commences his preliminary attempt at the theory of speech acts is a specific observation counter-indicating what has often been called the 'descriptive fallacy'. Although, once having explored this preliminary theory, Austin constructs a second theory that supersedes the first, it will be instructive to review both theories here.

4.2.2   Performative Utterances

The fallacy referred to as the 'descriptive fallacy' consists in the belief that all sentences are (perhaps by definition) *assertive*, that is, that they are all used for the purpose of 'stating facts'. The extremely interesting observation whose effects Austin brings to bear on this belief is an observation leading to his preliminary isolation of the category of performative utterances.

Austin notes that what is important about such examples as (a) 'I do' (as part of the marriage ceremony); (b) 'I name this ship the Queen Elizabeth'; (c) 'I give and bequeath my watch to my brother'; is not that they report facts (until they have been uttered, there are no facts for them to report), but that the performing of a valid marriage ceremony, the naming of a ship, and the settling of a valid bequest (respectively), depend largely on the uttering of the appropriate sentences. In other words, these sentences are uttered not for the sake of, or certainly not primarily for the sake of, stating or describing what the speaker is doing; the utterances are, rather, actions that constitute the doing itself.

The examples, and the conclusion Austin draws from them, are certainly suggestive, and command the impression that here we have something unusual about certain types of utterance that sets them apart from others. For, after all, not all utterances (and not even the majority of them) constitute the whole or part of performing a non-descriptive action – at least, not in the sense in which promises, contracts, christenings, and so on can be performed, either by performative utterances, or by other 'symbolic' acts conventionally designated for the purpose.

The starting-point of Austin's preliminary theory is the apparent isolatability of *performatives* as a special class of semiotic acts, making them entirely different from 'constative' semiotic acts (that is, semiotic acts whose function is merely, or primarily, the stating of some real or imaginary fact).

4.2.3 Functions and Malfunctions of Semiotic Acts

Given that performatives are a well-defined subgroup among semiotic acts, their very contrast with 'constative' semiotic acts paves the way to developing a special theory to cover the functioning of performatives. In order to set this theory into proper context, a comparison with Prieto's theory of signals and messages turns out to be unexpectedly informative. Prieto – who is a semiotician by virtue of being a linguist – seeks to clarify the mechanisms by which sender and hearer link signals with messages. His interest is, therefore, in the process of comprehension, and its various disorders (see Chapter 3). Austin – who becomes semiotician (*malgré lui?*) by virtue of being a philosopher and logician – inherits, naturally, the interest philosophers have in the nature of the link between messages and corresponding factual states in the 'real' world. His theory, unlike Prieto's, is typically that of a philosopher, concentrating as it does on the fit between what a semiotic event imputes to states of affairs in the world, and the actual states themselves. Traditionally, a proper fit between a 'message' and an actual state of reality is said to guarantee the truth of the statement in which that message is embodied. Disorders in the correspondence of 'message' and 'reality' are said to manifest themselves in terms of falsity. In short, Austin is, in fact, essentially concerned with that aspect of semiotic acts which is traditionally covered by the notion of 'truth' and 'falsity' of statements. Prieto, on the other hand, is chiefly concerned with the actual transmission (including disorders or failure of transmission) of 'messages', whether they be true or false. However, it is only fair to point out that both Prieto and Austin are in the business of exploring the proper functioning, and the malfunctions, of links between certain aspects of semiotic acts – albeit they deal with different links between different aspects.

4.3 'Felicity' and 'Infelicity'

4.3.1 Performatives versus Constatives

The chief import of the difference Austin establishes between 'performatives' and 'constatives' is that the normal concepts of 'truth' and 'falsity', while they may be appropriate to explaining the function and malfunction of 'constatives', do not fit the bill for discussing the proper functioning, or the malfunctioning, of 'performatives'. As he points out, it makes little sense to call a semiotic act whose function is the making of a contract, or the naming of an object, either 'true' or 'false'. Even where one may speak of a promise being 'false', what is meant is not that the semiotic act itself is 'false', but rather that, by not keeping a promise, the maker of that promise was not 'true to his word'.

This leads to the suggestion that a different pair of notions is required for expressing with respect to 'performatives' what the notions 'truth' and 'falsity' express with respect to 'constatives'. The pair of notions offered by Austin is that of 'felicity' and 'infelicity'. That is to say, from the dichotomy between 'constatives' and 'performatives', Austin (tentatively) proceeds to the following complex analogy.

felicity : performatives :: truth : constatives
infelicity : performatives :: falsity : constatives
felicity v. infelicity : performatives ::
    truth versus falsity : constatives

As there is reason to believe that not all semiotic acts function as either constatives or performatives, we may have expected Austin to provide pairs of notions analogous with those of 'truth' v. 'falsity' and 'felicity' v. 'infelicity' – a pair to cover the proper functioning and the malfunctioning of each type of semiotic act. The overall semiotic theory would then have assumed the character of an exhaustive categorisation of semiotic acts into 'functional' categories (for example, constative, performative, interrogative, and so on), together with appropriate notions for capturing the different conditions for the proper functioning, and malfunctions, of each of the categories.

In his preliminary theory, however, Austin chooses to stay with the category of performatives, developing a complex framework of notions in terms of which the various types of malfunction of performatives can be assessed. This framework is then extended to other types of semiotic act, as we shall see below.

4.3.2 Types of 'Infelicity'

The conditions of 'felicity' (or 'happiness-conditions') apply to performatives that successfully achieve their intended effects. Such a characterisation, which may sound vacuous, is rendered meaningful by the fact that 'felicity' receives a negative definition by contrast with 'infelicity' (that is, 'felicity' may be called the absence of any form of 'infelicity').

The scheme shown in Figure 4.1 tabulates the definitions of the various types of 'infelicity' that may affect performatives.

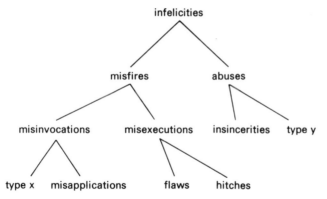

Misfires = semiotic act is null and void by virtue of being *incorrectly* performed.
Misinvocations = semiotic act is disallowed due to being performed in unsuitable circumstances.
Misinvocations of type X = semiotic act is null and void because it lacks the backing of the appropriate conventions to bring about the desired effects.
Misapplications = semiotic act is disallowed by virtue of being performed in a situation that precludes the possibility of its success.
Flaws = semiotic act is vitiated by virtue of being incorrectly performed by at least one of the participants.
Hitches = semiotic act is vitiated by virtue of being incompletely performed.
Insincerities = semiotic act is hollow by virtue of being performed by someone whose feelings and intentions, at the time of performance, are not congruent with the purported effects of the act.
Abuses of type Y = semiotic act is hollow by virtue of the fact that its purported effects are not congruent with subsequent events.

(Austin does not provide special terms for the categories I have labelled Type X and Type Y.)

Figure 4.1

4.3.3 'Infelicity' in Performative Utterances

Examples of the six major categories of infelicity as applied to 'performatives' will illustrate not only what Austin intends by the definitions found in the scheme above, but also some of the inherent imprecisions of the theory. These imprecisions are clearly enough recognised, and amply exemplified, by Austin himself. As such they may contribute to some degree to his own rejection of the preliminary theory we are considering at the moment.

Example I
Semiotic act: performative
Purported effect: 'to promise to give a horse to a person x'
Misinvocation of Type X: (*a*) if the speaker utters the sounds [bleŋ frip] when there are (obviously) no conventions allowing for the attribution of any conventional effect to such an utterance (But note that it does not make logical sense to maintain that a semiotic act has actually taken place in this case; i.e. this type of misinvocation does not so much affect the felicity of semiotic acts as *prevent* a semiotic act from taking place at

all.) (*b*) if the speaker utters the sound [žvupRɔmɛmõšval] (*Je vous promets mon cheval*), but the person addressed does not know (the conventions of) French; (*c*) if the speaker utters the sounds [k'ʌmhiə], which utterance does not, given the conventions of English, have a conventional effect of the purported type. (But note that this type of infelicity could equally well be classed as a 'Flaw'.)

Misapplication: (*a*) if the speaker does not have a horse at all. (But note that this could equally well be classed under 'Insincerity'.) (*b*) if the speaker has already promised his one and only horse to someone else. (But note that such an infelicity is again hard to distinguish from a case of 'Insincerity'.) (*c*) if the person addressed has previously made it clear that he does not want, and will under no circumstances accept, the gift of a horse; (*d*) if the person addressed is deaf.

Flaw: (*a*) if the speaker makes a slip of the tongue and says 'I promise to give you my hearse' instead of 'I promise to give you my horse'. (But note that the borderline between 'Flaws' and 'Misinvocations' can be extremely tenuous. So is, here, the borderline between 'Flaws' and 'Hitches' – the act of promising a horse is here 'incompletely' performed.) (*b*) if the speaker erroneously addresses the utterance, 'I promise you a horse' to a person other than the intended recipient. (But note that this could also be interpreted as a 'Misapplication', especially if, say, the conversation took place on the telephone and circumstances conspired to lead the speaker to believe that he was addressing the intended recipient of the gift horse.)

Hitch: (*a*) if the speaker is unable to complete his utterance, and manages only to say 'I promise to give you . . .'. (But note that this could be interpreted as a 'Misinvocation' resulting from the fact that there are no conventions by virtue of which the interrupted utterance can bring about the purported effect.) (*b*) if the person addressed blocks his ears to prevent himself from hearing the speaker's utterance. (But note that in such a case, one could equally well speak of 'Misapplication' or even of a 'Flaw'.)

Insincerity: (*a*) if the speaker intends all along to keep his horse; (*b*) if the speaker intends to give his horse to someone else, but wants the person addressed to think that he will be the recipient. (But note that the borderline between 'Insincerity' and 'Misapplication' is extremely tenuous here, especially if the speaker has already promised his horse to someone else.)

Abuse of Type Y: (*a*) if, for some reason beyond his control, the speaker is unable to fulfil his promise which was made in good faith, and the intended recipient does not in the end get the promised horse.

4.3.4 'Infelicity' in Non-Linguistic Performatives

For the sake of comparison and for illustrating the range of application of the types of infelicity listed by Austin, we shall take as a second example a performative semiotic act of a 'ceremonial', as opposed to 'linguistic' nature.

Example II
Semiotic act: performative
Purported effect: 'to enter into a Christian marriage'
Misinvocation of Type X: (*a*) if the groom, instead of placing a ring on the bride's finger, puts a thimble on it when there are (obviously) no conventions that would allow for this act to have any conventional effect. (Arguably, this is not so much a case of the performance of an infelicitous semiotic act, as a case where there is simply no *semiotic* act performed at all.) (*b*) if the groom places a crown on the bride's head, but none of the participants is aware of the conventions of a Russian Orthodox wedding ceremony; (*c*) if the groom, instead of placing a ring on the bride's finger, shakes hands with her. (But note that this could just as easily be classified as a 'Flaw'.)
Misapplication: (*a*) if the religious ceremony is performed by someone who is not really a priest; (*b*) if, at the time of going through the ceremony, either of the parties is already married. (But note that, on the part of the person who is already married, this also constitutes an 'Insincerity'.) (*c*) if, by accident, the best man happens to change places with the groom, or one of the bridesmaids with the bride, during the proceedings. (But note that this implies both a 'Flaw' and a 'Hitch' in the ceremony.)
Flaw: (*a*) if, by mistake, the bridegroom puts a key-ring, instead of the wedding-ring, on the bride's finger. (But note that the boundary between 'Flaws' and 'Misinvocations' is extremely tenuous.) (*b*) if the bride holds out the wrong finger of the wrong hand for the groom to put the ring on. (But note that this could also be interpreted as a 'Misinvocation of Type X'.)
Hitch: (*a*) if the best man forgets to bring the ring. (But note the tenuous borderline here between 'Hitches', 'Flaws' and 'Misinvocations'.) (*b*) if the ring is too small to fit on the bride's finger. (But note that this could be interpreted as a 'Misapplication'.) (*c*) if the bride refuses to let the ring be placed on her finger, say, because her finger is injured. (But note the tenuous distinction here between 'Hitches', 'Flaws' and 'Misapplications'.)
Insincerity: (*a*) if the groom goes through with the ceremony knowing full well that, half an hour later, he will be on a plane bound for South America with one of the bridesmaids; (*b*) if the groom has deliberately brought in a de-frocked priest to perform the ceremony, intending thereby to deceive the bride. (But note that this implies a 'Misapplication' and, probably, also a 'Misexecution'.)
Abuse of Type Y: (*a*) if the groom decides, after the ceremony has just been completed, that he cannot after all 'go through with it', and boards a plane for South America.

The examples cited not only show the kinds of disorder from which semiotic acts may be said to suffer, but also the overlapping and lack of sharpness in the typology developed in Austin's preliminary theory. It is not, however, the poor quality of the distinctions between categories of *infelicity* that makes Austin abandon his preliminary theory and look for a better alternative, using the lessons learnt from the preliminary theory. The shift to a modified theory is due rather to the realisation that almost as soon as the contrast between 'constatives' and 'performatives' is crystallised into the analogy

truth and falsity : constatives :: felicity and infelicity : performatives

evidence appears to indicate that both (*a*) felicity and infelicity (as opposed to *just* truth and falsity) are applicable to 'constatives' and (*b*) truth and falsity (as opposed to *just* felicity and infelicity) are applicable to 'performatives'. This means, in fact, that the originally assumed contrast between 'constatives' and 'performatives' is itself refuted (and becomes, at best, a matter of degree).

4.3.5 'Infelicity' in Constative Utterances

The following example will illustrate the applicability of felicity and infelicity to 'constatives':

Example III
Semiotic act: constative
Purported effect: 'to inform an interlocutor that this book is about semiotics'
Misinvocation of Type X: (*a*) if the speaker utters the sounds [liɔ frip] when there are (obviously) no conventions for the attribution of any conventional effect to such an utterance; (*b*) if the speaker utters the sounds [lsyžedsəli:vR elʌsemjɔlɔži] ('*le sujet de ce livre est la sémiologie*') but his interlocutor does not know (the conventions of) French; (*c*) if the speaker utters the sounds [k'ʌmhiə], which, according to the conventions of English, cannot have a conventional effect of the purported type.
Misapplication: (*a*) if there is no book anywhere in the vicinity; (*b*) if there are several books and the speaker fails to indicate to which one he is referring; (*c*) if the interlocutor has already read the book, and does not, therefore, need to be informed of its contents.
Flaw: (*a*) if the speaker makes a slip of the tongue and says 'This boot is about semiotics' instead of 'This book is about semiotics'; (*b*) if the speaker makes an utterance that can be heard by a third person, but not by the intended interlocutor.
Hitch: (*a*) if the speaker stops in mid-utterance; (*b*) if the speaker, erroneously, uses an intonation that makes the utterance sound more like a question than a statement; (*c*) if the interlocutor blocks his ears during the time of utterance.
Insincerity: (*a*) if the speaker actually intends to keep the interlocutor in the dark about the contents of the book, but accidentally says something that 'lets the cat out of the bag'; (*b*) if the speaker is merely talking aloud to himself, and has no intention of informing the interlocutor about the contents of the book (or, for that matter, about anything); (*c*) if the speaker is actually totally indifferent as to whether the interlocutor finds out about the contents of the book or not, and merely talks

about the book in order to distract the attention of the interlocutor, or to side-track him.

Abuse of Type Y: (*a*) if (and probably only if) the book indicated is, in fact, not about semiotics. (Note that this is the type of case that is normally interpreted under the traditional heading of 'Falsity'.)

4.3.6 Truth and Falsity in Performatives

From noting that when we apply the notion of *infelicity* to 'constatives', the traditional notion of falsity is interpreted as an 'Abuse of Type Y', it is fairly clear that, if 'performatives' can suffer from 'Abuses of Type Y', then criteria of truth and falsity can be re-introduced into discussion of 'performatives', simply by equating 'Abuse of Type Y' with 'falsity'.

Thus, for instance, if a speaker utters the 'performative' 'I promise to give you a horse' and, for whatever reason, this promise is not kept, then the utterance will be deemed infelicitous on account of a lack of correspondence between what the speaker imputes to a real situation – which, at the time of utterance, is still in the future – and the actual (future) state of affairs. While such a lack of correspondence would, in terms of 'felicity', be called an 'Abuse of Type Y', it is a situation clearly covered by the traditional notion of 'falsity'. From this, we can see that truth and falsity are, after all, applicable (among other considerations that are no less applicable) to 'performatives'.

4.3.7 The Value of Austin's Preliminary Theory

It might almost seem that this brings Austin's preliminary theory round in a full circle until the initial position on which it is based – namely the isolatability of 'performatives' as against 'constatives' – has been demolished. If that were the case, one might ask what was to be gained from such a costly detour into the ramifications of a theory whose first premiss is, in the end, shown to be unsound. Fortunately, certain other gains can be laid claim to – claims, that is, beyond giving Austin the opportunity to remark that 'it is time . . . to make a fresh start on the problem' (Austin, 1962).

Perhaps the most important of these gains are the notions 'felicity' and 'infelicity' themselves. The retention of the various types of 'infelicity' from which semiotic acts may suffer obviates the need to indulge in various contortions in order to make the notions of 'truth' and 'falsity' do all the explaining, to make all types of semiotic act solely and equally answerable to 'truth conditions'. It also provides a wider framework within which the very notions of 'truth' and 'falsity' can be accommodated – 'falsity' being interpreted, as we have seen, as just one particular type of 'infelicity'. Thus, rather than trying, unsuccessfully, to assimilate all types of semiotic disorder to the notion of 'falsity', we can assimilate 'falsity', itself, to types of 'infelicity'.

The question of positive gains bought, perhaps at the expense of occasionally excessive hair-splitting, by Austin's preliminary theory has, in the final event, to be considered in the light of the alternative theory he constructs from the ruins of his preliminary theory. We pass on, therefore, to Austin's 'final' thesis.

4.4   Austin's Revised Theory

4.4.1   Foundations of the Revised Theory

The starting-point of Austin's revised theory is a point so blatant that, on reading his *How to do things with words*, one cannot help a slight feeling of frustration at his having spent ninety pages of text just in getting to it. The answer, perhaps, is that as long as one is mesmerised by examples of 'performatives', in which there appears to be an ingredient of *practical action* of a sort not to be found in the mere reporting of 'facts', it is all too easy to overlook the obvious: namely that whoever performs a semiotic act is, in the 'full normal sense', *doing something*. (This is perhaps less obvious in Austin's terminology where 'utterances', or even 'sentences' are the objects under discussion, rather than 'semiotic *acts*'.) From this realisation, it becomes mandatory to look at *all semiotic acts* as performances of specific actions. It also becomes inescapable that semiotic acts should fall heir to general properties of *action*; i.e. that certain general pragmatic or 'axiological' considerations should directly affect *semiotic acts* (by virtue of their being acts, as opposed to by virtue of their being 'semiotic').

4.4.2   Locution, Illocution and Perlocution

From viewing 'semiotic acts' as acts, it emerges that saying something just for its own sake, or, for that matter, using any conventional sign for its intrinsic communicative value, is to perform a locutionary act pure and simple. Using a conventional sign with some ulterior motive (intention) in mind, that is, with the intention of thereby creating a particular effect (for example, asking a question, uttering a warning, making a promise, and so on), is to perform an illocutionary act. Thirdly, achieving a particular effect or producing a particular response in an interlocutor (for example, frighten, amuse, persuade, and so on) is to perform a perlocutionary act.

These three types of act generally go hand in hand. There is, however, a threefold ambiguity in the relationship that holds between them.

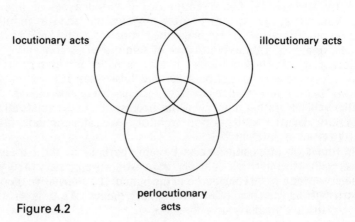

locutionary acts   illocutionary acts

perlocutionary
Figure 4.2   acts

First, the terminology used would tend to suggest that we are dealing with three largely separate, even if not wholly disjunct, classes of act, of a locutionary, illocutionary and perlocutionary type, respectively.

Secondly, Austin's explanation of the terms 'locutionary', 'illocutionary' and 'perlocutionary' suggests that he is on the way to developing a 'triangular' view of semiotic events, with 'locution', 'illocution' and 'perlocution' as three separable aspects that coincide in any given semiotic act.

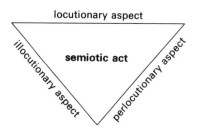

Figure 4.3

The distinction between (*a*) saying something (locutionary), (*b*) *in* saying something intending the performance of another (illocutionary) act, and (*c*) *by* saying something causing a particular effect or response (perlocutionary) creates the impression that, of the three aspects, the locutionary aspect is primary and basic, with the other two aspects being dependent on the basic one.

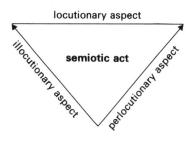

Figure 4.4

Alternatively, one might even find hints at a successive hierarchical progression in the relationship between the three aspects, in such a way that illocution presupposes locution, and perlocution, in turn, presupposes illocution (that is, intending to perform an illocutionary act *in* saying something presupposes that one says something; achieving an effect *by* saying something presupposes that one intended to, or was understood as intending to, perform an illocutionary act). The hierarchy could be diagrammed as in Figure 4.5.

locutionary aspect

↑

illocutionary aspect

↑

perlocutionary aspect

Figure 4.5

Thirdly, from further discussion, it transpires (or, at least, a strong impression is created to this effect) that, not only are the locutionary, illocutionary and perlocutionary acts (or aspects) separable, but they can be found to have mutually independent manifestations in isolation (for example, 'Four nines are thirty-six' might be uttered as a *purely* locutionary event, 'Good morning' as a *purely* illocutionary event, expressing polite or friendly intentions, and 'Hey, you!', as a *purely* perlocutionary event, attracting an interlocutor's attention). It is at no point completely clear just to what extent Austin believes locutionary, illocutionary and perlocutionary acts to be in practice independent, as opposed to merely 'isolatable' in theory.

Another grey area in the theory concerns the allocation of properties of given semiotic acts to one or other of the aspects. For instance, just how much of the 'interrogative' nature of 'How is your father?' belongs to the intrinsic locutionary aspect of the utterance, and how much, if any, should be attributed to the illocutionary aspect consisting in the speaker's intention, in uttering the words 'How is your father', of asking a question? Should one, perhaps, paraphrase the basic *locutionary* aspect of 'How is your father?' as 'Your father is in a state *x*', and have all the interrogative force of the utterance shunted off onto its illocutionary aspect? This would imply an analysis along the lines of Figure 4.6.

Overall event	*Locutionary aspect*	*Illocutionary aspect*	*Overall meaning*
'How is your father?'	Your father is in a state *x*	I am asking for information concerning *꜀*	I intend to ask for information as to the state your father is in

Figure 4.6

4.4.3   Semiotic Import of Austin's Theory

From a semiotic viewpoint, the chief import and contribution of Austin's theory of 'speech acts' must reside in the fact that, instead of being constrained to treat semiotic acts in just one dimension – that of 'meaning', 'sense', 'reference', 'truth' and 'falsity' – a framework is offered in which each semiotic act can be evaluated in the three dimensions of *locutionary*, *illocutionary* and *perlocutionary* acts. Of the three, the first two are notably speaker-orientated and conventional, whereas the third (perlocution) is hearer-orientated and non-conventional. Strictly speaking, therefore, perlocutionary acts (the realm of actual effect and actual response) might be considered as falling outside the scope of pure semiotics, for neither the speaker's communicative intention, nor the force of conventions, affect them in a direct, predictable and necessary way.

The *locutionary* dimension – that of 'meaning', 'sense' and 'reference' – corresponds more or less to the traditional preserve of linguistic semantics and of the philosophy of meaning, with the very important difference, however, that the burden which this dimension normally has to cope with is considerably lightened by being shared out between the three dimensions isolated by Austin. The real semiotic innovation, which enables one to distinguish between the import of the utterance of a conventional sign, and the purport of the utterer's intentions in uttering that conventional sign, is the dimension of *illocution*. It is here that Austin has the greatest claim to having originated a valuable field of research, as we shall see illustrated by further developments of the notion of 'illocutionary force' in the work of Searle.

4.4.4 Illocutionary Force

While the locutionary dimension is associated with meaning (in the 'normal' linguistic, philosophical and lay sense), and the perlocutionary dimension with *actual effects* (including *response* in the behavioural sense), the *illocutionary* dimension concentrates on the *force* that a particular semiotic act is intended to have on the particular occasion of its occurrence. Thus, although *illocutionary force* is a general, even 'generic', notion, actual illocutionary forces are properties of particular semiotic acts (that is, of 'tokens' rather than of 'types'). The success of the theory as a means of semiotic description depends largely on the extent to which the unlimited range of particular illocutionary forces can be reduced to categories or 'types'.

In the preliminary theory sketched by Austin, he stated the aim of listing (?exhaustively) the set of 'explicit performative verbs' (that is, words that make it conventionally explicit what force a particular utterance is intended to have, for example, 'promise', 'warn', 'tell', and so on in 'I promise . . .', 'I warn you . . .', 'I tell you . . .'). This task is, in the light of the revised theory, modified to the compilation of 'a list of illocutionary forces' (Austin, 1962).

Discussion of the categories and subcategories of *illocutionary force* tentatively advanced by Austin is reserved to a later stage, where these are compared with Searle's taxonomy. Suffice it to say here that Austin does attempt such a categorisation, but remains extremely cautious both about the actual categories he puts forward, and about the exhaustiveness of the list. On this score, I would add that the actual exhaustiveness or otherwise of Austin's proposed list is relatively unimportant beside the question of whether, in principle, an exhaustive list could be compiled by using the inductive-enumerative strategy that Austin seems to regard as appropriate to the task. For my part, I only know of one method of exhaustive categorisation, namely, the successive 'deductive' application of relevant distinctions by which a general category is partitioned into sub-sets. This strategy – illustrated by the schematic form in Figure 4.7 – is not employed by Austin.

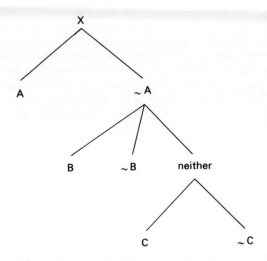

Figure 4.7

Equally serious, in a critical sense, is the question: to what extent has Austin succeeded in converting his earlier aim of listing 'explicit per-formative verbs' (in the preliminary theory) into a different task (in the revised theory) of making 'a list of *illocutionary forces*'? The point is that the former task is specifically and categorically part of a description of English, whereas the latter is not only not language-specific, but must, surely, apply to semiotic acts in general (for example, a traffic sign consisting of a blue circular field enclosing a white arrow does not contain an 'explicit performative verb' – except in translation into English – but such a sign has the illocutionary force of creating an obligation for motorists). It would be highly suspicious, to say the least, if the general categories of illocutionary force valid for all semiotic acts turned out to correspond closely to 'explicit performative verbs' of English. This would create the suspicion that the theory of speech acts had allowed itself to be caught in the trap that so many other theories have lately fallen into – that of implicitly giving English the status of the privileged language *par excellence*, the language which, above (or even to the exclusion of) all other languages holds the key to universal linguistic and semiotic prin-ciples and truths.

4.5 Searle's Elaboration of the 'Theory of Speech Acts'

4.5.1 Introductory Remarks

Starting with the basis that 'semiotic acts' belong to the category of rule-governed actions dependent on *constitutive conventions* (see below), Searle's most natural task is to extend the theory in the direction of an analysis of constitutive conventions seen as conditions for the performance of certain types of 'semiotic act'.

While there is much in Searle's work that, from our point of view, seems to be pure philosophy – and, therefore, out of place in a discussion of semiotics – there is also much that can be seen as the elaboration of a 'theory of speech acts'. Such a theory, once again seen from our point of view, qualifies as a theory of (certain aspects of) semiotics.

4.5.2 Semiotic Acts in Austin and Searle

As I have said, Searle's intention is to elaborate appropriate sets of conditions as a means of describing the constitutive conventions by which certain types of semiotic act are governed. The import of such analyses and descriptions is that they specify how, given a fixed number of fulfilled conditions, a particular act will 'count as' a specific type of 'semiotic act'. The actual types of 'semiotic act' closely resemble Austin's earlier typology, as we can see in Figure 4.8.

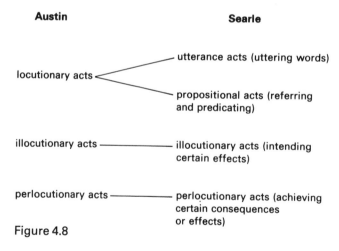

Figure 4.8

4.5.3 Semiotic Acts as 'Rule-Governed' Activity

There is a fundamental difference between semiotic theories that relate acts of communication directly to action (and 'theories of action') in general (for example, behavioural approaches), and theories that place acts of (deliberate) communication within the much narrower and more specific framework of conventional (or 'rule-governed') activity.

It would, in broad terms, be valid to suggest that just such a difference holds between the exploratory ideas of Austin and the more precisely restricted theory of Searle. In the latter, it is made clear virtually from the start, that not all properties of action are of direct relevance to 'semiotic acts' (that is, to so-called 'speech acts'), and that 'semiotic acts' belong to the specific category of 'rule-governed' activity.

An important, and neat, distinction is, furthermore, drawn by Searle between conformity to 'regulative' conventions and conformity to 'constitutive' conventions. The distinction is an interesting and fundamental one, and merits some discussion.

4.5.4   'Regulative' Conventions

Conventions may exist whose sole function is to control (within the limits of willingness to conform, of course) the manner in which a particular activity should 'ideally' be performed. The activity in question is, however, perfectly easily performed without conformity to any conventions whatsoever, in fact without observing anything other than the practical exigencies of the situation. Thus, for instance, one can eat with a knife and fork, or with one's bare hands, or, if need be, by attacking the food with mouth and teeth. The man who holds a chicken-leg in his right hand just so that he can wield his fork with his left is not acting in conformity with conventions any more than is a prisoner who is forced to eat with his right hand because his left hand is tied behind his back.

If, however, the manner of 'polite' eating is laid down in a given cultural group by the convention that one should never use one's left hand, then eating with the right hand becomes, in that instance, a matter of conformity with regulative conventions. Such regulative conventions may motivate the manner in which one eats in given social situations, but, of course, conformity remains subject to matters of feasibility, convenience, and so on. What is important, however, is that eating is an activity one can perform completely out of context with any conventions whatsoever. In short, there is only a weak dependence between certain ways of eating and certain conventions that are observed in given cultural situations. It is this weak form of dependence that characterises conventions of a purely regulative nature, as against constitutive conventions.

4.5.5   'Constitutive' Conventions

Naturally, constitutive conventions are also 'regulative' in the sense that they prescribe and control the manner in which an activity is to be performed. They are, however, not merely regulative, for, rather than being rules imposed on independently existing activities, they alone make it possible for the appropriate activity to exist at all.

The most compelling examples through which constitutive conventions can be explained come from the realms of sports and of games in general. Compare, for instance, the foregoing example of eating in a way prescribed by etiquette with such familiar actions as (*a*) scoring a goal in a game of soccer; (*b*) checkmating an opponent in a game of chess; (*c*) incurring four penalty-points for knocking down a fence in a show-jumping competition.

In each of these cases, the striking feature is that the action designated can only be conceived of in the context of the rules of the appropriate game or sport, and can only be performed in ways that are carefully circumscribed by conventional rules. Observance of these rules is not merely a matter of choosing, out of all the innumerable ways in which a given action can be performed, a way that satisfies certain cultural requirements of 'acceptable' behaviour. In particular, the competitor who incurs four penalty-points certainly does not choose to do so and would rather not have done so. The penalty is imposed upon him because his participation in the competition is entirely conditional on his accept-ance of all the rules of that competition. Furthermore, outside of the rules of show-jumping competitions, there is no way of incurring four penalty-points for knocking down a fence.

Equally, there are no extra-conventional, let alone contra-conven-tional, ways of scoring goals, or of checkmating an opponent. If the conventions are seen to have been contravened, the action in question simply does not count as 'scoring a goal', or as 'giving checkmate'. That is to say, while one can eat in non-conventional, as well as in conventionally approved, ways, one can only score goals, checkmate opponents or incur penalty-points in a conventionally defined and approved manner – non-observance of the rules simply disqualifies the action, making it null and void. It is in this sense that observance of all the appropriate conventions 'creates' or constitutes (by definition) what we describe as 'scoring a goal', as 'checkmate' or as 'incurring four penalty-points'. While it would be wrong to say that such conventions do not also 'regulate' the appropriate actions, this is only half the story, and not the most important half at that. Far more importantly, there is an absolute (mutual) dependence between the conventionally acceptable ways of scoring goals, and so on, and the actual scoring of goals, and so on. It is this absolute mutual dependence – as against the weak dependence noted in the cases of regulative conven-tions – that characterises constitutive conventions.

4.5.6 Semiotic Acts and 'Constitutive' Conventions

If it were the case that semiotic acts were mere physical actions that one could perform, either by choosing to ignore, or by choosing to adhere to, conventions that regulate their performance, it would be appropriate to treat them by analogy with all other practical actions in general, and to explore, from this general standpoint, the regulative conventions which may be imposed upon them. However, the production of a certain physical 'utterance' (be it vocal noise, or any other audible, visible, tangible, etc. manifestation) does not by any means amount to the issuing of a signal. The difference between, for instance, vocal noises and speech utterances is analogous with that between 'kicking the ball over the goal-line' and 'scoring a goal'. Only as a signal with a particular message associated to it by convention does the issuance of an 'utterance' qualify as a semiotic act. There is, in other words, an absolute mutual dependence between 'performing a semiotic act' and the appropriate conventionally regulated ways of performing that semiotic act. The conventions may, of course, allow considerable latitude, both in the variations between physical manifestations that count as 'the same' semiotic act, and in the variations between interpreted messages. Notwithstanding the potential lack of rigidity in conventions that govern semiotic acts, everything points to the conclusion – Searle's conclusion – that 'semiotic acts' are acts governed by *constitutive conventions*. This conclusion has important repercussions on the appropriateness of drawing the borderline between 'semiotic acts' and other significative acts of a non-semiotic nature – and, in fact, between 'semiotics' and other disciplines – precisely on the boundary between acts governed by constitutive conventions and acts governed by regulative conventions, or by no conventions at all. Significative acts that convey messages by virtue of constitutive conventions form a homogeneous and well-defined set of phenomena that can reasonably be expected to function according to analogous principles and mechanisms.

(The analogy between 'games' and 'languages' is not original or unique to the work of Searle. Saussure and Wittgenstein are just two outstanding scholars who have found this a profitable analogy, and who have seen the rule-governed nature of speech activity as being closely allied to the rule-governed nature of games and sports. I credit Searle, however, with the particularly lucid distinction between regulative and constitutive rules.)

4.6 Types of Semiotic Act

4.6.1 Utterance Acts and 'Literal' Meanings

The four major types of semiotic act – utterance act, propositional act, illocutionary act and perlocutionary act – were briefly outlined and characterised in Section 5.2 (Figure 4.7). It would be reasonable to expect all four types to be dealt with in equal detail in speech-act theory. As a matter of fact, however, the theory is concerned primarily (and almost exclusively) with illocutionary acts, and, in second instance (but almost incidentally), with propositional acts. Of the remaining two types, perlocutionary acts have the advantage over utterance acts, in that it is at least completely clear how perlocutionary acts are to be understood: as acts that succeed in producing specific effects on their receptors (for example, hearers). The concept of utterance acts not only remains in practice nebulous in the theory – for instance, their relation to 'literal' meaning (see below) is obscure – but there is reason to wonder how this concept, as it appears to be envisaged, can avoid being a contradiction in terms.

If, as seems likely from what Searle has to say on the matter ('Utterance acts consist simply in uttering strings of words'; Searle, 1969), an utterance act is constituted by the mere production of the physical trappings associated with the issuing of a signal, it is certain that such physical acts can be performed totally out of context with any constitutive or conventional rules. If, in other words, an act of utterance (the uttering of a string of words) is what is common between (*a*) the production of the sequence [k'ʌm hiə] ('Come here!') by an English speaker; (*b*) the production of 'the same' sequence by a Chinese speaker with no knowledge of English; (*c*) the production of 'the same' sequence by a parrot, then it is not tenable that utterance acts are a type of semiotic act at all. Yet, if an utterance act is not just an act of producing mere sequences completely isolated from acts of referring, predicating, and so on, that is, if it necessarily involves any of the latter, then it is hardly possible to see it as a type of act *separate* from referring, predicating, and so on. In those instances where a speaker of English utters [k'ʌm hiə] without in any way intending it as an utterance of 'Come here!' (perhaps when talking in his sleep), where a Chinese speaker tries to copy the sounds made by an English speaker (but without any idea of any aspect of their meaning), and those instances where a parrot produces a passable imitation of the human voice, we have, indeed, acts that would answer the definition of utterance acts as the mere uttering of strings of 'words'. Therefore, it is not the possibility of conceiving of a category of pure utterance acts that is in question, but whether it is conceivable to include such acts in the category of semiotic acts. Such acts would, by definition, be devoid of any conceivable form of semiotic significance – for, what form could such semiotic significance take, if it is neither propositional, nor illocutionary, nor perlocutionary? Nor could such acts come under the sway of constitutive rules – a fact that further emphasises their non-semiotic nature – for their very character is to be 'parrot-like', and parrots do not learn to operate with the constitutive rules of human intercourse.

We recognise, of course, that the reasonable way to construe utterance acts is as the issuing of physical signals to convey messages in accordance with certain 'literal' meanings, as determined by the semantic conventions of a given system. In this case, we could say that the semiotic significance of utterance acts is to be found primarily in their 'literal' meanings, rather than in the propositional acts they realise, or the illocutionary and perlocutionary acts that accompany them. But then we could hardly say that utterance acts 'consist simply in uttering strings of words', as there is nothing simple about the question of uttering words with their 'literal' meanings.

The long and the short of all this is that the notion of 'utterance acts' is an extremely shaky one in 'speech act theory'. This means, however, that there are difficulties with accommodating in the theory the vital and fundamental aspect of 'literal' meanings.

'Speech act theory' captures (*a*) the 'causal' (effective) aspects of semiotic acts under the aspect of *perlocution*; (*b*) the 'intentional (purposive) aspects of semiotic acts under the aspect of *illocution*; (*c*) the 'logical' (truth-functional) aspects of semiotic acts under the aspect of *propositional content*; leaving the 'literal' (and semiotically speaking most central) aspect to be captured under some other heading. In the case of Austin, one could identify this aspect with that of locution, but we cannot identify it, as we have seen, with Searle's 'utterance acts'.

The question of *propositional content* can, strictly speaking, only be approached by way of the 'literal' meaning of the expression used in conveying a proposition. In blunt terms, nothing short of the semantic conventions of English, by virtue of which 'this', 'book', 'is' and 'long' hold the 'literal' meanings they hold, can guarantee the range of propositions that can be conveyed by using the sentence 'This book is long'. Far from having to assimilate propositional content to 'literal' meaning, the problem is that the establishment of propositional uses of a 'literal' meaning presupposes that one knows in advance what those 'literal' meanings are. If the basis of 'literal' meaning is left unanalysed and undecided – in fact, left obscure – propositional content can only be discussed by begging the question.

The situation is only aggravated by those exponents of 'speech act theory' who, turning things upside down, insist on seeing the 'pragmatic' aspects of semiotic acts (propositional acts, illocutionary acts, perlocutionary acts) as being basic to 'litéral' meanings, and not vice versa.

4.6.2   Illocutionary Acts and Illocutionary Forces

Just as propositional acts must be functions of clearly established 'literal' meanings, so illocutionary acts, with their attendant illocutionary forces, constitute an additional dimension over and above the locutionary and propositional dimensions. (In fact, the formula $F(p)$, symbolising illocutionary force, explicitly indicates illocutionary force to be a function over a proposition.) The additional dimension of illocutionary acts is brought into play in order to register aspects of semiotic acts that are, in a sense, 'residual'. For instance, if the sentence 'This book is long' is uttered by you with the intention of dissuading a third party from reading it, then that intention (or 'ulterior motive'), although a very real aspect of your semiotic performance, cannot be registered either as part of the 'literal' meaning, or as part of the propositional act performed. After all, you did not actually express (in so many words), and could justifiably deny, your insinuated ulterior motive. (In this connection, illocution has been referred to as 'suggestion', by, for instance, R. Posner; cf. Searle, *et al.*, 1980. In my own view, 'insinuation' is an even better term for bringing out the difference between what is expressed and what is hinted at.) It is in this sense that the illocutionary force which is parasitic on, and is more or less concealed behind and beyond, a locutionary and a propositional act, can be said to be 'residual': factors are shunted onto illocutionary force when they are part of the global semiotic act, but are not contained in either the locutionary or the propositional act that has been performed.

Supposing, however, that you were to say instead: 'This book is too long for you to read.' Would it still be correct to say that the intention of dissuading a third party from reading the book is here an illocutionary force behind and beyond the locutionary and propositional acts? Clearly not, for '*too* long *for you to read*' is quite explicitly and literally endowed with a meaning of which the element of 'intending-to-dissuade-someone-from-reading-something' is an intrinsic part. What is mere illocutionary force ('insinuation') in an act involving the sentence 'This book is long' has become a matter of 'literal' meaning and of propositional content, in another act involving the sentence 'This book is *too* long *for you to read'*. The lesson to be learnt from this example is that acts, no matter how much they are motivated by the performer's inner intention, should only be assimilated to illocution in the event that there is nothing in the 'literal' meaning or propositional content to which their actual force and interpretation can be attributed. This is what I mean by saying that illocutionary force is a 'residual' notion – but this makes it all the more obvious that illocutionary acts can only be satisfactorily dealt with by examining what is left over when everything belonging to the 'literal' and propositional aspects of semiotic acts has been duly identified.

4.6.3 Illocutionary Force Indicating Devices

In this setting, we can detect a serious methodological flaw in working with the notion of illocutionary force: in the absence of a clearcut theory and methodology for identifying 'literal' meanings and propositional contents, it cannot be easy (if at all possible) to sift out the illocutionary aspects of semiotic acts. In his article on 'literal meaning' (Searle, 1979), Searle seems to be making matters worse by denying the hypothesis that there is a constancy of 'literal meaning' as abstracted from individual contexts.

Furthermore, my contention that illocutionary force must be, by definition, 'residual' has a completely destructive effect on the so-called 'illocutionary force indicating devices' (IFIDs) of speech act theory. The argument may run as follows: any force that is systematically and regularly carried by some explicit, conventional device is expressed as (a part of) the 'literal' meaning of that device (that is, the 'literal' meaning of that device contributes that force to the 'literal' meaning of the overall semiotic act), and cannot, therefore, be called an illocutionary force. IFIDs are just such devices, giving a 'literal' expression to what may, in their absence, appear only as 'suggestive' or 'insinuated' forces. Therefore, paradoxically enough, IFIDs – for all that they are called 'illocutionary force indicating devices' – do not indicate illocutionary forces, but express locutionary ones. They may, of course, 'translate' the illocutionary forces of other utterances, utterances, that is, in which they do not appear; as, for instance, 'I would like' translates the illocutionary force of an utterance 'An apple', when the latter is uttered with the same force as 'I would like an apple'.

Take also the following example: In an examiners' meeting, Dr A informs Professor B that all the papers written by Candidate X are outstandingly good. In this situation, we may contrast two alternative rejoinders on the part of Professor B: (1) 'Candidate X should be given a First Class Honours Degree;' (2) 'I agree (that) Candidate X should be given a First Class Honours Degree.'

In the light of Dr A's earlier remarks, either of Professor B's alternative replies has the force of agreement with Dr A. But while in alternative (1), agreement is not expressed as part of the 'literal' meaning, and is, therefore, something to be assigned to illocutionary force, in alternative

(2), the 'literal' force of 'I agree' constitutes an expression of agreement by locutionary means. In alternative (1), it would be said that, besides the locutionary and propositional acts constituted by uttering the sentence in question, there is also an illocutionary act of agreement. If, however, one were to register 'I agree' as an IFID in alternative (2), this would have the paradoxical effect of attributing an illocutionary force of agreement to an utterance in which agreement is expressed by locutionary means. While 'I agree' may 'translate' the illocutionary force of alternative (1), it should be clear that 'I agree (that) Candidate X should be given a First Class Honours Degree' does not constitute an illocutionary act of agreement, but a locutionary one.

Setting aside all the reservations that follow from objections to the development of a theory of propositional and illocutionary acts in the absence of an adequate background theory of 'literal'/locutionary constants, we shall now concentrate on Searle's theory of propositional acts and illocutionary acts, for it is almost exclusively in this area that the theory-building efforts of 'speech act theory' are to be found.

4.7 Propositional Acts as Acts Governed by Constitutive Conventions

4.7.1 Constitutive Conventions for Propositions

The description of propositional acts (as indeed of any semiotic act) takes the form, in Searle, of an analysis of the constitutive rules governing such acts. These constitutive rules are the conventions by virtue of which semiotic acts of the appropriate type 'count as' propositional acts. The constitutive rules are expressed in the form of a set of conditions that all and only propositional acts must satisfy. Therefore, the statement of a set of conditions is fully equivalent to a characterisation of 'what makes a semiotic act a propositional act'.

4.7.2 Reference and Predication

Propositional acts are dealt with under two separate headings corresponding to two types of propositional act: (1) Acts of *reference* and (2) Acts of *predication*.

Acts of reference are the characteristic acts performed through the use of 'referring expressions' such as personal pronouns ('I', 'you', and so on), descriptive phrases that serve to identify an object ('the present Queen of England', 'the book you have in your hand', names ('Elizabeth II', 'John R. Searle'), and the like. An act of referring may, however, also be accomplished by pointing at an object with one's index finger.

Acts of predication are typically performed by the use of such expressions as 'is good', 'is red', 'will read', 'have finished', and so on. Such acts must, however, be carefully distinguished from assertion which is an illocutionary act performed over and above a complete proposition. An act of predication may also be accomplished by such gestures as the 'thumbs-up' sign, meaning 'O.K.'.

4.7.3 Conditions for Reference

The performance of a semiotic act of referring is characterised, in the work of Searle, by a set of seven conditions that together sum up the constitutive rules of reference:

(1) *Normal input and output conditions obtain.*
This includes such conditions as eliminate impediments to an exchange of communication, among others stipulating that sender and receiver share knowledge of the same code, and that there is no serious interference with the channel of transmission (for example, the sender can make recognisable and audible vocal sounds, and the receiver is not prevented from hearing these sounds). I may add that, at one nigh-on magical stroke, this condition, stipulating 'normal' communication, disposes of a multitude of complexities. As for lumping 'knowledge of a code' among this multitude, this is little short of begging the question, especially where one of the main tasks of semiotics should be precisely the analysis of semiotic codes.

(2) *The referring expression is uttered as part of a sentence.*
It seems from this condition that by itself (that is, unaccompanied by a predicating expression) a referring expression cannot be used to make an act of referring. This is both counter-intuitive (examples of referring expressions used successfully without being parts of a larger sentence abound in everyday conversation), and theoretically unsound (predication should not be a necessary condition for reference, if the two are intended to be independent notions).

(3) *The sentence of which the referring expression is a part is uttered with the intention of performing an illocutionary act.*
In other words, an act of referring never takes place for its own sake, but only in connection with some ulterior illocutionary purpose.

(4) *The object identified by the referring expression, or by another expression that the sender can supply on demand, is an existing object.*
There would seem to be two major problems with this condition. One concerns the problem of how one is to interpret the term 'exist': in a strictly physicalist interpretation, only objects that directly emit physical stimuli qualify, but what, then, happens to 'the snows of yesteryear', to 'unicorns', or, for that matter, 'the present King of France' (to mention but a few of the 'objects' whose potential 'existence' has continued to exercise the minds of philosophers)? The second problem concerns the question of how important to the success of an act of reference it is that it uniquely identifies just one object in the real world, to the exclusion of all others. It seems to me that, on this strong requirement, no act of reference is ever likely to be successful, for there is no description of an object so precise that a more precise one could not be invented, thereby showing up the inherent imprecisions of the former description. For instance, the expression 'Mr John Smith' is relatively imprecise (in

identifying one specific individual to the exclusion of all others) as compared to 'Mr John Smith, who lives in London', the latter more imprecise than 'Mr John Smith, who lives at 52, Blank Street, London, England', the latter still not as precise as 'Mr John Smith, who lives at 52, Blank Street, London, England, and is aged 42', and so forth. If any such expression happens to eliminate all other existing John Smiths, this is no more than a happy accident – in principle at least, there could always be two or more John Smiths answering the same description, and requiring further distinguishing marks. Perfect precision of a descriptive expression that, in principle, uniquely identifies one individual is illusory.

(5) *The sender intends to use the referring expression for the purpose of identifying a particular object for the benefit of the receptor.*

(6) *The sender intends that the receptor should make the above identification by recognising his (the sender's) intention to affect that identification, and by means of an interplay between the receptor's knowledge of the literal meaning of the referring expression and his knowledge of the context.*

The phrasing of this rather tortuous condition places sender and receptor in a typical 'I–know–that–you–know' situation – each must be aware that they are 'playing the same game' according to the same constitutive rules, with the aim of communicating – unless this intention is clear to both parties, a deliberate act of reference cannot be made. (Condition 6 is, incidentally, strongly reminiscent of Prieto's 'notificative indication'.)

(7) *The literal meaning of the referring expression is such that it precludes a correct use of the referring expression unless the above Conditions 1–6 actually apply.*

The purport of the final condition seems to be that the referring expression must have the built-in potential to be used as a referring expression, and do so according to the definition of 'acting as a referring expression' that is given in the set of Conditions 1–6). Paraphrasing Condition 7 in this way highlights its rather circular appearance.

4.7.4 Conditions for Predication

The performance of a semiotic act of predication is characterised, along the same lines as are acts of reference, by a set of eight conditions.

(1) *Normal input and output conditions obtain.*
(See 7.3.)

(2) *The predicating expression is uttered as part of a sentence.*
Similar remarks apply here, *mutatis mutandis*, as apply to Condition 2 on referring (see 7.3).

(3) *The sentence of which the predicative expression is a part is uttered with the intention of performing an illocutionary act.*

(4) *The sentence of which the predicative expression is a part contains a referring expression which is successfully uttered.*

This condition further deepens the dependence of acts of predication on the success of accompanying acts of reference, and on the success of overall propositional acts. We may say that neither acts of predication, nor acts of reference, can be successful, except as complimentary aspects of successful propositional acts.

(5) *The object referred to is such that, in principle, it is possible for the predicative expression to be applied to it.*

This condition is imposed in order to guarantee that predications such as 'This sentence weighs twenty pounds' can never be successful. As a matter of fact, metaphorical interpretations apart, there is a lot to be said for allowing 'nonsensical' sentences like 'This sentence weighs twenty pounds' a degree of predicational success – if the sentence cannot be uttered as a fully fledged proposition, on what basis do we explain the fact that it is understood and judged to be false? To suggest that an utterance such as 'This sentence weighs twenty pounds' cannot successfully predicate is tantamount to saying that there is nothing for the hearer to understand. This is falsified by the evidence of hearers' reactions.

(6) *The sender intends to use the sentence of which the predicative expression is a part for the purpose of raising the question of the truth or falsity of that predicative expression as applied to the referent of the utterance.*

That is to say, predication is that aspect of a propositional act which, by definition, makes the proposition an act to be assessed on the dimension of truth versus falsity.

(7) *The sender intends that the receptor should recognise the utterance as raising the question of truth and falsity by being aware of his (the sender's) intention of raising that question, and by means of the receptor's knowledge of the literal meaning of the predicative expression.*

Once again, we are in the typical 'I–know–that–you–know' situation that is necessary when sender and receptor are engaged in an activity constituted by the same set of constitutive rules.

(8) *The literal meaning of the predicative expression is such that it precludes a correct use of that expression unless the above Conditions 1–7 actually apply.*

(See Condition 7, in 7.3.)

4.8 Illocutionary Acts

4.8.1 Analysis of Illocutionary Force

Searle's idea is to describe each type of illocutionary act, from the point of view of the illocutionary force that characterises it, in terms of an analysis of the appropriate constitutive rules on which it depends. As in the case of acts of referring and acts of predicating, the description takes the form of stating a set of conditions that together add up to a defining criterion. (The use of the same descriptive technique for illocutionary as for propositional acts tends to maximalise the similarity and affinity between the two types of act.)

We can use certain prototypes of illocutionary act to illustrate, without going into details, the principle and technique of illocutionary description. In all cases, the illocutionary act is conceived of as a 'force' – in fact, the essence of an illocutionary act is captured in its inherent illocutionary force (symbolised by F; note that illocutionary force is not to be identified with illocutionary point or purpose). An illocutionary force is seen as a function over a particular propositional content. This gives us

$$F(p)$$

as the general formula for a semiotic event having a particular propositional content and a particular illocutionary force.

Examples:

	F	p
'I shall bring you a tame tiger.'	Promise	that speaker do X
'This crocodile is green.'	Assert	that x has a property y
'You are going to stand on your head!'	Command	that hearer do X

4.8.2 Constitutive Conventions for Illocutionary Acts

In what follows, we shall try to examine what Searle means by stating the constitutive rules governing and defining a given type of illocutionary act. What is involved, in simplified terms, is a scanning of the factors without which it would not make sense to construe a given act as having such-and-such an illocutionary force. To set us on the right track, let us consider – in a rather oversimplified form – what is involved in construing 'I shall count to three . . .' as a threat (that is, with an illocutionary force to the effect that, by the count of three, the speaker intends to physically assault the hearer).

We can, by simple common sense, make a start on listing some of the factors which would make the force of the threat null and void:

the speaker is separated from the hearer by a soundproofed wall;
the hearer is stone deaf;
the speaker obviously has no intention of attacking the hearer;
the speaker is obviously in no position (physically speaking) to assault the hearer;
the speaker intends his utterance to be taken literally (as a description of what he is about to do);
the hearer enjoys and is looking forward to being beaten, and the speaker is aware of this strange predilection;
etc.

The purpose of a set of conditions on illocutionary force is to ensure that all nullifying factors are eliminated from the definition of acts having that illocutionary force.

4.8.3 The Illocutionary Act of Promising

Given that there are, if not an indefinite number, at least many different types of illocutionary act, the best we can hope to do by way of elucidation here, is to present Searle's own example of the set of conditions by which illocutionary acts of *promising* are governed. Other sets of conditions defining other types of illocutionary act are to be imagined as being constructed on similar lines.

4.8.4 Conditions for an Illocutionary Act of Promising

(1) *Normal input and output conditions obtain* (see 7.3).

Propositional Content Conditions

(2) *The utterance to which the illocutionary force of a promise is attributed contains the performance of a propositional act.*
That is to say, the illocutionary force of a promise (symbolised Pr.) is a function over a proposition.

(3) *The propositional content (i.e. the content of the proposition over which Pr. is a function) is some future act of the sender.*
This, in crude terms, means simply that one can only promise to do something in the future. (But this only works if one denies the *illocutionary* force of a *promise* to such utterances as 'I promise you you will be able to pass the exam'. Granted, such an utterance could be construed as having the illocutionary force of an 'encouragement'.)

Preparatory Conditions

(4) *The action mentioned in the proposition would be to the receptor's advantage, and the sender knows this fact.*
This condition prevents one from confusing promises with threats. To put it bluntly, 'promising someone a beating' is either ironical or requires unusual (not to say 'kinky') circumstances, whereas 'promising to give someone a birthday present' only fails to be a genuine promise in special circumstances.

(5) *It is likely that the sender would not perform the promised action in the normal course of events, and both sender and receptor are aware of this fact.*
It would certainly seem odd, not to say pointless, to make an express promise concerning a future event about which there is obviously no choice. To take an extreme example, an utterance such as 'I promise that I will die some day' could not fail to be infelicitous. Condition 5 eliminates such illocutionary acts from the status of promises.

Sincerity Condition

(6) *The sender really intends to perform the promised action.*
Without this, at least temporary, intention on the part of the sender, a genuine promise cannot have been sincerely meant. Thence the term 'sincerity condition'. The condition includes also a genuine belief on the part of the sender that he will be in a position to perform the promised act. In other words, not only 'insincere' promises, but also what one might call 'irresponsible' or 'unrealistic' ones are eliminated.

Essential Condition

(7) *The utterance with the illocutionary force Pr. counts as an obligation on the part of the sender to perform the future action mentioned in that utterance.*
This captures the 'performative' aspect of the utterance, which is the way, *par excellence*, for undertaking to do something.

(8) *The sender intends that the receptor should be aware of his (the sender's) intention to undertake an obligation, and he intends that the receptor should recognise this by virtue of the meaning of the utterance in question.*

This condition is of the same type as Condition 6 for referring and Condition 8 for predicating. As such, it probably belongs to semiotic acts in general – in fact, it probably does so by definition, given that semiotic acts are defined as acts governed by constitutive conventions (see also 4.7.3).

(9) *The meaning of the sentence uttered in making a promise is such that it can be correctly and sincerely uttered as a promise given that Conditions 1–8 obtain.*

This, to my mind, rather circular condition is admittedly intended to mean just that only sentences conventionally suited for use in making promises can be used in making promises. (The statement could be put in a worse light still, if paraphrased as: 'an utterance *x* can be used for making a promise, if and only if it is an utterance of the kind of sentence that can conventionally (but how else) be used for making promises.')

4.9   Types of Illocutionary Act; the Taxonomies of Austin and of Searle

4.9.1   Searle's Revision of Austin's Taxonomy

In no other area is the continuity between the work of Austin and of Searle more clearly visible than in that of the classification of types of illocutionary act (Searle, 1975). Searle's taxonomy is presented as a way of correcting certain weaknesses in Austin's original classification, which, incidentally, was described by Austin as not being 'in the very least definitive' (Austin, 1962).

Rather than following through Austin's five-way classification, the objections raised by Searle with regard to this classification, the proposed taxonomy as refined by Searle, and, finally, the weaknesses that seem to remain in the latter, I propose to present Austin's and Searle's taxonomies side by side, drawing attention to correspondences between categories wherever possible.

Austin, 1962	Searle, 1975

(1) Verdictives:
'consist in the delivering of a finding, official or unofficial, upon evidence or reasons as to value or fact so far as these are distinguishable', i.e. the expression of a judgement purportedly on the basis of evidence.
e.g. 'acquit',
     'describe',
     'estimate'
	(1) Assertives:
	commit the sender to the truth of a proposition
	     formula: $\vdash\downarrow B\,(p)$
	e.g. 'affirm', 'deny', 'report', 'describe', 'estimate'

(2) Exercitives:
'the giving of a decision in favour of or against a certain course of action'; 'a decision that something is to be so, as distinct from a judgement that it is so'
e.g. 'order', 'request',
	(2) Directives:
	attempts to get receptor to do something;
	     formula:
	     $!\uparrow W\,(H\ \text{does}\ A)$
	e.g. 'order', 'request', 'ask', 'advise'
	also 'dare', 'defy', ? 'protest'

'ask', 'advise'
also 'appoint', 'veto',
'announce', 'warn'

(3) Commissives:
'the whole point of a commissive is to commit the speaker to a certain course of action'
e.g. 'promise', 'vow', 'contract'

(3) Commissives:
(as in Austin)
commit sender to some future action
formula:
$C \uparrow I$ (S does A)
e.g. 'promise', 'vow', 'contract'

(4) Expositives:
'used in acts involving the expounding of views, the conducting of arguments and the clarifying of usages and references'
e.g. 'affirm', 'deny', 'report', 'illustrate', 'identify', 'call'

(4) Expressives:
express a psychological state about the state of affairs in the propositional content
formula:
$E \emptyset (P) (S/H + prop)$
e.g. 'apologise', 'thank', 'commiserate', 'welcome'
? 'protest'

(5) Behabitives:
'reaction to other people's behaviour and fortunes and of attitudes and expressions of attitudes to someone else's past conduct or imminent conduct'
e.g. 'apologise', 'thank', 'commiserate', 'welcome'
also 'dare', 'defy', 'protest'

(5) Declarations:
('performatives')
bring about truth of propositional content automatically
formula: $D \updownarrow \emptyset (p)$
e.g. 'appoint', 'veto', 'announce', 'warn', 'illustrate', 'identify', 'call'

(5a) Assertive declarations:
a category with the joint properties of assertives and declarations
formula:
$D_a\downarrow \updownarrow B (p)$
e.g. 'you are out'
(cricket or baseball),
'you are guilty'
(court of law),
'acquit'
(court of law)

Figure 4.9

4.9.2 Critique of Austin's and Searle's Taxonomies

Austin's tentative classification suffers from a great deal of overlapping between categories. Thus, for instance, the illocution, 'acquit' (listed as a Verdictive) also answers the definition of an Exercitive, whereas 'describe', 'estimate' (listed as Verdictives) have as much right to be listed as Expositives. While Austin classifies 'appoint', 'veto', 'announce' and 'warn' among Exercitives, it would be equally possible to make out a case for classifying them as Commissives. All the examples cited by Austin as Expositives are only tenuously distinguishable from Verdictives, the distinction depending essentially on the far from clear borderline between statements based on evidence (Verdictives) and statements that are matters of opinion (Expositives). As for 'dare', 'defy' and (perhaps even) 'protest' (which Austin lists along with the Behabitives), these do not seem to fit readily into any of Austin's existing categories; if anything, they might be more suitably classified together with 'order', 'ask', 'request' and 'advise'.

While Searle's taxonomy is a distinct improvement on Austin's, one could, at the price of being accused of quibbling, argue that Commissives are a subcategory of Assertives (not a separate category) in that the sender, by committing himself to the (future) truth of a proposition (designating a future action, granted) is asserting the truth of that proposition, that is, all Commissives are assertive in a rather special sense.

It would also be possible to argue that, since belief is a psychological state, and since belief is a necessary ingredient of Assertives, it is not only Expressives that 'express a psychological state about the state of affairs in the propositional content'. In other words, Assertive might be seen as only a special kind of Expressive, with 'belief' on one side, and all other psychological states on the other. At any rate, Searle's taxonomy – for all that it claims to put right whatever Searle sees as wrong in Austin's categorisation – is not, itself, exempt from criticism.

There is genuine doubt, for instance, about the placing of 'protest'. In both Figure 4.8 and Figure 4.9, I have been obliged to assign this item, with a question-mark, to two categories between which I am unable to decide.

Also, the category of Assertive Declarations could be said to create an anomaly; Assertives and Declaratives are mutually exclusive categories, but Assertive Declaratives belong with equal right to *both* these categories.

4.9.3 Comparison of Examples from Austin and Searle

Correlations between Austin's and Searle's taxonomies of illocutionary acts can be conveniently drawn by noting the distribution of Austin's examples into the various categories found in Searle's scheme (see Figure 4.10).

4.9.4 Searle's Illocutionary Categories

Finally, for a fuller understanding of Searle's categories of illocutionary act – and especially of the *formulae* into which he crystallises the definitions of these categories – we should take a closer look at the dimensions on which Searle locates definitionally crucial differences between types of illocutionary act. Searle lists and discusses twelve such dimensions (Searle, 1975), but his taxonomy makes actual use only of four of these:

(1) *point* or purpose of the illocutionary act;
(2) *direction of fit* between *words* (the proposition underlying the illocutionary act) *and the world*;

Examples	Classified by Austin as	Classified by Searle as
'acquit'	Verdictive	Assertive Declaration
'describe', 'estimate'	Verdictive	Assertive
'order', 'ask', 'request', 'advise'	Exercitive	Directive
'appoint', 'veto', 'announce', 'warn'	Exercitive	Declarations
'promise', 'vow', 'contract'	Commissive	Commissive
'affirm', 'deny', 'report'	Expositive	Assertive
'illustrate', 'identify', 'call'	Expositive	Declarations
'apologise', 'thank', 'commiserate', 'welcome'	Behabitive	Expressive
'dare', 'defy'	Behabitive	Directive
'protest'	Behabitive	?Directive/ ?Expressive

Figure 4.10

(3) *psychological state* constituting the *sincerity condition* for the illocutionary act;
(4) the type of *proposition* of which a given type of illocutionary force may be a function (i.e. *propositional content*).

The most crucial differences between illocutionary acts fall into the dimension of point or purpose of the act. Since illocutionary acts are purposive, it is only natural that this should be so. Thus, the defining purpose of Assertives ($\vdash$ = assertive illocutionary point) is to commit the sender to the truth of some proposition; that of Directives (! = directive illocutionary point) is to aim at getting a receptor to perform some action; that of Commissives (C = commissive illocutionary point) is to commit the sender to some future action; that of Expressives (E = expressive illocutionary point) is to convey the psychological attitude of the sender to some state of affairs; that of Declarations (D = declarative illocutionary point) is to perform, *eo ipso*, an action (cf. Austin's performatives); that of Assertive Declarations (D_a = assertive-declarative illocutionary point) to assert and declare, simultaneously, that something is so, and is to *count as* being so.

The notion of *direction of fit* between words and world concerns the nature of the relationship between an underlying proposition expressed alongside the illocutionary act and reality. There are two opposite possibilities in direction of fit: either the expressed proposition applies to a past or present reality which it purports to describe, or the expressed proposition alludes to a future state of affairs which the illocutionary act hopes to bring about. A further intermediate possibility is realised in the case of 'performatives' which serve to bring about a particular state of affairs and in the case of which therefore, there is a simultaneous fit between words and world (for example, 'I name this ship the *Blank*' at once declares the name of the ship and makes it true that the ship is so named).

Accordingly, there are three symbols used for representing direction of fit:

$\downarrow$ = words-to-world ('descriptive')
$\uparrow$ = world-to-words ('predictive')
$\updownarrow$ = simultaneous ('performative')

Assertive declarations, oddly enough, display at once two types of direction of fit, being both 'descriptive' and 'performative' (symbolically: $\downarrow \updownarrow$).

The *psychological state* dimension is important to the definition of illocutionary acts, since it is in this dimension that one has to assess whether such acts have been performed sincerely, as genuine attempts at the purported illocutionary point. Unless the appropriate psychological state obtains, the illocutionary act is the (illocutionary) equivalent of a lie, or piece of (self-) deception.

The major types of psychological state separated out by Searle are *belief* (symbolised B), *want or desire* (symbolised W), *intention* (to do something) (symbolised I), and *all other possible psychological states* (lumped together and symbolised by the variable P).

The fourth dimension, that of propositional content, examines the types of proposition that may be accompanied by a given illocutionary act type. Accordingly, any proposition (symbolised (p)) can form the background to an assertion; only propositions whose content is a (future) action on the part of the receptor (symbolised (H does A)) can form the background of a Directive; only propositions whose content is a (future) action on the part of the sender (symbolised (S does A)) can form the background to a Commissive; only propositions ascribing some property (in a very wide sense, including the attribution of actions, and so on) can form the propositional background (symbolised (S/H + prop)) of an Expressive, while declarations, including assertive declarations, can be served, in general, by any proposition (cf. Assertives).

Each complete formula symbolising a type of illocutionary act can be conceived as having four 'slots', one for each of the above dimensions as follows:

illocutionary point	direction of fit	sincerity condition	propositional content

Where a particular dimension is not relevant to, plays no role in, the definition of a particular illocutionary act type, or is characteristically absent from that definition, the appropriate slot is filled by Ø. This makes for an interpretation of the formulae as show in Figure 4.11.

	I. P.	Dir. of fit	Sincerity	Prop. cont.
Assertive ⊦ ↓ B (p)	⊦ commitment to truth	↓ words-to-world	B belief	(p) any proposition
Directive ! ↑ W(H do A)	! make the receptor act	↑ world-to-words	W want or desire	(H do A) proposition about some future act of receptor
Commissive C ↑ I(S do A)	C commitment to future act	↑ world-to-words	I intention to do	(S do A) proposition about some future act of sender
Expressive EØ(P) (S/H +prop.)	E expression of psychological state	Ø (truth of proposition *presupposed*)	(P) any one of a range of variable psychological states	(S/H+prop.) proposition attributing some property or action to sender/receptor
Declaration D ↕ Ø (p)	D performative	↕ automatic fit in both directions	Ø cannot be insincere	(p) any proposition
Assertive Declaration D_a ↓ ↕ B (p)	D_a to assess *and* pronounce 'judgement'	↓ ↕ from world to words in assessment, automatic fit in both directions for pronouncement	B belief (in correctness of assessment)	(p) any proposition about past event/state or present event/state

Figure 4.11

As a last word of explanation, I should add that Expressives have a zero (Ø) value for direction of fit because they do not – as do normal propositional acts – raise the question of the truth or falsity of a given proposition. Truth of the propositional content is presupposed, as, for instance, in the infuriating utterance, 'I deplore the way you beat your wife' (which takes it strictly for granted that you *do* beat your wife).

5

Semiology as an Ideology of Socio-Cultural Signification: Roland Barthes

5.1 General Remarks

To the reader who has successfully worked his way through the preceding chapters, the overall 'ethos' of Barthesian semiology will probably come as something of a surprise.

Whatever the differences between the various semiotic approaches hitherto discussed, these approaches share at least the uniformity offered by a scientifico-rational attitude both to the development and to the presentation of ideas.

As to the more immediately obvious matter of presentation, the relatively 'dry', expository mode, reminiscent of the neutral voice of philosophical treatises and scientific papers, gives way, in Barthes, to a more 'literary', frequently image-laden – not to say, 'purple' – style of discourse. It is as if, instead of a direct appeal to the intellect, Barthes were trying to gain access to the minds of his readers by the back door, capturing their imagination rather than their precise comprehension. From the smooth journalistic effects of *Mythologies* (Barthes, 1957) to the heavily ornamental excesses of *S/Z* (Barthes, 1974), the writings of Barthes put into service means of exposition that conjure up ideas rather than pinning down their scientific constancy. In this respect – though not in this respect alone, as we shall see – Barthes emerges as the reaffirmation of that 'arts–and–humanities' mentality whose virtual banishment from the field of study of language and communication has marked modern semiotics (and linguistics) off from its ancestral forms.

As for the development of Barthesian ideas, it is only the inherent vagueness of the term 'theory' that would persuade one to describe this as 'theory-building'. For one thing, while the theories discussed in previous chapters were clearly formulated with the intention of being subservient to the aims of 'objective description', Barthesianism is conducive, instead, to the formation of certain habits of evaluation – a mode of thinking, at once didactic and judgmental, that refuses to be pinned down, as opposed to a methodology that can be precisely prescribed.

Although the dogma of Barthesian semiology achieves a certain coherence, amounting at times to 'one-track-mindedness', this coherence is less of the order of a logical consistency than of an insistence on a quasi-obsessional perceptual perspective through which everything is to be viewed. The Barthesian framework is not content merely to select from the realm of acknowledged phenomena those events or objects that, according to a point of view adopted, qualify as 'semiological'. It proceeds, on the analogy of Freudian psychology, to 'discover', and, by the very act of 'discovery', to create novel 'semiological' phenomena in places where one might not have suspected their existence.

Ironically, both the *rationale* offered by Barthes for this 'unveiling' of 'signs', and the most forceful criticism offered (Mounin, 1970) against the unscientific nature of reading semiological interpretations into phenomena that are not manifestly semiological, stem from the same Saussurean source: namely, the famous Saussurean *dictum*, according to which *'c'est le point de vue qui crée l'objet'*.

A conservative and scientifico-rational interpretation of this *dictum* sees in it a reminder – essential to scientific rigour (Mounin, 1968), as against letting one's imagination run riot – that objects of description are not directly provided by nature alone, but also by a conscious act of selection and observation into which the observer's point of view should enter as a known constant, not as an uncontrolled variable. In other words, this reading of Saussure's *dictum* treats it as an admonishment and not as an invitation. It warns would-be describers to formulate their point of view in the explicit form of a theory, and to apply that theory with the utmost rigour in the pre-selection and processing of 'objects' they intend to describe.

Barthes' interpretation of the same dictum wilfully exaggerates the one vague term found in the Saussurean formulation of *'c'est le point de vue qui crée l'objet'*, namely the term 'create'. Accordingly, he treats the *dictum* as an open invitation (if not exhortation) to invent and intuit objects of observed fact through the sole authority of an original way of looking at things (*point de vue*). Where 'point of view' is not an explicitly formulated theory, but a personally held feeling or bias (which is largely the case with Barthes), Saussure's *dictum* becomes a licence for letting the imagination create phenomena more or less at will. In this respect, once again, Barthesianism reasserts the values of 'arts–and–humanities' scholarship: imagination, sensibility (the 'feel' and instinctive 'flair' for a subject), intuition and 'creativity'.

In the scientifico-rational approaches, too, the factuality of phenomena is postulated (facts are *given* through observation, thence the term *data*, used interchangeably with the term *phenomena*). However, before such 'facts' are accepted as objects suitable for a certain kind of description, they are required to answer explicit specification, as laid down by definitions stipulated in given theories. Consequently, the association of 'skull–and–crossbones' with 'piracy', or of the 'tail-wagging dance' of bees with 'location of a source of nectar', are not semiotic facts by mere postulation (because–I–say–so), nor because they can be imagined to be so (surely–you–can–see–how), but because the repeatable, systematic and communicative aspects of these associations can stand up to objective testing (Mounin, 1968).

By contrast, a minor example of the kind of semiological phenomenon 'created' by a Barthesian vision of the reality of social intercourse will illustrate the rather different status that 'facts' have in Barthes' semiological descriptions. When Barthes contends (Barthes, 1957) that the wearing of a beard 'can . . . be the attribute of a free man', he is in fact postulating that the association of 'the wearing of a beard' (a formal 'mark') with the message (or *signification*) 'I am an independent person' is a matter of experiential fact. Now, as there is no question for Barthes of 'testing' the regularity, systematicity and communicative value of this association, it follows that its 'factuality' can only be a matter of intuitive plausibility. For those who believe, no demonstration is necessary; for those who do not, no demonstration is possible.

The phenomena postulated by Barthes are, admittedly, endowed in most cases with a degree of plausibility. Just as in the case with the supposed association between 'the wearing of a beard' and a (quasi-conscious) message, 'I am an independent person' – where one's reaction is to admit that 'there *is* something in it' – so Barthes succeeds, in general, in evoking the response that his observations are certainly not without foundation. In fact, once thoroughly exposed to Barthesian habits of observation, one finds oneself unable to turn on a television channel, read a book, or listen to a conversation without 'discovering' Barthesian facts of one's own. However, it must also be admitted that positive response to the plausibility of Barthesian associations between supposed *signifiers* and alleged *significations* is frequently tinged with an afterthought of scepticism, the feeling of having to accept facts on someone else's say-so. Accepting the factuality of phenomena created by a Barthesian point of view requires (even when one intuits such facts for oneself) that 'willing suspension of disbelief' which lends to this kind of 'semiology' something of the character of an intellectual parlour-game. Here again we encounter in Barthes a reaffirmation of a typically 'arts–and–humanities' mentality, as opposed to a scientifico-rational one.

Barthesianism is a point of view that – like Marxism, or Freudianism, both of which have had a profound influence on the ideas of Barthes – has the power to create its own phenomena, that colours a whole pervasive mode of perception, that (unlike scientifico-rational semiological theories) is loaded with socio-political value-judgements, and that, finally, is more ready to diffuse itself into an intellectual fashion than to concentrate itself into an exact theory. Such a point of view can only be correctly described as an 'ideology'. We have good reason, therefore, to attach to it the label of 'semiology as ideology' – a designation which, incidentally, receives support from Barthes' own conception of his own aims (Barthes, 1957).

The ideological nature of Barthesian semiology is further bolstered by the claim that it has as its domain the sum total of ideas perpetuated and transmitted in the social life of every culture. This claim is an exaggerated interpretation of Saussure's description of semiology as a science '*qui étudie la vie des signes au sein de la vie sociale*' (cf. Chapter 1, Section 1.2.6, p. 15), an exaggeration that trades on the somewhat bombastic vagueness of the Saussurean formulation. Only an ideology could be as ambitious, as bombastic and, at the same time, as delightfully vague about its precise limits of applicability as Barthes' adaptation of Saussure's projected semiology.

The double distinction of 'ideology' versus 'theory' and of an 'arts-and-humanities' versus a 'scientifico-rational' attitude goes a long way towards setting Barthesian semiology apart from other semiotic approaches. It also paves the way to my choice of outlining the salient ideas of Barthes in the form of a series of paradoxes. In the scientifico-rational approaches, such a presentation would have had the automatic effect of a (rather cheap) polemical device for the instant belittling of a theory. (For instance, to have set out the ideas of Searle, or of Prieto, as a series of paradoxes would have been to imply, from the start, that they fail to make logical sense.) In terms of an 'arts–and–humanities' attitude, uncovering and dwelling on the (allegedly) essentially paradoxical nature with which reality is inherently endowed are descriptive virtues: there is no criticism, but rather a favourable opinion, implied by calling attention to paradoxes. Barthesianism treasures paradox, seeing it as part and parcel of an ideology of contradiction whose very essence is the dialectic of paradoxes. In terms of an ideology of contradiction, paradox is not a negative, but a positive, explanatory property.

5.2 Paradoxes of scope

A salient feature of Barthes' semiological ideology is the imperialism of signs (by 'signs', Barthes means all sorts of entities endowed with signification) established over the whole range of modern social life. Not only the obvious cases like advertising, literature, propaganda and linguistic communication, all of which have enjoyed an unprecedented flowering through the escalated development of the mass media, but also a host of more unexpected areas, among them photography, spectator sports, cinema, cuisine, clothes, and so forth, are laden, according to Barthes, with semiological-ideological signification. Sometimes this signification is analogous for those who 'produce' and those who 'consume' the signs concerned; at other times, it is the very discrepancy between a contrived transmission and a gullible reception that constitutes an object of special interest. In either case, Barthes' position is that in all the social life that acts out the features of a culture, there is, probably, no 'innocent' event or fact, but that events and facts constantly 'speak' to their culturally conditioned observers. (Cultural conditioning is neither more nor less than a repertoire of received signs constituting a particular orthodoxy.) If we accept the Barthesian metaphor, whereby the signification of facts and events (for example, 'long hair' as a sign of 'revolt against authority') is described as a kind of 'speech', then we should continue that metaphor by adding that in such signification, the message is generally oblique, and the mode of its delivery is that of a 'whisper'. This metaphor is not without its own paradoxical content, which we can crystallise in the words of a recent North American advertisement: 'If you want to capture someone's attention, whisper!' The paradox, that of an unexpected inverse ratio between 'volume' and 'effectiveness', between 'explicitness' and 'expressiveness', is not only one of the paradoxes of scope, but has important repercussions in the paradox of signification (Section 5.3,

p. 133) and the paradoxes of literature (Section 5.6, p. 148). At present, however, we are only concerned with looking at it as a paradox of scope. In this light, it has the effect of asserting that those areas where messages are most oblique and evidence of their transmission the most faint are actually the most firmly established parts of the scope of semiology. According to this, logically speaking at least, the highest degree of semiological effectiveness should belong to silence. At the same time, the usually central cases of highly explicit communication (the conveying of a literal message by unsubtle means, for example, putting up a 'No entry' sign to prevent entry, or simply saying 'Stay out!') are made to seem more peripheral to the scope of semiology than cases that are usually considered 'doubtful', or at least 'indirect' (for example, pinning a picture of a skunk on the door, as a way (?) of preventing entry). In short, the first of the paradoxes of scope is that standard, clearcut cases of *communication-as-the-literal-conveying-of-information* are hardly (if at all) objects of interest for Barthesian semiology. The scope of Barthesian semiology can be represented (by analogy) as a diagram indicating the shadow cast by a circular object, but with the terms 'full shade' and 'half shade' reversed (see Figure 5.1).

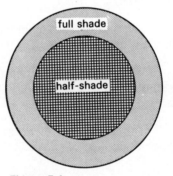

full shade

half-shade

Figure 5.1

The paradox whereby the core and the margins of semiological scope change places with one another is but one of the paradoxes of scope. A second paradox consists in Barthes' inversion of the relationship established by Saussure between the scope of semiology and the scope of linguistics. The Saussurean position is by no means paradoxical, and rests on a piece of common sense: both human languages and many other systems are semiological, therefore semiology covers a wider field, languages a narrower (no matter how privileged) section of that wider field; and semiology is the inclusive discipline while linguistics is one of its specialised branches.

Barthes does not try to deny the common-sensical nature of the position so far, but at the same time, he has, typically, no tolerance for received opinions dictated by common sense. He declares, therefore, his rejection of semiology as the inclusive master-discipline of which linguistics is only a part, insisting that it is rather semiology that is part of linguistics. Since he does this without denying the Saussurean view that natural languages are not the only semiological systems (which should, logically speaking, imply that there are semiological systems outside of languages), but at the same time, by claiming that there are probably no extensive sign-systems outside of human language (Barthes, 1967a), we are left with a definite paradox. It is, accordingly, not human languages that are instances of semiological systems endowed with a particular kind of semiological significance (though, to add to the paradox, Barthes also endorses the special semiological significance of human languages), but it is semiological systems at large that are special instances of languages, and that possess particular kinds of linguistic significance. As a result, we are presented with a paradox of the parts being greater than the whole; in every sense, it is through the parts (human language) that the whole (semiology) is to be understood and explained.

Two main ideas are cited as the underpinnings of this 'trans-linguistic' view of semiology (Barthes, 1967a). First, we are given to understand that, while human languages are in no way dependent on other semiological systems, other semiological systems are probably inconceivable without languages (for example, if there were no languages, it would be impossible to conceive of the existence of the Highway Code). This observation at once underlines the 'parts–to–the–whole' relationship (between, on the one hand, languages and other semiological systems, and, on the other, the whole of semiology), and lays emphasis on the notion of one of the parts (human language) being greater than the whole.

Secondly, Barthes insists that the signified elements of other semiological systems are almost inconceivable unless human language creates them: 'the world of signifieds is none other than that of language' (Barthes, 1967a). In other words, we are given to understand that semiological systems cannot convey comprehensible messages except through the intermediary of a human language, which, logically speaking, implies that there is in fact no message that is not linguistic, for no meaning can be seized until translation into a language has (automatically) taken place: signification only exists in so far as it is named by language (Barthes, 1967a). For instance, the message conveyed by a red traffic-light is not a 'traffic-light-message', but the *linguistic message* 'stop'.

For the benefit of those who, unlike Barthes, find paradoxes intolerable, it might be pointed out that the underpinnings of a 'trans-linguistic' view of semiology lack force as arguments. In the first place, the 'probably's and 'almost's with which Barthes qualifies them are, when it comes to argumentation, points of weakness. But even apart from that, two simple analogies – one for each of the main ideas backing the subservience of semiology to language – will readily show why Barthes' 'trans-linguistic' semiology is unconvincing.

There is, to take a first analogy, a 'parts–to–the–whole' relationship between, on the one hand, *trunk*, *branches* and *leaves*, and, on the other hand, a whole *tree*. To point out that a tree is (probably) inconceivable without a trunk, though it is quite conceivable without branches, or without leaves, is justifiable, and remains consistent with the 'parts–to–the–whole' relationship. To use this as a stepping-stone towards maintaining that, therefore, a tree-trunk is greater, and more inclusive than a whole tree, would, however, be absurd. It would be just as absurd to progress to the claim that branches and leaves are really modified or disguised forms of a tree-trunk. Yet it is the exact analogue of this that Barthes asks us to believe when he claims that, since there are no significant sign-systems that do not bring us right back to human language, all such semiological systems are modified or disguised forms of language.

Another simple analogy will clarify the fallacy behind the idea that messages exist only through the intermediary of language. I can bet you, as I go to see you off in the front hall, that you cannot put your coat on unaided, wait till you are half-way into the garment, and then forcibly 'help you on' with it. Have I really demonstrated that you are unable to put your coat on by yourself, without outside aid? Surely not! Now, to say that non-linguistic sign-systems (like ladies surrounded by a host of attentive gentlemen) are unable to act as autonomous agents in the conveying of messages merely because human language is always ready (not to say 'over-solicitous') to interpret these messages (like polite gentlemen forcing their attentions on un-liberated ladies), is simply to confuse 'helpability' with 'helplessness'. Sign-systems are by no means 'helpless' – it is, for instance, a driver's practical reactions to a red traffic light that constitute his understanding of the appropriate message, not his linguistic ability to register that message as meaning 'stop' (it does not mean 'stop', it is merely translatable as 'stop').

In theoretical terms, only an active enjoyment of paradoxes could fully motivate a 'trans-linguistic' view of semiology. In practical terms, however, it must be admitted that, while there is little profit to be gained from saying that languages have semiological properties, there is a great deal of profit to be had from saying that semiological systems partake in various linguistic (that is, language-like) properties. This option offers considerable borrowing-facilities in the way of a stock of linguistic notions that can be re-applied in semiology at large at the simple cost of describing all systems of signification as forms of 'speech'. To the critical eye, such a description may appear extremely metaphorical, elastic and tenuous (Mounin, 1968), but its winsomeness is undeniable.

One further paradox of scope deserves mention, a paradox so deep and inexplicit that it tends to escape notice altogether. It involves a notion of the defining property that circumscribes the domain of sign-systems. Normal semiological practice (and, on the face of it, Barthes keeps to this practice) sees the defining property of sign-systems in their actual or at least potential ability to transmit signification, to convey messages, to provide means of communication. It is part and parcel of this normalcy to acknowledge that the communicative potential of a sign-system carries the implication of a *classification* to which the domain of signifieds is automatically subjected. In simple terms, if a child can use a sign-system consisting of 'mama', 'dada' and 'doggy', it is automatically implied that the range of things he can communicate about is *classified* into three categories of object. Strictly speaking, then, the child 'knows' of four categories of things, the fourth category being that of 'unclassified' objects (but these fall outside his *communicative* range for the time being). Also, strictly speaking, the child does not speak about things as such, but as 'objects–conceived–as–belonging–to–a–given–class'. Conceiving of objects as belonging to one or other linguistically labelled class is an acknowledged side-effect (necessary, but secondary) of linguistic communication; other semiological systems are, likewise, acknowledged to have analogous side-effects.

If we look upon this side-effect as a way of organising ideas (our hypothetical child has his ideas organised into the 'mama', 'dada' and 'doggy' categories), and connect the organising of ideas to the notion of an ideology (a world-view), we can sympathise with Barthes' view of semiological systems as creators, repositories and Procrustean beds of ideology. What is paradoxical in Barthes, however, is that this ideological, or 'ideologising' character of sign-systems – seen as a secondary side-effect in orthodox semiology (Martinet, 1973) – is made to assume the role of defining property. In blunt terms, Barthes recognises as a sign-system anything that creates and embodies an ideology. In fact, what makes, for him, an object worthy of semiological-ideological description is none other than the 'ideologising' effects of that object.

The elevation of side-effects into *the* defining property of everything that is semiological in essence is a true paradox: since the very scope of semiology hinges on it, it ranks among the paradoxes of scope. It may be noted, in passing, that Barthes exaggerates the extent to which semiological systems are 'ideological straight-jackets': while it is true that, for instance, languages tend to fossilise certain ideologies, it is not true that they do so in an inescapable fashion. If the latter were true, English speakers would be forced, by the expressions 'sunrise' and 'sunset', which fossilise a conception of the sun moving round the earth, either to believe literally in the meanings of 'sunrise' and 'sunset', or to abandon the use of these signs altogether.

5.3 Paradoxes of Signification

In so far as one can speak of 'defining properties' in an approach that seldom, if ever, offers definition-like statements, the notion of *signification* constitutes for Barthes the defining property of signs. That is to say, anything is a sign to the extent that it is endowed with signification. So far, there is nothing unusual in this position. However, as we shall see, the Barthesian conception of signification itself is built on a paradox.

Allusion was made in the foregoing section to the paradox of an inverse ratio between semiological 'effectiveness' and semiological 'explicitness'. We should remember that, in an 'orthodox' semiotic view, the ideal of effectiveness is normally taken to be that of maximum explicitness and unambiguity; communication is effective when 'I'm receiving you loud and clear'. Accordingly, a 'stop' sign that declares a specific interdiction without equivocation – or, perhaps even more clearly, a sign expressing a logical function (for example, p & q) or a mathematical operation (for example a + b) – represents the epitomy of an ideally effective sign. Through Barthesian paradox, such signs are scarcely of semiological interest (Barthes, 1967a) at all, being as totally devoid of signification as any sign can be. This is because *signification is a property of objects that do not declare openly their possession of signification*, nor serve to pinpoint what that signification might be.

Explicit codes (traffic signs, logical or mathematical codes) are the least likely, therefore, to provide paradigm examples of signification. On the contrary, they could be used, if anything, as examples of the areas most resistant to being affected by signification in the Barthesian sense.

Paradigm examples are more likely to be found in the realm of clothes-consciousness, but even here, it is not the standard semiotic examples of institutionalised uniforms that we should look to, rather to 'ordinary' clothing that usurps the role of a kind of 'uniform' by historical accident. To wear the institutional uniform of a policeman, traffic-warden or staff-nurse is to engage in a form of explicit and unequivocal communication that closely parallels the expressive directness and clarity of the 'stop' sign, the logical & sign, the mathematical + sign. Signification is not a property of such signs. On the other hand, going round 'dressed like a plain-clothes cop' (this in itself is nigh on a paradox: how is a plain-clothes cop supposed to dress?) is a case of endowing particular forms of dress with signification. Similarly, if I turned up to give my lectures wearing patched jeans, a floppy and worn pullover and open sandals, the various implied 'messages' to which this might give rise would constitute excellent examples of signification. The very substance of these 'messages' is equivocation, summed up in the paradox that, by wearing such clothes, I have 'said' nothing about myself, and yet have said more than I could in hours of talking. The fact is that, regardless of my communicative intentions (or their absence), it would be 'natural' for my audience to reconstruct a host of information – in the form of an 'impression' – from my clothing about my personality and views, for example, that I am an eccentric/a Bohemian/a beatnik/a nonconformist/a radical/a 'pseud', and so on. Such 'information' is, by its very nature, very hard to pin down (this is part of the essence of the paradox of signification), since it is not underwritten by any firm commitment to communication: the clothes I wear don't have to mean anything. Whatever semiological properties may automatically attach themselves to my excessively informal attire in the eyes of the beholder are, however, all the more interesting and important for being somewhat vague – from the Barthesian point of view, they epitomise the notion of signification. Their importance would increase, and their signification undergo modification, on an ascending scale, if I wore the same apparel to the vice-chancellor's sherry-party, the university graduation ceremony, the Lord Mayor's dinner, and so forth, with the 'message' verbalised as 'I don't care a fig for your stupid, snobbish social conventions' crystallising in more and more undeniable fashion. Yet at no point would equivocation completely disappear; there is never a certainty that I will admit to an interpretation of what I 'mean' by wearing such clothes, with the result that interpretation of a message remains pure guesswork. (In Prieto's terms, one would say that such signs lack 'notificative indication', and have a dubious 'significative indication'.) In typically paradoxical fashion, signification can both be denied objective existence and be claimed to be insidiously operational.

Similarly, the signification of an advertisement – another type of example epitomising the notion of signification – is generally something that is 'left unsaid' in the actual text. Once again, the basic paradox of 'information–conveyed–and–yet–not–conveyed' is found to be the very essence of signification. So oblique and 'underhand' is signification in the Barthesian sense that one is tempted to identify it, not with information conveyed, but with impressions created by insinuation. Signification as insinuation is, in short, related to the kind of interpretation referred to in common parlance as 'reading between the lines'. Yet the attribute 'hidden' cannot be applied to this insinuated signification (for all that the object does not declare openly its signification), since its function is, like that of a whisper, to attract attention. To say (rather metaphorically) that objects with signification attract attention typically in a coy manner may make more intuitive sense of the paradox according to which signification is a meaning at once invisible and active, clear and implicit (Barthes, 1977).

In the two paradigm examples cited – clothes as an 'expression' of one's persona (or of a deliberately chosen 'image') and advertising copy – we recognise two types of object into which signification can insinuate itself. A metaphorical coinage, whereby signification is described as being 'parasitic' on the objects that carry it, will be used in further examination of these two types of 'carrier' of significance.

First, signification can be 'parasitic' on objects that have, in themselves, no semiological status, that is to say, objects that, on the face of it, are not meant to serve a communicative purpose at all. Reverting to the example of wearing patched jeans, floppy sweater and open sandals, if these items are taken at their face value, they are simply objects of clothing with a purely pragmatic function. (In fact, critics of Barthes are apt to deny that there is any justification for reading any more into them.) It is only their 'inappropriateness' in terms of what one is 'expected' to wear on given occasions, according to given social norms, that endows these articles with a 'parasitic' signification.

It is, however, no exaggeration of the Barthesian position to point out that, wherever a society or culture (with received and 'hallowed' values) exists, there can hardly be any object that is not in some way made (at least on occasion) into a carrier of a 'parasitic' signification. (Even the use of logical and mathematical signs can signify as a form of 'showing off'.) As it was pointed out earlier, there are probably no wholly 'innocent' objects, facts or events that can completely resist 'contamination' by a 'parasitic' signification. This is the upshot of Barthes' much-publicised remarks concerning the universality of what he calls *semantisation* of ordinary everyday objects that become derivatively used to signify by insinuation.

Secondly, an 'ulterior' signification may be 'parasitic' on objects that have, in themselves, the status of meaningful signs. In other words, semantisation can result when something already functioning as a sign with an explicit, literal meaning becomes overlaid with a further oblique signification acquired by insinuation.

The use/abuse of this potential for signs to mean one thing, but to hint at some other, perhaps even directly contradictory, signification beyond their literal meaning is characteristic of advertising texts. Whatever the actual words may be, the unspoken but 'real' (that is, 'ulterior') meaning of many advertisements can, for instance, be summed up fairly well as: 'if you use this product, you will be admired by your peers.'

To say that semantisation is universal means, in this context, that signs (linguistic signs *par excellence*) can never be used in a wholly 'innocent' way merely to convey their literal meanings and without insinuating, at the same time, a 'parasitic' signification that is hinted at (presupposed?) above and between the lines. (The inevitability, according to Barthes, of such semantisation contains the seeds of the paradox of 'realism' and 'mimesis' in literature.)

The term 'connotation' is appropriately used in cases where a sign acquires a 'higher' level of signification, functioning thereby as a 'secondary' sign that hints at a partially concealed, but all the more conspicuous, not to say, insidious, message. Barthes appears to adopt the notion 'connotation' wholesale from the Danish linguist, Louis Hjelmslev (1957) – but not, however, without departing from the rigorously circumscribed scope it has in Hjelmslev's original conception. It would seem that, at least some of the time, Barthes treats 'connotation' and 'signification' as synonymous terms, whereas in Hjelmslev 'connotation' is applied only to the 'secondary' signification of objects that are already signs in their own right. The signification of objects that are not, in themselves, coded signs (clothes, food, photographs, and so on) should not, strictly speaking, be referred to as 'connotation', since there can be no question here of that signification being 'secondary' to some underlying literal meaning.

A paradox develops from Barthes' adoption of the Hjelmslevian notion of 'connotation'. On the one hand, Barthes reiterates the precise Hjelmslevian definition of 'connotation' as 'secondary', as opposed to 'primary' meaning (see Figure 5.2), a definition that hinges on both 'primary' signifieds ('denotations') and 'secondary' signifieds ('connotations') being linked to their respective signifiers by the same type of conventional sign-relationship (symbolised by R in Figure 5.2). On the other hand, Barthes is already fully committed to seeing a completely different bond between signifiers and 'denotations' (conventional and explicitly communicative) and signifiers and their 'connotations'/significations ('accidental' and insinuative).

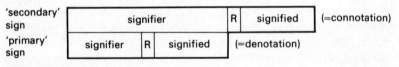

Figure 5.2

The second half of this paradox is the idea that 'normal' conventional sign-function (for example, the sign-function by virtue of which 'refuse disposal officer' conventionally denotes neither more nor less than the word 'dustman') does not operate in cases of signification (for example, the 'connotation' by virtue of which 'refuse disposal officer' is semantised as a sign of respect and flattery). This idea harbours a further paradox: if 'normal' signs denote by convention, but objects with signification, being different, do not signify either by virtue of convention, or by virtue of nature, then the very fact that they can signify at all assumes the character of a paradox. Yet Barthes is particularly insistent on the point (a point that epitomises the mystique of signification) that connotations/significations are not sanctioned either by being accepted as conventions or by being the natural interpretations of reality. (If 'refuse disposal officer' is interpreted as a sign of respect and flattery, this is neither because there exists a convention that makes this signification part of the literal meaning of the phrase, nor because the use of this phrase has respect and flattery as its natural corollaries.) What we have here is neither like the rules of chess, nor like the law of gravity, but rather a mechanism that, in the manner of a confidence trick, plays convention and nature off against one another. The only way to understand this – rather a metaphorical way, as is frequently the case with Barthesian notions – is to think of signification as the product of an 'illusion', rather like a mirage, or a dream. The paradox remains, however, in that signification shimmers between conventionality and naturalness without sharing the properties of either. It would not be too far-fetched to describe it as a 'mystery' rather than a 'concept'.

5.4 The 'Structuralist' Paradox

Along with paradoxes of his own making, there is an important paradox that Barthes inherits (ultimately from Saussure, via subsequent 'structuralist' interpreters of Saussure) and that he shares, up to a point, with other major 'structuralist' thinkers (for example, Lévi-Strauss, Foucault, Lacan). The paradox concerns the whole question of the explanatory value of the structures that are laid bare through the methods and techniques associated with 'structuralism' – it is, in other words, a fundamental paradox.

In order to set the scene, we should remind ourselves of the Saussurean origins of 'structuralism'. There is already in Saussure's *Cours de linguistique générale* a duality between two strands of thought: (*a*) a conception of *structure* as being strictly inherent – though in a virtual, rather than actual form – in conventional codes (for example, the structured conventions of languages are analogues of the structured rules of chess) and (*b*) a conception of structures as networks existing in a 'communal mind', that is, as mental properties. The duality can be crystallised, if we consider it in dichotomous terms, as: 'structure as a reflex of abstract conventions underlying overt behaviour' versus 'structure as a reflection of an underlying mental (socio-psychological) reality'. That this duality exists in Saussure is a direct result of the fact that, at the same time as championing an autonomous semiology, Saussure was enthusiastic about the prospects of attaching semiology to the recently initiated discipline of social psychology.

Ideas of a 'collective unconscious' (cf. Jungian psychology) as the repository of deep-seated 'concepts' common to sections of humanity have persisted in post-Saussurean thought, and it is not surprising that, as one of the major forms of neo-Saussureanism, 'structuralism' should have adopted both sides of Saussure's dual view of the explanatory relevance of structures.

In Barthes, the value attachable to structural patterns that are disentangled from groups of objects endowed with signification presents itself in a particularly paradoxical form.

On the one hand, an adherence to the pure abstractionism of a structural view – unless we were to put this down to mere lip-service – demands that structures should stand up by themselves as reflections of a systematic code. Thus, for instance, the structures Barthes uncovers as virtual underlying constants operating in the domain of food-consumption should constitute neither more nor less than a systematic alimentary code: 'the agglomeration of people's habits of eating makes up the alimentary language' (Barthes, 1967a).

It is, however, only by accepting a paradox that one can speak of a code (a system of conventions) in connection with structures whose defining feature is their signification, as is the case with habits of food-consumption. As we saw earlier, the whole point about signification is that it is not sanctioned by conventions. Since a structure based on signification cannot be rooted in convention – and it cannot be rooted in the 'laws of nature' (not even 'human nature') either – the paradox lies in the absence of candidates as to what such a structure might reflect. The 'normal' structuralist answer, according to which structure represents the underlying constancy of conventions, or, alternatively, the constancy of certain 'laws of nature', will serve only if we accept the paradox that constancy on the level of signification is of the same ilk as both constancy of conventions and constancy of 'laws of nature' without actually being equivalent to either of them.

On the other side of the coin, the structural analyses made by Barthes could be very readily interpreted as instances of socio-psychological diagnosis, in fact, a kind of sociological psycho-analysis in which structures reveal social 'obsessions' of a collectively subconscious nature. Enhancing this impression are the facts that (*a*) many of the exposed structures have a 'pathological' look about them (for example, the 'compulsive' aspects of following fashion in one's habits of dressing and eating), and (*b*) Barthes frequently presents himself in the role of a social 'therapist' (viz. 'change the world rather than preserve its images', Barthes, 1967a). Whether the significative signs found in Barthesian structures are conscious or unconscious, deliberate or spontaneous, natural or artificial, it is tempting to see them as reflecting underlying socio-psychological patterns, and, if so, to think of a 'collective mind' as the obvious candidate for a repository of these patterns. Barthes seems, however, to be quite convinced that these structures require no repository. He even appears to disclaim a socio-psychological interpretation of his structures. He disclaims an interest in anything further than the repetition of coherent patterns whose exposition simultaneously reproduces and dissects the ethos of a particular domain of signification. His structures are abstract codes, existing on the level of form (Chapter 1, Section 1.2.1, p. 9), for which no mental reality is claimed.

The disclaimer of a socio-psychological import for the structures diagnosed in, for instance, the various modern 'myths' exposed by Barthes are virtually without force in the eyes of many of Barthes' followers, as well as many of his critics, who, not unnaturally, take the attitude that 'actions speak louder than words'. If one infers, as Barthes does, backwards from an agglomeration of significative objects the existence of recurrent tastes, obsessions, passions, emotions, attitudes, and so on, then these inferred properties cannot be attributed to an abstract virtuality in the significative objects themselves; they can only be suitable attributes of some individual or collective mentality. In other words, if Barthesian semiology is an exposé of hidden social attitudes, then, logically speaking at least, one should agree with Mounin who labels and criticises Barthesian semiology as a (highly speculative and suspect) attempt at social psycho-analysis (Mounin, 1970). But to agree with Mounin – which is tempting – is to underestimate the role of paradox in Barthesian thought. It seems preferable, therefore, to interpret Barthes' position in terms of a paradox built on what Barthes sees as only an apparent contradiction: semiological structures both (directly) reflect virtual/abstract systems of forms and (indirectly, perhaps even unintentionally) tell us something about social psychology and a collective unconscious.

5.5 Paradoxes of the 'Myth'

Barthes is definitely at his best, and most obviously in his element, when exposing the way that the signification of certain objects reflects 'myths' harboured in the unspoken ideology of a given culture. To a layman's understanding, 'myth' probably means simply a belief in something fictional. For Barthes, however, a 'myth' is not a mere belief, but the embodiment of a belief in a form that subtly hints at its ideological content through its signification.

If we are to form a relatively clear idea of what Barthes understands by the term 'myth', we need, on the one hand, to consider some of Barthes' own examples, and, on the other hand, to take stock of the paradoxes that characterise the propagation of 'myths'. In each case, we should remember that it is not what objects serve to preserve 'myths' that matters (any object may do so, by 'semantisation'), but how objects preserve, or even create, 'myths'.

As a way of entering into the spirit of Barthesian 'mythology', it will be found extremely instructive to look at the particular case of 'photographic messages', especially of press photographs. While the example does not immediately involve the exposing of any particular 'myth', the extremely full discussion Barthes gives (Barthes, 1977) of the *connotative/significative* potential of photographic images will provide us with most of the main ingredients of 'myths' in general. Furthermore, what Barthes refers to as the 'photographic paradox' sheds light on, and epitomises, the 'myth'.

A press photograph is a vehicle of a message (signification) whose source of emission, channel of transmission and point of reception are readily identified. Emission, by the staff of a newspaper, and reception, by a reading public, are of sociological relevance; they are matters of determining motives and attitudes in a society. The photograph as such is an object of semiological interest; as it goes through its channel of transmission (which is the newspaper itself), it achieves a degree of structural autonomy as something separate both from its source of emission which it has left, and from its point of reception which will be its ultimate destination. It is at this in-between stage that the photograph becomes, for Barthes, an object of 'immanent' analysis; that is to say, at this point, one should be able to determine what is in the photograph itself, as opposed to what is in the motives or attitudes either of the newspaper staff who are its producers, or of the reading public who are its consumers. (There is a minor paradox here, in so far as the analyst cannot but become, himself, a point of reception – nor can he avoid attributing the messages he finds to some conscious/unconscious motives on the part of the source of emission.)

The central paradox of the photograph is that its content is by definition a literal reality: a photograph visually represents something, and does so in so far as physical/chemical processes enable it to record a concrete visual reality. Consequently, the relationship between photographic object and photographic image is not mediated by a code. On the other hand, each photographic message spontaneously develops an immediate supplementary message. The 'style' of the photograph signifies a particular treatment of the image, giving rise to what one might call 'stylistically induced' connotations. This is paradoxical in that, above all other visual images, a photograph appears to leave no room at all for connotation; if any image is objective and truly 'mimetic' (imitative of reality), then a photographic image must be. However, the very objectivity of a photograph carries the probability of being 'mythical'. The paradox here comes across in the nature of a confidence-trick: the photograph openly declares its objectivity, even to the point of helping to conceal any evidence of contrived techniques (trick effects, retouching, faking) and trades on its special credibility to make its supplementary message (acquired by insinuation) at once implicit and justified by objective reality.

In Barthes' own assessment, the photographic paradox is that the connoted message develops a message without a code; that is to say, the photograph is both wholly natural/mechanical and culturally contrived. It is because the photograph is objective that it succeeds in fulfilling a non-objective, 'rhetorical' function of signification. This subversion of the relationship and the difference between nature and artifice is the core of the 'myth'. By further paradox, the 'rhetorical' code of photographic messages (messages without a code) is neither natural nor artificial, but merely a matter of historical accident.

The 'hypocritical' aspect of 'myths' (in which the tendency is to confuse 'motives' with 'reasons') can be fully appreciated by noting, in particular examples, the way that a deliberate juggling with nature and artifice obscures the role of historical accident as the only real factor that sanctions a 'myth'. One of Barthes' examples that brings out this 'hypocrisy' particularly clearly is the case of a press photograph (the fact that it was faked is almost immaterial) in which an American Senator is shown in animated and friendly conversation with a known Communist leader. Such a photograph needed no caption to lose the Senator a vast number of votes due to the 'tetchy anti-Communism of the American electorate' (Barthes, 1977). It is, in spite of appearances to the contrary, neither a natural link between the photographic image and its insinuated message (translatable perhaps as: 'Senator X is a lousy commy-lover'), nor an artificial-conventional link associating the image and its interpretation, that makes the photograph successful. Its being interpreted as indicating Senator X to be favourable to Communism results from the touchy and hysterical suspiciousness of a prevalent 'Reds-under-the-beds' mentality, which is, itself, a purely historical phenomenon. That it should have served to discredit the Senator (doubtless the ulterior motive behind the insinuated message) hinges, again, purely on historical accident. The example – and, of course, the study of 'myths' in general – reveals the 'hypocrisy' of 'mythical' signification as a way of tricking people into jumping to conclusions by a sneaky use of their prejudices, not unlike a kind of mental *ju jitsu*.

Another well-known Barthesian photographic example (Barthes, 1972) brings out similar aspects of the perpetration/propagation of 'myths'. This is the example of a French press-photograph showing a black soldier saluting the French flag. Objectively, that is all there is to the photograph in question, but, of course, in the context of the Algerian controversy (and the political issues of French colonialism as a whole) the photographic image is easily transformed into a vehicle of signification (the message might be something like: "Look! This black soldier is happy to salute the French flag. He likes French colonialism.'). By the process of 'mythification' – in fact, through the paradox of the 'myth' – the photograph thus becomes a mythical sign of loyalty to French colonialism. The play on nature and history is obvious: the photograph masquerades as natural (there really *is* a black soldier photographed while saluting the flag), but, beyond this, it subtly signifies the excellence of, and 'naturalises', a purely historical colonial *status quo*.

In this example, we see, furthermore, that the paradoxical function of 'myth' is to signify covertly, and yet be eye-catching; thus, instead of either saying literally: 'French colonialism deserves the loyalty of all true Frenchmen', or making such a message hidden to the point of inaccessibility, the photograph catches the eye, makes its message known, but distorts it to read, to all intents and purposes, as: 'French colonialism, and loyalty to it, belong to the *natural* order of things.' (This aspect of 'myths' is of the greatest relevance to Barthes' 'semioclastic' ideology.)

Three ways of looking at the 'myth' embodied in the above example further help to analyse the intrinsic paradoxality of 'myths' (Barthes, 1972):

(*a*)   if our attention is focused on the photograph purely as an image, the black soldier serves literally as an example of French imperialism;

(*b*   if our attention is focused on the relationship between the photograph and its signification, the black soldier serves as a contrived, propagandistic 'alibi' for French imperialism – the imposture cannot be overlooked from this point of view;

(*c*)   if our attention is focused on the totality of the photograph and its implications, we become gullible consumers of the 'myth'; the black soldier will thus carry conviction as the very embodiment of French imperialism (and of a favourable attitude towards it).

From all this, we see that, above all, 'myths' are truly 'chameleon-like'.

One further point we can acquaint ourselves with at this juncture is the 'euphoric' ingredient generally found in 'mythical' signification. In affirming (however surreptitiously) a positive attitude to French colonialism ('the black soldier is happy to salute the flag'), the press photograph is a source of reassurance to the effect that all is well with the colonial *status quo*. The idea of referring to this reassuring quality as 'euphoric' implies, of course, that 'myth' reconciles its consumers with an order of things that is a typical 'fool's paradise'. Be that as it may, the ideological repertoire of a culture is, according to Barthes, largely constituted of 'myths' that are forms whereby society preserves its integration and ensures its peace of mind.

While it would be misleading to pretend that I can provide anything like a systematic classification of Barthesian 'myths' – after all, Barthes discusses 'myths' anecdotally, without even a hint at their categorisation – nevertheless, a vague outline of certain types of 'myth' does suggest itself. It will be just as well to avail oneself of such a framework, no matter how imperfect for, on the one hand, I am pressed by the need to be terse, and cannot afford to be anecdotal while, on the other hand, I cannot hope to deal with the notion of 'myth' without giving some idea at least of the various types of 'myth' in which Barthes is interested. Thus, for instance, alongside the 'myths' embodied in the press-photographs discussed above, which seem to be typically political 'myths', one should place also advertising 'myths', social 'myths', national 'myths' and dramatic (spectator) 'myths'. The category of those, in the eyes of Barthes, most insidious 'myths' to which he regularly alludes as bourgeois 'myths' will also need separate mention.

Advertising 'Myths'

Images and texts in advertising lend themselves particularly well to a Barthesian semiological analysis, since the signification they assume is undoubtedly intentional and achieves, by their strategically exaggerated character, a kind of paradoxical frankness. So, for instance, an advertisement showing a bonanza of Italian food-stuffs (Barthes, 1977) owes its semiological (and psychological) success to the way it is transmuted into a mythical sign of 'Italianicity' – the embodiment, as it were, of 'all that is good in the mystique of Italian cuisine'. It is obvious, in other words, that the advertisement works by preserving, propagating and taking advantage of an idea that exists in many people's minds in prejudicial form.

The advertising 'myths' of soap powders and detergents (Barthes, 1972) – surely an old chestnut by now – are more distorted in their signification. In a way that is, of course, wholly 'mythological', they create and trade on images that disguise and ennoble the real nature of the products advertised: fluids are made out to be something in the nature of 'liquid fire' that consumes germs and dirt; powders drive out dirt, restore the order (as good as new) of fabrics, putting softness (comfort/luxury) or whiteness (purity) into it. Fabrics themselves are often 'mythologised' by making them out to be deep, foamy and luxurious substances. The overall effect of all this is obviously intended to be 'euphoric'; the consumer is invited to share in the image of the products as substances endowed with somewhat magical, and definitely benevolent, properties.

Everyone is, doubtless, familiar with the infamous 'whiter-than-white' syndrome, which is an out-and-out 'myth' *par excellence*, and a few evenings spent in front of any commercial television channel could easily provide each and every one of us with hosts of advertising 'myths' suitable for Barthesian analysis. Whether, after a while, anything new and interesting would emerge or not is another question; suffice it to say that recognising the fundamentally 'mythical' functioning of the whole of advertising is a salutary, if not wholly original, lesson.

Social 'Myths'

Certain 'myths' propagated in the *media* seem to assume a fairly clearly functional aspect as soon as one sees that function as one of perpetuating and stereotyping certain groups or classes in society. From among the 'myths' analysed by Barthes, perhaps the most clearcut example is the 'myth' of royalty (Barthes, 1972); the example is of further interest in the way that it illustrates a 'mythical' technique that is one of Barthes' recurrent themes. The technique, as far as the royalty 'myth' is concerned, consists in

(*a*)   showing royalty in the pursuit of ordinary, pedestrian activities;
(*b*)   by expressing interest in the ordinariness of these activities, creating the impression that this ordinariness is actually in some way surprising;
(*c*)   by the paradoxality of making out the ordinariness of royalty to be unexpected, implying that royalty is not really ordinary, but only assumes ordinariness by condescension and artifice.

Thus, ultimately, the message of the 'blue-blood myth' comes out as a denial of what is superficially portrayed: the common humanity of royal personages. In fact, the 'myth' serves to confirm the not too uncommon suspicion that royalty is, by nature and by birth, superior to the common herd.

It is interesting to note how the same technique – say, the trick of showing Prince Charles 'playing at a prince playing at being a helicopter pilot' – produces, along with a 'deification' of royalty, a certain state of 'euphoria' whereby the consumer is made to feel happy to keep royalty on a pedestal (it is nice to believe in fairy-tales, especially when they are mixed up with reality), and to integrate himself willingly at a lower level of society.

'Myths' preserving the position of women in society can also be placed among social 'myths'. The particular technique Barthes analyses (Barthes, 1972) and which he qualifies, by a revealing and appropriate epithet, as a 'patronising myth', consists in

(*a*) presenting the successful authoress (a rather smug prototype of the successful career-woman, in any case) as the equal of any man;
(*b*) interpolating throughout the presentation references to her womanhood (children, household, and so on);
(*c*) suggesting, by this paradoxical mixture, that women are successful outside the home in spite of what nature had intended them for (that is, childbearing and sweet domesticity).

The final message manages to cancel the initial face value presentation of the authoress as the equal of man: by nature and by birth, it is implied, this can never be. The effect, when the 'myth' is successfully swallowed, should be one of double 'euphoria': first, there is the reassurance that women are not being unfairly discriminated against and secondly, there is the consumer's reassuring confirmation in the happy knowledge that the real place of woman (as he/she had always suspected) is in the home. Because the 'myth' serves to integrate, by stereotyping, woman on a less favourable level of society than man, and helps to maintain a male-oriented social *status quo*, it is appropriate to class it as a social 'myth'.

Dramatic (Spectator) 'Myths'

The genre of dramatic 'myth' is of particular interest for two main reasons. On the one hand, the interest lies in Barthes' rather unusual choice of paradigm examples of this genre; on the other hand, his view of dramatic 'myth' contains the seeds of an approach to theatrical art and to literature. Who but a professional 'iconoclast' (one is tempted to say) would have thought of all-in wrestling and strip-tease as ideal topics for a semiological analysis, let alone for the breeding-ground of an ideology of values in art criticism?

I do not mean, of course, that Barthes' ideas on drama, literature and the arts in general were suggested to him by what he observed in the 'lower' forms of entertainment and public spectacle, but rather that, for the reader of Barthes, there is a fairly complete genetic imprint of a theory of art contained in more readily accessible form within the analyses of these 'lower' forms. Barthes profits from the occasions offered by his rather unexpected analyses of all-in wrestling and of strip-tease for explicating and driving home certain of his major themes as regards a semiological/ideological view of art.

The case of all-in wrestling is interesting in itself, and Barthes' analysis is in many ways plausible. The 'mythical' aspects lie primarily in the paradox that is acted out in the ring: the paradox whereby an activity that should, on the face of it, be a sport, turns out, in fact, to be a kind of 'pantomime', and yet not a pantomime with a 'mimetic' purpose of re-creating outward physical actions. The physical actions are there; they even look like those of a sport, but their main impact is significative – the dramatic presentation of basic, inner passions: hate, cruelty, trust, betrayal, triumph, defeat, suffering, and so on. By a typically 'mythical' paradox, while the face value of all-in wrestling is that of a competitive sport, its most blatantly (though insinuatively) self-advertised feature is in complete contradiction with the ethos of competition, and is pure artifice. Wrestlers use extremely exaggerated motions, precisely as means of self-advertisement, assuming thereby a larger than life appearance that makes them suitable stereotype representations of basic human charac-ter-types (for example, the strong, silent, kindly giant, who is only terrifying when aroused; the treacherous, cowardly bastard, whom one is so pleased to see demolished, and so on). The physique, as well as the 'grandiloquent' gestures, facial expressions and vocal outbursts of wrest-lers are all made to serve as signs externalising and advertising emotions that are put on for show – signs that are excessively clear although their intention of clarity must remain concealed. Here, then, we can put our finger on a central paradox that wrestling shares with art: no matter how great its verisimilitude, it must not be taken for real, or else it loses its signification as a dramatic 'myth', and becomes identified with sport, but it must maintain the illusion of naturalness, or else it forfeits its dramatic and psychological effectiveness by becoming intolerably 'rigged'. Wrest-ling, like art, must be 'rigged', must be understood to be 'rigged', but must be plausibly and tolerably rigged. If successful in this 'mythical' capacity, a wrestling-bout becomes, so Barthes suggests, an image of the transparency of a reality in which all signs make perfect sense. This is surely a source of 'euphoria' since the experience of perfect intelligibility is a luxury not afforded by the real world, and since there is pleasure to be derived from the resolution of a fight between 'good' and 'evil' through the exercise of 'poetic justice' (the cliché seems so peculiarly apt here that Barthes might well have regretted not having used it).

The paradox of strip-tease is no less explicit. In it, woman is de-sexualised (*sic*) at the very moment of being stripped naked, while the venal side of sex is first magnified and advertised, but only in order to be all the more thoroughly exorcised. It is not the fulfilment of a perverted form of sexuality that the consumer of the 'myth' finds in strip-tease, but an externalisation and a dispelling of erotic evil.

Within this quasi-ritualistic *milieu*, woman is established, right from the start, as an object of disguise – from the shedding of a frequently exotic, and certainly incongruous costume (how different from the purely functional act of undressing in order to go to bed), woman emerges in a perfectly chaste state of the flesh, as if, at least by stereotyping, her natural vesture were nakedness. The element of dance (which also gives the show the alibi of 'art') merely serves to enhance both sides of a paradox: the concealment of real nudity under an artistic nakedness that is symbolic rather than functional, and the advertising of a symbolic nakedness that transforms woman into a symbol of pure decorativeness, an object that, like a jewel, serves no other purpose beyond its beauty.

The relevance of both these 'myths' as regards a theory of art will become apparent once more in the section devoted to 'paradoxes of literature'. It must, however, be underlined here that Barthes has a favourable view of the 'myths' of strip-tease and all-in wrestling, as opposed to the cynical and condemnatory attitude he displays towards practically all other 'myths'. This is not simply *pour épater les bourgeois* (though an element of the latter may have given Barthes a degree of 'euphoria', on the side). The explanation lies rather in the fact that Barthes, from the point of view of his theory of art, has good reason to admire the comparatively frank and innocent (certainly not too surreptitious), honestly significative, and yet by no means too didactic, nature of these two 'myths'. In this sense, they represent, at least in part, the ideal of his semiotic ideology of art:

(a)   an art that does not pretend to be 'mimetic' of actual reality;
(b)   an art that thrives on the paradox of signification;
(c)   an art that signals its artificiality;
(d)   an art that is understood to be (tolerably and plausibly) contrived;
(e)   an art that creates its own 'reality' by endowing artifice with an illusion of naturalness;
(f)   an art which remains vague enough in its 'moral' to allow the consumer to recreate, through his own imagination, the details of the 'myth' it embodies (in fact, there is then no precise, single, public 'myth', but rather a cluster of related personal 'myths');
(g)   an art that produces psychological effects (even if 'euphoric') that are neither risible nor ideologically reprehensible.

Bourgeois 'Myths'

Barthes is at his most scathing when he is taking apart 'bourgeois myths', which he considers to be the most insidious and objectionable. In short, he finds them shallow in their presuppositions, cheap in their repertoire of effects, and both hypocritical and harmful in their intentions.

For illustrating the genre, it will suffice to take, from among a host of examples (Barthes, 1972), the two cases labelled 'Operation Margarine' and 'The Great Family of Man'.

What Barthes calls 'Operation Margarine' is, in fact, a whole genre of 'myths' in itself: 'myths' based on the same familiar technique of presenting an object by emphasising its faults, but only in order to let its excellence emerge all the more clearly. As a technique for advertising a product, the basic paradox can be sketched as follows:

(a)   the advertisement portrays an emphatically (preferably exaggeratedly) critical attitude to the product (the 'Ugh! It's disgusting *margarine*, not real butter!' stage);

(b)   an element of doubt and debate is introduced, leading towards 'putting the product to the test' (the 'See if you are really right in saying that margarine is disgusting!' stage);

(c)   the advertisement culminates in letting it be understood that, after all, the product is admirable (the 'Yum! Yum! I should have known all along that margarine was delicious!' stage).

In other words, by enacting the 'conversion' of a sceptic or of a violent critic, the 'myth' moves from running down the product and exposing its shortcomings to exalting its ultimate excellence. (The recent North American advertisements for decaffeinated coffee are, for obvious reasons, a classic in this genre.)

The technique of 'Operation Margarine' is particularly suited to the complacent portrayal of the evils of an Established Order, aiming, paradoxically, at exalting that order. The example of the film, 'From Here to Eternity', is typical (Barthes, 1972). The first part of the film presents a grotesquely critical image of life in the United States Army (the 'Ugh! It's disgusting . . .' stage), leading into a time of testing with the outbreak of Japanese hostilities. The film culminates in the final 'message' that, for all its faults, when it comes to the crunch, the established order of the US Army deserves to command one's highest admiration – an ideal way of using 'bourgeois sentimentality' for the achievement of a double 'euphoria' (reminiscent of the 'myth' of the authoress in this respect): the 'euphoria' of free criticism of established institutions and the 'euphoria' at being reassured that (as one probably suspected deep down) these institutions are still the best available manifestations of a fundamentally natural order of things.

The background of the 'myth' referred to as 'The Great Family of Man' is a photographic exhibition held in Paris in the 1960s, originally entitled 'The Family of Man'. The change of title itself connotes a sentimentalisation of the unity of the human species as one 'great, big, happy family'. In fact, the semiotic/ideological content of the exhibition is seen by Barthes to be the ambiguous proposition of a human 'community' between 'brothers beneath the skin'. (Note how various clichés offer themselves in the description of the 'myth'.)

The technique creating and reinforcing this 'mythical' signification is suitably paradoxical:

(a)   everything in the presentation of the exhibition is laid on in order to emphasise a Babel-like diversity, enhanced by a striking exoticism of treatment;

(b)   from this exaggerated diversity, there arises the ethos of a magically produced 'essence' of human existence – the 'message' cries out that the human condition is fundamentally the same all over the world.

The sentimental humanism of this culminating message prevents the observation (obscured in the photographic material exhibited) of historically produced economic and social injustices. The consumer of the 'myth' is more than encouraged to take the unfair effects of historical accident for the equity of nature.

Within this 'myth' of placing nature at the bottom of history, there is a lyrical exaltation of Birth, Work and Death (recurrent themes in the exhibition, whose names deserve to be capitalised). This 'myth within a myth' leaves no room for considerations of the historical realities behind cruelly different conditions under which people live, work and die in different parts of the world.

The 'euphoric' elements are not difficult to find. One of them is, ironically enough, summed up by a remark found in an official introductory leaflet to the exhibition: 'this look over the human condition must somewhat resemble the benevolent gaze of God on our absurd and sublime ant-hill.' What could be more complacently 'euphoric' than the conceit of sharing, if only for a few moments, a divine view of the entire globe?

Furthermore, the intellectual defeatism of naturalising a historical situation (in blunt terms, there is no point in trying to change things, if they are as they are because it is natural for them to be so) is converted into the triumph of complacency (all is for the best in the best of all possible worlds, to use yet another cliché). There is reassurance for the consumer of the 'myth' in the 'euphoria' of knowing that (as he had probably always suspected) the existing order of things is as nature had intended it to be.

One might disagree with Barthes that the type of propagandism described in the two instances above (including its nauseating aspects) is necessarily, or even characteristically, 'bourgeois'. Western 'middle-class' mentality does not have a monopoly either on the techniques and effects of this type of 'myth', or on being nauseating. It is by looking to his background as a left-wing French intellectual that we can best understand why Barthes qualifies such 'myths' as pertaining to a 'bourgeois' mentality: a contemptuous attitude to the (lower) middle classes, not to mention an indulgence in the sport of 'bourgeois'-baiting has, for centuries, been a common attribute of French 'free-thinkers'.

5.6   Paradoxes of Literature

Without wanting to stray too far into the technical aspects of Barthes' theory of literature – related though they may be, in his own estimation, to his central semiological themes – I have to admit that even a sketchy introduction to Barthesianism cannot avoid some discussion of literary criticism and textual analysis. Consequently, it will be necessary to outline in what follows some of the major themes in Barthes' ideas on literature.

The first theme – leading, as usual, to a paradox – concerns a Barthesian ideal of literary honesty. Like the actors of classical Rome indicating their masks as a reminder of their play-acting role, the ideal author should constantly call attention to the artificiality of his text. If, however, these reminders were indeed continuous and blatant, the text would become the equivalent of a wrestling-match that is so obviously 'rigged' as to invite the booing and whistling of a revolted audience. There is, in this, an element of what, to me at least, is a mystery: just how exactly is the honest author to be frankly artificial at the same time as carrying conviction in the semiological/ideological 'signification' of his text. Presenting the dilemma in terms of a degree of 'alienation', whereby the 'audience' is made to see (or imagine) things happening, as opposed to (*sic*) being made to enjoy vicarious emotions, does not seem to resolve the paradox in the least.

Barthes is equally ready to attribute to 'bourgeois literature' (it would seem that very few texts escape this classification) the hallmarks of intellectual dishonesty, especially those of a pretence at re-creating reality from an 'objective' point of view, and to attribute to 'bourgeois literary criticism' the fault of maintaining this very 'myth' of expressionistic writing. However, his conception of a 'zero-degree of literature' (Barthes, 1953) – that is, of a neutral style which is maximally innocent of deception – suffers, surely, from the paradox that a lack of affectation is the ultimate form of affectation (Barthes, 1972). In effect, this conception of a text that offers to the reader maximal freedom in interpreting significations over and beyond the text, while all the time the reader is held aware of the artificiality of both text and interpretations, does not even wholly explain Barthes' relative enthusiasm for Chaplin films, nor his more committed approval of Brecht.

What seems to appeal to Barthes in the style of Chaplin (Barthes, 1972) is his portrayal of a character unaware of the extent of his poverty and helplessness (Barthes talks in terms of this character being below the level of 'proletarian awareness'). Thus the imagination – and the sign-interpreting faculty – of the audience supplies, by sympathy, what the 'little tramp' has no notion of, and does so all the more effectively. Barthes sees in this a proto-form of the Brechtian technique, the centre of which is the paradox that, to see someone who does *not* see, is to see all the more clearly *what* it is that he does not see. Be that as it may, a view of Chaplin and Brecht as producers of something approaching a 'zero-degree of writing' is, itself, only tenable in the form of a paradox; there is a hidden (therefore, by definition, not frank) artifice underlying both Chaplin and Brecht, which is rather the illusion of a neutral 'zero-degree' of style.

The whole of this theorising is caught up in the central literary paradox: a literary text portrays something at the same time as inventing it; for example, Hamlet is not a person outside of Shakespeare's play who is described within the play; he is simultaneously invented and portrayed inside the play as such. (One is forcibly reminded of the paradox of dreams as 'memories' of something that never happened.) Consequently, Barthes' insistence that literature should not conceive of itself, nor be conceived of from the outside, as having a 'mimetic' function – the representation of some external, pre-existing, objective reality – is a paradox within a paradox. Granted that realism is built on an absurdity, and that even its most expressionistic attempts must be interpreted as significative, rather than deictic, awareness of that absurdity does not suddenly transpose into a significative mode something that cannot in any case avoid being significative. If we posit the contrast between 'bourgeois' literature and 'zero-degree' literature in the form of an 'expressionistic' versus an 'impressionistic' style (which is admittedly only part of the picture), we are still left with two different nuances of one artificial genre, not with two sharply differing genres.

Further complications ensue with the Barthesian idea of the 'death of the author', that is to say, with the idea that texts cease to be connected with their authors the moment they have been finished. Making allowances for the obviously strategical exaggeration through which this slogan challenges 'traditional' literary criticism of the biographical/historical type, there still remains the fact that, according to Barthes, style forms a 'language' (that is, a semiological/ideological system) which is rooted in the personal and secret 'mythology' of the author (Barthes, 1953). In that case, Barthes must want to maintain both that the text minus the author is the repository of style and of signification, and that the decoding of the author's secret 'mythology' is the main semiological/ideological task of literary analysis. As it happens, such analysis is more often than not couched in terms of a language of conscious or subconscious intentionality. Now, if a text 'reflects' the results of what may pass for a kind of psycho-analysis, to whom – unless it be to the author – do we attribute these 'reflections'?

It is said, however, that, far from literary signification being tied to the author's conscious or subconscious intentions – or even being strictly limited by a single constancy of the text – all texts are 'infinitely re-writeable' by their readers. The text contains, of course, the wherewithal for this infinite re-creatability, but this can hardly serve as a constant signification within the text, since the readers' interpretations are infinitely variable within unknown limits. This provides us with a notion of infinitely meaningful texts, a notion which, if it can be used as an argument at all, would at best argue for the indescribability of texts (an ineffable ethos whose complexity defies analysis). As we shall see shortly, this pluralistic and infinite-faceted view of literary texts does not deter Barthes from offering means of textual analysis or, indeed, from attempting such analyses.

There is a mystery also when it comes to the relative importance of form and content in a literary text. In one direction, Barthes is wholly committed to the signification (content) of texts as objects suitable for semiological/ideological analysis – in another direction, that of the structuralism espoused by Barthes, he is driven to seeing in literature the triumph of form over content. Especially when it comes to modern French poetry – described both as pure and absolute style (form) and as pure signification (content) – which seems to display a submersion of content in a form that is a joy to itself, the double-edged nature of Barthes' theory comes into sharp relief. There is, in short, both a tendency towards pure formalism and towards extreme 'semantisation'. Only by some paradoxical statement, such as the slogan that 'form *is* signification', can these tendencies be reconciled.

Without providing very much in the way of information about the basis of literary 'codes' – except that they are, apparently, neither conventional nor natural, but historical and 'artificial' – Barthes presents us with a categorical statement to the effect that texts are constructed on the principle of language-like 'codes'. This, of course, opens the way for the discovery of units and structures within literature, conceived as 'organised discourse' above the level of sentences, and to a wholesale borrowing of linguistic concepts for pseudo-linguistic purposes (cf. Mounin, 1970). For instance, it is proposed that the 'grammar' (*sic*) of narrative analysis is organised on a hierarchy of levels containing units of decreasing magnitude (from top to bottom) (see Figure 5.3).

Figure 5.3

   The narration (which is the totality of the text) contains actions as its direct constituents, within which character-types, and the actual *dramatis personae* (as agents of the actions) are like phrases in a sentence. Presumably (though Barthes is somewhat vague on this point) actions give the narration the kind of structure that it might have in a *précis* of the plot (if so, this is hardly original).
   Actions can be further analysed into smaller constituent units of two different types: functions and indices. Indices proper are the formal means of hints referring to the character of a narrative agent (for example, in Hamlet's monologue, 'Oh that this too, too solid flesh . . .', the unit 'solid flesh' is an index of Hamlet's obsession with physical self-disgust). Another category of indices, that of *informants*, provides the minutiae of setting the action in an apparent space-time location (for example, Horatio's lines in *Hamlet*, Act I, Scene I: ' 'Tis bitter cold and I am sick at heart' contain, in the unit ' 'Tis bitter cold', an informant connoting a cold winter night in Denmark).
   Functions are also of two types, defined on a linguistic analogy with nucleus and expansion: namely, cardinal functions and catalysts. The former, like a linguistic nucleus, is an element that could not be deleted without altering the action-level structure of the narration (for example, if Hamlet did not happen to kill Polonius, the whole play would have had to be written differently). Cardinal points, in other words, are the 'joints' at which the action has to be 'carved', for they represent important alternatives, where the choice of what happens is crucial to the unfolding of the narration as a whole. In contrast, catalysts expand the bare bones of the narration, providing it with functional padding: functional, because without them the relationship between text and reader would be signi-

ficantly altered (one does not read Lamb's *Tales from Shakespeare* in the same spirit as one reads the plays themselves); yet 'padding', because they flesh out the skeletal structure of the action.

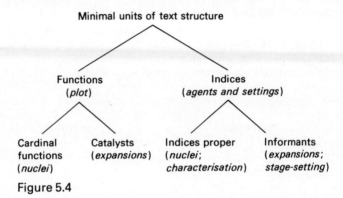

Figure 5.4

Without going into further details or exemplification (Barthes, 1974), I close this section on Barthes' literary paradoxes with the reminder that his most sophisticated textual analysis is based on the suggestion that such analysis can be exhausted (or so it would seem) by disentangling within a text the units of five different codes:

(1)   Hermeneutic code (the art of deciphering 'mysteries');
(2)   Semic code (semantic analysis of the text into units of signification);
(3)   Code of actions (analysis of elements of premeditation in the action);
(4)   Referential code (describes the denotative-conventional meaning of the sentences in the text);
(5)   Symbolic code (a 'Freudian' level of psycho-symbolic units).

The paradox of this 'five-code' approach is neatly summed up in Thody's ironical remark (Thody, 1977): 'to provide only five codes for an infinitely meaningful text is a shade miserly.'

5.7   The Paradox of 'Semioclasm'

A suitable way of closing this section on Barthes is by pointing to the ironical consequences of ideological semiology – an irony of which, incidentally, Barthes was not unaware in his later writings (Barthes, 1977).

In a nutshell, the irony is that Barthesianism has been overtaken by the natural fate of successful ideologies; it has become a dogma – but for an approach whose mainstay has always been a fundamental objection to all that is given out as 'self-evident' dogma, this fate is little short of 'poetic justice'.

Analysing the situation in a little more detail, this 'poetic justice' resolves itself into several clauses. Thus, for instance, there is the basic intention of creating a semiology that applies analytic techniques to works of art and to other cultural/social phenomena (in order to see 'what makes them tick, *not* to judge them') as against the fact that Barthes' semiology is ideological, and ideology is always judgemental. This dualism forces Barthesianism into an uneasy position of being divided between description of facts and prescription of ideals.

In particular, language and semiological systems (for example, 'myths') become targets viewed with a double vision: descriptive targets of structural analysis, and political targets in changing the world by breaking down its images. Since 'languages' (in the widest sense) imprison their uncritical users in the particular 'world' they create, the ideological task of the semiologist (inseparable from his descriptive task, it would seem) is to change society by altering its habits of thought. This latter, in turn, is to be achieved by overthrowing and dismantling the 'languages' in which people think.

In other words, semiology (pure and simple) has to be replaced by semioclasm – a deliberately irreverent descriptive destruction of signs: 'It is Western speech as such in its very basic and elementary forms that we have to destroy' (Barthes, 1970). This de-mythification (that is, *semioclasm*) is ideologically motivated by analogy with the therapeutic and self-freeing effects of psycho-analysis. However, semioclasm is not without its paradox: the 'world' of Barthesian analysis is no less than any other mythical 'world' an ideological, mythical invention that threatens to imprison those who fall under its influence.

Furthermore, if the missionary role of the semiologist/linguist/literary critic is to cure society of distortions created by a predigested presentation of reality through 'language', it is also evident that Barthesian analyses are, themselves, predigested presentations of a semiological reality. Besides, as Barthes sometimes suggests (cf. Lévi-Strauss: '*les mythes se pensent dans les hommes et à leur insu*'; 'myths think themselves out in people, without people's knowledge'), it is perhaps language that uses us, rather than we who use language. If this is so, then Barthes is considerably abused by his own 'language'. For, as an anonymous critic remarked in the *Bulletin critique du livre français* (cited in Thody, 1977), the 'language' of Barthes yields 'deliberately obscure pages, in which the ideas constantly hide themselves away behind an exaggerated, grandiloquent, metaphorical and wholly illogical mode of expression'. Here, in addition, Barthes' own idea of the 'infinite re-writability of texts' reflects unfavourably on his own texts which, through their own variable transcribability, put Barthesians in a weak position as regards intellectual solidarity between adherents of 'the same' theory.

Just as, say, spectator sports create 'myths' by over-simplifying the complex issues of life, so the spectacular semioclastic analysis of Barthes creates, also, its own 'myth', by over-simplifying the complex issues of cultural and literary signification. An instance of this over-simplification is the intellectual condescension manifested, throughout Barthes' analyses of 'advertising-myths', in the signal over-estimation of the gullibility of 'consumers' of such 'myths'. (How many people, for instance, *really* fall for the cheap tricks of the 'Operation Margarine' technique in advertising?)

The Barthesian 'semioclastic myth' has its own 'euphorics', notably (*a*) the 'euphoria' created by the inevitable insinuation that the Barthesian eye sees more deeply than ever before into cultural phenomena; (*b*) the reassuring effects of the feeling that, through semioclasm, one is assuming social-ideological responsibilities of diagnosing and curing social ills – responsibilities that others abdicate due to complacency.

Finally, the fusing of the two processes of ideological criticism and semiological dismantling, together with the denunciation of 'myths', has, since the early days of Barthes, become a fashion and a mythological dogma. This is a fact that Barthes' later writings note with a degree of cynicism (Barthes, 1977). With the 'myth of semioclasm' firmly established among classical twentieth-century myths, Barthesian semiology 'finds itself a little in the same situation as psycho-analysis before it' (Barthes, 1977), to wit, the way everyone goes around talking about 'Freudian complexes'. Thus, semiology finds itself diffused in popular culture, where it takes the form of a pastime that is scarcely more than an intellectual parlour-game, or a mode of making interesting conversation at cocktail parties.

6

Semiology as a Theory of Semiological Systems and of Indices: Functionalism

6.1 Introductory Remarks

In foregoing chapters, we have been dealing with approaches that can be presented, *par excellence*, by singling out the ideas of one or (at most) two principal exponents. This method of presentation will not serve our purpose in the present chapter. Instead, we shall need to discuss a movement, and to discuss it by forming a composite picture made up of the ideas of a number of important contributors. Even when they are attributable to particular sources, or, for that matter, when they constitute areas of disagreement within the movement as a whole, these ideas cluster round a fairly well-defined nucleus. The main exponents of the functionalist movement – those, at least, in whose writings the theses of functional semiology should be sought – are Eric Buyssens, André Martinet, Jeanne Martinet, Georges Mounin and Luis Prieto. From among these scholars, André Martinet is undoubtedly the centripetal force of the movement, while Eric Buyssens remains, for all his considerable influence on functionalist semiology, the furthest removed from the actual orbit of the movement.

6.1.1 The Scope of Functional Semiology

Functional semiology concerns itself primarily with two aspects of communication, in connection with which two strands of the theory are developed from general principles, separately and to an equal degree:

(1) semiological systems (by some, referred to as 'codes', for example, Prieto, by others, as 'sémies', for example, Buyssens): abstract structures that are the embodiment of all that is virtual, mandatory, systematic and heterogeneous in the particular domain of communication (cf. Saussure's notion 'system', Chapter 1, Section 1.2.3, p. 12). 'Semic acts' are of crucial, but none the less secondary, interest to the theory. These acts are tokens (cf. Chapter 1, Section 1.3.11, p. 34) of the types that are the (abstract) elements of 'semiological systems'. Consequently, the development of a model for concrete 'semic acts' is not a particular concern of functional semiology, which approaches such acts from the angle of systems,

rather than approaching systems, 'inductively', from the angle of acts (cf. Chapter 2, Section 2.1.2, p. 38; Chapter 3, Section 3.1.1, p. 59). For a model of 'semic acts', functionalists generally have recourse to Prieto's theory (discussed independently in Chapter 3).

(2)   a typology of 'indices': abstract entities that are the embodiment of particular systematic message-bearing capacities (cf. Saussure's notion 'sign', Chapter 1, Sections 1.2.4, p. 13 and 1.2.5, p. 14; also compare Peirce's typology of signs which is a similar endeavour, Chapter 1, Section 1.3.10, p. 33).

These two concerns of functionalist semiology can be illustrated by using, yet again, the analogy of chess. The interest in semiological systems is analogous with concentrating on the (abstract) rules of chess: viewing individual games from the angle of these rules, rather than 'inductively' viewing the rules from the angle of particular moves in particular games. The interest in a typology of 'signs' is somewhat analogous with concentrating on the various capacities of chess-piece types, these being the (abstract) elements of the 'systems of chess' whose uses are manifested in individual games.

Functional semiology attaches itself closely to the Saussurean dictate according to which 'semiology is the science that studies the life of signs within society' (Saussure, 1916). In consistent fashion, it interprets this dictate as logically implying that *semiotics includes linguistics* within its scope. Functionalists explicitly reject the Barthesian position according to which the 'universe' of language is greater than, and inclusive of, that of all other semiological systems (Barthes, 1967a). Thus, for functionalism, semiology is, strictly speaking, the parent-discipline – for all that, to date, more care has been lavished on its daughter-discipline, linguistics, with the result that the latter has a more highly developed and sophisticated range of notions and models to offer.

Where some functionalists fail to be wholly consistent is in the conception of semiology as falling into two categories: (1) languages, (2) (other) semiological systems. The inconsistency does not reside, of course, in this perfectly valid dichotomy, but in what some functionalists make of it (for example, Martinet, 1973), that is, in the 'shifted' position according to which the eventual scope of semiology is formulated as comprising only non-linguistic semiological systems. While in practice it may be true that it is linguists who describe languages, while semiologists only describe non-linguistic semiological systems, it is none the less clear that the original Saussurean position attaches languages and linguistics to the domain of semiology, whereas the 'shifted' position contradicts this by placing languages and linguistics outside that domain.

The problem is closely connected with a strategical dilemma, formulated by Jeanne Martinet in the following terms (Martinet, 1980): (*a*) 'Should we start with the study and analysis of the simplest and most rudimentary sign-systems and proceed gradually toward more elaborate ones . . .?' Or (*b*) 'should we concentrate first on a very complex but well delimited object, namely language [and then] . . . widen our field and test the adequacy of our methodology and conceptual apparatus, revise them when necessary and emerge with an original semiological theory derived from our initial linguistic one?'

Although the second alternative actually makes linguistics the parent-discipline of semiology (which is not in line with the explicit rejection of trans-linguistic semiology), it is this alternative that is chosen by Jeanne Martinet. As it happens, one's choice need not fall on either of the above alternatives; the preferable alternative would be to start out by building a theory (from general semiological considerations) that is powerful enough to permit the development of notions and models for the description of any semiological system, whether linguistic or non-linguistic. (This is what is attempted in the theory of axiomatic functionalism; see Chapter 7, pp. 186–8.)

6.1.2 Buyssens' Definition of the Scope of Semiology

With a view to the somewhat controversial nature of the way some functionalists solve the problems connected with the relationship of languages to semiological systems of a non-linguistic type, I propose to concentrate on Eric Buyssens' more 'purist' exposition of the scope of semiology (Buyssens, 1943).

For a start, Buyssens adheres strictly to a logical interpretation of the Saussurean position: '*Seul le point de vue sémiologique permet de déterminer scientifiquement l'objet de la linguistique.*' (Only the semiological viewpoint can lead to the scientific determination of the objectives of linguistics.)

Secondly, Buyssens' exposition leaves us in no doubt that the scope of semiology is intended to be strictly limited to those phenomena in which the following three characteristics coincide: (1) conventionality, (2) intention to communicate, (3) membership of a set. That is to say, the scope is set at a fairly restricted (though by no means over-restricted) level – which invites comparison with other, more elastic, conceptions of the domain of semiology – excluding from the domain phenomena that happen to communicate without depending on conventions implying a degree of social accord (compare Searle's notion of 'constitutive conventions'; Chapter 4, Section 4.5.3, p. 107). For instance, although the action of a dog scratching at the door may convey the message that the dog wants to be let in, although this action displays an intention to communicate, and although 'scratching at the door' may constitute a *type* of behaviour belonging to a canine repertoire (membership of a set) along with other types of intentionally communicative behaviour, this action falls, nevertheless, outside the scope of semiotics proper, since it lacks the third necessary ingredient: that of being determined by a convention.

On the other hand, if I use a system of classifying my lecture notes, no matter how conventional this system may be, and no matter to what extent it constitutes a repertoire (set) of types of classificatory index, the phenomenon will fall outside the scope of semiology proper, since its use lacks the ingredient of an intention to communicate.

Equally, if I agree, on a particular occasion, with a particular friend that I will signal to him that the plan to rob a bank is on, by hanging my wig out of the window – a signal that will undoubtedly depend on the convention agreed between the two of us, and that will undoubtedly manifest an intention to communicate – this phenomenon will fall outside the scope of semiotics (which is just as well, for otherwise that scope would become quite unmanageable), for the reason that there is no particular repertoire, set, or system of which this one-time signal forms a part.

The criterion of conventionality seems to be relatively easy to operate, types of action depending on ('constitutive') conventions being fairly sharply distinguished from other types of action. The criterion of intention to communicate raises certain 'metaphysical' questions concerning the difficulty of positively demonstrating the existence of an intention (though it must be said that many philosophers are relatively happy to work with this notion; see for example Searle, Chapter 4, Section 4.7.3, pp. 115–6). However, in practical terms, this criterion seems to be capable of a fairly clearcut operation.

The criterion of membership of a set seems to me to require the most difficult decisions and to be most in need of explanation in this outline of the position contributed to functional semiology by Buyssens. Even by reflecting back on my example of hanging my wig out of the window in order to signal that the bank robbery is on, we can begin to appreciate the problem when we note that, effectively, there are two types of signal, and two types of message involved in this once-off convention: (*a*) hanging the wig out of the window = robbery is on, (*b*) *not* hanging the wig out of the window = robbery is off.

These two possibilities are interdependent and mutually determine each other's values by being opposed to one another. Consequently, there is a kind of minimal 'network of values' involved here, which implies that the signal in question does belong to a repertoire, in fact, is a member of a set of two types of behaviour which cannot be isolated from one another without both of them losing their identities and their ability to function in a communicative manner.

In short, membership of a set is to be understood as 'belonging to a network of values' such as is envisaged in the Saussurean conception of a 'system' and exemplified in the relationship that holds together the types of chess-piece in the system of chess to the exclusion of everything else. However, chess is a very simple analogy which does not do justice to the difficulties of deciding the extension of semiological 'networks'. The example of 'Christian names' illustrates this difficulty admirably: (*a*) Is there one single network to which all 'Christian names' (used in all communities that have such things) should be assigned? (*b*) Is there a separate network of 'Christian names' for each linguistic community, but each forming a set that is not part of any given language? (c) Is there a separate network of 'Christian names' for each linguistic community, forming a subset, in each case, of a particular language?

The second problem is that it seems that any conventional and intentional signal, no matter how isolated and individualistic it may appear to be, implies the possibility of an 'on'-state and an 'off'-state, without which it could not, in principle, have a value at all. While it may be difficult to convince people that a single entity can constitute a set (yet in terms of set-theory this is perfectly allowable), it is equally difficult to see how, as soon as two entities are involved, one can be prevented from being convinced that both of them are members of a set. (The same consideration will come up again when we consider Prieto's *'code à sème unique'* as one of the possible types of semiological system.)

It seems, in short, that, even in Buyssens' excellent definition, the borderline of semiology stays somewhat indistinct in the one respect of deciding when to assign types of phenomenon to sets that constitute interdependent networks, and belong to the domain of semiology by virtue of this membership of a set.

In contrast with the restrictive attitude of Buyssens, an attitude shared by Georges Mounin (1968, 1970), there is a tendency within functional semiology to treat the scope of semiology as elastic and expandable. Thus while Buyssens and Mounin would offer resistance to extending semiology to cover, for instance, the description of art (paintings, music, sculpture, drama, dance, architecture, and so on; Buyssens, 1943), or the description of genetic codes or animal behaviour (Mounin, 1968), there is an identifiable directive within functionalist semiology to attempt semiological analyses in various of these, from a 'purist' viewpoint external, areas. The tendency is understandable if one observes that functionalist semiology needs to compete with semiological approaches that have no scruples about extending the empire of semiology virtually over the whole of culture (cf. Barthes, Chapter 5).

6.2.1 Types of Semiological System

The pioneering ideas of Buyssens offer three main dimensions (or parameters) for the classification of semiological systems (in Buyssens' terminology called *'sémies'*): (1) *systematic* versus *asystematic;* (2) *extrinsic* versus *intrinsic*; (3) *direct* versus *substitutive*.

The resulting classification has been, to a large extent, adopted (sometimes adapted, or further developed) within functionalist semiology as a whole.

In order to attempt an explanation of Buyssens' categories of *'sémie'*, we need both to refer back to what has been said in the foregoing section and to make use of a notion of *'sème'*, which, however, cannot be completely clarified until we come to the section dealing with the typology of indices. The notion *'sème'* can perhaps best be understood as referring to any element that can be used *as it stands* for the conveying of a message – an element, of course, that is dependent on a convention, and that must manifest an intention to communicate, if it is to function at all. That is to say, a 'complete' sentence of a particular language, a sign in the Highway Code, the green light in the set of traffic lights – all these are examples of *'sèmes'*.

A *'sémie'* is a set, a network, of interdependent *'sèmes'* – interdependent in the sense that their values can only be conceived of in terms of the oppositions within the set in question. In Buyssens' terminology (unlike in Saussure's), this interdependence does not define a 'system', but only a semiological set, that is, a *sémie*' is simply a repertoire of elements ready-made and complete for use in communication. This leaves open the at first sight rather unexpected possibility of a distinction between 'systemic' sets, and 'asystemic' sets. The distinction is made on the basis of the observation that some '*sémies*' allow for the decomposition of their '*sèmes*' into separately and constantly meaningful component units (in Buyssens' terminology 'signs', which makes for a certain confusion with the notion 'sign' in Saussure). So, for instance, the words and affixes in a linguistic sentence are separately and constantly meaningful units into which that sentence can be decomposed; but these component units, while they share with '*sèmes*' the property of a constant signification, are not like '*sèmes*', because, in themselves, they are not ready-made for use in communication.

Likewise, a '*sème*' of the Highway Code may be decomposable, say, into a blue circular field (with the constant meaning of 'obligation') and a white arrow (with the constant meaning of 'follow direction indicated'). These component 'signs' resemble '*sèmes*' in their constancy of conventional meaning, but differ essentially from '*sèmes*' by not being capable, as they stand (that is, unless they are in combination with some other, appropriate 'sign'), of immediate use in communication.

In fine, what makes a '*sémie*' systemic is the fact that its '*sèmes*' are systematically (shall we say, according to certain 'rules') constructed out of 'signs' belonging to a basic inventory. For this is what is implied by saying that '*sèmes*' are decomposable into 'signs', in view of the fact that the 'analytic' notion of decomposition and the 'synthetic' notion of construction are merely two sides of the same coin.

As opposed to '*sémies*' that are systemic in this sense of making use of ('rules' of) combination, there are '*sémies*' that are no more than simple lists of alternative, uncombinable (and unanalysable) '*sèmes*'. Such '*sémies*' constitute the category of 'asystemic' semiological systems (an unfortunate usage, especially in translation, but perfectly sensible once the terms are understood). In fact, traffic lights constitute such an 'asystemic' repertoire – a '*sémie*' consisting simply of a set of four alternative types of element, each with its conventional meaning, each a complete '*sème*':

(1)   red light = stop,
(2)   red and amber lights = prepare to go,
(3)   green light = go,
(4)   amber light = prepare to stop.

The second dimension of the classification of '*sémies*' in Buyssens is one that, strictly speaking, has its proper place in the typology of indices (where it will be more fully discussed), but which makes its influence felt on the '*sémies*' of which particular types of '*sème*' are the message-bearing members. For instance, a '*sémie*' whose '*sèmes*' are designed as schematic diagrams of objects (say, the stylised picture of a man and of a woman, to indicate 'gentlemen's toilet' and 'ladies' toilet', respectively), would be considered a different type of '*sémie*' from one in which there is no representational motivation at the root of the design of the '*sèmes*' (for example, algebraic formulae are totally lacking in such 'iconic' motivation; cf. Peirce, Chapter 1, Section 1.3.8, p. 30). Semiological sets ('*sémies*') of the former type are called 'intrinsic', those of the latter type, 'extrinsic'. It seems that Buyssens does not make explicit allowances for a type of 'mixed' semiological set with members that are 'iconic' as well as members that are wholly arbitrary.

The third dimension of the classification functionalism inherits from Buyssens is based on the observation that some '*sémies*' provide '*sèmes*' whose messages are perceived, interpreted and reacted to in an immediately practical way, that is, these '*sèmes*' directly convey information about reality, without needing to be further processed through the intermediary of some other semiological system. On the other hand, it appears that other '*sémies*' require the subsequent interpretation of their '*sèmes*' in some further semiological system before the ultimate message intended can be deciphered. '*Sémies*' of the first type are referred to as 'direct', those of the second type as 'substitutive'.

Thus, for instance, the messages of the Highway Code are immediate, and do not need the intermediary of any other system (they need neither be 'translated', say, into a language, nor deciphered through the application of any other semiological system) to be fully grasped and appropriately responded to. This is not to say, of course, that one cannot 'translate' a '*sème*' of the Highway Code by saying, for instance, that it '*means*' *drivers must follow the direction indicated by an arrow*, only that this 'translation' is unnecessary; the Highway Code '*sème*' has that 'meaning' quite independently of the linguistic 'translation'.

A written language, however, seems to require two stages for the full interpretation of its '*sèmes*': in the first stage, the '*sèmes*' of the system are read, that is to say, converted over to the appropriate '*sèmes*' of the appropriate spoken language; in the second stage, the final messages are comprehended through the meanings of the '*sèmes*' of the spoken language. Accordingly, written languages, understood through the intermediary of a spoken language for which they 'substitute' (whose '*sèmes*' they 'record' in written form), would be classed as 'substitutive' semiological systems. (This, however, is only correct if reading – not necessarily reading aloud – actually necessitates the intermediate reconstruction of the '*sèmes*' of a spoken language, which can hardly be the case with a really accomplished reader, or with a foreign reader who has only a 'reading' knowledge of a language he cannot speak at all. In other words, written sentences could be argued to have meanings reconstructable independently of their conversion into speech, that is, directly accessible meanings.)

A '*sémie*' such as the Morse code would be classified as 'substitutive to the second degree'. In a first stage of operations, the '*sèmes*' of Morse are converted (deciphered) into alphabetic letters of a particular written language; the resulting sequence of letters is then, in a second stage, interpreted as a '*sème*' of a written language, and accordingly converted into speech; in the third stage, the final message intended emerges through the interpretation of the meanings of sentences of a spoken language. (While, operationally speaking, this account seems to be plausible enough, it is also true that the Morse code only communicates letters and numbers which are, in fact, its ultimate messages – and it can do this perfectly successfully even if the sequence of letters so communicated cannot be further processed in a written, and then a spoken, language. Such a use of Morse code, without an ultimate linguistic message, would still be a perfectly correct use of the Morse code – that is to say, the Morse code does not depend for its operation on the presence of messages beyond the conveying of alphabetical letters, numbers, and so on.)

Apart from the three valued dimensions of classification, Buyssens recognises also a number of possible dimensions (Buyssens, 1967), dimensions to which functionalists, in general, give little weight, since they are based on considerations not directly linkable to the functioning, and the functional structures, of semiological systems.

One such dimension is, of course, that of the *medium* in which a particular system is realised: vocal, auditory, colour, gestural, visual, tactile, gustative, and so on. A classification in this dimension is, indeed, quite possible (in common parlance, systems are often referred to according to their medium, for example, 'the language of *flowers*'), but it is not of very great interest, since it is clearly based on secondary matters of 'substance' (which is incidental to 'form'), as opposed to primary considerations of 'form'.

Equally, one could classify semiological systems (Buyssens, 1967) from a point of view of their pragmatic use in society; the everyday terms for such systems are, in fact, often conceived in this dimension: *traffic* lights, *Highway* Code, *deaf–and–dumb* language, and so on. Once again, however, the classification is, arguably, based on incidental considerations, the structure of a system being a primary and central factor presupposed by accessory details of the range of its social uses.

A further classificatory possibility (Buyssens, 1967) strikes me as less trivial, touching as it does on what is almost a 'controversy' between those functionalists who refer to semiological systems in general as 'codes' (Prieto, for example) and those who insist on an intrinsic difference between 'codes' and semiological systems that are not 'codes' (Buyssens, for example). The dichotomy is, in fact, between (*a*) *'sémies'* that operate with tacitly acquired conventions (such as languages); (*b*) *'sémies'* that operate with explicitly codified, written conventions (such as the Highway Code, Morse code).

Undoubtedly, true codes are of the second type, and the affiliation of *'sémies'* having tacit conventions to the category of 'codes' having explicit conventions could be rather misleading, for instance, in the sense of minimalising (wrongly) the descriptive problems of trying to 'reconstruct' the tacit 'code' underlying a *'sémie'* whose conventions have never been codified (this is, for instance, exactly what a linguistic description of an 'exotic' language tries to do). Thus, in so far as one is invited to take sides, it would be clearly preferable to come down on the side of those functionalists who refuse to extend the application of the term 'code' to semiological systems in general.

6.2.2 Prieto's Typology of Semiological Systems

Further elaboration of a functionalist classification of semiological systems is found in its clearest form in Prieto's formulation of the background to André Martinet's idea of the 'double articulation'. In this formulation (and indeed also in Buyssens, 1967), 'asystematic' semiological sets become 'systems with no economy', and finally (but in exactly the same sense), '*sémies*' with *no* articulation'. Likewise, 'systemic' semiological sets are explained as 'systems with some measure of economy', eventually to be identified as 'articulated semiological systems'.

Using Prieto's manner of presentation – but remembering that on this point we are dealing with a fundamental thesis common to functionalist semiology as a whole – a 'code' (semiological system) lacks economy as long as it is a mere list of '*sèmes*', with no possibilities of analysis into smaller elements, elements whose deployment in constructions would permit the system to be richer in the range of messages it can convey than it is in units requiring separate memorisation. Thus, for instance, a 'code' by which room numbers in, say, a hotel are indicated simply at random, has as many unrelated '*sèmes*' as there are rooms, each having to be memorised separately in a fashion that is in no sense 'labour-saving', that is, it is 'uneconomical'. The uneconomic nature of such a system is directly, and tautologically, related to the fact that each '*sème*' is an unanalysable whole (not a construction made up of 'factorial' units); that is to say, there is *no 'articulation' of 'sèmes'* in the system.

By contrast, if the rooms of a hotel are numbered (Prieto, 1966) in such a way that the left-hand index stands for the number of the floor on which the room is located, whereas the right-hand index stands for the serial number of the room, indicating its distance from the main staircase, then each '*sème*' of the system is a combination of two factors into which it can be articulated. Thus a '*sème*', say, '311' (indicating the eleventh room along the corridor on the third floor) is articulable into the two *factors*: '3—' = room on third floor, '–11' = eleventh room from main staircase.

The entire set of '*sèmes*' in this system can, in fact, be conceived of as logical multiplication of the set of left-hand units indicating floor number, and the set of right-hand units indicating sequence along the corridor (see Figure 6.1), producing, systematically and 'logically', the complex '*sèmes*': '11', '12', etc., '21', '22', etc., '31', '32', . . . '311', etc. Needless to say, working out where a room is by noting, from the left-hand factor, what floor it is on, and from the right-hand factor, how far along the corridor it is, clearly is a more 'effort-saving' and economical process than having to memorise, one by one, where to find 'the green room', 'the bridal suite', 'the Presidential suite', and so on. It is equally clear that the economy is directly attributable to the 'factorial' nature of the '*sèmes*' in the system, this latter being neither more nor less than the analysability – the so-called 'articulation' – of those '*sèmes*'; that is to say, 'economy' = 'articulation' (but compare the axiomatic functionalist view of 'articulation', Chapter 7, Section 7.3.3, p. 193). As we see ('rules' of) combinability of component units connect the '*sèmes*' of an 'economical', or 'articulated' semiological system, making this type of system the exact

$$\left.\begin{array}{l} \text{'1--'} \\ \text{'2--'} \\ \text{'3--'} \\ \text{etc.} \end{array}\right\} \quad \mathbf{\times} \quad \left\{\begin{array}{l} \text{'--1'} \\ \text{'--2'} \\ \text{'--3'} \\ \text{'--4'} \\ \text{etc.} \end{array}\right.$$

Figure 6.1

equivalent (though differently named and more precisely explained) of the type earlier called 'systemic *sémie*'.

The notion of 'economy of cost' (Prieto, 1966), to which the above examples of 'economy' belong, has further ramifications that are a reconstruction of the implications of André Martinet's historic concept of the 'double articulation' of language. These ramifications can be tabulated, in advance of further explanation, in the following scheme shown in Figure 6.2.

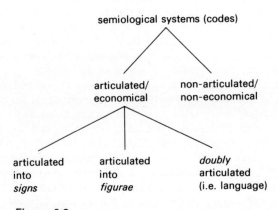

Figure 6.2

In order to make the scheme comprehensible, it must be pointed out that each '*sème*', by analogy with the Saussurean 'sign' – and also each component sign into which a '*sème*' is analysed (where such analysis is possible) – is to be conceived of as an entity with two integrated facets: content (the 'signified' aspect) and expression (the 'signifier' aspect). Thus a global (unanalysed) '*sème*' can be represented as in Figure 6.3.

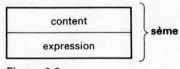

Figure 6.3

Now, if, as in the case of the articulated system of room-numbering, the factors of the '*sèmes*' of the system are signs with a constancy in their 'signified', not only in their 'signifying', aspects, then the articulation cuts across the whole of the '*sème*', producing articulated units in which content and expression are still integrated (these are the units that Buyssens and Prieto call 'signs'). The situation can be visualised as in Figure 6.4.

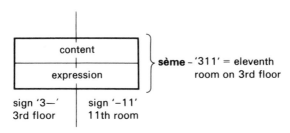

Figure 6.4

However, there are other, highly economical semiological systems (for example, Morse code) which exemplify a second type of articulation (Martinet's 'second articulation', cf. Martinet, 1960), an articulation that affects only the expression side of a '*sème*'. That is to say, the '*sème*' is not constructed out of signs (into which it could again be articulated through a 'factorial' analysis), and yet it is neither isolated from other '*sèmes*' by being totally different from them, nor uneconomically constituted. It is linked to other '*sèmes*' whose expressions are different (systematic and 'rule-governed') combinations of one and the same, relatively small, set of basic units of form (but no corresponding 'meaning'). These basic units of form, participating only in the expression aspect of '*sèmes*' are referred to as *figurae* (cf. axiomatic functionalism, Chapter 7, Section 7.5.1, p. 205). The economy achieved by means of an articulation of expression into figurae is illustrated by the example of Morse code, where all expressions of '*sèmes*' are, in a highly economic way, constructed out of combinations of two figurae: 'short' and 'long'. Thus, the articulation of the expression of 'long–short' = letter 'n' is an example, *par excellence*, of an articulation into figurae: Martinet's 'second articulation' (see Figure 6.5).

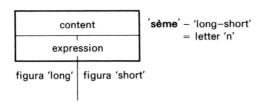

Figure 6.5

The final category of semiological systems in the scheme (Figure 6.2), that of 'doubly articulated' systems, is, according to the Martinetian theory, the category of true languages (but see the discussion in Chapter 7, Section 7.3.5, pp. 197–9). This is a category of semiological systems that make use, not only of an articulation into signs (the level of economy of Martinet's 'first articulation'), but also of a further articulation into figurae (the level of economy of Martinet's 'second articulation'). Since languages are identified with this type of doubly-economical system, we can illustrate the representation of a 'double articulation' through an example from English (see Figure 6.6).

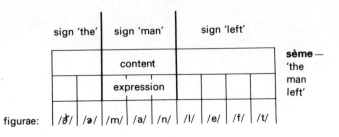

Figure 6.6

6.2.3   Further Categories of Prieto's Typology

Prieto increases the repertoire of semiological classification by adding a number of further categories, which are of sufficient interest to merit discussion here.

First, alongside the 'economy of cost' which is at the root of the classification discussed in the foregoing section, Prieto also discusses another type of economy, which he calls 'quantitative', but to which I shall refer as 'economy of specificity'. This criterion establishes a dichotomy between semiological systems with no 'economy of specificity', and systems that offer means of 'economy of specificity'.

In order to explain the notion of 'economy of specificity', it will be most convenient to take a linguistic example (languages have the greatest potential with respect to this type of 'economy'). Supposing I want to make a date with a friend on 'July 1st at 2.00 p.m.'. According to my needs to be specific, and in view of what I know my friend will take for granted, I have at my disposal a number of *'sèmes'* of English, some of which I shall list in order of increasing specificity (that is, precision in details communicated):

(a)   'See you, you know when.'
(b)   'See you in July.'
(c)   'See you on July 1st.'
(d)   'See you at two o'clock on July 1st.'
(e)   'See you at two p.m. on July 1st.'

From this set of alternatives, it is quite clear that languages, *par excellence*, offer various more or less specific and detailed ways of referring to what is basically the same piece of information: it is the same rendezvous to which I am referring, no matter which of these alternatives I use. However, if I think that my interlocutor needs to have 'everything spelt out', I may need to expend more energy by using the most clearly circumscribed, and therefore most specific of the alternatives listed. The 'specificity' of the information (for Prieto, the 'quantity') depends on the effort made in carefully circumscribing and limiting the range of potential messages that a '*sème*' could be understood to convey – an inverse ratio of the range of messages excluded (Prieto, 1964) from possible consideration. Thus the '*sème*' 'See you at 2 p.m. on July 1st' is more specific, more restricted, more circumscribed than the '*sème*' 'See you at 2 o'clock on July 1st' because, while the latter admits the possibility of the rendezvous being either at 02.00 hours or at 14.00 hours, the former only admits the possibility of 14.00 hours. It is the former, therefore, which has the greater specificity (for Prieto, 'quantity') of information.

As opposed to the additional effort needed in achieving a higher degree of specificity, languages, *par excellence*, offer more and more 'lazy' ways of 'saying the same thing'. From among the alternatives listed, it is the '*sème*' 'See you, you know when' that most clearly illustrates the way the speaker can save himself trouble by counting on the situation and the hearer's knowledge and memory to enable the hearer to reconstruct 'you know when' as '14.00 hours on July 1st'. (This is a case where speaker's 'economy' is liable to imply hearer's extra 'effort'.)

While languages – and, in principle at least, other semiological systems (though Prieto does not seem to think so) – offer choices between more or less specific '*sèmes*' that could answer the same referential need (see Figure 6.7), in other semiological systems, only one particular '*sème*' can convey a particular type of message (see Figure 6.8).

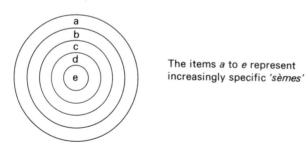

The items *a* to *e* represent increasingly specific '*sèmes*'

Figure 6.7

Such systems with no 'economy of specificity' are typified by codes like the Highway Code: in this code, there are no choices between more or less specific, more or less circumscribed, more or less 'effort-saving' ways of conveying, say, the message 'no parking', or 'no entry'. Systems of this type lack richness, and stylistic alternatives that can be used to 'vary the

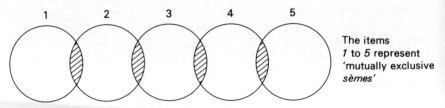

The items
1 to *5* represent
'mutually exclusive
sèmes'

Figure 6.8

tempo' of communication; 'bits of information' from '*sème*' to '*sème*' all have the same 'weight'. A code like this does not lend itself to literary/ artistic manipulation.

In the case of '*sémes*' regarded by Buyssens as being 'isolated' and falling outside of semiological systems, Prieto talks, instead, of two different types of code: (*a*) 'code with a Ø expression' ('*code à signifiant zéro*'), (*b*) 'single-*sème* code' ('*code à sème unique*').

The former category covers those systems which, although they appear to contain only one positive '*sème*' among their members, actually contain an 'on'-state and an 'off'-state (that is, *two* members). The 'off'-state, manifested simply as the absence of the positive features of the 'on'-state – as, for instance, not switching on the red light at a level crossing (which indicates that the track is meant to be clear), or, in my earlier example, not hanging my wig out of the window (which means the robbery is off) – is, for all its apparent 'zero-ness', ' meaningful '*sème*' indicating the negation of the meaning of the 'on-'state. A '*sème*' of this type – with an expression that requires 'doing nothing' (thence the idea of a Ø expression), but with a perfectly explicit meaning – is a '*sème*' with zero expression', and the code of which it is a member is a 'code with Ø expression'. (As a matter of fact, it is not only codes with just the two possibilities of an 'on-'state and an 'off-'state that may contain a '*sème*' with zero expression' as one of their members. However, the presence of an 'off-'state is only crucial when this is the only alternative '*sème*' opposed to an 'on-'state.)

The situation is rather different where there is an 'isolated' signal that carries a definite message when manifested, but whose absence is not normally interpreted as conveying any message at all. Thus, for instance, if I put a 'do not disturb' sign on my door, this indicates without a shadow of doubt that visitors will *not* be welcome; however, if I do *not* put out the sign, I am in no way conveying the opposite message, namely that visitors *will* be welcome. Or, to use Prieto's example, the carrying of a white stick positively indicates that the bearer has defective eyesight, whereas seeing someone *not* carrying a white stick does not indicate at all. Consequently, in examples like these, there is no question of a system (or set) containing an 'on'-state balanced by, and set off against, an opposing 'off'-state (manifested by Ø). There is nothing but an isolated '*sème*' that does not form even a rudimentary 'network' of two mutually opposed alternatives. Although Prieto refers to such '*sèmes*' as constituting 'single-*sème* codes', there does not seem to be sufficient logical justification for talking about a 'code' (semiological system) at all – if the facts are indeed correctly interpreted, and the '*sèmes*' in question are wholly isolated, then Buyssens' way of dealing with them as elements outside of '*sémies*' (*not* members of sets) and outside of semiology, is probably to be preferred.

Where Buyssens classifies '*sémies*' into 'direct' and 'substitutive' categories, Prieto contributes to functionalist semiology a three-way classification: (*a*) direct codes, (*b*) parallel codes, (*c*) substitutive codes.

Both direct, and substitutive, codes are to be understood in the way explained above. However, an intermediate category is proposed for those codes which are intrinsically direct – they can actually function perfectly well without one another – but are in a specially privileged relation of structural 'isomorphism'; that is, the structures of one 'reflect' or 'represent' (or even in a sense 'record') the structures of the other. This special relation of 'parallel' codes is proposed in particular with a view to the 'isomorphism' between, say, written English and spoken English. There is no '*sème*' of the one system that cannot be 'duplicated' by a particular '*sème*' of the other, which gives a very real basis to the idea of parallelism. (As for the degree of structural 'isomorphism', the well-known pecularities of English spelling effectively put a limit to the 'structure–to–structure' correspondence as soon as this is assessed on the level of Martinet's 'second articulation' into figurae.)

The notion of parallel codes allows functional semiology to posit a special relationship between a given spoken language and the appropriate corresponding written language; and to do so without the unfortunate implications of treating a written language as 'substitutive', whereas its comprehension is perfectly possible without going through the intermediary of speech.

By way of an 'appendix', it should be pointed out briefly, that Prieto's notions of 'notificative indication' and 'significative indication' (discussed in the independent chapter on Prieto's '*acte sémique*', Chapter 3, Sections 3.2.2 and 3.2.3, pp. 70 and 71) play a role in his conception of 'codes', especially with regard to the distinction between 'codes with Ø expression' and 'single-*sème* codes'. For instance, the fact that the red light at a level-crossing is not on contains as much notificative indication (that is, an intention to communicate) as does the flashing of that red light itself – and both, of course, have a significative indication (meaning). On the other hand, failing to put out a 'do not disturb' sign, or failing to carry a white stick, not only do not have significative indication, but cannot, in principle, do so, because they lack even a notificative indication (they are not likely to be interpreted as manifesting an intention to communicate).

6.3.1 The Typology of 'Indices'

The title of this section has caused me some terminological embarrassment for, while one knows perfectly well what subcategories are established by the typology, and the sum total of these subcategories makes it perfectly clear what kind of entities are being subclassified, one is at a loss to know what to call the main category at the apex of the typology. I have referred to the typology so far as being that of 'indices' (Jeanne Martinet refers to it as being that of 'signs'; Martinet, 1980), considering the term 'index' to be the most suitable general term for all types of entity whose generic function is the indication of some specific type of information. (The category corresponds to all intents and purposes to the wide sense of 'sign' as used by Peirce, but this latter term has a very much narrower sense in the Saussurean tradition, and is used in that narrow sense in the functionalist typology). Though 'index' would serve conveniently as a generic term, it is, unfortunately, already taken up as a term for one of the subcategories in the functionalist typology, which does not seem to leave any term available for designating the *genus* whose typology we are concerned with here. Using such terms as 'indicator', or 'signal' – which are also within the currency of a functionalist-type terminology – would not do either, for this would create the false impression that the typology belonged to the level of a theory of semiotic acts. This is obviously not the case; the typology does not classify tokens, but types: we are not dealing with individual acts, but with abstract, virtual entities that are, in the Saussurean sense, values or forms. (Using, once more, the analogy of chess, the typology is not one referring to the kinds of move that one might make in particular games, but to the types of piece that figure in the rules of the game in general.)

The terminological predicament in which I find myself leaves me no alternative (unless I resort to the confusing use of 'index' in two different senses, a wider and a narrower one) but to continue using the term 'index' in a way that is not typical of functional semiology, and to substitute the term '(natural) index' where functionalists would simply use the term 'index'. (I add merely that it is not my strange manner of exposition, but the improvidence and incomplete terminological rigour of functionalist semiology, that is responsible for the predicament, and for the contortions necessary for getting out of it.)

6.3.2   Foundations of the Typology of 'Indices'

The considerations made use of in classifying indices have somewhat eclectic origins – the notion of 'extrinsicness' comes from Buyssens, the notion of 'arbitrariness' from Saussure, the notion of 'iconicity' from Peirce. Functionalist semiology does, however, manage to integrate these notions into a fairly consistent scheme, and one that also succeeds in being fairly consonant with functionalism as a whole (but see the discrepancy between 'sign' as a subcategory in the typology, and 'sign' as a 'factorial' component of a *'sème'*, Section 6.3.4, p. 180).

As a preliminary to examining the definitions of subcategories of index – '(natural) index', 'icon', 'symbol' and 'sign' – it must be remembered that any index, though conceived of as an entity, is actually a correlation in which are integrated *two* aspects – in the manner of the Janus-like nature of the Saussurean 'sign'. These two aspects we may, at some slight risk of imposing too much of the conventional nature of 'signs' on the category of '(natural) indices', continue to call expression and content (in French *'signifiant'* and *'signifié'*, respectively). At any rate, the expression aspect of an index, while necessarily implying its relationship to a content, captures the formal properties of the index; the content aspect, on the other hand, while necessarily implying its relationship to an expression, concentrates on the meaning–bearing properties of the index. For instance, in the case of the warning lights at a level crossing, the expression aspect (symbolised where convenient as *EA*) is 'the flashing of a red disc' (implying, of course, a certain type of message); whereas the content aspect (symbolised where convenient as *CA*) is 'stop at the barrier' (implying, of course, a particular form for its expression).

Given what we have so far, the following questions arise almost automatically (thence the degree of integratedness in the typology that results from different answers to these questions, according to different types of index):

(*a*)   What is the nature of *EA* (in a particular index)?
(*b*)   What is the nature of *CA* (in a particular index)?
(*c*)   What is the nature of the relationship by virtue of which *EA* and *CA* are linked in a particular index?

With a view to these questions, the properties of 'naturalness', 'arbitrariness', 'intrinsic motivation', 'convention' and 'intentionality' begin to find the level on which they can operate, and by their operation, take care of the entire typology of indices.

As for 'naturalness', this property is best understood, perhaps, in contradistinction with 'artificiality'. Types of phenomenon whose explanation hinges entirely on 'physical' (in a wide sense, that is, including biological, chemical, electrical, and so on) chains of cause and effect are to be designated as 'natural'. As soon, however, as a chain of cause and effect is, in some way, incomplete – in such a way as to necessitate the role of some additional, not purely causal, factor in the explanation of a phenomenon – that type of phenomenon is interpreted as 'artificial'.

In functional semiology, 'non-naturalness' (= 'artificiality') is not equated with 'arbitrariness', for this latter (according to the functionalist way of interpreting Saussure) is set off, rather, against the notion of 'motivation'. That is to say, in this approach, 'arbitrariness' = 'absence of motivation'. Now it so happens that indices – especially with regard to the choice of a particular expression being linked to a particular content – may display various degrees of 'motivation' (and various types, for that matter, for example, historical, political, social, educational, and so on). The type of motivation, however, that is of interest to the typology of indices in functional semiology is particularly that of a 'resemblance' (or some similar mental link-up) between properties of form involved in the *EA* of an index and properties of objects involved in the *CA* of that index. That is to say, the type of motivation in question is at least strongly reminiscent of Peirce's 'iconicity' – though, of course, such motivation has also been signalled by Saussure, especially in connection with *onomatopoeic* words.

Buyssens' distinction between 'extrinsic' and 'intrinsic' categories of '*sème*' is, in fact, a way of presenting the difference between indices motivated by an internal 'naturalness' that links a particular *EA* with a particular *CA* (for example, there would seem to be something of a 'natural' motivation in referring to a particular kind of noise as a 'bang') and indices motivated completely extrinsically, by imposing a wholly arbitrary convention (for example, what else but the imposition of a convention could link the shape 'Ø' with its mathematical signification of 'zero'). While on the subject of examples of 'intrinsic' and 'extrinsic' indices, it is worth mentioning – merely in the form of a suggestion, for the moment – the possibility that the association of 'red' with danger (in traffic lights, highway signals, level crossing lights, flags, and so on) may constitute a borderline case between extrinsically imposed conventions and intrinsically 'natural' motivation.

The property of 'extrinsicness' – but not that of 'arbitrariness' – is equated with that of total 'conventionality'. An index is 'extrinsic' if, and only if, it depends entirely on a wholly arbitrary convention, while indices motivated up to a point by arbitrary and conventional factors may still possess sufficient 'naturalness' of motivation to count as 'intrinsic' indices. Conventions presuppose an 'agreement' (which may be entirely tacit) between at least two conscious participants who know and share that convention. Thus, in any realisation of a conventional index as a concrete semiotic act, it is always and by necessity possible to identify both a sender and a receptor.

Conventionality (in the sense of a shared 'consciousness') sharply distinguishes between two types of index: one resembling the interpretation of symptoms, the other, the production and interpretation of signals (Buyssens, 1943). Thus, for instance, interpreting the purring of a cat as indicating that the said cat is contented is not essentially and qualitatively different from what a doctor does when diagnosing an illness by interpreting certain classic symptoms. Furthermore, first appearances apart, when a dog scratches at the door and is understood to be 'expressing a wish' to be let in, we are still not in the presence of a fully-fledged signal, for the dog cannot be supposed to constitute the kind of conscious participant with whom, by tacit 'agreement', one may share the knowledge of a convention.

For fully-fledged signals manifesting conventionality, therefore, we probably have to look uniquely at 'agreements' – both tacit and explicit – concerning shared conventions between human subjects. Yet, we may well be slightly at a loss when confronted by communication behaviour in social bees. Bees certainly appear to share a 'knowledge' of what might be interpreted as the 'conventions' of a system for communication – unless we insist that this 'knowledge' is purely instinctual, and that instinctual 'agreement' is not consonant with the possibility of shared conventions.

The property of 'intentionality' – which, incidentally, distinguishes the purring of a cat from the case of a dog deliberately scratching at the door – implies the assured place, in a particular index, of an intention to communicate on every occasion of the use of that index. In this respect, not only conventional, man-instituted, indices, but also indices such as those underlying the communicative behaviour of a dog scratching at the door to be let in, or the communicative behaviour of social bees in indicating a source of nectar to other members of the hive, fall clearly into the same category. (Intention to communicate is so much part of, say, the action of a dog scratching at the door that if, on the door being opened, the dog does not fulfil the 'expressed wish' of coming in, we are liable to conclude that the dog has 'changed its mind'.)

6.3.3 Functionalist Categories of 'Index'

Having filled in the background, we are now in a fair position to explain, illustrate and examine the four categories of index: (1) (natural) index, (2) icon, (3) symbol, (4) sign.

(Natural) Index
In the case of (natural indices, the defining properties, according to functionalist semiology (Martinet, 1973) are the following:

(*a*)   EA is a phenomenon occurring naturally (independently of a contrived or artificial production for semiological purposes); that is to say, EA is *not arbitrary*;

(*b*)   CA is a natural phenomenon (existing independently of semiological purposes or effects); that is to say, CA is *not arbitrary*;

(*c*)   the link between EA and CA is *not arbitrary* (it exists, in this case, by virtue of *causality*);

(*d*)   the phenomenon (that gives substance to) EA and the phenomenon (that gives substance to) CA are natural and necessary corollaries – the link between EA and CA depends on this *necessary coexistence*;

(*e*)   EA and CA are separate in reality and in one's consciousness of reality – their identities cannot be confused, since these *identities do not coincide*;

(*f*)   EA and CA *do not resemble one another* (or, at any rate, if they do so, this is not pertinent to motivating the link between them);

(*g*)   the index *cannot presuppose an intention to communicate* (the fact that the link between EA and CA is natural/causal precludes this possibility in any case).

Example: '(natural) index': $\dfrac{\text{smoke}}{\text{EA}}$ (indicates) $\dfrac{\text{fire}}{\text{CA}}$

(*a*)   *smoke* (EA) is a naturally occurring phenomenon – independent of semiological artifice;

(*b*)   *fire* (CA) is a natural phenomenon – existing independently of semiological purposes or effects;

(*c*)   the link between *smoke* and *fire* (as EA and CA of an index, respectively) is assured by virtue of *causality* – it is not arbitrary;

(*d*)   *smoke* (the phenomenon giving substance to EA) and *fire* (the phenomenon giving substance to CA) *must* coexist side-by-side – the working of the index depends on this *necessary coexistence*;

(*e*)   *smoke* and *fire* are separate phenomena in reality and in one's consciousness of reality – their identities do not coincide in spite of their temporal co-occurrence, and cannot be confused;

(f) *smoke* and *fire* do not resemble one another (in any pertinent way) – at any rate, the link between them is not motivated by a resemblance;

(g) *smoke* indicates *fire* regardless of, and in the absence of, any intention to communicate. (The fact that fire causes smoke in a wholly natural way precludes the interference of a communicative intention – on whose part?)

Icon
The defining properties of *icons* as understood in functional semiology (Martinet, 1973) are the following:

(a) EA is a phenomenon occurring independently of contrivance or artifice *for semiological purposes*; that is to say, EA is *not arbitrary*;

(b) CA is a phenomenon existing independently of *semiological* purposes or effects; that is to say, CA is *not arbitrary*;

(c) the link between EA and CA is *not arbitrary* (it exists, in this case, by virtue of a strong natural motivation);

(d) the phenomenon (that gives substance to) EA and the phenomenon (that gives substance to) CA must be comparable in a situation of spatial coexistence, but the index can function when the two are not side by side – that is to say, the question of whether coexistence is necessary has the answer 'yes and no';

(e) EA and CA are separate in reality, and separable in one's consciousness, but they are also liable to be confused – that is to say, one cannot categorically answer the question of whether their *identities coincide or not* (another 'yes and no' answer);

(f) there is a *positive resemblance* between EA and CA, and this resemblance is the motivating factor, *par excellence*, for the link by which EA represents CA;

(g) the index *may or may not* manifest an intention to communicate, but does not depend on such an intention.

Example: 'icon': $\dfrac{\text{photograph of Nessie}}{\text{EA}}$ (represents)

$$\frac{\text{Nessie}}{\text{CA}} \qquad \text{(the Loch Ness monster)}$$

(a) The *photograph* – no matter how much contrivance and artifice may go into it – is essentially a natural object, and what is more to the point, is *not contrived for semiological purposes* from which it is independent; in this sense, then, the *photograph* is not arbitrary.

(b) *Nessie* is (understood to be) a natural phenomenon – definitely one that exists (if at all) independently of semiological purposes and effects.

(c) The link between the *photograph of Nessie* and *Nessie* is assured by a strong natural motivation (along the lines that the *photograph* is a visual recording of *Nessie*).

(d) If one wanted to be satisfied that the photograph is really a 'good likeness' of Nessie (that is, that the representational link really holds), one should have to compare the photograph (EA) and its object (CA) by having them side by side, that is, as coexisting objects. Also, for the genuineness of the photograph, it must be supposed that, at the time of the photograph being taken, the film in the camera was actually exposed to the light-waves reflected by the *real* Nessie. Thereafter, however, the photograph continues to represent Nessie even if she disappears forever. Thus, in a way, coexistence of photograph and subject are necessarily presupposed, yet, in another sense, this coexistence does not need to occur for the photograph to continue representing its subject; thence the 'yes and no' answer to the question of whether coexistence of EA and CA is necessary.

(e) The *photograph of Nessie* and the 'real' *Nessie* can be separated in reality, but are separated with somewhat more difficulty in one's consciousness of reality, since it is only a (genuine) *photograph* that could, to date, give credibility to the identity of *Nessie*, as such. Thus, the problem of the genuineness of *Nessie* may in general boil down to that of the genuineness of *photographs of Nessie* – an indication of some degree of coincidence between the two identities.

(f) There has to be a positive resemblance between the *photograph* and *Nessie*, for this resemblance is the motivating factor for the link by which the photograph is taken to represent Nessie.

(g) The photograph of Nessie may manifest, but does not depend on, an intention to communicate – since its representative function is already fully motivated by a natural resemblance.

The example of photographs, although frequently cited by functional semiologists, is actually rather a special case. As it happens, one could make out an equally good case for attributing the motivation of the link between photograph and subject to a causal relation, or for attributing this motivation to a resemblance. The case for the latter has already been pointed out, since this is how photographs come to be interpreted as icons and not as natural indices. The case for the former simply needs a reconstruction of the causal chain of events from the moment that light from an object penetrates the open shutter of a camera, for, from then on, there is a perfect causal explanation of the photographic process leading to the point when one is finally in possession of the finished photograph. This would be sufficient reason for suggesting that the link between EA and CA is no less guaranteed by causality here than in the case of the (natural) index smoke indicating fire. It would seem, therefore, that photographs may constitute an in-between category of indices that are both iconic and indexical.

In order not to base our exemplification entirely on a case that is somewhat peculiar, it will be just as well to give a second example, this time of an icon that is unequivocally iconic.

Example: 'icon': $\dfrac{\text{portrait of Elizabeth I}}{\text{EA}}$ (represents)

$$\dfrac{\text{Elizabeth I}}{\text{CA}}$$

(a) the *portrait* exists as a natural phenomenon, independent of any semiological contrivance or artifice – in this sense, it is not arbitrary;

(b) *Elizabeth I* is (was) a natural phenomenon existing independently of semiological purposes or effects;

(c) the link between the *portrait* and *Elizabeth I* is assured by a strong natural motivation (that is, the belief that the portrait is *of* Elizabeth I);

(d) the only way to be sure that the *portrait* is a 'good likeness' would be to put it side by side with the real *Elizabeth I*, but, in the absence of this possibility, we have to be content with the supposition that at least the artist who painted the portrait had access to both the picture and its subject at one and the same time (that is, in coexistence with one another). At the same time, we have to admit that the portrait continues to represent *Elizabeth I* out of context of any possible coexistence between it and its subject. Thus, the question of whether coexistence is necessary for this icon is again 'yes and no';

(e) the *portrait* and *Elizabeth I* are separate in reality, and separable in one's consciousness, but as *Elizabeth I* (as a visual entity) is known only through her portraits, there is likely to be a certain amount of confusion between the two identities. This confusion is evidenced, perhaps, by the fact that, on being presented with the portrait, one is likely to say 'oh, that's Elizabeth I', rather than (the strictly correct) 'oh, that's a *portrait* of Elizabeth I'. In other words, continued consciousness of the appearance of Elizabeth I is, at the very least, 'parasitic' on contemporary portraits in a way that trades on a partial coincidence between the identity of the real Elizabeth I and the identity of her *portraits*;

(f) there has to be a positive resemblance between the *portrait* and Elizabeth I, for this resemblance is the (and, in this case, really *the*) motivating factor for the link by which the portrait is taken to represent Elizabeth I;

(g) the *portrait* of *Elizabeth I* may manifest, but does not depend on, an intention to communicate – its representative function is already fully motivated by (and this time *only* by) a natural resemblance.

Symbol
In functionalist semiology (Martinet, 1973), the defining properties of symbols are listed as follows:

(a) EA *may or may not* be *arbitrary* (that is to say, it may be a phenomenon that can occur without being artificially produced for *semiological* purposes, or it may be a phenomenon that one is unlikely to encounter out of context with a need to convey a message);

(*b*)   CA is a phenomenon existing independently of *semiological* purposes and effects; that is to say, it is *not arbitrary*;

(*c*)   the link between EA and CA is *partly motivated and partly arbitrary*; at any rate, in spite of its degree of motivatedness, it also displays a considerable degree of *conventionality*;

(*d*)   EA and CA *do not need* to coexist side by side for the index to be effective;

(*e*)   EA and CA are separate and *non-coincident* objects in reality – no one in his right mind would for a moment confuse the identity of the one with that of the other;

(*f*)   EA and CA *do not resemble one another* (in any pertinent way) – and if they did so, this would be irrelevant to motivating the link between them;

(*g*)   the index necessarily presupposes an *intention to communicate*, this intention being its very *raison d'être*.

Example: 'symbol': $\underset{\text{EA}}{\text{🚹}}$ (symbolises) gentlemen's $\underset{\text{CA}}{\underline{\text{toilet}}}$

(*a*)   It is virtually impossible to decide whether 🚹 is, as such, arbitrary or not – it could, perhaps, occur independently of any communicative corollaries; on the other hand, it is hard to maintain that it is just an ordinary, naturally occurring phenomenon. Fortunately, it is not necessary to decide the issue since symbols belong to a category of indices that *may or may not* be arbitrary (that is, the issue is not crucial).

(*b*)   A *gentlemen's toilet* (CA) is a perfectly ordinary, functional object that is in no way dependent on semiological considerations (it does not even have to be labelled as to what it is in order to be what it is) – consequently, as an object, it is not semiologically arbitrary.

(*c*)   The link between 🚹 and *gentlemen's toilet* is both conventional (an extrinsic convention is needed in order to impose the link, which is otherwise not all that obvious) and motivated (it is not wholly arbitrary that, of all possible EAs, the choice fell on a schematic figure representing, in a distantly iconic way, the shape of a man). It may have been said that a symbol is, in a manner of speaking, 'indirectly iconic' – at any rate, it seems clear enough that symbols form, in this respect, a category falling in between icons and signs.

(*d*)   A gentlemen's toilet does not have to display a figure 🚹 on it, nor does the figure 🚹 have to appear necessarily on a genuine gentlemen's toilet in order to be interpreted as a symbol with the appropriate meaning – the link is sufficiently conventionalised not to require actual coexistence of its terms in order to have its desired semiological effects.

(*e*)   As objects in reality, and in one's consciousness of reality, the figure 🚹 and the object, *gentlemen's toilet*, are so distinct as to preclude any possibility of coincidence or confusion between the two identities.

(f)   The use of 🚹 to indicate a *gentlemen's toilet* necessarily presupposes an intention to communicate, an intention which is the *raison d'être* for the very invention of the symbol.

At this point it is worth referring back to a suggestion made earlier, by noting that functionalist semiology would probably recognise – in the system of traffic-lights – the index 'red light' as a symbol (while 'green light' and 'amber light' would be identified as signs). For, in view of the undecidability of whether 'red light' is 'arbitrary', 'conventional' or 'motivated', or some mixture of these, the frequency of a connection between 'red' and danger would be sufficient for supporting the position that the index 'red light' is partially conventional and partially motivated at one and the same time. This 'in-between-ness' would place 'red light' into the category of symbols.

Sign
Functionalist semiology is interested, *par excellence*, in the category of signs: the indices that, above all others, conform to the ideal of the functioning of semiological systems (Saussure, 1916), and belong to the hard core of semiology. The defining properties of this category of index are as follows:

(a)   EA is *arbitrary* (it is semiologically artificial, being specifically produced for semiological purposes, and its occurrence without a communicative purpose is, to say the least, improbable);

(b)   CA is *arbitrary* (that is to say, the signified aspect of the sign is 'created' by the sign itself, and is hard to conceive of in isolation from the sign);

(c)   the link between EA and CA is totally *arbitrary, conventional and* (intrinsically) *unmotivated*;

(d)   EA and CA do not need to coexist side by side – if anything, the *raison d'être* of signs is to convey information about objects *in their absence*;

(e)   EA and CA are so strongly associated as to form a virtually indissoluble mental union – this *coincidence* makes for frequent confusion between the reality of (the phenomena that give substance to) the sign and the reality of (the phenomena that give substance to) the CA;

(f)   EA and CA *do not resemble* one another in any pertinent way;

(g)   the index necessarily presupposes an *intention to communicate*, and this intention is the *raison d'être* of the sign.

Example: 'sign': $\dfrac{\text{the written form)}}{\text{EA}}$ PIG (signifying)

$$\frac{\text{the species pig}}{\text{CA}}$$

(*a*) The configuration of letters *PIG* is *arbitrary* – out of context with its occurrence as a piece of semiological artifice, its probability of occurrence is infinitesimal and negligible.

(*b*) *The species pig* (CA) is an abstraction resulting from a particular semiological classification of reality – it is, therefore, said to be *arbitrary*.

(*c*) The link between the figure *PIG* and *the species pig* is totally *arbitrary, unmotivated*, and imposed by an *extrinsic convention*.

(*d*) The written figure *PIG* is especially efficacious in being capable of referring to the species (or to a member of it) in the total absence of any *pigs* (that is, no coexistence required).

(*e*) It is extremely hard to dissociate *the species of pigs* from the linguistic sign 'pig', whose effect is to 'create' (as we noted in (*c*) immediately above), and to fix in our consciousness, the concept of that species. Consequently, the figure PIG is almost inextricably entwined with the concept of *the species of pigs*. Although we know these to have separable and separate identities, we find it virtually impossible to approach the concept except through the EA of the sign – this implies a coincidence between the two identities (EA and CA), which is frequently manifested in naïve confusions between 'the word "pig" ' and 'the species *pig*'.

(*f*) The shape of the letters PIG does not in any pertinent way resemble a *pig* (let alone the whole species), and even if it did, this would be wholly immaterial for the functioning of the sign.

(*g*) Unless we recognise, in each occurrence of PIG, an intention to communicate about the species in question (or a member of it), we cannot provide any explanation (let alone a semiological one) of how or why such a configuration of lines could ever have come into being – the only *raison d'être* we can attribute to PIG is that of fulfilling an intention to communicate.

The rather extended presentation of the defining properties of the four types of index can now be brought together into compact form in Figure 6.9. The properties listed in the figure correspond to those listed from (*a*) to (*g*) in the foregoing discussion – the prefixed '+' affirms a particular property, the prefixed '−' negates it, the prefixed '±' means 'yes and no' and the prefixed 'Ø' means 'undecidable'.

(*Natural*) *Index*	*Icon*	*Symbol*	*Sign*
(*a*) − Arbitrary EA	− Arbitrary EA	± Arbitrary EA	+ Arbitrary EA
(*b*) − Arbitrary CA	− Arbitrary CA	− Arbitrary CA	+ Arbitrary CA
(*c*) − Arbitrary link	− Arbitrary link	± Arbitrary link	+ Arbitrary link
(*d*) +Coexistence	± Coexistence	− Coexistence	− Coexistence
(*e*) − Coincidence	Ø Coincidence	− Coincidence	+ Coincidence
(*f*) − Resemblance	+ Resemblance	− Resemblance	− Resemblance
(*g*) − Intention	± Intention	+ Intention	+ Intention

Figure 6.9

6.3.4 Critique of the Functionalist Typology of 'Indices'

There are certain weak points in the typology which, while an attempt had to be made to ignore them in the course of presenting the categories of index, cannot go entirely without remark. I shall list them in somewhat laconic fashion, accompanied by as few remarks as possible.

(1) What exactly is meant by 'EA is arbitrary/non-arbitrary'? In my exposé, I took the attitude that this was a matter of absence/presence of a potential for occurrence in the course of nature, and independently of semiological implications. It is, however, far from clear from my readings in functional semiology whether this conforms exactly with the ideas I am presenting.

(2) Similarly, what exactly does it mean for 'CA to be arbitrary/non-arbitrary'? In my presentation, I took the attitude that 'arbitrary CA' means that the CA itself is a semiological abstraction 'created' through the formation of concepts by signs; conversely, I interpreted 'non-arbitrary CA' as one that exists (at least in substance) independently of the concept-creating function of indices. If, however, this interpretation is reasonably correct – and I do not see any other interpretation at present – I must admit that I find it somewhat tenuous; there is a very strong sense in which *all* indices select (and in this way 'create') the domain of their referents.

(3) Symbols receive a ± prefix for the property of 'arbitrariness of the link between EA and CA'. But, can a typology of indices permit a 'yes and no' answer when it comes to deciding the nature of the relation that mediates between EA and CA, making the association effective as an index? And does the dichotomy 'arbitrary' versus 'motivated', apparently conceived through the mutual exclusivity of these alternatives, permit, logically speaking, that one and the same index be both 'arbitrary' and 'motivated'?

(4) What exactly is meant by the property of 'coexistence'? I have interpreted it as an analogue of 'displacement' (Hockett, 1958) – the ability for an index to convey information about objects absent from the situation in which that index is observed – but this implies a distinction between *necessary* and *incidental* coexistence (an index may be potentially 'displaced' for all that it frequently occurs side by side with its referent). The notion of 'coexistence', and its ramifications, are not clearly expressed in functional semiology.

(5) What precisely is meant by 'coincidence' between EA and CA? As soon as EA and CA are discussed in terms of an index, it is automatically implied that the two are separate, distinguishable identities, but that they 'coincide' in the index in question. I have tried to make out a case that the CAs of all index-types *except signs* are significantly more independent (non-arbitrary) in their extra-semiological existence than are the CAs of signs (arbitrary), and that 'coincidence' between EA and CA results from the distinction between them being significantly less clearcut where identification of the CA is wholly dependent on the sign itself. This point seems,

however, to be rather tenuous – and, besides, I am not all that sure that my interpretation of 'coincidence' is the intended one.

(6) The typology stipulates that, for instance in symbols, there is no resemblance between EA and CA. Now, it is never possible (though the point may be a hair-splitting one) to maintain that two objects have no resemblance. I have therefore altered the stipulation to read 'no pertinent resemblance', and added that the crucial point is that, even if a resemblance were found, this would be irrelevant to the motivating of the link between EA and CA.

(7) In symbols and signs, there is not only an intention to communicate – there may be such an intention in icons also – but, far more importantly, this intention to communicate is the *raison d'être* of symbols and signs, while it is not the *raison d'être* of icons. If the question had been formulated in this way – that is, is the *raison d'être* of this index an intention to communicate? – there would not have been a 'yes and no' answer to the question of intentionality in icons.

A further weak point – in the form of a lack of complete (terminological) consistency – is the discrepancy between sign viewed as a general category of index, and sign viewed as a constituent of a '*sème*'. Explained in terms of an example, the discrepancy consists in the fact that, from the point of view of *typology of indices*, the Highway Code elements ⊝, ○ and ⇨ answer, all three, to the definition of *sign* (as can be easily checked out in Figure 6.9, p. 179); whereas, from the point of view of a *theory of 'codes'*, ⊝ is a '*sème*', and only ○ and ⇨ are signs. Putting it bluntly, according to the theory of indices, both '*sèmes*' and signs are 'signs', whereas, according to the theory of 'codes', '*sèmes*' are not 'signs'. This points to the imperfect integration of the two strands of the theory: 'theory of indices' and 'theory of semiological systems'.

For all the incompletely answered questions, incompletely explored ramifications and the occasional not wholly consistent decision, the typology of indices offered by functionalist semiology ranks among the most important and powerful theories of indices – one of the few that are truly worthy of notice.

6.4.1 Hard Core of Descriptive Applications of Functional Semiology

Both with regard to recognising signs (as defined in Figure 6.9, p. 179) as representing the ideal of semiology, and with regard to the economy-based theory of the functioning of semiological systems, the hard core of semiological description can be identified with the description of *systems containing signs and manifesting functional economy*. This is not to say that systems with a zero degree of economy do not fall within the scope of the descriptive applications of functional semiology – only that such systems will seem relatively uninteresting, since their descriptions will be no more than simple lists of signs to which appropriate meanings are attached (that is, no more than a kind of 'dictionary').

Functional semiology is particularly applicable, therefore, to the descriptions of such systems as:

(1)   Highway Code,
(2)   Morse code,
(3)   Braille,
(4)   Finger-spelling codes,
(5)   American Sign Language (for the deaf),
(6)   Semaphore (see Prieto, 1966),
(7)   Gestural sign systems,
(8)   Heraldic signs (see Mounin, 1970),
(9)   Number-writing systems (Arabic and Roman),
(10) Ideographic writing systems (for example, hieroglyphics, classical Chinese),
(11) Syllabic writing systems,
(12) Alphabetic writing systems (see especially Mounin's analysis of alphabetic letters into component features; Mounin, 1970),
(13) Musical notation systems,
(14) Drum codes,
(15) Smoke-signal systems,
(16) Shorthand writing systems,
(17) Whistle codes (such as that used in the Canary Islands),
(18) Secret codes and cryptographic codes, etc.

Some caution is advised (Mounin, 1968) in the application of functional semiology to the description of, for instance:

(1)   Communication in social bees,
(2)   Communication in apes in the wild,
(3)   Communication in apes under experimental conditions,
(4)   'Bird song',
(5)   Communication in dolphins and porpoises (Mounin, 1968).

Even more doubtful – and possibly wholly misconceived – is the appropriateness of semiological description to the 'transmission of genetic information' (see Mounin's discussion in Mounin, 1968). In the same category of doubtful cases, I would include also 'kinesic' and 'paralinguistic' phenomena (so-called 'body-language').

The fact remains that functional semiology is not wholly content to remain within the hard core of its descriptive applications – in spite of the fact that it has a clear enough and wide enough scope of hard core applications (to which, strictly speaking, all *spoken languages* also belong). The following section will deal, very briefly, with areas to which functional semiology is tempted to 'extend' its application, descriptions of further areas of 'communication' that do not belong to the hard core (see Mounin's excellent discussion on 'communication' versus 'communion'; Mounin, 1968).

6.5.1 'Extensions' of Functional Semiology

In a semiological climate in which the ambitions of semiological analysis frequently seem to know no bounds – and such, in general, is the present semiological climate – it is understandable that no competing semiological theory wishes to be outdone in the matter of the scope of its applications. There is, of course, an alternative attitude, which is to argue that excessive 'extension' costs loss of rigour, descriptive precision (and, perhaps, even loss of plausibility), and is therefore to be resisted by the more exact approaches to semiology (Mounin, 1968, 1970). This 'purist' attitude is, however, not easy to adhere to. Functionalist semiology, as a whole, tends to vacillate (from scholar to scholar, or even within the attitude of one particular scholar) between the two alternatives.

Be that as it may, it is possible to pinpoint certain areas of description which belong to an 'extended' use of functional semiology. These areas lie especially in the field of the 'arts'. The main problem, of course, is whether 'art' can be, plausibly and appropriately, viewed as being the manipulation of systematic sets of conventions for communication. If, however, this problem is glossed over, or if the assumption is made that functional semiology is 'extendable' in this direction (Martinet, 1980), a range of 'extended' applications is created, including:

(1)   the analysis of paintings (Martinet, 1980),
(2)   the analysis of sculpture,
(3)   the analysis of poster art,
(4)   the analysis of musical works,
(5)   the analysis of prose and poetry,
(6)   the analysis of architectural artefacts, etc.

In so far as it is possible through the types of analysis listed from 1 to 6 to identify clearly determined indices (preferably signs), and to show that their functioning is systematic and conventional, and has communication for its *raison d'être*, the 'extension' of functional semiology to such analyses justifies itself. It does not seem, however, that such analyses can ever belong to the hard core of functional semiology in the way that, for instance, writing systems or 'substitutive systems' belong to that hard core.

7

An Integrated Theory of Semiotics: Axiomatic Functionalism

7.1 Introductory Remarks

In the case of the semiotic theory discussed in this chapter, we shall be dealing with an approach – not unrelated to functional semiology, but, as it will be seen, quite significantly different from it – initiated by the ideas of Jan W. F. Mulder and developed chiefly by Mulder and the present author. This being the case, the presentation will, in the main, avoid references to the authorship of particular ideas, except, of course, for textual references, where they are deemed to be useful. Furthermore, it should be understood that, in general, the views of Mulder and of myself coincide sufficiently not to present significant alternatives, even where these views are expressed in different ways. On the other hand, I do not feel bound, in the outlining of these views, to adhere strictly to already published material – that is, I reserve the right to introduce certain 'innovations' where they seem to be appropriate. Consequently, I take full responsibility for my version of axiomatic functionalist semiotics (henceforth referred to as 'axiomatic semiotics') on all points where it may not do justice to the ideas of Mulder.

7.1.1 The Scope of Axiomatic Semiotics

In functional semiology, we encountered two tendencies: one towards 'extensions' of semiology that encompass areas outside its hard core, the other towards a 'purist' attitude, insisting on a narrow application of semiology within a scope that, after all, is already extensive enough. It is the latter of these attitudes that is unequivocally espoused by axiomatic semiotics.

We also saw in functional semiology that the 'purist' position, as expressed by Buyssens (1943), regards the scope of semiology to be restricted to phenomena in which coincide the three characteristics of *conventionality*, *intention to communicate* and *membership of a set* (that is, belonging to a system of interdependent values). While axiomatic semiotics takes an even more 'purist' stance, Buyssens' position provides an excellent background to explaining that stance.

Of the three characteristics listed by Buyssens, axiomatic semiotics retains two in more or less the same sense: (1) convention; (2) membership in a *self-contained* set (see Mulder's *Axiom A: 'All features in semiotic sets are functional'* and the definitions accompanying this axiom; Mulder, 1968, Mulder and Hervey, 1980).

The characteristic of 'intention to communicate' is, however, replaced by the less psychologically and more philosophically oriented notion: (3) communicative *raison d'être*. That is to say, phenomena within the scope of axiomatic semiotics are required to (1) function on the basis of (constitutive) conventions; (2) be tokens of types that are, themselves, members of particular semiotic sets (self-contained systems); (3) be not merely incidentally communicative (as most phenomena can be), but to have communication as their *raison d'etre*. The definition of the scope of axiomatic semiotics is crystallised in the shape of the definition of the term 'semiotic system'. This definition is formulated (Mulder, 1968) as: 'semiotic system' for 'system of conventions *for* communication'.

A further point of comparison with the approach of Buyssens reveals an important difference between functional semiology and axiomatic semiotics.

On the one hand, the characteristics stipulated by Buyssens are applied, and their presence in particular phenomena is checked, one by one: (1) Is this phenomenon conventional? (2) Does this phenomenon manifest an intention to communicate? (3) Is this phenomenon a member of a set of mutually interdependent values?

On the other hand, the three characteristics stipulated by axiomatic semiotics are applied in pairs: (1) Does this phenomenon function on the basis of conventions whose *raison d'être* is communication? (2) Does this phenomenon constitute a token of a convention-based type that is a member of a particular self-contained semiotic set (system)? (3) Is this phenomenon a token of a type belonging to a self-contained semiotic set (system) whose *raison d'être* is communication?

7.1.2   Phenomena within the Scope of Axiomatic Semiotics

Apparent hair-splitting apart, the fact of the matter is that, checking for three characteristics one by one does not give the same results as checking for them in pairs; the two methods do not agree in what phenomena they admit to the scope of semiotics. For instance, the possibility arises that a particular phenomenon is, indeed, conventional, but its conventionality relates to something other than communication, while its communicative content is undeniable, but arises from sources other than convention.

In terms of a concrete example, a polite bow is, separately, both conventional and communicative, but its conventionality is a matter of polite behaviour (not communication), while its communicative content is a matter of a 'natural' expression of submissiveness (not of convention).

In this example, therefore, the method of checking one by one would tend to give an affirmative answer to both the question of conventionality and the question of intention to communicate – although a discrepancy of some sort would be felt, making the phenomenon 'marginally' semiological. On the other hand, the method of checking in pairs, which poses the question 'does this phenomenon function on the basis of conventions whose *raison d'être* is communication?', would give a clearcut negative answer. As we see from the example, there are phenomena which belong (actually in a rather paradoxical way, which is why they are 'marginal') to the scope of semiology as formulated by Buyssens, but which would be strictly, and for good reason, excluded from the scope of axiomatic semiotics. The latter avoids, as much as possible, the inclusion of 'marginal' or 'paradoxical' cases.

7.1.3 A Comparison of Semiotic Theories

Further to the matter of the scope of axiomatic semiotics, the 'deductive' nature (that is, proceeding always from general to particular, from abstract to concrete, from theory to phenomena) of the approach makes its centre(s) of interest similar to the centre(s) of interest in functional semiology. That is to say, while functional semiology is interested chiefly in developing a theory of types or values (cf. Chapter 6, Section 6.1.1, p. 155), and not of 'acts', axiomatic semiotics also concentrates much of its interest in developing a theory of types or values – with the one main difference that, in one part of that theory, a subtheory is evolved in which the level of 'semiotic acts' is incorporated. The incorporation of this level in the theoretical model implies that the theory includes a 'theory of semiotic acts'.

We may at this point usefully compare, in schematic form, the 'skeletons' of Morris' theory, of functional semiology minus Prieto, of functional semiology in Prieto's version, and of axiomatic semiology (Figure 7.1).

The comparison of axiomatic semiotics with other approaches hints at the reason why, in the title of the present chapter, axiomatic semiotics is described as 'an *integrated* theory'. This issue of integration, the point of departure for separate discussions of the 'subtheories' integrated within axiomatic semiotic theory, will be taken up in more precise detail in the following section. For the time being, we conclude the comparison sketched out in Figure 7.1 by noting that, while Morris' semiotic has no clearly definable scope, functionalist semiology taken together with Prieto's theory of '*l'acte sémique*' has three largely, but not completely, overlapping scopes (determined from the angle of 'theory of codes', 'theory of indices' and 'theory of *l'acte sémique*', respectively), axiomatic semiology has a single definition of scope in which all three subtheories coincide. This, in itself, is an aspect of 'integratedness'.

7.1.4 Semiotics and Linguistics

Finally, on the matter of scope, it must be mentioned that axiomatic semiotics is wholly inclusive of linguistics (that is to say, axiomatic functionalist linguistics). The approach neither chooses to extend itself from analysing rudimentary semiotic systems to analysing, finally, 'languages', nor does it content itself with first analysing 'languages' and then widening the scope to non-linguistic systems. Nor does it accept any kind

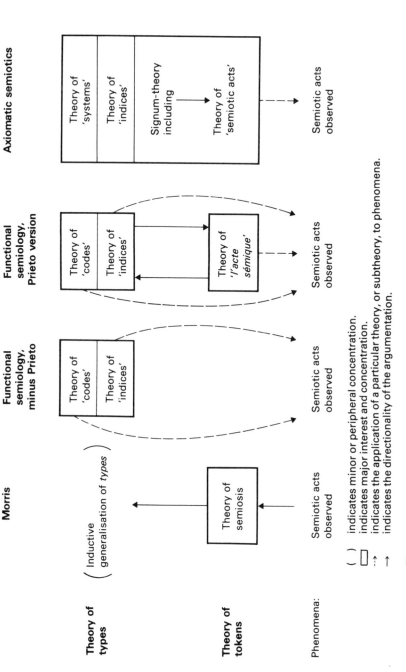

Theory of types

Theory of tokens

Phenomena:

Morris

$\left(\begin{array}{c}\text{Inductive}\\\text{generalisation of } \textit{types}\end{array}\right)$

Theory of semiosis

Semiotic acts observed

Functional semiology, minus Prieto

Theory of 'codes' | Theory of 'indices'

Semiotic acts observed

Functional semiology, Prieto version

Theory of 'codes' | Theory of 'indices'

Theory of 'l'acte sémique'

Semiotic acts observed

Axiomatic semiotics

Theory of 'systems'

Theory of 'indices'

Signum-theory including

Theory of 'semiotic acts'

Semiotic acts observed

( ) indicates minor or peripheral concentration.
▢ indicates major interest and concentration.
⤏ indicates the application of a particular theory, or subtheory, to phenomena.
↑ indicates the directionality of the argumentation.

Figure 7.1

of discrepancy between non-linguistic semiology and linguistic semiology; there is only one *semiotics*, which is equally applicable to any semiotic system, including any language (cf. Chapter 6, Section 6.1.1, p. 155). In other words, the approach simply back-tracks to general principles (axioms, definitions, theorems) that are appropriate (Mulder, 1980) to semiotic systems as a genus, a genus of which 'languages' do not *a priori* constitute a norm-setting species. (If, after all this, axiomatic functionalists happen – because of their particular linguistic interests – to develop in more precise detail those implications of the semiotic theory which yield notions applicable to 'languages', and go into less detail over implications that might only affect non-linguistic systems, this is merely accidental, and can be easily remedied without transcending the original scope of the theory, or 'extending' it in any way. Filling in the details of a pre-established framework should not be confused with 'extending', that is to say, 'stretching' – perhaps to breaking-point – that framework.)

7.2.1   The Integration of Axiomatic Semiotics

As Figure 7.1 indicates, axiomatic semiotics is constructed in the form of three 'subtheories'. These 'subtheories' are developed separately, but are mutually complementary in a theory with the single aim of describing 'semiotic acts'. The three 'subtheories' – which are, as it were, the 'pillars' supporting the overall structure of the theory, and of the (both linguistic and other semiotic) descriptions based on that theory – can be designated (in order to emphasise the comparison with other approaches): (1) theory of semiotic systems ('systemology'; Mulder, 1980); (2) theory of indices ('semantics'; Mulder, 1980); (3) *signum*-theory ('ontology'; Mulder, 1980).

From the angle of 'theory of semiotic systems' (henceforth 'systemology') is obtained a deductive classification of functional types of semiotic system. In these systems, an important part is played by the *internal deployment* (that is, combinability/analysability; Mulder, 1979) of *signa* – along with the internal deployment of *figurae*. The notion of *signum* is, however, not a matter for 'systemological' definition; the definition is provided by the 'theory of indices'. Furthermore, the notion is 'analysed' together with that of figura, and the interplay between signa and figurae, in 'signum-theory' (see below, Section 7.5.1, p. 205). (Incidentally, because 'systemology' merely uses the notion signum, 'theory of indices' defines it and 'signum-theory' makes an 'analysis' of it, it is theoretically impossible for the three 'subtheories' to operate with discrepant senses of signum. This is a feature of the 'integratedness' of the semiotic theory.)

From the angle of 'theory of indices' is obtained a deductive classification of information-conveying types (that is, of indices; note that indices are types and not tokens). Among the various categories of index distinguished by the classification, the category signum is a particular species. The deductive nature of the classification implies an automatic setting-off of signum against all other species of index – a procedure that yields, equally automatically, a definition of the species signum. As for the internal 'structure' of a signum – used as a starting point for its definition – this is not a matter of 'theory of indices', but of 'signum-theory'. It is 'signum-theory' also that is responsible for determining the relation signa bear to 'semiotic acts'. (Integration is manifested here too, in that the notion signum is equally dependent for its definition on 'theory of indices' and 'signum-theory'.)

From the angle of 'signum-theory', the notion signum – seen as an entity with two 'faces' – is analysed into its mutually inter-related aspects ('faces'), each of which is put in relation with its (physical) 'substance'. At the same time, signum is set in context with figura, and put in relation, via its tokens (see below Section 7.5.2, p. 208) with its concrete manifestations in the form of 'semiotic acts'.

7.3.1 'Systemology' – the Deductive Classification of Semiotic Systems

There are two factors required for the construction of a deductive classification: (1) a point of departure that defines precisely the *genus* to be subclassified; (2) a principle of relevance that selects the properties in terms of which subcategories are set off against one another and, in this manner, are defined within the classification itself.

Both the point of departure, and the principle of relevance adopted by axiomatic semiotics for the classification of semiotic systems, are significantly similar to those of functional semiology. But we have seen already the extent of a discrepancy between the scope of semiological systems (*conventionality, intention to communicate* and *membership of a set*, applied one by one) and the scope of semiotic systems (*conventionality, membership of a self-contained set* and *communicative raison d'être*, applied in pairs) – a discrepancy that sets apart the points of departure of the two approaches. We shall see, with regard to a principle of relevance, that axiomatic semiotics is somewhat more strict and rigorous in classifying systems only with regard to that principle – whereas functional semiology frequently makes use of classificatory properties (or 'dimensions') falling outside the domain of its principle of relevance.

The point of departure of 'systemology' is, of course, the notion of semiotic system itself, defined as '(any) system of conventions *for* communication'; it is the genus of semiotic systems that is to be subclassified.

It is, of course, absolutely correct to say that, from a theoretically uncommitted viewpoint, all observable differences between one system and another are equally deserving of consideration, and valid as means of subcategorisation. However, a semiotician does not speak from a theoretically uncommitted viewpoint – not even when he claims to, or pretends to do so. The properties he elevates to classificatory status presuppose implicitly – and should presuppose explicitly – a particular theoretical commitment.

In general, and for the moment, fairly vague, terms, the principle of relevance for functional semiotics – and also for axiomatic semiotics – is *functionality*. This notion of functionality is traceable right back to Saussure's notion of *valeur* (cf. Chapter 1, Section 1.2.2, p. 12) –

functional elements are values defined by their oppositions (to one another, and/or to their simple absence). Semiotically functional elements are oppositional values defined by the communicative differences their oppositions are capable of producing. Furthermore, while (real) values are given concrete 'realisation' by particular 'substances', these values are, as such, forms and not substances.

It should follow, therefore, that a theoretical commitment to semiotic function (communicative differential) elevates all properties traceable to that function to the status of relevant classificatory properties, whereas all properties that do not derive from semiotic function – but, say, from mere 'accidents' of substance, or from other functions – are automatically demoted to a non-pertinent, at best quasi-pertinent, status.

With the above considerations in mind, axiomatic semiotics can justify (in terms of its own theoretical commitment, of course) the position – already explicit in functional semiology – that certain popular forms of classification of semiotic systems are not pertinent. Thus, for instance, a classification in terms of the medium used by a semiotic system (vocal, visual, and so on; cf. Chapter 6, Section 6.2.1, p. 162) is non-pertinent because it derives from accidents of substance. This is just as well, otherwise one may have to classify Morse code separately in every one of the media: vocal, auditory, visual, light, tactile, and so on, for that system can function equally well in all these media, given the appropriate circumstances.

Similarly, a classification according to the pragmatic use of a system (for example, for the deaf, for the blind, for directing traffic, and so on; cf. Chapter 6, Section 6.2.1, p. 162) would be only quasi-pertinent (at best), since it derives from considerations of a function other than semiotic function as explained above.

At the same time, these considerations would also demote the categories of 'substitutive *sémie*' (Chapter 6, Section 6.2.1, p. 161) and 'parallel code' (Chapter 6, Section 6.2.3, p. 169) to a non-pertinent status, since

(a)   the *semiotic function* of a system is completed before that so-called 'substitutive' system comes into contact with the system for which it is said to 'substitute' (for example, Morse code is said to be 'substitutive' for 'written languages', but Morse code has already finished its semiotic function as soon as the appropriate letters have been distinguished – what the 'writing system' does with these letters subsequently has nothing to do with the semiotic function of Morse code);

(b)   the semiotic functions of 'parallel codes' may resemble each other, and may be 'isomorphic' in certain respects, but they are separate and independent (for example, no one would deny a degree of 'parallelism' between 'written English' and 'spoken English', but, equally, everyone is aware of the 'aberrations of spelling' that manifest the discernible discrepancies between these two systems).

Of the available dimensions for classifying semiotic systems, only the dimension of economy (cf. Chapter 6, Section 6.2.2, p. 163) can be fully connected to semiotic function. Accordingly, this dimension is treated as the sole pertinent dimension of classification in the 'systemology' of axiomatic semiotics.

7.3.2 Semiotic Economy

As a first step in establishing this classification in the dimension of economy, it must be remembered that every semiotic system operates with two levels of entity: figurae and signa. For the time being, it is sufficient to note that, while signa are essentially 'two-faced' (endowed with properties both of form and of meaning), figurae are entities with distinctive formal properties, but have, as such, no meaning. (Both signum and figura will be made more precise in subsequent sections.)

In some systems, the two levels of figurae and signa are isomorphic (that is to say, there is an exact one–to–one correspondence between figurae and signa). This helps to obscure the general conclusion that, in all semiotic systems, the levels of figurae and signa are separately relevant. For example, the shower attachment in a bathroom may display the use of a small semiotic system with the figurae: /H/,/W/ and /C/ (figurae whose connection with any meaning is, on this level, not yet relevant). In the same semiotic system, however, there are also three signa: 'H = hot water', 'W = warm water' and 'C = cold water'.

Evidently, in this system, three figurae are associated with three signa – each figura with only one signum and each signum with only one figura. Separating out the levels, and listing their separate inventories (of figurae and signa, respectively) appears redundant (see Figure 7.2). None the less, this very appearance of redundancy pinpoints a characteristic of the semiotic system in question: the lack of economy resulting from the one–to–one isomorphism between the two levels. These two levels will henceforth be referred to as 'cenological' (the Greek root 'ceno-' denotes 'empty'; figurae are 'empty' of meaning) and 'plerological' (the Greek root 'plero-' denotes 'full'; signa are 'full' of meaning).

A discrepancy between the inventory of cenological units and the inventory of plerological units is an instant pointer to semiotic economy. The British system of traffic-lights provides a simple example of this.

The system disposes of three basic figurae: /red/, /amber/ and /green/, but of four basic signa: 'red = stop', 'amber = prepare to stop', 'green = go' and 'red + amber = prepare to go'. The system makes up for the three to four discrepancy between the basic cenological and plerological inventories by allowing the production of a cenological combination: /red/ +

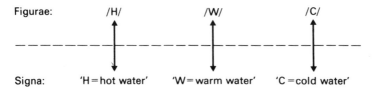

Figurae: /H/   /W/   /C/

Signa: 'H = hot water'   'W = warm water'   'C = cold water'

Figure 7.2

/amber/. (In fact, we may say that the system creates a discrepancy between its basic inventory of three simple/unanalysable figurae and its overall inventory of four figurae – three simple and one complex. By means of combining /red/ and /amber/ into the complex /red + amber/ the system provides, in an economical way, for the ability to distinguish the forms of four signa.)

Figurae: /red/, /amber/, /green/   /red + amber/
           simple   complex

basic inventory

overall inventory

Signa: 'red = stop', 'amber = prepare to stop',
'green = go', 'red + amber = prepare to go'

Figure 7.3

Quantitatively speaking, the above system has a very low numerical index of economy, expressible as a ratio of 3:4 between the basic inventory of simple figurae and the overall inventory of figurae capable of being used in communication. However, as we shall continue to see below, axiomatic semiotics takes a qualitative view of economy – the mere presence or absence of economy distinguishes between 'complex' semiotic systems and 'simple' semiotic systems, respectively.

The example of traffic lights allows us to make two further observations: (*a*) economy is always measured as a ratio between the basic inventory of simple (that is, not complex) units on a given level (cenological or plerological) of a semiotic system and the overall inventory of units on that level: (*b*) economy is always tautologous with the creation of complex units.

Semiotic systems that have no economy (on either of their two levels) are designated as simple systems; semiotic systems with some degree of economy on at least one of their two levels are complex systems (Mulder, 1968).

Complex systems may be cenologically complex (for example, the traffic-lights discussed above), plerologically complex (for example, the Highway Code discussed below), or they may also be 'doubly complex', having both a cenological and a plerological economy.

Before moving on to further ramifications of the notion of economy, we shall take the example of the Highway Code to illustrate a type of semiotic system that has economy only on one level; this time, a system with a plerological economy (that is, a plerologically complex system). In the case of the Highway Code, a large number of the signa in this system are actually analysable into constituent signa; that is to say, they are complexes made up by a combination of signa belonging to a basic inventory. In each of the combinations in which a particular basic signum occurs as a constituent, that signum has the same constant denotation – that is to say, it is not only certain 'forms' that enter into combinations, but 'two-faced' entities that are fusions of 'form and meaning' (that is, signa). The basic signa of the Highway Code are such semantically constant entities as: 'arrow = follow direction indicated', 'circular blue field = obligation', 'rectangular blue field = permission', 'P = parking', 'circular red field = interdiction', and so on. The complexes formed out of combinations of these basic signa are the familiar 'signs' of the Highway Code: 'arrow in circular blue field = obligation to follow direction indicated', 'arrow in rectangular blue field = permission to follow direction indicated', 'P in rectangular blue field = permission to park', 'arrow in circular red field = interdiction to follow direction indicated', and so on. (The quantitative measure of economy is unimportant; what matters is that the semiotic system in question operates with the construction of complex signa out of simple signa, that is, it is a plerologically complex system.)

7.3.3 'Simultaneity' versus 'Articulation'

Alongside the first qualitative dichotomy (that between systems with no economy and systems with some economy), we shall now place a second qualitative dichotomy: that between the formation of simultaneous bundles and the formation of articulated constructions. In order to emphasise the qualitative differences, I shall make use of hypothetical examples in which there is also a striking quantitative difference.

Let us suppose that we have three hypothetical semiotic systems, each of them having three basic signa:

System I: 'a = keep hot', 'b = keep warm',
             'c = keep moist'
System II: 'a = hop', 'b = skip', 'c = jump'
System III: 'a = push', 'b = pull', 'c = lift'.

Furthermore, each of the three hypothetical systems contains a convention (rule) limiting each signum to one occurrence (maximum) in each construction. This effectively limits the extension of complex signa to a maximum of three constituent signa.

In System I, there is a further convention according to which 'a = keep hot' cannot, in a construction, follow either 'b = keep warm' or 'c = keep moist' in linear succession, and, similarly, 'b = keep warm' cannot succeed 'c = keep moist'.

Limited by these combinatory conventions, the overall inventory of System I will be:

'a   = keep hot', 'b = keep warm', 'c = keep moist' (basic signa)
'ab = keep hot and/or warm'
'ac = keep hot and/or moist'
'bc = keep warm and/or moist'
'abc = keep hot and/or warm and/or moist'

The system, with an economy ratio of 3:7, could be used to give seven types of instruction about the conditions under which, say, particular plants should be kept.

In System II, the convention about linear succession of signa in complexes is replaced by a convention of free variance – that is to say, the constituent signa may occur in any sequence; their sequential arrangement does not affect the identity (and the meaning) of the complex, only their presence/absence is significant.

Given these conventions, the overall inventory of System II will be:

'a = hop', 'b = skip', 'c = jump' (basic signa)
'ab/ba = hop and/or skip'
'ac/ca = hop and/or jump'
'bc/cb = skip and/or jump'
'abc/acb/cab, etc. = hop and/or skip and/or jump'.

It is interesting to note that, from the point of view of economy – in fact, of 'functional structure' – System I and System II are virtually equivalent (there is only a 'realisational' convention governing linear sequence that differentiates between them). System II has also an economy ratio of 3:7, and disposes of seven possible types of instruction that could be issued, say, to a physical education class.

Let us now add a third system, in which not only is each permutation of basic signa permitted, but also each such permutation is differentiated from every other permutation. The convention in this third system will be that every constituent in a complex is subordinated to the preceding one.

Given these stipulations, the overall inventory of System III will be:

'a = push', 'b = pull', 'c = lift' (basic inventory)
'ab = first push then pull', 'ba = first pull then push'
'ac = first push then lift', 'ca = first lift then push'
'bc = first pull then lift', 'cb = first lift then pull'
'abc = first push then pull then lift'
'bac = first pull then push then lift'
'cab = first lift then push then pull' etc.

Without listing the overall inventory (which can be easily calculated), it is sufficient to note that System III has an increased economy ratio of 3:15, as against 3:7 in the previous two systems. System III could be used for giving fifteen different types of instruction about, say, how to open a strong-box whose lock is operated by a lever that can be pushed, pulled or lifted.

What, from a qualitative point of view, is even more significant than the more than doubled ratio of economy is the fact that, in the third system, the types of message that can be communicated and differentiated are very much more sophisticated than in the other two systems. In System III, the messages conveyed by complex signa are not mere additive reflexes of the meanings of the constituent signa. For instance, the meaning of /ab/ is not 'push and/or pull', but the much more specific and sophisticated message, *'first* push and *then* pull'. Similarly, the system manipulates all the possible ways in which a maximum of three signa can be subordinated to one another (in constructions) in order to give specific instructions about the order in which the actions of pushing, pulling and lifting are to be performed. This is qualitatively different from, say, System II in terms of which one can give only much vaguer instructions, for example, /ab/ meaning 'either hop or skip, or alternate these activities in some unspecified way'.

One might say that Systems I and II are 'co-ordinative' in nature, while System III is essentially 'subordinative', and that 'subordinative' semiotic systems are structurally and functionally more powerful than 'co-ordinative' ones. In other words, systems that operate with a purely 'symmetrical' principle of construction, thereby producing simultaneous bundles, are of a qualitatively inferior type as compared to systems that operate with an 'asymmetrical' principle of construction, thereby producing articulated constructions.

A terminological and notional difference between functional semiology and axiomatic semiotics must be noted and kept in mind, in connection with the term 'articulation' (and its derivates). As a term in functional semiology, 'articulation' is synonymous with 'complexity/analysability'; that is to say, any analysable semiological complex is said to be 'articulated' into its constituents. In axiomatic semiotics, with the further addition of a qualitative dichotomy between 'symmetrical' and 'asymmetrical' constructions, the term 'articulation' is reserved only for constructions of the second (higher) type. Simultaneous bundles, while they are analysable semiotic complexes, are not said to be 'articulated'.

A semiotic system that operates with articulated constructions on the plerological level is the system of Arabic number writing. The very fact that '2418', '24.18', '18.24', '81.42', and so on, while containing exactly the same constituent signa ('1', '2', '4', and '8'), are different numerical expressions, indicates that number writing produces articulated plerological constructions.

For a better understanding of the structures of this semiotic system, it should be noted that every complex numerical expression has a nucleus (either the rightmost number, or the number marked with a decimal point) to which all other numbers in the complex are subordinated in various ways (directly or indirectly, pre-nuclearly or post-nuclearly). Furthermore, each numerical expression is interpreted on the basis of (*a*) the face value of the numbers that are its constituents; (*b*) the subordinative relations between the *nucleus* and the various constituents subordinated (in different ways) to that nucleus. In other words, the actual value of a given number in a numerical expression is a function of (calculable from) the basic meaning of that number as a signum in the inventory of numbers (zero to 9), and the position of subordination of that number *vis-à-vis* the nucleus of the numerical expression.

Generalising and systematising matters, a pattern emerges as a model for the articulated constructions of Arabic number writing as shown in Figure 7.4.

While on the one hand, the examples of Arabic number writing and Highway Code illustrate the difference between articulated constructions and simultaneous bundles of signa (that is, on the plerological level), on the other hand, the plerological articulation of Arabic number writing can be set off against the cenological articulation of Morse code.

Morse code is an example, *par excellence*, of a highly economical semiotic system whose economy is exclusively achieved by means of a cenological articulation (that is, the production of articulated constructions of figurae). The basic cenological inventory of the system contains only two figurae: 'short' and 'long'. From these two basic figurae are produced all the complex figurae that are subsequently (that is to say, on the plerological level) used for differentiating the forms of the signa belonging to the code. (The denotations of these signa are alphabetic letters, numbers, and so on; combinations of these denotations may be further interpreted in an alphabetic writing system – these further combinations do not, however, form part of the Morse code; they belong to an appropriate system of alphabetic writing.)

←							→
etc. ×1000	×100	×10	nuclear	1/10	1/100	1/1000	etc.
position	position	position	position	position	position	position	
2	4	1	8				
		2	4	1	8		
		1	8	2	4		
		8	1	4	2		

Figure 7.4

(The numerical expressions represented in the model are: '2418', '24.18', '18.24', and '81.42'.)

7.3.4   Economy and Semiotic Subsystems

We noted right from the start that a semiotic system is always 'compounded' of a cenological level and a plerological level, and have also mentioned, in connection with the possibility of a system being 'doubly complex', that both these levels may display their own measure of economy (that is, both levels may be capable of a systematic production of complex entities). When this is the case, each of the levels is said to constitute a subsystem of the semiotic system in question. The cenological subsystem and the plerological subsystem out of which a given semiotic system is 'compounded' are autonomous, mutually complementary 'compartments' of one and the same semiotic system.

Subsystems of a semiotic system can be classified in two dimensions: (1) cenological subsystems versus plerological subsystems; (2) componential subsystems versus articulations. The term 'componential subsystem' refers to a subsystem producing complex entities of the simultaneous bundle type; 'an articulation' refers to a subsystem capable of producing complexes that are articulated constructions.

A matrix can be formed from the two dimensions listed above, leading to the establishment of four types of subsystem (see Figure 7.5).

	Componential subsystem	Articulation
Cenological subsystem	Cenematics	Cenotactics
Plerological subsystem	Plerematics	Plerotactics

Figure 7.5

7.3.5 'Interlocking' of Semiotic Subsystems

At this point, we are in possession of all the ingredients required for classifying semiotic systems according to the way they are 'compounded' of a cenological level (that may be a simple inventory with no potential for producing complexes, or may, itself, be 'compounded' of cenological subsystems) and a plerological level (that may be a simple inventory with no potential for producing complexes, or may, in turn, be 'compounded' of plerological subsystems).

The compounding of a semiotic system out of 'interlocking' subsystems is particularly clearly illustrated by human languages:

(1) Cenematics: a small closed inventory of basic figurae – the so-called *distinctive features* (e.g. /labial/, /occlusive/, /voiced/, etc.); a cenematic subsystem operates on these distinctive features, combining them into simultaneous bundles, the so-called *phonemes* (e.g. /labial/ + /occlusive/ + /voiced/ = /b/, /labial/ + /nasal/ = /m/, /dorsal/ + /occlusive/ + /voiced/ = /g/, etc.).

(2) Cenotactics: the *phoneme-output* of the cenematics provides an inventory of basic figurae (this constitutes the interlock between cenematics and cenotactics: an output–input relation); a cenotactic subsystem operates on the phonemes, combining them into *articulated constructions*, the so-called *phoneme-chains* (e.g. /t→r→a←m←z/, /s→t→r→a←p/, /l→e← ŋ← θ ←n←z/, etc.).

The combined output of the two cenological subsystems provides the means whereby the forms of the signa of the human language in question (i.e. English) can be differentiated (this constitutes the interlock between the cenological level and the plerological level).

(3) Plerematics: a closed and relatively limited inventory of basic signa – the so-called *monemes* or *morphemes* (e.g. 'man', 'boy', 'walk', 'quick', 'plural', 'past', '-ly', etc.); a plerematic subsystem operates on these *monemes*, combining them into *simultaneous bundles*, the so-called *words* (e.g. 'boy' + 'plural' = 'boys', 'walk' + 'past' = 'walked', 'quick' + '-ly' = 'quickly', etc.).

(4) Plerotactics: the *word-output* of the plerematics provides an inventory of basic signa (this constitutes the interlock between plerematics and plerotactics: an output–input relation); a plerotactic subsystem operates on the words, combining them into articu-

lated constructions, the so-called syntactic combinations (e.g. (the→man)→(has→taught)←(many→boys), (that→girl←(in← (the→garden))), (((his→father)→s)→brother), etc.).

The compounding of human languages out of subsystems that interlock in a fixed order can be sketched in the scheme shown in Figure 7.6.

(1) Cenematics (2) Cenotactics   (3) Plerematics (4) Plerotactics

Figure 7.6

In comparison, to take yet another example of a different type of semiotic system, a written language such as English is compounded out of the interlocking of three subsystems (see Figure 7.7).

(1) Cenotactics (2) Plerematics (4) Plerotactics

Figure 7.7

The lowest level of economy in this system is that subsystem of which the basic inventory is the graphemes (alphabetic letters). These, however, do not enter into a cenematics forming them into simultaneous bundles, but directly into a cenotactics producing articulated constructions (that is, chains of alphabetic letters). As for the signa-level of an alphabetically written language, this operates, analogously with a spoken language, with monemes combined into simultaneous bundles: the words; and with words combined into articulated constructions of a syntactic nature. (There is, in other words, a high degree of isomorphism between, say, the plerological subsystems of written English and of spoken English. Such an isomorphism presupposes, however, that we have two *a priori* separate systems to compare, and that we have well-established ways for comparing them. Looking upon the written system and the spoken system as separate semiotic systems, each compounded out of a certain number of subsystems, brings out both the differences and the correspondences between the two systems.)

A systemology (theory of semiotic systems) distinguishing between (*a*) simple semiotic systems; (*b*) complex semiotic systems with only one economising subsystem (but in this category, there are already four types according to the type of subsystem); (*c*) complex semiotic systems with *two* economising subsystems (this time there are six logically possible types); (*d*) complex semiotic systems with three economising subsystems (three logically possible types), and (*e*) complex semiotic systems with four economising subsystems (one logically possible type), is a powerful way of classifying semiotic systems according to their structural/functional properties. (All the more so as the classification is directly geared to systematic ways of describing semiotic systems.) The overall classification, in which only some of the categories have been filled in by concrete examples, requires the matrix-type representation shown in Table 7.1.

Table 7.1: logically possible types of semiotic system

	simple figurae only	simple and simultaneous complex figurae only	simple and articulated complex figurae only	simple, simultaneous and articulated complex figurae
simple signa only	Simple system e.g. system of map 'symbols'	An inventory of signa plus a cenematics to provide some of the forms of signa, e.g. traffic lights, semaphore	An inventory of signa plus a cenotactics to provide some of the forms of signa, e.g. Morse code	An inventory of signa plus a cenematics and a cenotactics working together to provide some of the forms of signa
simple and simultaneous signa only	A plerematics with the forms of simple signa provided by an inventory of figurae, e.g. Highway code	A plerematics with the forms of simple signa provided by a cenematics	A plerematics with the forms of simple signa provided by a cenotactics	A plerematics with the forms of simple signa provided by a cenematics and cenotactics working together
simple and articulated complex signa only	A plerotactics with the forms of simple signa provided by an inventory of figurae, e.g. Arabic number writing	A plerotactics with the forms of simple signa provided at least partly by a cenematics	A plerotactics with the forms of simple signa provided at least partly by a cenotactics	A plerotactics with the forms of at least some simple signa provided by a cenematics and a cenotactics working together
simple simultaneous and articulated complex signa	A plerematics as well as a plerotactics with the forms of simple signa provided by an inventory of figurae, e.g. ideographic writing	A plerematics and a plerotactics with the forms of simple signa provided at least partly by a cenematics, e.g. classical written Chinese	A plerematics and a plerotactics with the forms of simple signa provided at least partly by a cenotactics, e.g. alphabetic writing	A plerematics and a plerotactics with the forms of at least some simple signa provided by a cenematics and a cenotactics working together, e.g. spoken languages

7.4.1   Theory of Indices

In 'systemology', an extensive use was made of the notion of signum, provisionally understood as a 'two-faced' entity constituted by a fusion of formal and semantic properties (reminiscent, that is, of the Saussurean *'signe'*). A definition of this notion will be seen to emerge from a deductive classification in which various types of index (of which signum is one type) are compared.

Once again, the working out of a deductive classification presupposes a search for a pertinent dimension in which different types of index are to be compared. As a preliminary to this search, we should note that, by an 'index' is meant any 'two-faced' entity (that is to say, strictly speaking, a relationship) in which a type of signifier (manifested as an observable 'form') acts in a capacity of conveying a certain type of information (registered in the form of a 'message'). Adopting the convention of representing the mediating relationship 'acts in a capacity to convey' by the symbol '→', the general formulaic representation of 'index' will be: *signifier→information*.

There being three 'components' involved in an 'index' – the signifier manifested by observable forms, the information registered as messages of a certain kind, as well as the mediating relationship represented by the '→' – there are three logically possible ways of classifying indices. Of these, however, two can be immediately eliminated as being possible but relatively trivial and unilluminating: (1) the substance that happens to manifest the signifier and (2) the substance of the message registered. (It has already been argued sufficiently that 'accidents' of substance do not provide pertinent dimensions of functional classification.)

The pertinent dimension we are left with is that of the mediating relationship that holds together the two 'faces' of an 'index' (and without which there can be no such thing as an 'index', nor a 'signifier', nor, for that matter, any 'information'). The basis of classification in this dimension boils down to inquiring as to the factors by virtue of which the mediating relationship has come about between a particular signifier and a particular information in a particular 'index'. As we shall find, there are, essentially, two types of factor that can bring about such a mediating relationship: natural (basically causal) links and conventions. The classification of indices takes off from this starting point and culminates (in a way that will be outlined subsequently) in the scheme shown in Figure 7.8.

In the case of a natural index, the mediating relationship between signifier and information can be said to hold by virtue of regular, essentially causal or co-occurrential, links in the 'physical' world between observable manifestations of the signifier and observable objects that 'give substance to' messages registered. Thus, for instance, when lightning acts as a signifier of the information: 'impending thunder', it does so by virtue of the regular 'physical' link that we have come to expect habitually between lightning and thunder. Similarly, 'indices' made use of in medical diagnosis operate by virtue of symptoms regularly associated (in our knowledge of 'nature') with particular diseases.

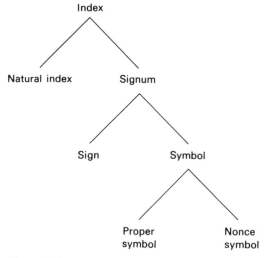

Figure 7.8

Natural indices can be put to artificial uses (without in any way changing their status as natural indices). Thus, artificial devices such as thermometers, pressure gauges, warning lights indicating the malfunction of machines, and so on, profit from natural links by virtue of which their indices convey the appropriate information. In the same way, photographic images must be classified under the category of natural indices, since they 'represent' their subjects by virtue of the photographic process that, link by link, establishes a causal chain whereby light reflected from that subject causes an image to appear on photographic paper.

As long as a causal, or co-occurrence, link can be maintained – no matter how complex a chain this may require – the index in question is identified as a natural index. However, as soon as such a chain is broken – be it only in one small detail – in such a way that some element of convention needs to be stipulated in order to 'explain' the connection between signifier and information, the index can no longer be called 'natural'. That is to say, the natural link by virtue of which a particular 'index' operates (as an index) must be conceived by analogy with an electric circuit; contact needs to be broken only at one point, and the lights go off. Thus, an index that is 'partially motivated' by natural links (for instance, by a natural similarity between signifier and information) is not a natural index – just as a partially connected electric circuit is not a functioning electric circuit. For instance, a pictorial representation drawn by hand, or reproduced in print, may be motivated, as an index of the object represented, by a strong natural resemblance. Yet, in the absence of a complete natural link justifying (motivation is always a case of partial justification) the mediating relationship between signifier and information, such an index must be removed from the category of natural indices. (It would be possible to establish a classification according to degree and type of motivation of indices, but this classification, apart from introducing a large number of imponderable factors, for example, what *is* the motivation, ultimately, of the sign ♀ for 'female', originally for 'Venus'?, would be applicable only to the category of 'conventional' indices. In short, motivation or no motivation, an index is 'conventional' if its 'explanation' requires the slightest reference to conventions.)

7.4.2 The Notion 'Signum'

The discussion so far has established a clearcut and uncompromising borderline between natural indices, and indices that operate (at least to some degree) by virtue of conventions. The fact that some of these latter indices may be guessed when we do not actually know for certain the conventions behind them (for example, the stylised drawing of a human figure wearing a skirt – or is it a Scotsman wearing a kilt? – displayed on a ladies' toilet) does not in any way alter the fact that, in the final analysis, such indices are mediated by virtue of conventions. (A category of visually, or audially, motivated index could, in principle, be set up – we may even call this category 'iconic' – but the fact remains that members of this category will be conventional indices, rather than belong to some third class intermediate between natural indices and conventional indices.)

The term signum refers in axiomatic semiotics to the total set of conventional indices; that is to say, indices in which the mediating relation between signifier and information hold by virtue of a convention (an 'arbitrary' element as opposed to the causal links in natural indices). Thus, for instance, even apparently 'marginal' cases such as

(a)   sunrise→'time to attack'
(b)   red→'danger'
(c)   [k'uk'uw]→'a particular species of bird'
(d)   [bæn]→'a particular kind of noise'
      etc.

fall fully into the category of signa, as they are dependent on conventions for their operation as indices.

7.4.3 Subcategories of 'Signum'

The further subclassification of signa into signs and symbols is based on a distinction between conventions that are 'fixed' within the semiotic system to which a given signum belongs, and conventions that are 'occasional' and 'extra-systemic'. Signa that are used (and understood) entirely in terms of intra-systemic conventions that do not have to be supplemented by the stipulation of 'operational' conventions of an occasional and extra-systemic nature are designated as signs. Signa that depend (for their use and interpretation as indices) on particular *ad hoc* conventions are classified as *symbols*.

Thus, for instance, the signum '[k'uk'uw]→a particular species of bird' is used and understood according to the intra-systemic (linguistic) conventions of English – once these conventions have been grasped, the information value (denotation) of this signum is fixed within certain limits (all and only the birds that belong to the particular species in question). In other words, 'cuckoo' is a (linguistic) sign in English.

In contrast to this, the signum 'sunrise→time to attack' does not belong to any established semiotic system; consequently, there is no question of the convention that makes it operational (as an index) being an intra-systemic one. We are dealing here with an *ad hoc* convention established for particular purposes and on a particular occasion (thence the term 'occasional' convention); the signum in question is a symbol.

For all that the example of 'sunrise→time to attack' – being dependent on an *ad hoc* convention explicitly agreed upon (by the attackers) – seems very different from the case of a 'nonsense word' such as 'jabberwock', the two instances both belong to the same category of symbols. The difference between them lies in the distinction between conventions that are explicitly stated, and conventions that are left *tacit*. The signum in Lewis Carroll's poem – '[džæbəwɔk]→a particular kind of fierce mythical beast' – has the context of the whole poem as the factor that tacitly establishes a kind of *ad hoc* convention, a convention that is 'occasional' and extra-systemic, because it does not belong to English, but to the peculiar 'world' of the poem itself. While within the category of signa wholly dependent for their mediating relationship on 'occasional', extra-systemic conventions one may further distinguish between explicit and tacit symbols, these symbols clearly belong, in the first place, to a single category. This category is designated in axiomatic semiotics by the term 'nonce symbol'. (Using the word 'nonce' acts both as a reminder of the 'occasional', 'one-time' nature of the conventions involved, and as a hint at the presence of so-called 'nonsense words' in this category of symbols.)

While sign and nonce symbol represent two extremes of signa – those whose mediating relation holds entirely by virtue of intra-systemic conventions, and those whose mediating relation holds entirely by virtue of extra-systemic, 'occasional' conventions – there is also an intermediate logical possibility. In short, there is a category of symbols whose information values depend in part on certain general, conventional limitations of an intra-systemic nature, but whose use and interpretation depend also in part on supplementary 'occasional' conventions that need to be separately stipulated. Once again, the 'occasional' conventions may be given explicitly (in the form of a 'naming' process, or a 'definition'), or they may be tacit from a context or situation. (We shall, for the most part, ignore this explicit–tacit distinction.)

For instance, conventions generally accepted within the system of algebraic symbols limit the information values that can (in algebraic indices) be connected to such signifiers as a, b, c, and so on – these are not variables over the whole universe, but only over numbers (the algebraic signifier a can stand for any number, but it cannot stand for, say, 'elephant'). The mediating relation in an index 'a→any particular number' is intra-systemically conventional; it is a matter of the conventions of algebra as such.

On the other hand, in given algebraic operations, the constant informa-

204 SEMIOTIC PERSPECTIVES

tion value (constant, that is, for that operation only) is not just any particular number, but some number different from all others. There is, however, nothing in the systemic conventions of algebra that can determine the particular values that algebraic symbols have in particular operations. This we can only know by virtue of 'occasional' conventions set up for the particular operation in question. Thus, when we say 'let a equal 235', we are explicitly establishing an *ad hoc* convention by virtue of which we create an 'occasional' index '$a = 235$'. (Similarly, when we place x in an equation in which it is the only unknown value to be calculated, we are tacitly creating an index in which x has the predetermined and calculable value attributed to it by the context of the algebraic equation in question.)

Superficial differences apart, there is a remarkable similarity between the case of '$a \rightarrow$ any particular number' and that of 'Peter $\rightarrow$ any animate male creature'. The fact of the matter is that, wholly unconventional uses apart, a system of first names conventionally limits the use of 'Peter' as a 'name for' animate (mostly, but not necessarily, human) creatures of the male sex. Once again, 'Peter' is not a variable over the whole of the universe, but only over a well-defined subset of it, a subset determined by intra-systemic conventions. On the other hand, to put it bluntly, not just any male individual can be, indiscriminately, addressed as 'Peter', only those who have been so named. There is, however, nothing in the systemic conventions of first names by virtue of which it is possible to know which particular individuals within the range of male creatures may, and which may not, be referred to as 'Peter'. The only way we can know this is by virtue of 'occasional' conventions that, in an *ad hoc* manner, establish a link between the symbol 'Peter $\rightarrow$ any animate male creature' and some particular human being, or domestic pet. The establishing of such *ad hoc* conventions for humans is considered important enough to constitute a ceremonial or official procedure (baptism, registration of birth, deed poll, and so on) in order to regularise and advertise these conventions.

The category we have been discussing includes, on the one hand, indices such as algebraic symbols, and, on the other hand, indices usually referred to as 'proper names'. This fact motivates the use of the term 'proper symbol' for designating the category in question.

Another way of explaining the category of proper symbols is by pointing to a 'discrepancy' between the messages they may carry (as far as systemic conventions are concerned) and the messages they do carry (in particular instances). The messages a symbol such as '$a \rightarrow$ any particular number' or 'Peter $\rightarrow$ any animate male creature' may carry are typically conceived as a range of variables. This, however, is also the case for *signs* such as '$\pi \rightarrow \frac{22}{7}$' or '[k'uk'uw] $\rightarrow$ a particular species of bird'. Where signs and proper symbols differ is in 'getting from' the range of variables that they *may* denote to the range of actual messages that they *do* denote. For signs, the transition is automatic within the system to which they belong: all and only measurements that conform to the value $\frac{22}{7}$ can be denoted by the sign 'π'; all and only members of the appropriate species can be denoted by the sign 'cuckoo'. For proper symbols, however, the transition needs to overcome a 'discrepancy': 'a' may denote any particular number, but the numbers it does denote are specific to the occasions of its use; 'Peter' may denote any particular male creature, but the creatures it does denote are only those who have been explicitly named 'Peter'. Without extra *ad hoc* stipulations (which we have called extra-systemic, 'occasional' conventions) it is impossible to overcome the discrepancy between 'may' and 'does' in the case of proper symbols. This is a typical feature by which proper symbols can be identified.

The distinctions drawn between the categories of *sign*, *proper symbol* and *nonce symbol* are an interesting and, I think, original, aspect of axiomatic semiotics. However, the category that is most important from the point of view of the integrated theory as a whole is that of signum, since it is in terms of this notion that the 'systemological' classification of semiotic systems is couched; semiotics is concerned with systems containing signa, not merely with systems containing signs. It is, accordingly, the more general notion of signum, and not the more restricted notion of sign, that is to be further analysed in 'signum-theory'.

7.5.1 'Signum-theory' – the 'Expression' Aspect

The *raison d'être* of a signum is the mediating relationship it creates (as an index) between a 'signifier' and an 'information value'. This mediation is, however, not a simple union of two irreducible entities, but rather a whole chain of successive relationships, for it is, ultimately, between (physical) emissions as the means of conveying messages, and messages conveyed by these physical means, that signa mediate.

'Signum-theory' requires, therefore, to analyse step-by-step the complete 'circuit' of relations linking the messages conveyed by realisations of a given signum (on particular occasions) and the physical means that are used to convey these messages (these concrete means are referred to as emissions). The two extremes between which the signum mediates as a central and abstract entity are emissions and messages.

Within the signum as such (an entity of a high degree of abstraction, it must be remembered) there is a fusion of two equally weighted facets: the aspect of expression (symbolically: E) facing in the direction of the physical means (that is, emissions) and the aspect of content (symbolically: C) facing in the direction of messages conveyed. The way to capture the relationship between these two facets of the signum is by insisting that the signum is the union of these facets, while these facets are each other's logical converses. (The analogy of monogamous marriage relationships may help to clarify this conception: a married couple, z is the logical union of two relationships that are each other's converses, that is to say, of 'husbandhood' $=$ *man x* in the capacity of husband of *woman y* and 'wifehood' $=$ *woman y* in the capacity of wife of *man x*.)

In the case of signa, the two converses are: expression (E) $=$ class of figurae x in its capacity of having the plerological value y, and content (C) $=$ plerological value y being the (semiotic) capacity of class of figurae x.

A signum is thus seen as the union of an expression and a content (like a bottle of wine is the union of a solid container and its liquid contents), but with each of the united terms being reducible to a relationship between identifiable factors. The class of figurae (symbolically $\{p\}^x$) – in its turn, further reducible, ultimately to concrete realisations of figurae in actual communication (as we shall see below) – is an abstraction and generalisation representing the range of physical means from which concrete emissions of the signum may be drawn. The plerological value is a relative and negative value (in the Saussurean sense) created by the network of oppositions to which a signum belongs by virtue of its membership of (the plerological level of) a semiotic system. In short, plerological value is definable as the set of oppositions between a given signum and all the other signa from which it differs within a given semiotic system (for example, the plerological value of '/red and amber/ = prepare to go' is determined in the system of traffic-lights as: $\{\sim$'/red/ = stop', $\sim$'/green/ = go', $\sim$'/amber/ = prepare to stop'$\}$). A particular plerological value is symbolically represented by s^y. Thus the formulaic representation of expression and content is: $E = \{p\}^x$ R s^y and $C = s^y$ Ř $\{p\}^x$, where R stands for the relation 'in its capacity of having', and Ř for the converse relation 'being the (semiotic) capacity'.

Converses mutually imply one another, as well as each of them being in mutual implication with the entity resulting from the union of the converses; that is to say, given that $S(ignum) = $ E and C, and that E and C are converses, it is also the case that S, E and C mutually imply one another (see Figure 7.9).

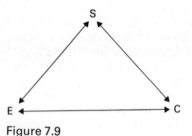

Figure 7.9

Reducing the expression of a signum to the concrete means by which that signum conveys individual messages on particular occasions is a complex matter that takes us through a whole scale of successive steps of reduction:

(1)   reduce $\{p\}^x$ R s^y (i.e. expression) to its members
      p^1 R s^y, p^2 R $s^y \ldots p^n$ R s^y (where $p^1 \ldots p^n = \{p\}^x$).
      Each of these members is a variant *allomorph* of the expression (for example, contextual variants '/iz/ R $s_{plur.}$', '/z/ R $s_{plur.}$', '/ən/ R $s_{plur.}$', etc. of the signum 'plural' in English, in the respective contexts of 'boxes', 'hills', 'oxen', and so on).

(2)   Reduce $\{p\}^x$ to its members (abstracting away from plerological value)
      $\{p^1, p^2 \ldots p^n\} = \{p\}^x$
      Each of these members is a figura (with a potential for differentiating signa, but now abstracted away from the realisation of that

potential (for example, /iz/, /z/, /ən/, etc. as abstracted from their plerological capacities, and viewed as mere means of systematic formal differentiation in English).

(3) Reduce each figura to a value in a cenological subsystem within which it is opposed to other figurae, and has its own range of variation over its appropriate domain of substance

$$p^1 = \{f\}^a \, R \, d^b$$

$\{f\}^a$ represents the class of units of substance that may have the same cenological value;

d^b represents a particular cenological value, defined by the oppositions between a particular figura and all the other figurae which it differs from within the (cenological level of the) same semiotic system (for example, the cenological value, in the Morse code, of the figura /short/ is '~/long/'). R continues to represent the relationship stated as 'in its capacity of having'.

(4) Reduce $\{f\}^a \, R \, d^b$ to its members

$$\{f^1 \, R \, d^b, f^2 \, R \, d^b \ldots f^n \, R \, d^b\} \text{ (where } \{f^1 \ldots f^n\} = \{f\}^a)$$

Each of these members is an *allo-figura*, a 'substantial' variant of the figura in question (for example, the Morse code figura /long/ can vary in substance from medium to medium, and can vary also in actual length according to the pace of transmission).

(5) Reduce $\{f\}^a$ to its members (abstracting away from cenological value)

$$\{f^1, f^2 \ldots f^n\} = \{f\}^a$$

Each of these members can be termed an '*etic* form' (in the case of languages, a 'phonetic form').

While reducing figurae to observably different variants in substance (for example, 'tongue-trilled' [r] and 'uvular' [R] are variant substances of French /r/), 'etic forms' are still not irreducible, concrete phenomena – they must be conceived, in turn, as 'classes of approximations' (for example, 'uvular' [R] is produced in more or less subliminally different ways on each occasion – these pronunciations 'approximate' to one phonetic specification, and are, by courtesy, said to be 'the same').

(6) Reduce each 'etic form' to a class of concrete phenomena

$$f^1 = \{i\}^x$$

$\{i\}^x = \{i^1, i^2 \ldots i^n\}$ where $\{i^1 \ldots i^n\}$ represents the class of actual, individual emissions approximating to the specification of a particular 'etic form' (for example, all individual pronunciations, by any speaker of French, on any given occasion, of the phonetic form [R]).

As we have seen, the reduction of the expression of a signum to a class of concrete and individual emissions, that class whose members can potentially realise the message-bearing means implicated in the given signum, involves a highly complex chain, taking us through a whole scale of abstractions. (Note that the notion figura finds its definition on this scale.)

A further scale of abstractions will be required for dealing with the content aspect of the signum, and the relationship this bears to actual messages. However, before we explore this 'semantic' side of the signum, we shall sum up in Figure 7.10 the scale of abstractions that systematically relates expression to concrete emissions.

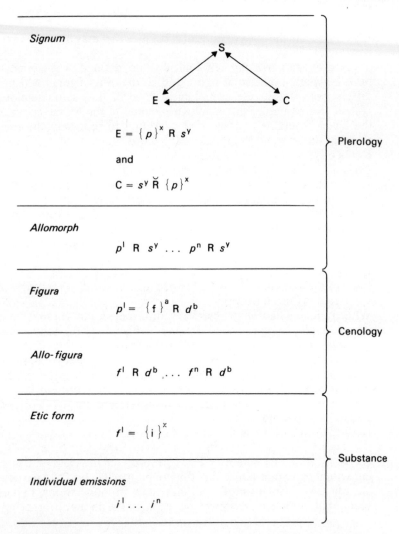

Figure 7.10

7.5.2   Signum-theory – the 'Content' Aspect

The content of a signum, while defined in terms of a plerological value (as the oppositional, negative property in terms of which the semiotic capacity of the signum is measured), has as its positive semiotic property the correspondence of the signum with a specific information value. Such a correspondence of a signum with its 'semantic' properties is most frequently represented as a 'triangular' relationship; for example, Ullmann's adaptation (Ullmann, 1957, 1962) of the famous 'Ogden and Richards triangle' (Ogden and Richards, 1923) (see Figure 7.11).

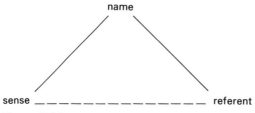

Figure 7.11

In axiomatic semiotics (Hervey, 1979), a *'rectangular'* model (henceforth referred to as the 'denotational rectangle') replaces the usual 'referential triangle'. The role of this 'denotational rectangle' is to relate, in clearly specified ways, the abstractions designated by the terms 'signum', 'information value', 'signum-token' and 'denotatum', both to one another, and to their concrete correlates in the realm of actual phenomena. In this exposition, the 'denotational rectangle' will be built up from a confrontation of the Peircean idea of type versus token with the Saussurean idea of form versus substance.

In connection with the Peircean idea of type, we note that types are both abstract and generalising – for instance, a type such as '£1.00' is both a 'notional figure', and a value comprised of a potentially unlimited class of its tokens (it is both an abstraction and a generalisation of all manifestations of a particular monetary value).

Tokens of a given type are members of the general category brought into one abstract entity by that type; that is to say, tokens are specific or particularising (as opposed to being generalisations). They stand for particular manifestations of a category. Since, however, it would be absurd to say that a category that is abstract consists in a class of members that are concrete, and since tokens, themselves, are descriptive of (stand for) concrete particulars, rather than being concrete particulars, it follows that tokens are also abstractions (for example, 'a £1.00 note', as a token of the type '£1.00', is a 'notional', though particular, representative of the type in question).

Tokens, in short, are abstract and particularising: particular by virtue of being individual members of a general category, but abstract by virtue of representing certain relevant aspects of a given concrete phenomenon (for example, the token 'a £1.00 note' represents the inherent aspect of financial value attached to a particular piece of paper bearing the appropriate physical markings).

In connection with the Saussurean notion 'form', we note also that forms are both abstract and generalising. A form is a value infinitely realisable in its (infinitely renewable) substance – for instance, the form

'£1.00' is both an abstraction and a generalisation over the whole range of substances (pieces of paper currency, sets of coins, and so on) that have the same value.

Substance – and the agglomeration of concrete physical entities that constitute the variable substances of a given form – concretely manifests form. It is, in other words, concrete (as opposed to being abstract). Since concrete entities are individual and particular in 'reality', the phenomena that constitute the substance of a form are concrete particulars.

When applied to the plerological level of a semiotic system, the notion type covers signum and the information value corresponding to a signum (that is, these two abstractions are plerological types, both being abstract, generalising, categorial entities). Similarly, and for the same reasons, signum and information value are the forms (values) pertaining to the plerological level of a semiotic system. Thus, in plerology, signum and information value belong to the highest level of abstraction, the level in which type and form coincide with one another.

These abstractions – signum and information value – need to be correlated both to their appropriate tokens and to their appropriate substances. Token and substance cannot, however, be incorporated on a single level, for, although both involve particulars, tokens are abstract, while substances are concrete phenomena.

Tokens of signa (designated, for lack of a better term, as 'signum-tokens') are one step removed from signa – they stand to a signum as members to a class. Analogously, tokens of information values (designated by the term 'denotatum') are one step removed from information values, standing to an information value as members to a class.

Substance is relegated to a further level – that of concrete phenomena.

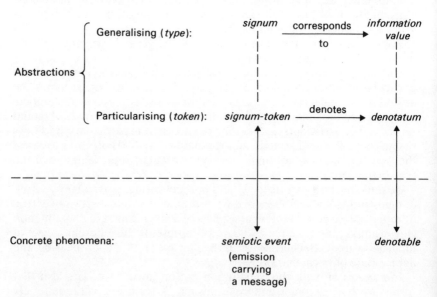

Figure 7.12

On this level, the particular phenomena corresponding to signa (realisations of signa) are semiotic events. Each such event is, itself, constituted of the interplay between an emission (cf. Section 7.5.1, p. 205) and the message it conveys. The concrete phenomena that are the substances of information values (that is, concretisations of denotata) are the 'objects' designated by the term 'denotable'. 'Denotables' are, on the one hand, the subject matter of messages and, on the other, entities susceptible to being experienced independently of communication (Hervey, 1979).

The 'denotational rectangle' built on the basis of the foregoing discussion can be diagrammatically represented as in Figure 7.12. The relationships between terms in the 'rectangle' in Figure 7.12 can now be precisely stated:

(1) *Signum* to *signum-token*: a relationship of class to member (that is, a signum is a class of its signum-tokens).

(2) *Signum* to *semiotic event*: a signum is a model for a particular class of concrete semiotic events;
conversely, a particular class of semiotic events constitutes the potentially infinitely repeatable realisations of a given signum. (For example, every time a driver observes a circular design with a blue field enclosing a white arrow, interpreting its message by following the direction of the arrow, the resulting event is, regardless of all its material differences from other such events, classified as a realisation of one and the same Highway Code signum).

(3) *Signum-token* to *semiotic event*: while signum is a model for a class of semiotic events, and signum-token is a member of the signum, a particular signum-token is a model for a particular semiotic event. That is to say, signum-token is an abstract model, but a model with an extreme specificity, standing in a one–to–one relation with a single *semiotic event* (for example, a cine-film recording of a driver observing a particular Highway Code signal on a particular occasion would be a model with the required degree of specificity).

(4) *Signum-token* to *denotatum*: a particular signum-token conveys a particular piece of information (in this way, the model reflects the message necessarily conveyed in the course of the semiotic event represented by the signum-token); we shall say that the particular piece of information conveyed is denoted by the signum-token (this piece of information is a denotatum). Since what is essentially the same denotatum can be conveyed by an unlimited number of tokens of the same signum, though a given signum-token can only denote one single denotatum, the relationship between signum-token and denotatum is a relationship of one-way implication (for example, the grapheme 'a' of English can be denoted by a signum-token involving a 'short' followed by a 'long' flash with the torch I bought last week, or by another signum-token I have just tapped out on my desk).

(5) *Denotatum* to *information value*: a relationship of member to class; an information value is the generalisation of a class of denotata, each of whose members can (according to the conventions gov-

erning a particular signum) be denoted by signum-tokens of the same signum; conversely, a particular denotatum instantiates (in the way that a specimen instantiates a species) a particular information value (for example, the grapheme 'A' of English, the grapheme 'a' of English, the grapheme 'A' of French, the grapheme 'a' of French, the grapheme 'A' of German, the grapheme 'a' of German, and so on, are all members of the same class of denotata, the class generalised as the information value ('the alphabetic letter "a" ') of the Morse code signum ('/short + long/→the letter "a" ').

(6) *Signum* to *information value*: a correspondence between two types; since (*a*) signum is conceived of as a determinate class of signum-tokens, (*b*) information value as a determinate class of denotata, and (*c*) each signum-token denotes its own determinate denotatum, it follows that the correspondence of signum to information value is not only conceivable as a direct correspondence between two types, but also as the result of the fact that each individual token of a signum denotes its own denotatum. A given signum determines its class of signum-tokens and each such signum-token determines its denotatum; consequently, the class of signum-tokens (= signum) determines a class of denotata: the information value of the signum, seen as the potential range of denotata that can be denoted by tokens of the signum. Once again, a one-way implication emerges between signum and information value: a signum implies the class of denotata designated as its information value. (This one-way implication allows synonymy between signa; two or more signa may have the same information value corresponding to them.)

(7) *Denotatum* to *denotable*: a denotatum faces at once in two directions: in one sense, it is the information-bearing capacity of a signum-token (that is, it is a term necessarily linked via a token to a signum); in another, it is an entity endowed with properties that make it a part of practical experience (that is, it is an 'object' that can be reacted to in terms of practical, non-semiotic behaviour; it is not just something that can be 'referred to' or 'talked about', but also something that can be 'experienced' in other ways). Outside of its functioning as the information-bearing capacity of a signum-token, a denotatum, while it does not lose its potential for being denoted, becomes a mere denotable. We may say that a denotable is the 'substance' that gives a denotatum its basis in extra-semiotic reality. (The wide sense in which the term denotable is to be used – including 'objects', 'qualities', 'processes', 'relations' and 'complex circumstances' that are networks of the former – can only be hinted at in the context of this discussion. Reference may be made to Harre (1970a, 1970b) and to Hervey (1979). Similarly, I can only allude to the notion of 'functional ostension' – the idea that 'experiential reality' should be viewed, by analogy with any 'functional' system, as a network of opposed values – as the basis for endowing denotables with an extra-semiotic identity. On this point, reference may be made to Hervey (1979, 1980).)

What is important about the 'denotational rectangle' for our present purposes is that it locates content as that aspect of signum that faces in the direction of information value, and that it 'analyses' both signum and information value, relating them, ultimately, to their concrete correlates in the realm of actual phenomena (semiotic events and denotables, respectively). In this way, the 'denotational rectangle' fulfils its purpose by setting up a scale of abstractions that link signum to its 'semantic' aspect.

7.6 Some Examples of Axiomatic Semiotic Analyses

7.6.1 Roman Number-writing

The system is analysed as the interlock of a simple cenological inventory with a plerological level containing a (rudimentary) plerematics and a (more sophisticated) plerotactics.

The cenological inventory contains the figurae: /I/, /V/, /X/, /L/, /C/, /D/, /M/ and /‾/.

The basic inventory of the plerematics consists of the signs: 'I→1', 'V→5', 'X→10'. 'L→50', 'C→100', 'D→500', 'M→1000' and '‾→ ×1000' (e.g. 'V̄→5 × 1000 = 5000').

For plerological purposes, this inventory forms a hierarchy, with 'I→1' having the lowest 'rank', and the hierarchy beyond 'M→1000' being continued in 'V̄→5000', 'X̄→10000', etc. Elements belonging to an odd 'rank' in the hierarchy behave differently (in constructions) from elements of an even 'rank' (odd 'rank': 'I→1', 'X→10', 'C→100', etc., even 'rank': 'V→5', 'L→50', 'D→500', etc.).

Rank 1	'I→1'	
Rank 2	'V→5'	
Rank 3	'X→10'	
Rank 4	'L→50'	Plerematic hierarchy
Rank 5	'C→100'	(in ascending order)
Rank 6	'D→500'	
Rank 7	'M→1000'	
Rank 8	'V̄→5000'	
Rank 9	'X̄→10000'	
etc.		

Plerematic constructions are of two types:

Type A: simultaneous bundles of two, or three identical signs (e.g. 'II→2', 'III→3', etc.). Such constructions only occur with signs belonging to an odd 'rank' in the hierarchy (e.g. 'XX→20', but not *'VV→10').

Type B: simultaneous bundles consisting of a sign from 'rank' 2 to 'rank' 7 (i.e. 'V→5' − 'M→1000') and the sign'‾ → × 1000' (e.g. 'V̄→5 × 1000 = 5000', 'X̄→10 × 1000 = 10000', etc.).

Plerotactic constructions operate with the subordination of a lower 'ranking' sign to the next higher 'ranking' sign with which it co-occurs in a given complex.

There are three types of position (one nuclear and two subordinative types) in the plerotactics of Roman number writing:

(1) *Nuclear* position (the semantic function of this position is simply to attribute the face value to the sign standing in that position; e.g. 'X→10' has its face value in 'XVII→17', where it stands in nuclear position with respect to 'VII→7').

(2) *Pre-nuclear* position (the semantic function of this position is to subtract the face value of the sign standing in that position from the face value of the sign standing in nuclear position; e.g. in 'XC→90', 'X→10' has the actual value '−10').

(3) *Post-nuclear* position (the semantic function of this position is to add the face value of the sign standing in that position to the face value of the sign in nuclear position; e.g. in 'XV→15', where it stands in post-nuclear position, 'V→5' has the actual value '+5').

Plerotactic conventions:

(a) Only simple signs, and pleremantic complexes of Type B (e.g. '$\bar{V}$→5000') can stand in nuclear position.

(b) If the pre-nuclear position is filled, the post-nuclear position can only contain signs of a 'rank' lower than that of the sign filling the pre-nuclear position (e.g. 'XCV→95', but not *'XCXI→101, nor *'XCL→140).

(c) Pre-nuclear position can only be filled by simple signs or pleremantic complexes of Type B (e.g. '$\bar{V}$→5000').

(d) Pre-nuclear position can only be filled by a sign one 'rank' below the 'rank' of the nuclear sign if that nuclear sign is of even 'rank'; if the nuclear sign is of odd 'rank', pre-nuclear position can only be filled by a sign two 'ranks' below that of the nuclear sign (e.g. 'XL→ − 10 + 50 = 40', but not *'VL→− 5 + 50 = 45'; 'XC→− 10 + 100 = 90', but not *'LC→ − 50 + 100 = 50', nor *'VC→ − 5 + 100 = 95').

(e) Post nuclear position can only be filled by signs of a lower 'rank' than that of the sign filling nuclear position (e.g. 'VI→ 5 + 1 = 6', 'LX→50 + 10 = 60', but not *'VX→5 + 10 = 15', nor *'XC→10 + 100 = 110').

(f) Post-nuclear position may be filled by (and is the only position that may be filled by) pleremantic complexes of Type A. It may also be filled by plerotactic complexes whose highest 'ranking' constituent is
   (i) of lower 'rank' than the filler of nuclear position, if pre-nuclear position is not filled (e.g. 'CXL→100 + (−10 + 50) = 140', 'CLXV→100 + (50 + (10 + 5)) = 165', but not *'LDXV→50 + (500 + (10 + 5)) = 565');
   (ii) of lower 'rank' than the filler of pre-nuclear position, if the latter is filled (e.g. 'XCVI→ − 10 + 100 + (5 + 1) = 96', but not *'XCXI→ − 10 + 100 + (10 + 1) = 101').

In terms of the foregoing inventories and constructional conventions, any Roman numeral expression can be described or predicted – the system is exhaustively described by these means. (I am indebted to Sheena Gardner, University of St Andrews, Scotland, for her collaboration in producing this semiotic description of the system of Roman number writing.)

7.6.2 Ideographic writing: Classical Chinese

There is, of course, no question of attempting here a full-fledged description of a complete writing system with all its inventory and conventions. We can only indicate the 'skeletal' structure of ideographic writing, as exemplified by classical Chinese, in terms of its constitutive *subsystems*, and of the partial isomorphism between these subsystems and subsystems of the corresponding spoken language. These indications will, however, be found to be revealing of the differences between types of writing system.

Classical Chinese has a fully fledged plerology that is the interlocking of a plerematics (forming written 'words' as simultaneous bundles of simple signs of the writing system) and a plerotactics (forming written complexes of a syntactic type from the 'words' produced by the plerematics). On the plerological level, therefore, classical (written) Chinese is structurally analogous with semiotic systems of the spoken language type. Furthermore, there is a close one–to–one isomorphism whereby simple signs of the writing system correspond to those of a spoken language, 'words' of the writing system with 'words' of a spoken language, syntactic complexes of the writing system with syntactic complexes of a corresponding spoken language. Both the inventories, and the structures of classical (written) Chinese and of a corresponding spoken language run closely parallel with one another on the plerological level (reading or writing can, on this level, take the form of a word–for–word transition from one system to the other).

On the cenological level, however, classical (written) Chinese shows only the most rudimentary degree of structural economy. Characters, as figurae, may be analysable into so-called 'radicals' (for example, / 他 / into /亻/ and /也/, /字/ into /宀/ and /子/) that are 'systematically' recurring cenological elements. These complex characters (figurae) can, consequently, be regarded as (economically constructed) simultaneous bundles of figurae (radicals). Accordingly, we recognise a cenematic subsystem in classical (written) Chinese; this subsystem, however, exhausts the cenological economy of the writing system.

While the presence of a cenematics in classical (written) Chinese argues for a degree of structural analogy between the cenological level of this system, and that of a spoken language (compounded of a *cenematics and* a *cenotactics*), there is no isomorphism whatever between the inventory and constructions of the written cenematics, and the cenematics of a corresponding spoken language. 'Radicals' cannot be transliterated into units of the spoken language (they cannot be 'read aloud' at all). As for the cenematics of the corresponding spoken language, culminating in the cenematic complexes that linguists call 'phonemes', its elements are not 'represented' in classical (written) Chinese in any way (this is our way of saying what, in common parlance, is often expressed as the 'non-phonetic nature of ideographic writing').

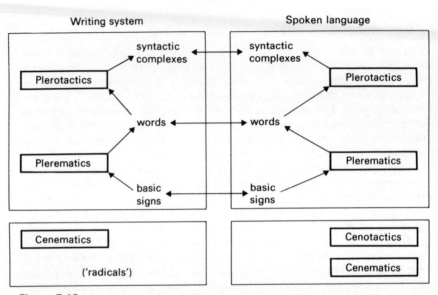

Classical Chinese

Figure 7.13

7.6.3   Syllabic Writing: Japanese Kana

The 'skeletal' structure of Japanese Kana is, as we shall see, somewhat different on the cenological level from that of an ideographic writing system. On the plerological level, however, such a system is both analogous with spoken languages (constituted by an interlocking *plerematics* and *plerotactics*) and displays a close one–to–one isomorph-ism (in terms of inventory and constructions of signs) with spoken Japanese. (Reading and writing take the form, on the plerological level, of a word–for–word transition from one system to the other.)

On the cenological level, Japanese Kana displays a highly systematic cenotactic economy: the basic figurae, for example,$|$か$/$, $/$ナ$/$, $/$ラ$/$, $/$オ$/$, and so on, can be combined into articulated constructions, for example, $/$かオ$/$, $/$オか$/$, $/$ナか$/$, and so on. Thus the system of Kana is actually a semiotic system with two articulations (both a plerological and a cenolo-gical articulation are instanced). Where the system differs from alphabetical writing, however, is the point of correspondence between written figurae and figurae of spoken Japanese: this point of correspond-ence is through the one–to–one isomorphism of basic figurae of the writing system with 'phoneme-chains' (cenotactic constructions) of spoken Japanese. (These 'phoneme-chains' are in fact the 'syllables' of spoken Japanese; thence the term 'syllabic writing' in token of the 'syllable–to–basic–written–figura' correspondence between the two systems.)

Japanese Kana and Spoken Japanese

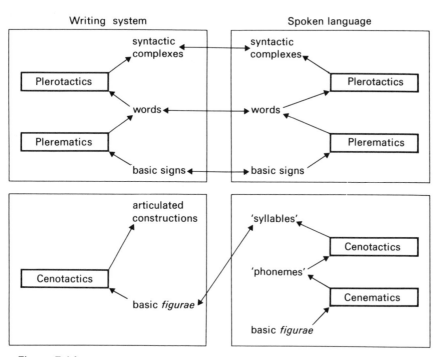

Figure 7.14

7.6.4 Alphabetic Writing: English

The 'skeletal' structure of written English (in terms of constitutive subsystems) is analogous with that of Japanese Kana: we find in it the same three subsystems (plerotactics, plerematics and cenotactics). Furthermore, there is a high degree of isomorphism between (a) basic signs of the writing system and those of the spoken language; (b) words of the writing system and those of the spoken language; (c) syntactic constructions of the writing system and those of the spoken language. (It is only relatively rarely that a written sign can be 'read' in alternate ways – e.g. 'e-i-t-h-e-r' as [aiðə] or as [iːðə]; or two written signs 'read' in identical ways – e.g. 'C-h-r-i-s-t-m-a-s' and 'X-m-a-s' as [krisməs]·)

On the cenological level, there is no qualitative difference between Japanese Kana and alphabetic writing (both have a cenotactic economy). Where there is a divergence is in the point of correspondence between figurae of written English and figurae of spoken English: this point of correspondence is through a degree of isomorphism (which we know to

Alphabetic Writing

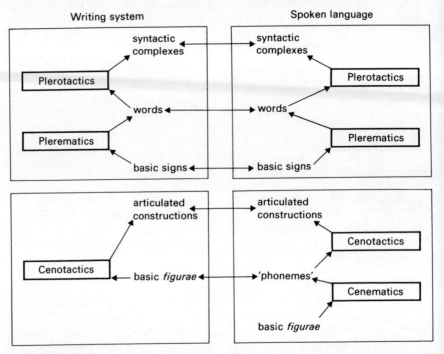

Figure 7.15

be far from perfect because of the vagaries of English spelling, a spelling that reflects too much of historically earlier stages of English to be able to stand in close isomorphism with present-day spoken English) between basic figurae (graphemes) of the writing-system and 'phonemes' of spoken English.

8

Semiotics as a Stylistic Theory: Bureau and Riffaterre

General Remarks

Attempts to fathom the mysteries of literary style span the whole history of Western thought. It is only recently, however, that style has been studied as a form of 'communication', a form sufficiently analogous with other communicational codes for it to be a potential object of semiotic study.

Since it is, currently, by no means uncommon to subscribe to the view that semiotics holds the key to matters of style, we might have chosen any of a number of semiotic approaches to stylistics (Granger, 1969; Guiraud and Kuentz, 1970; Jakobson, 1979; Kristeva, 1974; Todorov, 1967; and so on). Of course, a full discussion even of the salient points that unite or divide the most influential semiotic-stylistic theories of recent times is out of the question in this volume. At the same time, leaving the entire area of these theories completely unexplored would have an unfortunate effect on the balance of its contents; the fact of the matter is that, to many scholars, 'semiotics' connotes the stylistic-semiotic study of literary works.

The present chapter – in fact, the conjoining of two antithetical 'sketches' – is in the nature of a compromise by means of which I hope to convey some idea of the kind of theoretical and descriptive activity one might expect to encounter in a semiotic approach to literary style. Choice of the two authors selected is, in part, motivated by the very antithesis they offer between a 'text-based' (Bureau) and a 'reader-based' (Riffaterre) approach to stylistics. In addition, both theories recommend themselves by their relative accessibility, their up-to-dateness, and by the intrinsic merits of the ideas they encompass.

8 Bureau

8.1.1 Literature as a Semiotic Object; Background to Bureau's Stylistics

The identification of literature as an object of semiotic study is conditional, as pointed out by Bureau (1976), on the identification (both in principle and in practice) of various semiological levels that intermingle in constituting a literary work.

A text, taken purely on the level of its sentences (that is, its units of discourse), is a linguistic object – it does not become a literary object by mere 'osmosis', but only by the superimposition of further, and in that sense, 'higher', literary properties. The properties constitutive of the 'literariness' of a work should not be automatically assumed to be semiotic; what makes them so, however, is the fact that they – like other 'codes' – operate with recurrences and contrasts, and that – also like other 'codes' – these operations have communicative ends.

The functioning of 'superimposed' codes (surcodages, cf. Granger, 1969) over a linguistic text is made possible by two general factors: (*a*) the substance in which linguistic messages are necessarily realised (whether phonic or graphic) can, at the same time, be put to other uses (for example, in uttering the sentence 'I am keen', the phonetic substance can be so modulated as to convey reluctance – creating thereby a contrast between linguistic message and 'superposed' message; a poem about the Crucifixion can be typographically set out in the form of a cross – creating a recurrence between the linguistic message and the 'superposed' message); (*b*) the form (in so far as that form is a matter of choice) in which a linguistic message is couched can, at the same time, be put to other uses (for example, the particular form in which the linguistic message of 'Excuse me, but you make me sick' is couched, conveys, over and above the purely offensive linguistic message, a conciliatory message of polite apology – creating a contrast between the linguistic message and the 'superposed' message; choice of 'May I say how much I admire your work?' conveys, over and above the linguistic message, an expression of respectful admiration carried by the respectful manner of address, creating a recurrence between the linguistic message and the 'superposed' message).

It should be obvious that the 'non-primary' use of linguistic substance or linguistic form for the operation of a superposed code is conditional on the substance or form in question being primarily that of an underlying linguistic code. Equating literary style with the operation of superposed codes on a necessary foundation of a linguistic text makes it, furthermore, apparent that the key word of stylistics is 'strategy'; to say something is to avail oneself of a basic linguistic code – to say it in a strategically apt way is to avail oneself of a 'superposed' stylistic code.

Methodologically, as Bureau (1976) points out, a knowledge of the underlying linguistic code, and a full analysis of the text as a linguistic object, are a necessary condition for the subsequent identification and analysis of superposed codes operating over the linguistic text.

Admittedly, any level of linguistic form (or of the corresponding substance) may become available for 'strategic' use by a stylistic code. Thus, for instance, the structure of a text in terms of syllables, or in terms of 'graphemes', may give rise to contrasts and recurrences (rhymes, assonances, metric variation, and so on), each level of structure contributing thereby a level of stylistic coding. However, Bureau's attention is specifically focused on one particular linguistic level (though he is well aware of others), that of syntactic structure, and the strategic use of syntactic structure for stylistic purposes. It is in this area that Bureau's stylistic-semiotic theory is extensively elaborated and exemplified.

8.1.2 Syntactic Analysis and the Stylistic Aspects of Syntax

Bureau has a great advantage in being able to avail himself of a detailed functional analysis of syntactic structure (Bureau, 1978). We are, unfortunately, unable here to cover the principles and practices of Bureau's syntactic model, but must instead imagine that sentences analysed according to this model serve as a background to identifying the interplay, in a text, of syntactic forms and substances. This interplay constitutes the 'strategic' operation of syntactic features in the realisation of elements of a stylistic code. (It must also be understood that the text has been prepared for syntactic analysis by a segmentation into sentences – not necessarily in a way corresponding to the 'sentences' indicated by punctuation, but those that answer Bureau's syntactic definition of self-contained linguistic units; Bureau, 1976, 1978.)

On the basis of properties precisely specifiable as a result of syntactic analysis, there emerge three types of potentially stylistically relevant characteristic: (*a*) length (quantifiable from *1* to *n*); (*b*) complexity (quantifiable from $\emptyset$ to *n*) and (*c*) structure. These three characteristics will be discussed under separate headings below.

8.1.3 Syntactic 'Length' as a Potential Carrier of Style

The 'length' of a sentence is the numerical index of the number of its constitutive syntactically minimal elements (that is, the so-called *syntaxemes*). Thus, while the sentence 'Look!' contains only one syntaxeme (index of length = *1*), some sentences in literary texts may run into hundreds (for example, the Proustian sentence analysed in Bureau (1976) has an index of length of *222*). It is fairly obvious that the extent of maximum, minimum and average sentence length can be a salient 'strategic' feature of the style of a literary text.

While individuation of a literary style (that of a text, or, even more generally, that of an author) is, of course, never solely a matter of sentence length, sentence length is clearly one of the features that may play a significant role in characterising an individual style. An exact measure of sentence length contributes, for instance, to a specification of the syntactic aspect of Proust's literary style – a specification that is highly relevant to appreciating the particularities of that style.

Given an exact measurement of sentence length, a number of important statistical operations become possible: (*a*) computation of the average sentence length in a literary text; (*b*) comparison of maximum, minimum and average sentence length from one text to another, or from one author to another; (*c*) plotting of the distribution of shorter and longer sentences in a given text.

The latter may be of particular interest as a 'strategic' device establishing a kind of 'rhythmic' pattern in a text. In particular, the juxtaposition of a relatively short and a relatively long sentence creates a contrast in that pattern, whereas recurrences will be found in the distribution of sentences of (approximately) the same length at different points in the text. Where the contrasts and recurrences that make up this 'rhythmic' textual pattern can, furthermore, be put into correlation with a textual or thematic meaning that they serve to bring into relief, they constitute fully fledged carriers of stylistic coding. To take a crude example (the genuine examples furnished in Bureau (1976) are too extensive and complex to include here), in a text where a number of relatively long sentences are 'sandwiched' between two minimally short sentences, 'Birth.' and 'Death.', the patterning of sentence length could be correlated with a stylistic meaning paraphraseable as: 'the seemingly long-drawn-out efforts of Life are bounded by the decisive incidents of Birth and Death'.

Syntactic length may create a 'rhythmic' patterning between sentences. It may also lend a sometimes unexpected balance to the strategic construction of a text through the recurrence of structurally isolable groups of comparable length within sentences. On Bureau's analysis, for instance, Proustian sentences consisting of over two hundred syntaxemes – sentences that, on the surface, appear to be merely 'rambling' – turn out to be remarkably balanced in terms of a patterned distribution of internal syntactic groups of comparable length. Again, where such patterns can be put into correlation with thematic features (for example, they give stylistic emphasis to a particular 'privileged' *sign* in the text) these patterns are carriers of a superposed stylistic coding.

8.1.4 Syntactic 'Complexity' as a Potential Carrier of Style

Syntactic 'complexity' is a matter of 'depth' in the hierarchical syntactic structure of a sentence. In a sentence whose syntaxemes all belong to the nucleus, the 'complexity index' is said to be zero. In sentences that are 'expanded' by the addition of constituents subordinated to the nucleus as a whole, these subordinated elements constitute level 1 'expansions'. In an increasing hierarchical 'depth', part of a secondary expansion may, in turn, have a further 'expansion' appended to it, and so forth. Since an expansion subordinated to the nucleus is labelled level 1, the level of 'secondary expansions' (subordinative expansions of the second degree: SE 2) is given the index 2. 'Third level' elements of the sentence, which are subordinative expansions of the third degree (SE 3), are given the index *3*, and so on with each increasing level of 'depth' in syntactic structure. Sentences are given a complexity index according to the 'deepest' level of subordinative expansion found in them, thus a sentence containing one or more subordinative expansions of, say, the fourth degree (SE 4), would have a complexity index of *4*. It may be argued that a complexity index of $\emptyset$ is only appropriate to sentences such as 'Run!', 'Here!', 'Mary!', etc. while sentences like 'I ran.', 'I shot Mary.', which contain already one level of subordination ('I' is subordinated to the predicate 'ran'; both 'I' and 'Mary' are subordinated to the predicate 'shot'), should have a complexity index of *1*. In that case, 'secondary expansions' – that is to say, elements that are expansions of the nucleus of a sentence – would receive a numerical index of *2*, rather than *1*. Be that as it may, Bureau counts the level of other nuclear syntactic units clustering round a predicate as *level $\emptyset$*. Appendages to the nucleus as a whole are *level 1* expansions. Subsequent appendages of $\emptyset$ *level* constituents, appendages to parts of these appendages, and so forth, constitute 'deeper' levels of subordinative expansion that are numbered from *2* to *n*.

According to Bureau's procedures, the sentence 'This is the house.' (containing no subordinative expansions) is a sentence with a complexity index of Ø. (This may seem somewhat odd, since the sentence is obviously complex to some degree, unlike, say the sentence 'Run!' which is not.)

In 'This is the house *that Jack built.*', a subordinative expansion has been appended to the nuclear element 'the house'. This expansion is, in Bureau's terms, an expansion of the first degree of 'depth' (SE 1). Accordingly, the sentence has a complexity index of *1*.

In 'This is the malt *that lay in the house that Jack built.*', the unit 'that lay' is a first degree subordinative expansion of the unit 'the malt'. In turn, however, this subordinative expansion (SE 1) is further expanded by the unit 'in the house' (SE 2), to which 'that Jack built' is attached as a further, 'deeper' level of subordinative expansion (SE 3). The sentence, containing 3 subsequent levels of subordinative expansion, has a complexity index of *3*.

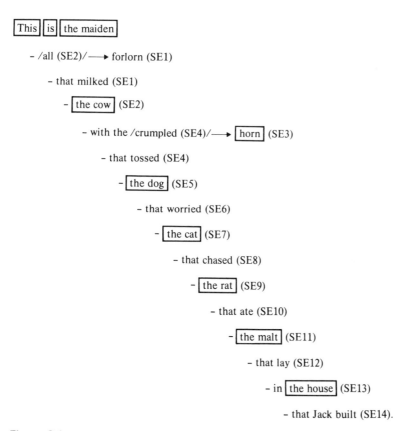

Figure 8.1

The complexity index of 'This is the maiden all forlorn that milked the cow with the crumpled horn that tossed the dog that worried the cat that chased the rat that ate the malt that lay in the house that Jack built.' is measurable in terms of the number of successive 'depths' of subordinative expansion that characterise the hierarchical structure of this sentence. Since the deepest level of 'embedded' subordinative expansion is of the fourteenth degree (SE 14), the complexity index of the whole sentence is *14*. (We should note, incidentally, that there is a closer connection between the intellectual effort required for the comprehension of a sentence and the complexity of that sentence, than there is between comprehensibility and sentence length. For instance, the more complex, though shorter, sentence 'He is my father's brother's wife's son.' is conspicuously more opaque than the longer, but less complex, sentence 'The fat old man must have drunk a few large gins on the way home.')

The nursery rhyme to which belongs the sentence represented in Figure 8.1 provides a crude example of a strategic-stylistic play on sentence complexity. The stylistic character of the nursery rhyme – in a sense its whole point is a piece of 'fun' – derives from the game it makes of its pattern of cumulatively increasing sentence complexity:

Sentence 1: Complexity index = *1*
Sentence 2: Complexity index = *3*
Sentence 3: Complexity index = *5*
Sentence 4: Complexity index = *7*
etc.

8.1.5 Structure as a Potential Carrier of Style

There are two properties of sentences that, together, add up to what Bureau refers to as syntactic 'structure': (*a*) the syntactic functions (relationships) responsible for the particular cohesion and organisation of the constituent units in a given sentence; (*b*) the linear succession in which these units are disposed.

The most immediately striking contribution of syntactic 'structure' to the level of 'strategic' stylistic functions is, of course, in terms of variety. Common sense alone tells us that substantially equivalent linguistic messages can be couched in sentences of varying length and complexity, sentences that are different in internal organisation and/or the linear disposition of their elements (compare, for instance, 'Death is our end.' with 'In the end, we die.' or with 'Our end is death.').

Structural variety (the spice of style) in a text is quantitatively measurable as a function of the number of sentences over the number of syntactic classes (or types) to which these sentences can be assigned. That is to say, the greater the number of sentence types, the greater the variety – the syntactic richness – of the text.

More importantly still, 'external' symmetry between sentences, and 'internal' symmetry within sentences – both matters of the manifestation of equivalent syntactic structures that 'mirror' each other in the text – impose a pattern of recurrences (and, of course, contrasts) on a given text. Our rather crude example of the nursery rhyme 'The house that Jack built' can again be used to illustrate such a patterning. Each sentence of the rhyme belongs to the same type ('This is the . . .'), from which comes the particular symmetry between sentences that is so characteristic of the text as a whole. There is, however, a more detailed structural patterning that emerges when the nursery rhyme is tabulated as in Figure 8.2.

The (admittedly rather childish) playfulness of the pattern of symmetries and contrasts in the example should not mislead us into denying that we are dealing with a basically serious stylistic device. In so far as Sentence 1 of the nursery rhyme contains the sign 'house', this sentence can be seen as the 'foundation stone' on which the whole nursery rhyme is built by successive extensions. Thus, stylistically speaking, 'house' becomes a privileged sign in the text. It may not even be too fanciful to suggest that the 'construction' of the nursery rhyme is in correlation with the theme of 'building a house'; in this way, we might view the whole nursery rhyme as 'miming' the process of building a house, by means of an analogy that shows up in the textual pattern represented in Figure 8.2. There is certainly some basis to the suggestion that this throws an interesting light on the playful stylistic strategy of the nursery rhyme.

Within sentences of this nursery rhyme, we find cases of total symmetry (designated by Bureau as isomorphism). For instance, in the sentence tabulated in Figure 8.1, there is isomorphism between several successive subordinative expansions:

that tossed the dog
that worried the cat
that chased the rat
that ate the malt

which are exact syntactic equivalents of one another. Not only does this isomorphism constitute an obvious part of the stylistic 'game' in which the nursery rhyme seems to indulge, but it may not be too fanciful to correlate the isomorphism of these sentence units with the uniformity of building materials in the construction of a house. If such a correlation is not too far-fetched, then we have here another stylistic instance of the way the nursery rhyme plays on an analogy with the theme of 'building a house'.

The nursery rhyme example, albeit crude when compared with the serious literary examples analysed by Bureau, has the advantage of illustrating the stylistic observations and generalisations that may be suggested by analysing the syntactic properties of a text. It also has the advantage of showing up the weaker side of this type of stylistic exercise, which is that, while patterns such as those in Figures 8.1 and 8.2 can, indeed, be objectively established, the placing of these patterns in correlation with thematic features or privileged signs of the text remains a matter of speculation, subject only to vague considerations of 'plausi-

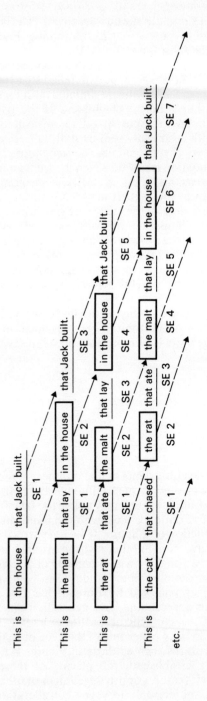

Figure 8.2

bility'. Although it might not be too far-fetched (and this is the most that one can say) to recognise in the syntactic patterns of the nursery rhyme the manifestation of a message-bearing (semiotic) code stylistically alluding to the theme of 'building a house', the putative analogy on which this suggestion rests is far from being objectively established. This correlation between syntactic patterns and a stylistic-semiotic function (as well as the exact nature and purport of that stylistic function itself) is an invention of the analyst – the critic may or may not find that 'there is something in it', according to his personal, subjective predilections.

8.2 Riffaterre

8.2.1 Literature as a Semiotic Object; Background to Riffaterre's Stylistics

Riffaterre's basic position with respect to the phenomenon of literature is to be found in the notion of a rule-governed dialectic between text and reader. In this dialectic, the text plays two roles that are seen as being balanced, one against the other: (*a*) the referentiality of the linguistic text expressing messages directly (literally) through linguistic-semantic convention; (*b*) the expression of concepts *by indirection* (that is, 'saying one thing and meaning another').

Riffaterre identifies the referential function of a text with the 'mimetic' aspect of that text – the purpose of referring is to reflect or mirror reality as exactly and literally as possible (thence the use of the term 'mimesis': the 'imitation' or 'copying' of reality). Since reality is perceived essentially as the variation or multiplicity of experiences – though in saying this, Riffaterre underestimates the way percepts are automatically classified by perceivers – the key word of the 'mimetic' aspect of a text is said to be variety.

In contradistinction (the result of an oversimplification, I fear), unity is to be the key word of literary style whereby concepts are expressed through indirection.

There are three possible ways in which a text can express concepts by indirection, namely (*a*) displacement (for example, metaphorical or metonymic usage of signs); (*b*) distortion (for example, ambiguity, contradiction, nonsense); (*c*) creation of meaning (that is, endowing with 'meaning' items in the text that are not meaningful in the normal linguistic sense, for example, assonance, synaesthesia). All three have in common the fact that they work counter to the referential function of the text (that is, they 'mean' something other than what the text, as a purely linguistic object, actually 'says').

For instance, the apparent referential nonsense of

> Mary, Mary, quite contrary,
> How does your garden grow?
> With silver bells, and cockle-shells
> And pretty maids all in a row.

is set off against the heavily insinuated concept that is left unsaid, but that, in spite of all, gives the quatrain its unity, namely, 'all the trappings of Roman Catholicism'. Of course, gardens do not literally grow silver bells, cockle-shells or pretty maids – however, the whole point of the verse is just this clash with referentiality, a clash that forces the insinuated 'meaning' to come to the surface.

In this process of giving force to an insinuated 'meaning' that lies behind the basic referential interpretation of a text, Riffaterre sees a particular manifestation of semiosis. The result of literary semiosis is to endow the text with a higher level of significance than that which it has as a mere juxtaposition of linguistic sentences operating on a referential level.

The reader enters into the dialectic of literature not only with his linguistic knowledge, but also his familiarity with all the presuppositions, biases, prejudices, 'mythologies' (cf. Barthes) current in a society or culture. The mentality of the reader must, therefore, be supposed to constitute a crucial factor determining literary semiosis.

The conflict or interplay between 'mimesis' and 'semiosis' (lower-level linguistic interpretation of a text versus higher-level interpretation of its signification) characterises the whole of literature. It is, however, especially in poetry that semiosis triumphs most completely over linguistic reference. It is in the area of poetics that Riffaterre's stylistics is extensively elaborated and exemplified.

8.2.2 Mimesis-cancelling Mechanisms as Devices of Literary Semiosis

Up to a point, mimetic representation (linguistic reference to reality) and semiotic innuendo are capable of existing side by side as opposed forces in a literary text. Beyond a certain level, attained by the piling-up of factors that work against a literal interpretation of the text (that is, that cancel mimesis), semiosis completely overcomes mimesis; the literal reading of the text becomes trivial and is abandoned for a higher level of 'signification'. This triumph of 'signification' over 'reference' reaches its epitomy in poetry. (Accordingly, it would seem that we should imagine prose and poetry as being located on a single continuum, one extreme being represented by such ultimately prosaic texts as one might find in medical textbooks, the other by, perhaps, 'surrealist' poetry.)

Considering our earlier example of 'Mary, Mary, quite contrary', we find that the text presents no referential difficulties up to the end of the second line – literal reading is perfectly feasible up to this point. The first 'mimesis-cancelling' device we encounter is in the item 'silver bells' – or, to be more precise, in the referential nonsense created by the literal interpretation of 'silver bells growing in a garden'. At this stage, however, attributing a 'displaced' signification could compensate for the 'mimesis-cancelling' effects; since 'bluebells', 'harebells', and so on may literally grow in a garden, the reader's reaction may be to convert (by semiosis) the item 'silver bells' into a metaphor signifying a flower.

The next 'mimesis-cancelling' device is the reference to 'cockle-shells growing in a garden'. This time, the referential nonsensicality is even more striking. In the absence of a possible metaphorical interpretation in line with the one proposed for 'silver bells', the reader abandons attempts at literal interpretation altogether in favour of semiosis. The verse, as we see, does not require a long 'detour' (Riffaterre, 1978) in order to force the reader to recognise the indirection of its allusive significance. Retroactively (this effect of retroactive reading is noteworthy), 'silver bells' is no longer taken to be a metaphor signifying a flower, but becomes the vehicle of a semiosis similar to that in which the item 'cockle-shells' is involved; that is, both items are interpreted as having an allusive signification that completely overlays their literal meaning. Similarly, 'pretty maids all in a row' – also 'mimesis-cancelling' in connection with 'things growing in a garden' – will be endowed with a higher allusive signification.

None of these allusive significations can be reconstructed unless the reader enters into the 'literary dialectic' through the use of his historical-cultural knowledge, the clue to which is contained in the word 'Mary'. Identifying the theme of the verse as being connected with the appropriate Queen Mary of English history leads to the realisation that the 'key phrase' underlying and epitomising the signification of the whole quatrain is 'the restitution of Roman Catholicism by Mary, Queen of England'. (It may be contentious and over-simplificative to assume, along with Riffaterre, that the significance of a poem can always be epitomised in a key word, phrase or sentence. This, however, is what we must assume if we are to believe that a poem is always essentially a derivate of a single, unified 'matrix' containing, in embryonic form, the whole being and growth-pattern of the finished text.) In the light of the thematic key phrase, in terms of which the verse in our example is made to signify a particular historical event, the allusive semiosis of 'silver bells' (= Roman Catholic Mass), 'cockle-shells' (= pilgrims) and 'pretty maids' (= nuns) replaces the gratuitous appearance of the text with a clear, if indirect, significative purpose.

8.2.3 Poems as Derivates from Single 'Matrices'

Owing to my inability and reluctance to follow Riffaterre into the realms of speculative reconstruction of the 'kernel' concept that – in the manner of 'genetic imprinting' – underlies the unity of a given poem, I shall resort to one of Riffaterre's own examples for illustrating his concept of a poetic 'matrix'.

Riffaterre cites the following four lines from Mallarmé as being epitomised by the word 'nothingness' (that is, this word is said to represent the poetic 'matrix'):

> *Sur les crédences, au salon vide: nul ptyx,*
> *Aboli bibelot d'inanité sonore*
> *(Car le Maître est allé puiser des pleurs au Styx*
> *Avec ce seul objet dont le Néant s'honore)*
> (freely translated as:
> On the showcases, in the empty front room: no ptyx,

> Knocked-out knick-knacks of sounding inanity
> (For the Master has gone to draw tears from the Styx
> With that sole object: the Void's self-flattery))

Riffaterre supports the identification of 'nothingness' as the *matrix* of this quatrain with a list of stylistic devices all of which hark back to the same semiotic function of signifying 'nothingness':

(i)   *'salon vide'*: provides a clue to the matrix by mention of the word *'vide'* ('empty', 'void'),

(ii) 'ptyx': a pure nonsense-word with no possible reference,

(iii) *'aboli bibelot'*: referentially problematic, a special kind of assonance made into a metaphor of 'worthless trash',

(iv) *'inanité sonore'*: referentially obscure, but makes a literary allusion to Latin *'inania verba'*,

(v)   *'Néant s'honore'*: punning with *'Néant sonore'*, referentially obscure, but parallels *'inanité sonore'*.

It would appear, from this illustration, that Riffaterre regards the matrix of a poem to be some 'word' or 'phrase' to which items in the poem constantly hark back, in terms of which these items are given a signification by the reader, and in terms of which that poem can be explained as the expansion of a single unified 'theme'.

It would appear also, however, that the identification of a matrix is a highly subjective, and rather question-begging operation. Who is to say that I am not more correct than Riffaterre in suggesting that the matrix of the Mallarmé quatrain should rather be summed up through an equivalence with the Shakespearean line 'full of sound and fury signifying nothing'? Let us say that the matrix (the epitomisation of the quatrain) is not merely 'nothingness', but the more elaborate idea of 'grandiose words (and actions) empty of content and value'. The devices noted in the poem could certainly be used to support this interpretation:

(i)   *'inanité sonore'*: virtually names 'empty grandiloquence',

(ii) *'aboli bibelot'*: metaphorically signifies 'showy but worthless trash', by assonance constitutes an example of empty sonority (why not a 'symbol' of 'empty grandiloquence'?),

(iii) 'ptyx': a fancy-sounding nonsense-word, with pretensions to a Greek origin (why not a 'symbol' of 'empty grandiloquence'?),

(iv) *'Néant s'honore'*: punning with *'Néant sonore'* – virtually names 'empty grandiloquence', at the same time as being an example of empty sonority,

(v)   *'puiser des pleurs au Styx'* – by classical allusion, signifying a grandiose but useless gesture (why not a 'symbol' for 'empty grandiloquence'?).

As for 'salon vide', there is, of course, nothing to prevent its continued interpretation as a device providing the first hint at the matrix of 'empty grandiloquence'.

Pushing the interpretation of indirect signification still further, one could bring '*crédences*' and '*salon*' more fully within the unity of the poem by further modification of the supposed matrix. It could be suggested that the former is a device involving a play on words ('*crédence*' = showcase, Latin '*credo*' = believe) whereby it signifies, on the one hand 'empty showiness' and on the other, 'vacuous beliefs'. At the same time, the juxtaposition of '*crédence*' and '*salon*' – associated in the reader's cultural presuppositions with a wealthy middle-class life-style – could act by semiosis as a signifier of 'middle-class pretentiousness'. On this basis, a modified matrix begins to emerge in the form of 'the empty self-deceit and grandiose vacuity of a showy middle-class existence'. Given this matrix, '*le Néant s'honore*' could be brought within the scope of that matrix as a 'symbol' of 'empty self-flattery and self-deceit'. Almost every item in the poem is now clustered, in one way or another, round the revised central 'motif' crystallised in the matrix.

Fanciful though these elaborations beyond Riffaterre's more bland suggestion of a matrix ('nothingness') may be, we may well ask: in what way precisely are they in essence more far-fetched or laboured? We may be sure, at any rate, that whatever matrix is suggested as the 'key' to the reading of a poem, there will always be potentially better alternatives. Nor will a single 'word' or 'phrase' ever succeed in exactly and exhaustively epitomising even a single reader's interpretation of the underlying significative unity of a poem.

8.2.4 Semiotic Operations on a Matrix

The assumption that a poem, as a fully-fledged literary text, derives from the unity of a single matrix implies the presumption that there are identifiable operations by which one can trace the growth of the matrix into the fully elaborated poem. (In other words, we must suppose the existence of a kind of 'chrysalis to butterfly' process between matrix and poetic text.)

In this connection, Riffaterre speaks of two types of operation: (1) conversion rules, (2) expansion rules.

'Conversion' is explained as the transforming of several (otherwise unconnected) signs into a 'collective sign', by endowing the components of that 'collective sign' with the self-same characteristic feature (Riffaterre, 1978). In other words, by conversion, the signs constituting the fleshed-out version of the text are all *modified by the same factor* under the influence of the matrix. Illustrated by our earlier example of 'Mary, Mary, quite contrary', conversion means roughly the following. When taken in isolation, the signs 'silver bells', 'cockle-shells' and 'pretty maids all in a row' form a heterogeneous and unconnected set. Conjoined in the text of the rhyme into a 'collective sign', these signs are brought within the scope of a single matrix, and are, as a result, transformed into a connected set with a unified, homogeneous signification. The transformation consists in modifying each of these signs by the same factor, namely '(allusion to) Roman Catholicity'. This example of 'conversion' can be represented as in Figure 8.3.

Matrix	Conversion		Text

'the restitution of Roman Catholicity' { 'silver bells' 'cockle-shells' 'pretty maids all in a row' } × 'Roman Catholicity' } = signifiers of Roman Catholicity

Figure 8.3

The chief agent in the formation of poetic texts, designated by Riffaterre (1978) as the 'principal generator' of textual signification, is the operation of 'expansion'. To put it crudely, a text is formed by taking an underlying matrix (definable as a 'word', 'phrase' or 'sentence' that may or may not be explicitly named in the text) as a 'theme', and elaborating sentences that are variations on that theme. In other words, 'expansion' transforms the contents of the matrix into more complex forms: the phrases and sentences of the poetic text.

Thus, for instance, the matrix of 'empty grandiloquence' – if we grant, for the sake of argument, that this is the appropriate matrix of the Mallarmé quatrain cited above – is multiply embroidered and elaborated by the successive variations on the theme of 'vacuity' and 'grandiloquence' that make up the phrases and sentences of the text. As Riffaterre puts it: 'the poem . . . results from the transformation of a word or sentence into a text . . . its form is felt to be a detour or circuitous path around what it means'.

The concepts of 'matrix', 'expansion' and 'conversion' in relation to poetic texts are intended as means of explaining the typical 'reader-perception modes connected with poetry' – that is to say, in blunt terms, the way that a poem is typically perceived and interpreted by readers. The non-finality of such perceptions and interpretations – varying in unpredictable ways from reader to reader – is but one of the weaknesses (briefly acknowledged and glossed over by Riffaterre) of the proposed approach to textual semiotics. More importantly, the concepts of 'matrix', 'expansion' and 'conversion' stand or fall together according to their appropriateness to poetry in general. Even if we accept the slogan (credited to Mallarmé and taken up by Riffaterre) that 'a poem is a mystery and it is up to the reader to look for the key', we are not forced to agree that the 'key' to a poem lies in an object smaller, more concise, more contracted than the poetic text itself (that is, a matrix that is expanded and converted into the text). It may well be, as in the case of epic poetry or of ballads where a prosaic (narrative) epitomisation of the theme would be more extensive than the poetic text, that a poem is a contraction and not an expansion of a 'theme'. Similarly, it is hard to imagine how the almost telegraphically economical style of classical Chinese lyrical poetry (for example, of the

T'ang and Sung Dynasties) could be the result of expanding an underlying matrix. Furthermore, in terms of purely abstract and general considerations alone, it seems hardly flattering to poetry as a *genre* to suggest that its essence is sheer circuitous embroidery on a theme.

8.3   Conclusion: Summary of the Antithesis between Bureau and Riffaterre

From among a number of antithetical features differentiating Bureau's stylistics from Riffaterre's textual semiotics, two general points emerge.

In the first place, Bureau's stylistics presupposes a recognition of well-defined semiotic levels superposed over a text, the performing of painstaking linguistic analyses, and the establishment of objectively (in general, quantitatively) identifiable patterns of recurrences and contrasts. Stylistic speculation enters into this method only where these patterns are subsequently put into correlation with 'thematic' features of the literary work under consideration.

In contrast to this, virtually no features are established by Riffaterre independently of the 'thematic' aspect of a literary work; that is to say, poetics is stylistic speculation from start to finish. The inventive specification of a matrix is primary and reflects back on the text where it illuminates, and is used to identify, a higher level of poetic signification. Instead of a correlation between textual features and signification, the matrix fabricates the poetically significative textual features. Such a method cannot be essentially different from reading into a text a particular signification by interpreting the putative 'connotations' of its contents. Consequently, 'textual semiotics' of this kind seems merely to offer a respectable (and new) pretext for indulging in an exercise that has for long been known under such names as 'literary appreciation', 'critical analysis', and so on.

In the second place, Bureau's stylistic correlations (between independently established patterns in a text and 'thematic' features of the literary work realised in that text) are hypothesised as inherent textual properties. In no way do these properties depend on, reflect, or otherwise relate to, processes that a reader (whether real or 'ideal') may perform (whether in principle or in practice). The approach abstracts away from potential readers and concentrates entirely on textual potential.

As for Riffaterre's poetics, the semiotic processes of 'mimesis-cancellation', the discovery of a matrix, the transformation of that matrix by 'expansion' and 'conversion', and so on, are all implicated in the interpreting of a text by a putative reader. The signification resulting from these processes takes shape only in the mentality of the reader – a mentality that cannot, unfortunately, be adequately scrutinised.

As a final summing up of the antithesis, we note that a non-initiate may learn Bureau's methodology, but, if he hopes to apply the procedures of Riffaterre, he must try to acquire the mentality behind, and enter into the spirit of, Riffaterre's approach.

9

Semiotics of the Cinema: Christian Metz

General Remarks

The publications of Christian Metz are particularly suited to the purpose of a brief review of film analysis as a form of applied semiotics. In the first place, the widely eclectic sources and references brought together (Metz, 1974a) allow for an interpretation of Metz's ideas as a 'crystallisation' of tendencies, attitudes and practices of cinema related scholarship at large. In the second place, Metz's ideas seem fairly representative of a type of 'semiotics applied to art' that is scattered over a considerable range of the humanities, and in which the shadows of Saussure, Lévi-Strauss and Barthes loom large.

Furthermore, Metz's relative restraint as against certain extremes in identifying films as being semiotic objects (in fact, as being language systems) makes it somewhat easier to avoid turning this 'sketch' into a 'caricature' portraying the excesses of a semiotics–run–wild.

9.1 The Basis of Cinematic Expression

In most cases of 'performances' aimed at an 'audience' (including literature, music, choreography, painting, sculpture, and so on), the immediate medium of expression is obvious, and common sense alone tells us a great deal about the nature of that expression (the aesthetic use of language, of sound, of dance movements, and so on). This is much less so, however, in the case of the relatively new genre of films. The closest relatives of this genre, in this respect, are, on the one hand, still photography and, on the other, theatrical performances. (We shall largely ignore, incidentally, the earlier genre of silent films.)

A photograph achieves its particular effects by establishing a special kind of credibility: it is primarily 'understood' to be the image of something (real or posed) that has been 'recorded' by photo-chemical means. Whereas Metz would refer to the recorded object as the 'signified' (of which the photograph itself is the 'signifier'), we shall not enter into the same terminological assumptions as Metz (for reasons that will become clear as the discussion unfolds), but will speak, instead, of the *subject-matter* of the photograph.

It can be immediately noted that the subject-matter of a photograph may be real in a full sense (though, perhaps, a reality rooted in the past, not in the present), or it may be fictional, witness posed or faked photographs that represent a subject-matter that has never existed as such. Be that as it may, the basis of expression (that is, the way in which a photograph 'conveys' a particular subject-matter) is of the order of 'seeing is believing'. The viewer sees the visual details of a recorded scene and (up to a point, at least) responds to it by investing it with reality. This process of investing an image with reality, a reality that is actually an illusion, is referred to in Metz's terminology as *diegesis*.

In the case of photographs, diegesis receives extra support from (*a*) the fact that photographs often are *genuine* records of a past reality; (*b*) the fact that a photograph really *looks like* an actual scene since one readily acquires the habit of transferring images seen in three dimensions to images seen in two dimensions, and vice versa; (*c*) the fact that the medium of a flat paper surface with an imprinted image presents few obstacles that obtrude by spoiling the illusion of the image.

Obtruding factors – apart from the absence of motion which makes a photograph less like reality – can come only from perceiving the photograph as being 'really' just a flat surface, or from touching that surface and finding its tactile properties to be wholly unlike those that one would expect from the subject-matter of the image. But, of course, only the very naïve would experience such obtrusions, since one learns to make abstraction of the flatness of the paper on which the image is imprinted.

Thus, in still photography, diegesis is effective up to the point of 're-creating' a scene invested with reality – and is effective to a considerable degree because of a very favourable balance between factors maintaining the illusion and (the few) factors that might obtrude to spoil it.

The kind of credibility established by a theatrical performance falls also under the concept of diegesis. The subject-matter is the closed sequence of events re-enacted on the stage, but, whereas this subject-matter may have strong roots in fact (the actors may be re-enacting a historical event that really took place), a theatrical performance is never a 'recording' of a reality. Where the theatre scores in diegetic illusion over still photography is, of course, in the portrayal of actions (including the action of speaking). The reinforcing of diegesis by actions visible in three-dimensional space, by accompanying sound-effects, and by an accompanying dialogue are, of course, factors that still photography is unable to reproduce. Since, however, the essence of diegesis is a balance between illusion-maintaining factors and obtruding factors working against the illusion, it does not by any means follow that theatrical performances are more credible than photographs (indeed, this would be hard to swallow). On the contrary, the presence of obtruding factors is much stronger, and makes diegesis much less complete, on the stage than in a photograph. The very real presence of a mock version of three-dimensional space ('can this cockpit hold the vasty fields of France'; Shakespeare, *Henry V*, Prologue) is a case in point; what little 'scenery' contributes to theatrical diegesis is easily cancelled out by its so obviously being 'scenery'. Similarly, the portrayed actions of the protagonists (belonging to the realm of the subject-matter) cannot add sufficiently to diegesis to hold a balance against the crude presence of the actors (for example, Laurence

Olivier in the flesh) who are 'ordinary' people in the same reality as the audience. Such physical beings as the actors breathe, blink, sneeze, and may even trip over objects, or stumble over their lines in their own right, not as protagonists in the re-enacted subject-matter. Consequently, the constant reminder of an interplay between two 'realities' – that of the present to which actors and audience belong together, as against the illusory, which only the actors participate in as protagonists in the subject-matter – makes for a relatively poor balance between illusion-maintaining factors and obtruding factors. The result is a low degree of diegesis.

Taking, initially, the position that a movie film consists of individual stills (we shall see that things are much more complex than this would suggest), we may note that some of the diegetic properties of still photography are shared by films; a film is 'understood' to be the image of something real or posed; the subject-matter may be (it *is*, for instance, in the case of documentaries and newsreels) a recorded reality rooted in the past (or even in the present, as with live TV coverage). Thus, diegesis receives a strong background support (psychologically speaking) from the fact that films often are genuine records of a minimally contrived visual reality. That visual record, two-dimensionally projected onto a flat screen, not only really looks like ordinary perceived objects, but the illusion is further enhanced by the fact that the film reproduces movement. (The technical fact that this is done through projecting a succession of still frames is neither here nor there – the successivity of frames is subliminal and is perceived as motion.)

In addition, the presence of a sound-track (we shall ignore 'incidental music', whose purpose is clearly not diegetic, but which is used for suggesting moods and heightening emotional atmosphere) adds both the supportive factor of sound-effects, and that of dialogue. The objects seen, by illusion, as moving objects make, in addition, the kinds of sound real objects would make in analogous circumstances; the acting protagonists of the subject-matter adhere to the same linguistic conventions as do real speakers.

As against stage productions, where the illusion-maintaining effects of movement and speech portrayed are cancelled out by the corporeal reality of the actors (as actors, rather than as protagonists), filmic presentation offers relatively little resistance to diegesis; in short, events portrayed in a film are not prevented from looking very much like genuine records of real events and, through this, like real events themselves.

Naturally, the awareness of the substance of the screen on which images are projected, and of the actual flatness (two-dimensionality) of the projected images, can and does obtrude in a way as to limit verisimilitude. (However, one learns easily and automatically to filter out and ignore such obtruding factors.) To an unusually high degree, watching through a film is like having participated – as a disembodied, sheltered, safe and privileged observer – in experiencing the events that constitute the subject-matter of the film; witness live coverage of sporting events as an extreme example. Where the subject-matter of the film is constituted by purely fictional events (staged and filmed artificially), the genuine background of real fact is, of course, known to be lacking – it is remarkable how little difference this makes, however, to the impression of having experienced something that is closely akin to a record of real events. One has, if anything, to remind oneself that what one has observed is 'only a film'.

This high degree of maintenance of illusion owes a lot to certain negative factors – namely, the absence of illusion-spoiling realities: mock scenery, corporeally substantial actors, spatial contiguity between the stage containing the world of the subject-matter and the real space in which the audience is located, and so on. The balance between illusion-maintaining and illusion-spoiling factors is more strongly in favour of diegesis than in the case of any other medium.

9.2   Cinema: Art or Discourse?

While for Metz, cinema is, obviously, both a form of art and a form of (narrative) discourse, only an uncritical rehash of what Metz has to say on the subject could register agreement with this position. (Apart from further considerations that will occupy us below, it is perfectly possible for a film to be neither art nor discourse, but a mere record, witness video-coverage of sporting events.)

One should not allow oneself to get carried away by the (in any case, somewhat naïve) observation that literature constitutes an object that is at once both a form of art and a form of discourse, rather than being primarily a form of discourse on which artistic considerations are super-imposed. In the light of this, it is even questionable whether, in general, a genre can be both art and discourse, let alone whether it is admissible to assimilate cinema to this type of genre.

That aspect of literature which gives it the nature of discourse accounts for the fact that it can 'tell a story' (among other things that may constitute the subject-matter of discourse). The aspect of literature as art resides elsewhere, not in the fact that literature can narrate, but in the 'choices' relating to the manner of narration. In short, the art-like aspect of literature is 'superimposed' on the basic discourse-like nature of the text (cf. Granger's notion of 'surcodage'; Granger, 1969). In order to under-stand a text on the most superficial and 'literal' level, however, one must first know the conventions of the appropriate natural language in which the text is couched. The discourse-like nature of literature is directly conditional on this. Its diegetic and art-like aspects are only partly and indirectly conditional on the underlying linguistic-conventional nature of the text. Thus, even in the rather unique case of literature, we are not faced with a genre that is simultaneously and equally both art and discourse – the discourse aspect is 'parasitic' on a language system (for example, English), whereas the art aspect transcends both language and discourse.

Reflecting this discrimination back on cinematic matters, we find no objection to saying that, in the case of films that are not mere unretouched records of real events, cinema becomes fundamentally a form of art. It is, in this respect, a particularly strongly diegetic art – its artistic aspect resides chiefly in the maintaining of illusion, regardless of the fictionality of the subject-matter. (Additional aesthetic, ideological, symbolic, etc. content is incidental.)

While accepting, therefore, that there is a whole branch of film-making that is fundamentally an artistic pursuit, we reject the position (that of Metz among others) that the cinema constitutes a form of discourse. First, the only thing that can guarantee discourse is a text couched in the medium of a spoken or written language – cinema is not couched in either of these media. Secondly, even if it were correct to designate the function of a film as that of 'telling' a story, this would not make cinema into a form of discourse, since 'story-telling' cannot be equated with discourse. Finally, we must remind ourselves that a film does not 'tell' a story, but projects it 'as though it were actually happening'. A story 'unfolds', perhaps – as it does also, for instance, when we watch a football match from the sidelines – but it is not told.

In fact, only an absolute and primary dependence on the medium of a particular natural language can constitute the literal 'telling' of a story – there must first be a text that is basically 'in a language' and, in addition, the 'telling of a story' must be the function of that text. Only then can we speak of narrative discourse. Needless to say, even the 'talkies' do not manifest an absolute and fundamental dependence on a natural language (it is only part of the sound-track that requires linguistic competence). Films are what they are not because they 'tell' (in the form of discourse) of events, but because they 're-enact' them through an illusion of recorded reality.

Metz rejects, and criticises as extreme and untenable, the attitude of those who see the cinema as basically analogous with language-systems (Saussure's *'langue'*). However, it is no less untenable, and only slightly less extreme, to classify films as a form of 'connected' speech (that is, as discourse). For one thing, speech exists as such only because it has a language-system as its organising principle; that is to say, one cannot claim that films are a form of speech without, implicitly (but necessarily) claiming at the same time that they have a kind of underlying language-system.

Furthermore, even though discourse proper may have its 'rules' (for example, rhetoric) that function over and beyond the conventions of a language-system, the 'rules' by which a film is structured – even if identifiably similar to the 'rules' of discourse – are *not* constitutive of discourse, in that cinematic 'rules' do not function over and above a linguistic text.

In fact, films are not structured by constitutive conventions on any level of their functioning; that is, their basis is in no way conventional. (The fact that they may be 'gilded' by stylistic-conventional devices of a 'symbolic' nature is not relevant, but merely incidental.) In the absence of fundamental constitutive conventions, one must not only disagree with Metz's designation of the cinema as a form of discourse, but also with the extended use of the terms 'signifier' and 'signified' for the 'film–as–image' and its portrayed subject-matter, respectively. If we call the relationship between what is projected on the screen and the portrayed subject-matter a relationship of 'signification', we are only one small step away from saying that the relationship between a real action perceived by the senses and a real action conceived by the mind is also a relationship of 'signification'. In view of diegesis, the psychological basis of 'interpreting' what is projected on the screen is virtually the same as that of interpreting the events that really happen around us. There is nothing 'sign-like' in this interpretation – consequently 'signification', 'signifier' and 'signified' (concepts specifically designed to make sense only in the context of 'signs') are wholly inept when applied in the context of films.

Even more inexcusable in Metz's terminology is the use of the term 'grammar' in connection with the structural analysis of films. Having been at pains to point out that the intra-linguistic conventions of 'grammar' should not be confused with the (supra-linguistic) 'rules' of discourse, Metz has taken a position against the myth of cinematic 'grammar'. One does not even need to refer to arguments beyond Metz's own in order to point to the theoretical contradiction behind Metz's own 'grammatical' analysis of films.

9.3   Structure of Narrative, Structure of Film

The most fundamental error in analysing films through a type of narrative analysis can be seen as a version of the 'translation fallacy'. This fallacy consists in translating the content embodied in a particular medium of expression, analysing the translation, and submitting the results of that analysis as the underlying structure of the original medium of expression. (A homely analogy will show the fallacious nature of such a procedure: the value £1.00 can be 'translated' – exchange is analogous with 'translation' – into, say, $2.73; $2.73 can be 'analysed' into two dollar notes, two quarters, two dimes and three cents, but to submit this latter as representing the 'underlying structure' of £1.00 would be risible.)

In Metz's analysis of Jacques Rozier's film *Adieu Philippine* (Metz, 1974a) we have a fairly typical example of the 'translation fallacy' in semiotic description. The 'events' observed on the screen are 'retold' in words; this retelling is organised into sections, making up what amounts to no more and no less than a *'précis* of the plot', in essence little different from the kind of schoolroom exercise by which 'salient' points of a narrative can be summarised and rehashed. Metz attaches *ad hoc* cinematic labels ('scene', 'sequence', 'autonomous shot', and so on) to the headings into which the plot is divided, attempting thereby to create the impression that the 'units' so labelled constitute the underlying structure of the film as a semiotic-artistic object. However, neither the attaching of these labels, nor the specification of the transitional camera devices that sometimes separate and connect the units ('fade', 'dissolve', 'wipe', and so on), can introduce a cinematic, let alone semiotic, relevance into what is a mere *ad hoc* outline of the 'plot'. The point is that anyone with a modicum of intelligence can 'retell' a sequence of events in a more or less telescoped and more or less structured form. There is nothing particularly semiotic, nor cinematically relevant, in such an exercise. Even on the assumption that 'grammar and rhetoric are not separate' in terms of a semiotics of the cinema, a *précis* of the important moments in a film is not *a fortiori* a semiotic analysis of the 'grammar' of that film. The merging of cinema with narration – itself a dubious proposition – does not provide a sufficient pretext for presenting a form of narrative analysis as the semiotic analysis of a film.

9.4   Units of Film Discourse: a Typology

In the foregoing we registered certain reservations with regard to the identification of film with discourse, and with regard to the aptness of semiotic analysis of films, since films do not signify their subject-matter, but portray it in mainly visual form. In spite of these reservations, we should acknowledge the interest inherent in the typology of filmic units established by Metz. This typology can be set out in the form of a deductive scheme (see Figure 9.1). Explanations to the terms used are as follows:

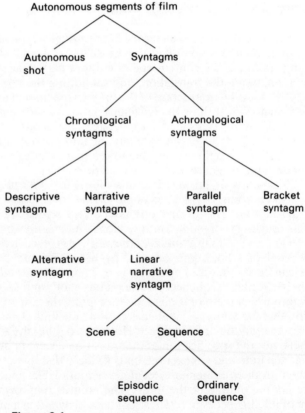

Figure 9.1

Autonomous shot: single shot that, within a particular film, constitutes the filmic equivalent of a complete statement (for example, a single shot of the White House, setting the *locale* of the subject-matter, much as though the film started with the 'statement': 'the following story happens in the White House').

Chronological syntagm: chain of shots in which the temporal sequence of projected images corresponds to the temporal sequence in which events are to be understood to have occurred in the plot.

Achronological syntagm: chain of shots in which the sequence of images projected departs from the normal temporal sequence in which events in the plot follow one another (for example, a 'flashback' follows in the projected sequence images that show later events in the plot).

Parallel syntagm: chain of alternating 'motifs' with no precise spatio-temporal relationship between them – initially, at least, it is only their juxtaposition in projected sequence that mediates a relationship between the 'motifs'; in terms of the subject-matter, this relationship is not chronological, but 'thematic' (for example, shots of an intimate household scene alternating with shots of wild stormy seas might be an effective parallel syntagmatic device in a film whose 'theme' is the conflict of life at sea and life on land in a seafaring man).

Bracket syntagm: series of non-chronological scenes representing activities typical of a certain *milieu* (for example, a series of shots showing race horses being groomed, trained, exercised, ridden in races, etc., as a way of 'setting the scene' for a film about a jockey; the bracket syntagm 'presents' the 'world of horse racing' in a nutshell).

Descriptive syntagm: chronological syntagm that constitutes the filmic equivalent of a descriptive passage in a literary narrative (for example, a sequence of shots that shows the White House from different, successively closer, angles and culminates in a close-up of the entrance to the President's quarters).

Narrative syntagm: chronological syntagm in which the protagonists of the film are shown as being engaged in action that significantly advances the plot (there seems to be no reason, in principle at least, why an entire film should not consist in a single narrative syntagm as defined here).

Alternate syntagm: alternation of sequences within which there are two or more series of events that are mutually temporally simultaneous (for example, in an escape sequence, the flight of the pursued is one series of events, the actions of the pursuers are one or more equally continuous series of events, but flight and pursuit are understood to be going on simultaneously in the plot, though their images are projected in alternation).

Linear narrative syntagm: narrative syntagm consisting of a single, continuous series of consecutive events consecutively projected.

Scene: linear narrative syntagm uninterrupted by significant changes of location or time lapse in the action.

Ordinary sequence: linear narrative syntagm characterised by temporal discontinuity; that is, 'the viewer skips the moments that have . . . no direct bearing on the plot' (Metz, 1974a).

Episodic sequence: linear narrative syntagm strung together out of brief episodic scenes following in chronological order, but interrupted by lapses in time and space.

The above typology is, to a large extent, based on an interplay between time and space as 'portrayed' in the projected sequences of a film and the spatio-temporal relationships in the plot (that is, the 'real' relationships that would hold if the plot were actually a real event).

There are certain notable features in the typology that reinforce the earlier mentioned criticisms in connection with the 'translation fallacy'. For instance, an autonomous shot and a descriptive syntagm are identified by translating their content and finding this translation to be equivalent to a 'statement' or a 'descriptive passage' respectively.

9.5   Conclusion: Semiotic Fallacies in Cinematic Analysis

It may seem unduly negative to equate the conclusion of this discussion on semiotics of the cinema with a list of assumptions that appear to be fallacious. However, one should not forget that the application of semiotics to the analysis of cinematic art is hardly an established and uncontentious notion, but one that must be met with considerable caution and a degree of scepticism. This is the final impression the reader is to be left with – thence the nature of my concluding remarks.

There are at least four fundamental assumptions that provide the semiotics of the cinema with a basis of misconceptions. First, in order to bring the cinematic genre within the scope of semiotics, it is necessary to assume that the overriding (primary) function of films is a communicative function. On this point, we note – in the spirit of the proverb 'all that glitters is not gold' – that not everything from which 'information' (in a wide sense) may be gathered is necessarily a form of communication. The observation of everyday reality, for one thing, is highly 'informative' in this wide sense, but it would be strange to suggest that this reality 'communicates' things to the observer. (This first assumption we may think of as the 'communication' fallacy.)

Secondly, in order to bring the mechanisms of the cinematic medium within the scope of semiotics, it is necessary to assume that the relationship that mediates between means of 'expression' employed in the films and their 'expressed' subject-matter is one of 'signification'. On this point, we note that the entire discussion on diegesis suggests a relationship that is much more akin to a direct visual presentation (of an illusion of reality) than to an arbitrary (sign-like) mediation between a 'signifier' and a 'signified'. 'Signification', 'signifier' and 'signified' are, none the less, concepts applied to the functioning of the filmic medium. (This second assumption we may call the 'signification' fallacy.)

Thirdly, in order to make the techniques of semiotic description apply to film analysis, it is necessary to assume that there is an analogy between the way films are structured and the way that ordinary semiotic objects (for example, 'sentences' in languages, or in other semiotic codes) are structured. It should not go unnoticed, however, that the structural analysis of ordinary semiotic objects is conditional on the notion of commutation, that is, the systematic alternation of each and every structural unit, one at a time, with another unit (or zero) that may replace that unit in such a way as to create another, well-formed, minimally different semiotic complex. There seems to be no evidence that, even if units of a film are subjected to alternation, they are all commutable, one at a time, or that their replacement with other units (or zero) corresponds to minimal differences between the complexes thus created. Furthermore, descriptive efforts in filmic analysis may assume the commutability of structural units, but do not perform the necessary operations to demonstrate it. (This third assumption of the presence of commutable units in films we designate as the 'structural analysis' fallacy.)

Fourthly, in order to maintain the notion of a fully-fledged structural analysis of films, it is necessary to assume that, in the same way that the units composing ordinary semiotic objects (for example, sentences) are drawn from a systematic inventory, so there is some systematic inventory of units underlying filmic structures. All we can say here is that there is very little evidence of underlying systematic constants upon which either the 'creation' or the 'consumption' of films is based. As is usual in the domain of 'art', it is underlying variety and not underlying constancy, that seems to be the fundamental characteristic of the cinema. However, any form of semiotic analysis of films necessarily implies the search for an 'underlying system' – an assumption that I venture to label the 'underlying system' fallacy.

It is not beyond the realms of possibility that what I have here referred to as various 'fallacies' may, if put in a new and different light, become justifiable tenets of the semiotics of cinema. At the present stage in the development of the 'discipline', however, this still seems to be a distant prospect.

10

Zoo-semiotics

General Remarks

A chapter dealing with a field of study as wide, as complex and as relatively new as zoo-semiotics (embracing communicative behaviour in all non-human species) is bound, for several reasons, to be highly impressionistic. There are, however, certain generalities, as well as certain specific points, that can be usefully picked out, if one hopes to reproduce for the reader some of the 'flavour' of recent and current zoo-semiotic research.

For a start, it will be noted that practical research work in this field is not usually undertaken by trained semioticians (let alone by 'armchair' semioticians), but by researchers whose training is in zoology, biology and the natural sciences in general. As a result, zoo-semiotics is hardly to be considered a branch of 'applied semiotics'; rather it is a part of natural science turned towards communication as an aspect (and an important one at that) of animal behaviour. The semiotic-theoretical background of researchers in the field is, understandably, rudimentary – studies are carried out rather against a background of biological and physical science and experimental methods. In some cases this has produced excellent results (for example, Von Frisch, 1950, 1967, and so on); in others (for example, in the literature on the 'linguistic' ability of apes) it has been responsible for an approach that is somewhat semiotically naïve, that fails, to a considerable extent, to ask the appropriate questions, and that, consequently, leads to inconclusive answers (cf. Mounin, 1968, 1970).

10.1.1 Physical Analysis of Communicative Behaviour

As indicated above, a large section of zoo-semiotics would be more suitably classed under the heading of a general study of animal behaviour (the fact that the behaviour concerned is 'communicative' is almost incidental). The task of such research starts with the detailed observation and recording of sounds, movements, or other (for example, chemical) 'emissions' produced by animals. The species studied range from insects, through fish and amphibians, to birds and mammals. These 'emissions', especially when found to occur in repeated patterns (for example, bird song) are put into correlation with effects they produce in a 'receptor' belonging to the same species. The study of these correlated effects triggered by particular 'emissions' supports (up to a point at least) the claim that the behaviour studied is 'communicative'. (However, not all behaviour that triggers a response is appropriately classed as 'communication'.)

The minutiae of detail in a zoo-semiotic study are generally those of a 'physical', rather than a semiotic, analysis. For instance, using the instruments and techniques of acoustics in recording and analysing animal sounds leads to a kind of 'animal phonetics' producing a very detailed and exact description of the sounds emitted. The spotlight, however, is on the analysis of 'physical' (acoustic) complexity – and this is where the rigour and scientificity of the research is concentrated. The communicative aspect of minutely analysed behaviour remains frequently tentative and is described in a relatively rudimentary manner.

The sophistication of the analysis of the physical, biological, and so on, aspects of animal 'signals' has, in other words, to be balanced against the somewhat fumbling nature of the research into the 'message' aspect. As a corollary of this, it would be fair to say that zoo-semiotics is zoologically advanced, but semiotically backward. For one thing, researchers in the field work with a very wide (not to say 'loose') conception of 'communication' – a conception that would not satisfy the requirements of a semiotic theory (for example, 'communication can be said to occur whenever the activities of one animal influence the activities of another animal'; Alexander, 1960).

From a semiotic viewpoint, zoo-semiotic studies establish, at best, a tentative inventory of behaviour patterns available to members of a particular species, behavioural patterns to which tentative 'meanings' are attached in terms of their assumed behavioural 'purpose', or in terms of the behaviour they trigger off as a response from other members of the species.

Example I: crickets
Inventory of communicative sounds:
(1)   Male 'calling' sounds: periodic rhythmic stridulation (operating at long range) described as a 'song'; correlates with the gathering of crickets in groups, thus acting as a kind of 'recognition signal' with a 'contact-maintaining' function; detailed acoustic analyses show species-specific variations.
(2)   Male 'aggressive' sounds: protracted rhythmic stridulation described as 'chirping'; correlates with aggressive behaviour, acting as a 'threatening' signal, and apparently is proportionate to male dominance; detailed acoustic analyses show species-specific variation.
(3)   Female 'calling' sounds: soft 'ticking' stridulation (not usually operative over long range); these sounds appear to be produced in response to male 'calling song', and attract male crickets; detailed acoustic analyses show species-specific variations.
(4)   Male 'courtship' sounds: 'wide frequency-band', continuous 'noise' described as 'mating song'; these sounds are directly correlated with approach for the purposes of copulation, to which they are a necessary prerequisite (that is, their 'meaning' lies in the fact that they stimulate female responsiveness permitting mating); detailed acoustic analyses show species-specific variations.

Example II: bird song
An 'average' inventory:

(1)   'Call notes': 'musical' motifs (of varying acoustic complexity); these motifs have the function of a kind of 'recognition signal'; detailed acoustic analyses (*spectrograms*) show evidence of variation between, not only species, but geographical subvarieties of the same species – a kind of 'dialect' – and between individual specimens – a kind of 'idiolect' – (cf. chaffinch 'dialects' described by Thorpe, 1958).

(2)   'Territorial' song: 'musical' motifs with the function of 'advertising' the boundaries to be respected by other members of the species; clearly connected with the repulsion of invaders; detailed acoustic analyses (*spectrograms*) show species-specific, 'dialectal', and specimen-restricted variation.

(3)   'Threatening' call: sharp 'cry' correlating with aggressive behaviour.

(4)   'Warning' call: sharp 'cry', or continuous 'chattering' sound, etc., acting as a kind of 'danger signal' at the approach of a predator.

(5)   'Mating' call: sounds produced with the specific function of predisposing approach for the purposes of copulation.

10.1.2   Animal 'Displays'

Whereas the methods and instruments of acoustics are productive of an 'animal phonetics' that measures with considerable exactitude the 'communicative' sounds emitted by animals, the use of photographic techniques and instruments is conducive to the recording and minute analysis of the 'ritual' movements involved in 'face–to–face' communication between animals. Such movement patterns are generally referred to as 'displays' (note the analogy between such 'displays', and so-called 'body-language' in humans).

The description of 'displays' – for example, bird 'courtship displays' – has benefited from the painstaking, 'frame by frame' examination to which movements (formerly too difficult to subject to minute observation) can be submitted. While terminological and representational problems of describing the minutiae of 'displays' (these problems affect even 'animal phonetics', where terms like 'chirping', 'song', and so on are but inadequate labels for the sounds recorded and analysed) make such descriptions either cumbersome or imprecise, stylised drawings abstracting the essentials of sequences of positions adopted in, say, a 'courtship display' can be made on the basis of photographic records. As a result, both exact observational details of 'displays', and generalised descriptions of species-specific patterns underlying individual 'display performances', can be provided by zoo-semiotic research. The connection between 'displays' and their biological functions remains to date relatively the weakest and most tenuous aspect of zoo-semiotic descriptions.

Where 'communication' is by means of glandular secretion by an animal organism, the physiological mechanisms of the production of chemical substances, and the chemical composition of these substances are, once again, open to the same kind of minute examination as are sounds and 'displays'. For instance, 'communication' by smell presents no great observational or analytical problems as far as the nature and mechanisms of 'emission' are concerned. A special descriptive vocabulary for such studies presents a relatively minor problem; the major area where developments are to be hoped for is, again, that of the connection between chemical (glandular) 'signals' and their 'meanings' (that is, the 'messages' they are alleged to convey), seen in terms of biological functions.

10.1.3 Characteristic Problems of Zoo-semiotic Research: a Summary

(*a*) The physiology of the *production* of 'signals' (for example, stridula-tion, vocalisation, visual 'displays', glandular secretions);

(*b*) the physiology of the *reception* of (and response to) 'signals' (for example, auditory, visual, olfactory, etc. systems in animals);

(*c*) the *physical* (observational) recording of 'signals' in sufficient detail, and the analysis of such recordings through the abstraction of salient features and relevant details (for example, spectrographic recording, analysis and comparison of animal sounds);

(*d*) the 'survival-value' and biological function of animal 'signals' (for example, of the 173 recorded motifs in the repertoire of a lark; how much of this rich variety is the exercise of an 'aesthetic' function and how much can be connected to biological functions?);

(*e*) the 'message' value of animal 'signals' in terms of 'sender's purpose' (if any) and 'receptor's' response (for example, the exact informa-tion a 'scout' bee can impart to 'foragers' concerning a source of nectar);

(*f*) the 'acquisition' of species-specific, regionally specific ('dialectal') and individually specific forms of 'signals'; learning versus genetic transmission ('instinct').

To this list we may add, tentatively, a further type of problem, one which, I venture to suggest, zoo-semiotics is as yet very far from being able to tackle in a systematic way:

(*g*) the degree of intelligence required for operating 'signals' of a particular type (for example, are bees, as a result of the complex system of communication they use for indicating sources of nectar, to be credited with more intelligence than the majority of bird and mammal species?).

10.1.4 Theoretical Considerations in Animal Communication: Hockett

One of the few attempts at introducing special, and systematically established, theoretical considerations into zoo-semiotics originates from C. F. Hockett. Hockett, essentially and primarily a linguist, became interested in non-human communication as a result of his research into the 'design features' ('defining' or 'key' properties) of human language, as compared with communication in other species (Hockett, 1958, 1959, 1960). From the initial list of six dimensions relevant for the comparison of communicative (including linguistic) behaviour in different species, an extended list of thirteen dimensions has been constructed (Hockett, 1960). These dimensions constitute a theoretical framework proposed by Hockett as a set of guiding principles for systematic zoo-semiotic research. Although discussion will be necessarily brief, we shall go through the list of these dimensions, giving examples where appropriate.

(1) Channel of Communication
While in the case of human languages, the channel of communication is entirely vocal-auditory, channels of communication may vary from species to species (as we have seen exemplified above) according to the anatomical-physiological make-up of the animals concerned. Furthermore, even the organs (lungs, larynx, tongue, palate, and so on) homologous in primates with human 'speech organs' are considerably different in structure. Such differences in 'vocal equipment' must play a strong preconditioning role in determining the precise medium in which communication is realised.

(2) Transmission and Reception
According to the medium of communication, the physical substances of signals have different properties that affect the use to which a particular channel of communication may be put (for example, sound-waves can travel round a corner, but cannot be heard at great distances; light-waves are easily cut off by obstacles, but can be perceived at greater distances than sound). Specialised ways of using a medium (for example, high-frequency sounds used by some birds and insects, where predators only have the ability to hear lower frequencies) may have a significant practical, biological function, or even 'survival-value'.

(3) Rapid Fading
Messages encoded in a given medium are more or less transitory according to the physical properties of the medium (for example, sound fades quickly and is unsuitable, as such, for recording information; a written medium, say, pictograms carved in stone, may endure for thousands of years, and is, therefore, highly suited for recording information). The problem of information storage can, in general, only be solved in non-human species by repeated transmission (for example, 'calling sounds' of crickets are repeated as long as the appropriate conditions hold; bee 'scouts' repeat the dance informing 'foragers' of a nectar source as long as that source holds out).

(4) Interchangeability
In certain forms of communication, there are signals that can only be emitted by, for instance, males of a species, and only be responded to by females. There is no question, then, with regard to such signals, of an interchanging of the roles of 'sender' and 'receptor' (for example, male

and female roles in 'courtship displays' are strictly defined and non-interchangeable). In other forms of communication, interchangeability is possible; one and the same animal may at one stage be the 'sender' of a given signal, at another stage, a 'receptor' of the same type of signal (for example, in bee 'dancing' all workers participate, now as 'senders', now as 'receptors'; human languages, highly suited to 'conversation' in which speaker and hearer are constantly changing roles, show a very high degree of interchangeability).

(5) Total Feedback

In some forms of communicative behaviour, the organism acting as 'sender' is precluded from perceiving the signals it emits (for example, the aggressive 'blushing' produced by Siamese fighting fish is a signal to other males, but cannot, of course, be perceived by the 'sender' itself; a mirror-reflection is responded to as an *id*, not as an *ego*). Such a situation typifies total absence of feedback; the 'sender' is not in a position to observe (or 'monitor') its own communicative output. At the other extreme, other forms of communication imply that the 'sender' perceives his own signals as well (if differently) as any potential 'receptor' (for example, a speaker almost always, in normal circumstances at least, hears his own vocalisations, even though they sound different to him than to others). This possibility of total feedback is significant when it comes to 'practising' or 'learning' to produce signals (not only humans learn to speak in this 'self-correcting' way, but many patterns of bird song are elaborated through a use of 'feedback'). Total feedback also has a significant connection with interchangeability – where the signals produced by a 'sender' are 'self-observed', the roles of 'sender' (active participant) and 'receptor' (passive participant) are not so clearly distinguished; the 'sender' always constitutes, at one and the same time, a passive participant in perceiving his own signals.

(6) Specialisation

In some forms of communication, the 'message' conveyed by a 'signal' is biologically connected with the causes of which the production of the 'signal' is a consequence (for example, the distended abdomen of a female stickleback is 'interpreted' by male sticklebacks as a 'signal' for breeding; the female does not, however, distend her abdomen to produce the 'signal'; it is her biological readiness for breeding, that is to say, the accumulation of roe in her abdomen, that is the cause of the distended appearance). Such cases typify non-specialised communication (indeed it is doubtful whether one should speak of 'communication' – that is, the production and reception of 'signals' – in such instances). At the other extreme, certain signals are produced in the total absence of a biological link between their production and their 'meaning' or 'message' (for example, the circular movements produced in the 'round' dance of bees, indicating a source of nectar near the hive, have a biological 'purpose', but are not produced through any conceivable biological causes connected with the nearness of nectar to the hive). Communication of this type is 'communication proper', designated as being *specialised*. (The explanation of the production of a specialised signal is 'purposive', but not 'causal'.)

(7) Semanticity

There are, on the one hand, forms of 'communication' that act as direct biological triggering for a response (for example, the 'courtship' behaviour of sticklebacks, cited above). In this type of communication, the link between the 'signal' and the appropriate response it triggers does not involve us in having to conceive of special semantic associations (? constitutive conventions) in order to explain how 'communication' takes place (the trigger-mechanisms are purely of a natural, 'causal' type, and do not presuppose any specialised 'mental' activity in the 'communicating' organisms). On the other hand, there are forms of communication – human languages are foremost instances – that can only be envisaged on the understanding that the participants are able to operate with (abstract and general) associative links between type of signal and type of information; that is to say, with associations that have the nature of special semantic conventions. The presence of such abstract links assures the semanticity of a particular form of communication. (It is, however, slightly odd that semanticity in bee-dancing should involve Hockett in the tacit claim that this form of communication is based on semantic conventions; presumably a corollary would be that bees are endowed with the 'mental' capacity to operate with such abstract conventions.)

(8) Arbitrariness (cf. Peirce and Saussure, Chapter 1)

Semanticity in a system of communication leaves open two possibilities: (*a*) iconic motivation, (*b*) absence of motivation (= arbitrariness) in the associative link between 'signal' and 'message'. Once again, human languages are at one extreme, that of *arbitrariness* (for most 'signals'). Bee dancing (according to Hockett) is 'iconic'; the angle of flight with respect to the position of the sun is 'iconically' represented by the angle of the dance from the vertical.

(9) Discreteness

Some forms of communication work with repertoires of signals arranged along a continuum, in such a way that every one of an infinite number of points along that continuum constitutes a different signal type (opposed to all others). Thus, for instance, the angle and rate of every bee dance makes it a unique signal correlated with a particular type of 'message' along the continuum of flight angle and flight distance. In other forms of communication, however, signals cluster round discrete types (for example, the inventory of bird song falls, in general, into five or six discrete types of signal – actual signals emitted are opposed to one another according to the type they fall into, and in-between possibilities are not admissible; for example, a given signal is either a realisation of the 'mating song' type, or it is the realisation of some other type, but never of some intermediate alternative).

(10) Displacement
In some forms of communication, the 'substance' of the 'message' is spatio-temporally removed from the context in which the signal is realised. This property is referred to as 'displacement' (for example, a signal whose 'message' amounts to a request for an apple, but which is emitted in the total absence of the stimuli of any apple, is a displaced signal). It is easy to see that displacement involves the role of 'memory' in the participants of this type of communication (for example, unless both 'sender' and 'receptor' can remember what apples are like and, of course, the appropriate signal used in asking for apples, displaced signals in requesting an apple are inconceivable). In most animals, displaced behaviour is infrequent ('out of sight, out of mind' seems to be the order of the day); signals are usually only emitted under the direct stimulation of the biological 'purpose' that constitutes their 'meaning' (for example, a 'danger signal' is only emitted by, say, a bird under the influence of immediately perceived danger). The virtual inability to produce displaced signals (at 'will') limits the possibility of 'uttering falsehoods'; in general, animals cannot use communicative behaviour for the purposes of lying. However, while the ability to 'tell lies' cannot be a matter of degree, the question of displacement does allow degrees. For instance, a 'scout' bee is no longer under the direct stimulation of a perceived source of nectar when it performs its dance inside the hive (some form of 'memory storage' must be involved); yet without a relatively immediate real stimulation by a perceived source of nectar, the dance will not be performed. This is to be contrasted to the human ability to talk about 'objects' that never have been observed (for example, I have never perceived the North Pole, yet here I am, writing about it).

(11) Productivity
Communicative systems 'designed' for the purpose of creating 'novel' signals by combination of existing basic signals (cf. *economy*, Chapter 6, 2.2, p. 163 and Chapter 7, Section 7.3.2, p. 191) are designated by Hockett as 'productive' (for example, bee dancing is 'productive' in this sense, since conveying information about a 'novel' source of nectar involves the production of a complex signal by combining one of the available flight-angle indicating signals (total available set is a continuum) with one of the available flight-distance indicating signals (yet again, the total available set forms a continuum). Other forms of communication merely draw on a limited and ready-made inventory (cf. simple systems, Chapter 7, Section 7.3.2, p. 191) that only allows the 'reproduction', not the 'production', of signals (for example, bird song).

(12) Duality
This property of Hockett's version is what, in functionalist semiology, is referred to as the 'double articulation' (Chapter 6, Section 6.2.2, p. 164). Some communication systems (primarily, perhaps exclusively, of the type of human languages) display economy of patterning not only on the level of meaningful elements (Hockett's 'pleremes'), but also on a second level of meaningless, but differential, units (Hockett's 'cenemes'). (Compari-

son may be usefully made between 'duality', and the notions of cenological and plerological economy, Chapter 7, Section 7.3.2, p. 192.)

(13) Cultural or Traditional Transmission
Some forms of communication involve an ability that is entirely genetically transmitted (for example, experiments with species of birds have
shown, more or less conclusively, that 'call notes' are 'instinctual', in the
sense that they are produced by specimens that have not had the
opportunity to learn them from adult members of their species). Other
forms of communication (and, once again, human languages stand first
and foremost in this category) require long periods of 'acquisition' and
'apprenticeship', and are transmitted entirely by learning, from generation to generation.

A study of animal communication (in a given species) that is organised
round these thirteen dimensions and sets itself the task of answering the
various questions that are raised by a consideration of these dimensions,
is liable to be of more theoretical (and descriptive) value than a study
lacking such principled guidance. In this lies the usefulness of Hockett's
theoretical attempt. (It is not to be precluded, however, that other
semiotic theories could provide at least as good a theoretical basis for
zoo-semiotic research.)

10.2 Communication in Social Bees: Karl von Frisch

10.2.1 An Appraisal of von Frisch's Research

The most impressive piece of research that I have encountered in the field
of zoo-semiotics is represented by the life-long work of Karl von Frisch on
the communication of bees. It is not merely as a 'representative sample'
that this research has been singled out for discussion here. It also
constitutes an outstanding example of what zoo-semiotic research can
achieve at its best, as well as acquainting the reader with a particularly
fascinating case in animal communication.

While the procedures used by von Frisch for testing and refining his
hypotheses about the communicative behaviour of bees are admirable
and interesting in themselves, we shall limit ourselves here only to the
general conclusions drawn from these procedures. Suffice it to say that
von Frisch's study is not merely an analysis of bee dancing as a 'performance', but that its correlations with 'messages' are carefully researched
and analysed, and wholly convincing. Von Frisch's experiments leave no
serious doubt as to the 'semantic' content of bee dancing, and establish
that semantic content with great precision – that is to say, the study is not
merely a behavioural one, but zoo-*semiotic* in the full sense.

10.2.2 The 'Round Dance'

When a 'scout' bee locates a source of nectar near the hive (at less than
100 m distance), she fills her honey stomach with the nectar. On returning

to the hive, she lets a drop of honey appear at her mouth. This 'sample' is taken up by other bees with which the 'scout' comes into contact. By these means, other 'foragers' are made aware of the precise quality of nectar discovered by the 'scout' (that is, by practical means, they are informed of what to look for). After distribution of the 'sample', the 'scout' bee performs the movements of the so-called 'round dance'; she describes circles, not more than three or four cells in diameter, on the surface of the honeycomb, reversing her direction after every one or two complete circles (see Figure 10.1). The 'dance' is usually interrupted by further distribution of 'samples', and resumed several times.

Figure 10.1

In response to the 'dance', closely attended by foragers to whom 'samples' have been distributed, these foragers set out and locate within minutes the source of nectar from which the sample has been drawn.

In communicative terms, therefore, the 'round dance' may be said to constitute an index in the inventory of the communication system of bees. This index may be represented ('translated' into English) as: 'round dance→presence of source of nectar somewhere near the hive'.

Experiments have shown the information value to be no more (but also no less) specific than this – there is evidence, however, that 'near the hive' may mean anything up to about 100 m from the hive. (The 'round dance' is always used up to a distance of about 25 m; it may give way to the 'tail-wagging dance' – either immediately, or through a 'transition' from 'round dance' to 'tail-wagging dance' – at 25 m to 100 m. At greater distances, the 'tail-wagging dance' is used exclusively. The transition from 'round dance' to 'tail-wagging dance' has its own interest; different species of bees perform different 'dialectal' variants in the way they change from the 'round dance' gradually over to the 'tail-wagging dance'.)

10.2.3 The 'Tail-wagging Dance'

After distributing 'samples' from a distant source (up to 11 km), the 'scout' bee performs a dance in which she repeats 'circuits' consisting of two sections: (1) a straight run during which she waggles her tail rapidly, (2) either (*a*) outward oval runs in alternate directions, or (*b*) S-bend runs.

Thus the shape of a complete 'circuit' of the 'tail-wagging dance' belongs to one of two types (see Figure 10.2).

(1) 'oval circuit'

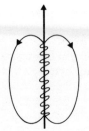

Wavy line represents 'tail-wagging'; arrow through it, direction of straight run.

(2) 'S-bend circuit' (represented by four types of variant recorded)

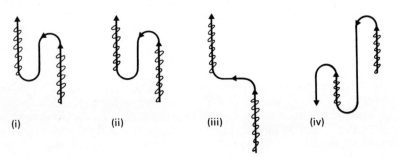

(i)   (ii)   (iii)   (iv)

(There does not appear to be any significant difference of 'meaning' between the variants.)

Figure 10.2

In response to the 'tail-wagging dance', those foragers that have taken 'samples' from, and have observed and attended the 'dance' of the 'scout' bee set out and locate (with remarkable directness and accuracy) the original nectar source of the 'sample'.

In communicational terms, the 'tail-wagging dance' contains two constitutive indices conveying two types of information, respectively 'dance tempo→flight distance', 'direction of straight run→direction of source of nectar'. The totality of a particular 'dance' (containing simultaneously the above two types of index) itself constitutes a complex index of a type we can represent as

'dance at tempo t^n with direction d^x of straight run→
→flight distance and direction of nectar source'

Though, of course, the distance-indicating and direction-indicating constituents always occur simultaneously within a 'dance', these factors are isolatable and independently manipulable variables. It will be convenient to discuss their expression and their information value under separate headings.

Indication of Distance

'Dance sequences' normally last about 13–15 seconds. During that time, the 'scout' bee completes several circuits at a more or less constant tempo – the number of circuits varying with the length of the straight run (which proportionately varies the overall distance covered in each circuit) and, of course, with the actual pace at which the 'dance' is performed. In short, however, the tempo of the 'dance' is calculated in circuits/15 seconds, taken as an average over repeated performances (each lasting about 15 seconds).

The informational content of the 'dance' tempo lies in the correlations that can be set up between that tempo and the distance from the hive of the nectar source discovered by the 'scout' bee. In general terms, the greater the number of circuits (per 15 seconds) – that is, the faster individual circuits are completed, on average – the shorter the flight distance to the nectar source. Figure 10.3 (von Frisch, 1967) illustrates the correlation.

Distance to nectar source	Average number of circuits/15 seconds
100 m	9.45
200 m	7.90
400 m	6.34
600 m	5.59
800 m	4.79
1000 m	4.62
1300 m	4.30
1500 m	4.06
2000 m	3.31
3000 m	2.77
6000 m	1.93
9500 m	1.36

Figure 10.3

The variation between 'oval circuits' and 'S-bend circuits' turns out to be in correlation with flight distance. At distances between 200 m and 4500 m 'S-bend circuits' may be observed, but are performed infrequently and in a random way. At around 4500 m of flight distance, however, 'S-bend circuits' substitute for 'oval circuits' in an average of one out of every three 'dance' performances, and over this distance 'S-bend circuits' are increasingly frequent. At great distances, there is a clear preponderance of the 'S-bend' variant over the 'oval circuit' variant.

There are certain complications with regard to the correlation between tempo and flight distance. If the latter is assumed to be simply the actual linear distance of the nectar source from the hive, the correlations turn out to be rather inexact. It is, however, not information about the real distance that is biologically relevant to forager bees that have to carry enough 'fuel' for the journey; what is relevant is the flight effort in which adverse weather conditions have to be compensated for (for example, additional 'distance' is incalculated to compensate for a head-wind). Furthermore, evidence indicates that, while the flight effort required for the outward run is the main factor in 'converting' actual distance into 'flight distance' allowance is made also for the homeward run. (Since the flight speed of bees in neutral weather conditions is relatively constant, one may be tempted to think that, in compensating for weather conditions, 'flight distance' is converted into 'flight time'. Von Frisch's experiments show that this is not actually the case – while 'flight distance' is a calculable factor on the basis of real distance, wind direction and speed, outward run, homeward run, it is not a straightforward mathematical average over these variables. It is, as it were, processed through 'weighting' that makes it a more complex, though still systematic and calculable function of the variables.) Once 'flight distance' is calculated in these more complex terms (von Frisch, 1967), its correlation with the tempo of the 'dance' shows itself to be remarkably exact, certainly exact enough to leave no other plausible explanation than that the tempo of the 'dance' is an index of 'flight distance'.

Indication of Direction

Two main variants must be considered here, and it will be helpful to treat them under separate headings: (1) indication of direction by 'dances' performed on a horizontal surface; (2) indication of direction by 'dances' performed on a vertical surface.

In both cases, the correlations (between index and information) are between the *direction of the straight run* portion of the 'dance' (represented by an arrow through a wavy line in diagrammatical form) on the one hand, and the direction of the nectar source (goal) from the hive on the other.

The correlation in the case of the horizontal surface variant of the 'dance' is relatively straightforward. Using the sun as a fixed point of reference both for the flight direction and for the direction of the straight run in the 'dance', the 'scout' bee simply reproduces the flight angle from the hive by the angle at which she performs the straight runs of the dance.

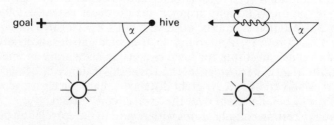

Figure 10.4

Nectar source at α degrees to left of sun

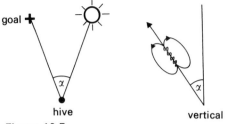

goal

hive

vertical

Figure 10.5

Nectar source at β degrees to right of sun

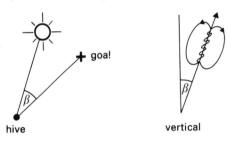

goal

hive

vertical

Figure 10.6

Nectar source in direction of sun

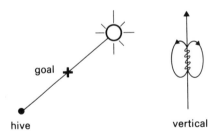

goal

hive

vertical

Figure 10.7

Nectar source in direction away from sun

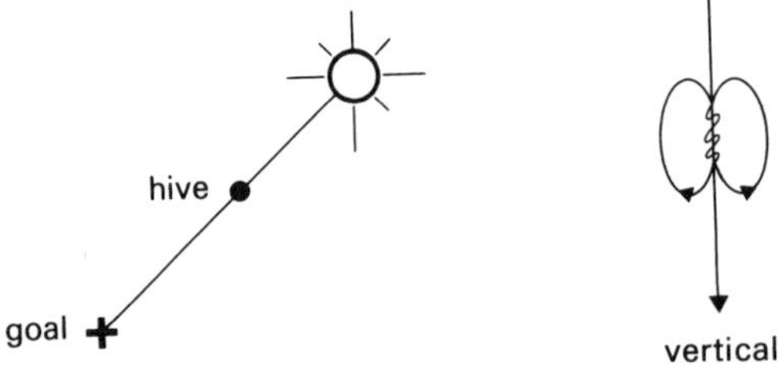

hive

goal

vertical

Figure 10.8

The correlation, in the case of the vertical 'dance' – performed, as is normally the case in non-experimental conditions, on the vertical surface of the honeycomb – is much less straightforward. Here the straight segment of the 'dance' is made to reproduce the same angle with respect to a vertical line (for which gravity is the point of reference) as the angle formed by the direction of the nectar source (goal) and the direction of the sun.

The 'tail-wagging dance' constitutes a semiological repertoire in which an index from the continuum of 'dance' tempo is combined with an index from the continuum of direction of the straight run – combined information is conveyed about 'flight distance' (itself a point on a continuum) and flight direction (a point on the compass). The repertoire can be represented as in Figure 10.9.

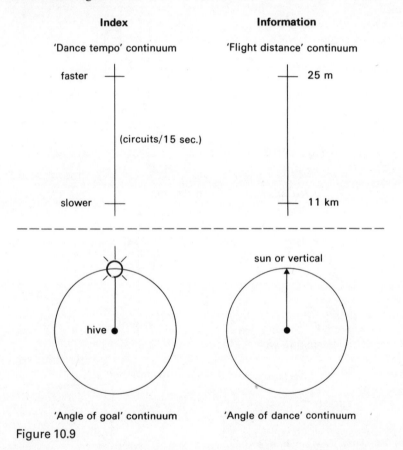

Figure 10.9

Points on the 'dance tempo' continuum are indices corresponding with points on the flight distance continuum; points on the 'angle of dance' continuum are indices corresponding with points on the 'angle of goal' continuum.

In principle, at least, any index from the 'tempo' continuum can combine with any index from the 'angle of dance' continuum to form a complex index (simultaneous bundle, cf. Chapter 7, Section 7.3.2, p. 192) indicating both flight distance and flight direction.

This complexity of indices – drawn from two continua; that is, non-discrete in Hockett's sense (cf. Section 10.1.4, p. 250 above) makes bee dancing a unique type of zoo-semiotic system.

10.3 Apes and 'Language'

10.3.1 An Appraisal of Research on the Linguistic Ability of Apes

The majority of zoo-semiotic research has as its objective the study of 'normal' communicative behaviour of animals in their natural habitat. Thus, even where experimental conditions are set up, these conditions seek to reproduce an environment conducive to discovering the behaviour patterns of animals in the wild, as opposed to the habits they might be induced to acquire in captivity.

There is, however, one branch of (recently much publicised) zoo-semiotic research that explores, and attempts artificially to push to the limit, the inherent capacities of certain species of primates to indulge in 'higher' forms of semiotic activity (that is, in 'linguistic' activity that could not be evidenced in the wild). This branch of research has been directed at studying the extent to which apes (especially chimpanzees, but also gorillas) are capable of being taught human-like language abilities.

Speculation about the possibility of teaching a language to an ape predates modern research in this area by at least two centuries. The success of such research was, however, initially blocked by the assumption that the vocal aspect of human speech is an essential ingredient of human language. As a result of this assumption, early research was directed at trying to teach apes to speak – the ability to speak (vocalise) being seen as inseparable from human linguistic ability in general.

The important lesson learnt from the failure of these experiments – even the chimpanzee Vicki, brought up in a home environment (and treated virtually as a human child) by Keith and Cathy Hayes between 1947 and 1954, only managed to learn four rough approximations to the words 'mama', 'papa', 'cup' and 'up' – can be summed up in the following points:

(1) apes appear to lack (genetically) the tendency to reproduce and imitate vocal speech sounds and, therefore, cannot be expected to learn human speech;
(2) the physiological and anatomical make-up of apes is (probably) unsuited to the production of human-like speech sounds;
(3) apes show a high degree of passive ability to 'understand' a large variety of vocal signs (though they are unable to reproduce them);
(4) there is a notable propensity in apes to communicate by way of manual gestures.

While the first two of these conclusions suggest an explanation, other than a total lack of linguistic ability (and intelligence), for the fact that apes are unable to learn to speak, the last two suggest the germ of an idea for divorcing the ability to speak (vocally) from linguistic ability in general and for testing that ability by the use of a non-vocal 'sign language' (for example, gestural 'sign languages' used by the deaf and dumb). This new direction of research proved to be a breakthrough in the field.

In the mid-1960s, R. Allen and Beatrice Gardner set up a project with the – now world-famous – chimpanzee *Washoe*. Using Ameslan (a gestural semiotic system for the deaf) as a substitute for vocal speech, the Gardners soon found that Washoe made considerable progress in learning signs, and in stringing them together to form simple 'sentences'. The eighty-five (basic) signs of Ameslan that Washoe learnt to use over a period of three years certainly contrast significantly with – and seem impressive when compared to – the four approximations of vocal words learned by Vicki.

Even more significant, in Washoe's use of Ameslan signs, are the following factors:

(*a*) she employed these signs not merely as a repertoire, but as the basic inventory for making up constructions (complex signs) for expressing messages by means of a system with a degree of (plerological) economy (cf. Chapter 7, Section 7.3.2, p. 192);

(*b*) her use of the signs was not a mere 'emotional' response to characteristic 'triggering' situations, but a genuine means of 'intellectual' expression (witness Washoe's ability to produce purely descriptive statements when being shown unfamiliar objects);

(*c*) her use of signs was not in the nature of a 'trick' or of a conditioned response performed in connection with the expectation of a reward (witness, again, Washoe's tendency to use the signs as a spontaneous means of making statements, even when unaware of being observed, apparently purely for their own sake);

(*d*) her use of signs was not the mere copying of rote-learned behaviour, but showed inventiveness and creativity (witness Washoe's readiness to make up a designation for objects whose names had not been taught to her, for example, denoting a duck as a 'water bird', by combining available signs known to her in a, for her, 'new' way);

(*e*) her use of signs was not a mere passive response to a training situation, but a form of behaviour whose usefulness she appeared to appreciate (witness the fact that, in contact with other apes, Washoe made attempts to teach them to communicate in Ameslan).

Other projects similar to the Gardners' work with Washoe – for example, David Premack's project with Sarah, the Lana project directed by Duane Rumbaugh (both started in the early 1970s) – have been designed round the use of specially constructed artificial 'languages'.

Sarah, for instance, learnt to manipulate a system with 130 'words', each of them represented by a piece of plastic of distinctive shape, size and colour.

The Lana project (Rumbaugh, 1977) also makes use of a specially designed 'language' (called 'Yerkish' in honour of the pioneering ideas of Yerkes). In this artificial semiotic system, a number of basic 'design features' (figurae) are combined to make up the forms of 'lexigrams' (basic signs). Each combination of 'design features' is used for labelling a key on a keyboard – 'sentences' are formed by pressing the appropriate keys in an appropriate sequence (for example, 'Lana' – 'drink' – 'juice', in that order, but not 'Juice' – 'drink' – 'Lana', nor, for that matter, 'Lana' – 'eat' – 'juice'.

Researchers in these (and yet other) projects have formed the opinions, in general terms, that

(*a*) apes are fairly adept in learning the use of arbitrary signs (e.g. ' ◇ →eat') – though, of course, quantitatively, their ability is considerably more limited than that of humans (compare the eighty-five signs learnt by Washoe over three years to the hundreds of words known by the average human 3-year-old, and to the thousands of words known by a reasonably educated 10-year-old);

(*b*) apes can form 'sentences' by stringing words together, and can 'compose' syntactically well-formed constructions beyond those they have been explicitly taught (for example, on the basis of using, in other contexts, 'coke', 'which is' and 'orange-coloured' – or rather their equivalents in 'Yerkish' – Lana was able to form, in a 'novel' situation, the combination 'coke which is orange-coloured' for denoting Fanta orange drink);

(*c*) apes can use their 'language' skills appropriately in situations far removed from the specific contexts which were used in teaching those skills (for example, the context in which Washoe learnt the sign for 'baby' had nothing whatever to do with toy animals, yet there is something particularly appropriate about her extended use of the sign for 'baby' in denoting toy animals);

(*d*) apes can use their skills 'creatively' to produce their own 'invented' designations for objects, on the basis of certain salient characteristics of those objects (for example, Washoe's designation of ducks as 'water birds', of Brazil-nuts as 'rock berries', and Lana's reference to over-ripe bananas as 'banana which is black').

10.3.2 Problems in the Evaluation of Ape Research

While the above conclusions are probably justified by the evidence, there are a number of 'strategic' difficulties that are liable to make the evaluation of research on the 'linguistic' ability of apes far from straightforward.

One source of difficulty is the lack of sufficient attention to a detailed semiotic analysis of the structural properties of the 'language' used in a given project. For instance, in projects working with Ameslan, it is all too easy to assume that Ameslan is simply an alternative form of human language used by the deaf and dumb. However, evaluation of what exactly has been learned by an ape 'educated' to use Ameslan depends on knowing precisely what the structural mechanisms of Ameslan are. (For this, it will not do merely to assume that Ameslan is a 'language'; the system may, for example, be structurally analogous with semiotic systems of the 'ideographic' type, or with the semiotic systems of the 'alphabetic' type, viz. Chapter 7, Sections 7.6.2 and 7.6.4, pp. 215 and 217.)

The Lana project is relatively sound in this respect – the system of 'Yerkish' is explicitly set out, so that one may properly evaluate with what underlying semiotic principles Lana was actually taught to operate.

Even in this project, however, the structural role of the 'design features' is insufficiently understood. Are we to understand by the way these 'design features' are combined to make up the forms of 'lexigrams' that 'Yerkish' operates with a cenematic-type subsystem (viz. Chapter 7, Section 7.3.4, p. 197) that 'duplicates' one of the levels of economy not found in Ameslan (as used by apes, at least), but found characteristically in human languages (cf. Hockett's 'duality', above, p. 251)? Is there any guarantee that Lana actually 'operates' with these 'design features'? Does she recognise keys representing 'Yerkish' signs by their global shapes, or is she aware of them as combinations of the 'design features'? These are still important questions that remain unanswered.

A difficulty, or rather danger, of the research is evaluating the 'utterances' of apes made in Ameslan or in 'Yerkish' by first translating them into English. The temptation to report that (to use an earlier mentioned example) Washoe called ducks 'water birds' illustrates a relatively harmless case of falling into this particular trap; Washoe certainly did not *say* 'water bird', this is merely an English translation of what she was understood to have conveyed by using a succession of Ameslan signs. It is easy to see how, translating from another system into English (we know translations to be frequently highly inexact), and reporting the message conveyed as though it had been uttered in English, could have a distorting effect on the scientific precision of descriptions of the 'meanings' of ape utterances.

A related problem is that of a discrepancy between complete proficiency in the *full* use of a semiotic system and a rudimentary ability to use a reduced (and distorted) version of that semiotic system. This problem can best be illustrated through the example of language-acquisition in human children. An infant's utterance, 'Mama go', may appear to give evidence of proficiency in the English language. However, if the infant uses 'mama' to denote several women that it sees – and obviously uses it without any understanding of the relationship that makes a woman 'mother' (to a particular child) – it is a fallacy to suppose that the infant has acquired the use of the English word 'mama' (compare 'mama = any woman' with 'mama = woman who gave birth to a particular child'; the two are obviously not the same sign).

Similarly, if the infant uses 'Mama go' as a request/command, but also uses it as a question, a supposition, the expression of a wishful thought, the constatation of an observed event, and so on, then it is only using an

Design features

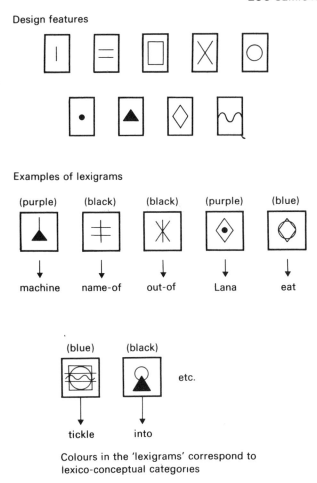

Examples of lexigrams

(purple) (black) (black) (purple) (blue)

↓   ↓   ↓   ↓   ↓
machine   name-of out-of   Lana   eat

(blue)   (black)

etc.

↓   ↓
tickle   into

Colours in the 'lexigrams' correspond to
lexico-conceptual categories

Figure 10.10

index that superficially resembles (but is actually substantially different from) the English sentence 'Mama, go!'.

In short, observing rudimentary sentences that superficially resemble, in the infant's usage, sentences of the English language, does not constitute evidence that the child is able to speak English (the latter implies a fully-fledged use of the system as used by adults).

By analogy, observing rudimentary sentences that *resemble* the use of Ameslan by completely proficient humans does not automatically guarantee that an ape capable of producing these rudimentary sentences is able to use Ameslan (the latter implies a fully-fledged use of the complete system). Just as a reduced version of (a few sentences of) English is not tantamount to the English language, so a selection of a few (eighty-five is relatively few) Ameslan signs does not make up Ameslan.

The ape that uses eighty-five signs drawn from Ameslan is, strictly speaking, operating with a different network of signs (that is, a different system) than the fully proficient user of Ameslan who operates with an at least quantitatively different network of signs. The quantitative difference between the performance of a human who can communicate more or less any message in Ameslan and the performance of an ape that can communicate a few messages by using a few of the signs drawn from Ameslan may conceal a very considerable qualitative difference, similar to that between 'baby talk' and 'adult speech'.

The main problem in evaluating the claims about 'linguistic' ability in apes – a problem that has not gone unnoticed by at least some researchers in the field – is the central question of whether, even if all the evidence of communicative ability in specially 'educated' apes has been correctly interpreted, these pieces of evidence are tantamount to demonstrating the use of a language. As Rumbaugh (1977) points out: 'Without a good and generally accepted definition of language, the questions cannot be answered definitively.'

Language may – in spite of the unexpected, and in a way spectacular, proficiency of apes in Ameslan or 'Yerkish' – still be unique to humans, depending on how exigently one defines its structural properties. For instance, if defined in the way proposed by axiomatic semiotics (Chapter 7) human languages remain unique in the use they make of cenological subsystems as means of structural economy. There is no evidence to date that apes are able to operate with semiotic systems that have a cenematic and a cenotactic economy as well as a plerological (probably plerotactic) one.

10.3.3   The 'Metaphysical' Implications of Ape Research

Reported assessments of the 'linguistic' ability of apes have met with a widely divergent response from scholars in various fields: anything from an outright dismissive attitude (regarding the performance of Washoe *et al.* as something in the nature of a circus trick), to wholesale acceptance without caution. Attempting to steer a middle course between these extremes, it would probably be fair to say that ape research has certainly served to narrow the gap between man and ape – the distinction between (both semiotically and intellectually) 'dumb' animal and linguistically and intellectually sophisticated man, does not appear to be as sharp in the light of this research as it did before. On the other hand, there are plenty of distinctions left, both on the semiotic and on the intellectual plane, to leave an evolutionary gap between primates and humans. The rudimentary semiotic ability of apes, even if it far surpasses all expectations prior to the breakthrough in ape research, does not even qualify as a missing link in terms of the evolution of human language.

Be that as it may, part of the impact of ape research – almost certainly the impact on popular knowledge – is the raising of the old 'metaphysical' question (with attendant moral implications?): how is man superior to animals? (Or, for that matter, is he?) I believe this to be in the nature of an over-reaction, but none the less recognise its importance as a major factor ape research is likely to contribute to 'philosophy'.

Another important side-product of ape research is the new lease of life it gives to evolutionary views of language. While twentieth-century linguistics represents, in general, a slump in scholarly interest in the origins of language, ape research constitutes an occasion for the revival of this field of enquiry. For, whereas speculations about these origins were turning somewhat stale in the absence of evidence that may shed new light on them, ape research may be taken to give an advanced slant and better vantage-point to theories of how a 'linguistic' ability may develop from more rudimentary semiotic abilities.

References

Alexander, R., 'Sound communication in Orthoptera and Cicadidae', in Lanyon, W. and Tavolga, W. (eds.) (1960).

Alston, W. P., *Philosophy of Language* (Englewood Cliffs, New Jersey: Prentice Hall, 1964).

Amacker, R., *Linguistique Saussurienne* (Geneva: Droz, 1975).

Austin, J. L., *How to Do Things with Words* (Oxford: Clarendon Press, 1962).

Bailey, R. W., *et al.* (eds), *The Sign; Semiotics Around the World* (Michigan: Ann Arbor, 1978).

Barthes, R., *Le Degré Zéro de l'Ecriture* (Paris: Editions du Seuil, 1953).

Barthes, R., *Mythologies* (Paris: Editions du Seuil, 1957).

Barthes, R., *Elements of Semiology* (New York: Hill & Wang, 1967a).

Barthes, R., *Système de la Mode* (Paris: Editions du Seuil, 1967b).

Barthes, R., *L'Empire des Signes* (Geneva: Skira, 1970).

Barthes, R., *Mythologies* (English translation) (London: Cape, 1972).

Barthes, R., *S/Z* (New York: Hill & Wang, 1974).

Barthes, R., *Image–Music–Text: Essays Selected and Translated by Stephen Heath* (Glasgow: Fontana/Collins, 1977).

Bentham, J., *Benthamiana*, edited by Burton, J. (Edinburgh: William Tait, 1843).

Benveniste, E., 'Communication animale et langage humain', *Diogène*, vol. 1 (1952).

Berlo, D., *Communication and Behavior* (Reading (Mass.): Addison-Wesley, 1975).

Bierwisch, M., 'Semantic structure and illocutionary force', in Searle, J. *et al.* (1980).

Bloomfield, L., *Language* (London: Allen & Unwin, 1935).

Bourne, G. (ed.), *Progress in Ape Research* (New York: Academic Press, 1977).

Bureau, C., *Linguistique Fonctionnelle et Stylistique Objective* (Paris: PUF, 1976).

Bureau, C., *Syntaxe Fonctionnelle du Français* (Quebec: Les Presses de l'Université Laval, 1978).

Buyssens, E., *Les Langages et le Discours; Essai de Linguistique Fonctionnelle dans le Cadre de la Sémiologie* (Brussels: Lebègue, 1943).

Buyssens, E., *La Communication et l'Articulation Linguistique* (Paris and Brussels: PUF/PUB, 1967).

Carnap, R., *The Logical Syntax of Language* (New York: Dover, 1937).

Carnap, R., *Meaning and Necessity* (Chicago: Chicago University Press, 1947).

Carnap, R., *Introduction to Semantics* (Cambridge (Mass.): MIT Press, 1964).

Cherry, C., *On Human Communication* (Cambridge (Mass.): MIT Press, 1957).

Cole, P. and Morgan, J. L. (eds), *Syntax and Semantics: Speech Acts*, Vol. 3 (New York: Academic Press, 1975).

Culler, J., *Structuralist Poetics* (Ithaca (NY): Cornell University Press, 1975).

Culler, J., *Saussure* (Glasgow: Fontana/Collins, 1976).

Eaton, T., *The Semantics of Literature* (De Proprietatibus Litterarum) (The Hague: Mouton, 1966).

Eco, U., 'Introduction to a semiotics of iconic signs', *Versus*, vol. 2, no. 1 (1972).

Eco, U., *A Theory of Semiotics* (Bloomington (Ind.): Indiana University Press, 1976).

Frisch, K. von, *Bees, their Vision, Chemical Senses and Language* (Ithaca (NY): Cornell University Press, 1950).

Frisch, K. von, 'The language and orientation of bees', *Proceedings of the American Philosophical Society*, vol. 100 (1956).

Frisch, K. von, *The Dance Language and Orientation of Bees* (Cambridge (Mass.): Harvard University Press, 1967).

Granger, G., *Essai d'une Philosophie du Style* (Paris: Colin, 1969).

Greimas, A., *Essais de Sémiotique Poétique* (Paris: Larousse, 1972).

Greimas, A. *et al.*, *Sign, Language, Culture* (Janua Linguarum Series Minor) (The Hague: Mouton, 1970).

Guiraud, P., *Semiology* (London: Routledge & Kegan Paul, 1975).

Guiraud, P. and Kuentz, P., *La Stylistique; Lectures* (Paris: Klincksieck, 1970).

Harré, R., *The Principles of Scientific Thinking* (London: Macmillan, 1970a).

Harré, R., 'Powers', *British Journal for the Philosophy of Science* (1970b).

Hawkes, T., *Structuralism and Semiotics* (Berkeley (Ca): University of California Press, 1977).

Hervey, S., *Functional Semantics; a Linguistic Theory, with Application to Pekingese*, Oxford D. Phil. thesis (1970).

Hervey, S., *Axiomatic Semantics; a Theory of Linguistic Semantics* (Edinburgh: Scottish Academic Press, 1979).

Hervey, S., 'Les postulats de la sémantique fonctionnelle axiomatique' (traduit de l'anglais et présenté par Paul R. Rastall), *La Linguistique*, vol. 16, no. 1 (1980).

Hjelmslev, L., *Prolegomena to a Theory of Language* (Bloomington (Ind.): Indiana University Press, 1957).

Hockett, C., *A Course in Modern Linguistics* (New York: Macmillan, 1958).

Hockett, C., 'Animal "languages" and human language', in Spuhler, J. N. (ed.), *The Evolution of Man's Capacity for Culture* (Detroit (Mich.): Wayne State University Press, 1959).

Hockett, C., 'Logical considerations in the study of animal communication' in Lanyon, W. and Tavolga, W. (eds) (1960).

Jakobson, R., *Selected Writings*, Vol. 3: *The Grammar of Poetry and the Poetry of Grammar* (The Hague: Mouton, 1961).

Jakobson, R., *Essais de Linguistique Générale* (Paris: Editions Minuit, 1963).

Jakobson, R., *Selected Writings*, Vol. 5: *On Verse, Its Masters and Explorers* (The Hague: Mouton, 1979).

Kristeva, J., *Semeiotike; Recherches pour une Sémanalyse* (Paris: Editions du Seuil, 1969).

Kristeva, J., *La Révolution du Langage Poétique* (Paris: Editions du Seuil, 1974).

Kristeva, J. *et al.* (eds), *Essays in Semiotics* (Approaches to Semiotics, Vol. 4) (The Hague: Mouton, 1971).

Lanyon, W. and Tavolga, W. (eds), *Animal Sounds and Communication* (Washington: American Institute of Biological Sciences, 1960).

Lévi-Strauss, C., *Structural Anthropology* (London and New York: Basic Books, 1963).

Lyons, J., *Structural Semantics* (Oxford: Blackwell, 1963).

Lyons, J., *Introduction to Theoretical Linguistics* (London and New York: Cambridge University Press, 1968).

Martinet, A., 'La double articulation linguistique', *Travaux du Cercle Linguistique de Copenhague*, vol. 5 (1949).

Martinet, A., 'Arbitraire linguistique et double articulation', *Cahiers Ferdinand de Saussure*, vol. 15 (1957).

Martinet, A., *Eléments de Linguistique Générale* (Paris: Colin, 1960).

Martinet, J., *Clefs pour la Sémiologie* (Paris: Editions Seghers, 1973).

Martinet, J., 'From linguistics to semiology', 'Index, icon, symbol and sign', 'From semiology to linguistics' and 'Semiology and the arts', lectures given at the University of St Andrews, Scotland (mimeographed) (1980).

Metz, C., *Film Language; a Semiotics of the Cinema* (New York: Oxford University Press, 1974a).

Metz, C., *Language and Cinema* (Approaches to Semiotics, vol. 26) (The Hague: Mouton, 1974b).

Metz, C., *Essais Sémiotiques* (Paris: Klincksieck, 1977).

Morris, C., 'Foundations of the theory of signs', *International Encyclopedia of Unified Science*, vol. 1, no. 2 (Chicago: University of Chicago Press, 1938).

Morris, C., *Signs, Language and Behavior* (New York: Prentice-Hall, 1946).

Morris, C., *Signification and Significance* (Cambridge (Mass.): MIT Press, 1964).

Morris, C., *Writings on the General Theory of Signs* (Approaches to Semiotics, Vol. 16) (The Hague: Mouton, 1971).

Mounin, G., *Clefs pour la Linguistique* (Paris: Editions Seghers, 1968).

Mounin, G., *La Communication Poétique* (Paris: NRF, 1969).

Mounin, G., *Introduction à la Sémiologie* (Paris: Editions Minuit, 1970).

Mulder, J., *Sets and Relations in Phonology; an Axiomatic Approach to the Description of Speech* (Oxford: Clarendon Press, 1968).

Mulder, J., 'The strategy of linguistics', *Estudios Ofrecidos a Emilio Alarcos Llorach*, Tomo 3, Oviedo (reprinted in Mulder and Hervey, 1980) (1979).

Mulder, J., 'Postulates for axiomatic functionalism', in Mulder and Hervey (1980).

Mulder, J. and Hervey, S., 'Index and *signum*', *Semiotica*, vol. 4, no. 4 (1971).

Mulder, J. and Hervey, S., *Theory of the Linguistic Sign* (Janua Linguarum Series Minor) (The Hague: Mouton, 1972).

Mulder J. and Hervey, S., *The Strategy of Linguistics* (Edinburgh: Scottish Academic Press, 1980).

Ogden C. and Richards, I., *The Meaning of Meaning* (London: Routledge & Kegan Paul, 1923).

Peirce, C. S., *The Philosophy of Peirce; Selected Writings*, edited by Buchler, J. (London: Routledge & Kegan Paul, 1940).

Peirce, C. S., *Charles S. Peirce's Letters to Lady Welby*, edited by Lieb, I. (Newhaven (Conn.): Whitlock's Inc., 1953).

Peirce, C. S., *Collected Papers of Charles Sanders Peirce*, Vols. 1–8, edited by Hartshorne, C. and Weiss, P. (Cambridge (Mass.): Harvard University Press, 1960).

Peirce, C. S., *Semiotic and Significs; the Correspondence Between Charles S. Peirce and Victoria Lady Welby*, edited by Hardwick, C. (Bloomington (Ind.): Indiana University Press, 1977).

Popper, K., *The Logic of Scientific Discovery* (London: Hutchinson, 1959).

Popper, K., *Conjectures and Refutations* (London: Routledge & Kegan Paul, 1963).

Popper, K., *Objective Knowledge* (revised edition) (Oxford: Clarendon Press, 1973).

Prieto, L., *Principes de Noologie* (Janua Linguarum Series Minor) (The Hague: Mouton, 1964).

Prieto, L., *Messages et Signaux* (Paris: PUF, 1966).

Prieto, L., *Etudes de Linguistique et de Sémiologie Générales* (Paris: Droz, 1975).

Prieto, L., *Pertinence et Pratique* (Paris: Editions Minuit, 1977).

Riffaterre, M., *Essais de stylistique structurale* (Paris: Flammarion, 1971).

Riffaterre, M., *Semiotics of Poetry* (Bloomington (Ind.): Indiana University Press, 1978).

Robey, D. (ed.), *Structuralism: an Introduction* (Oxford: Clarendon Press, 1973).

Rollin, B., *Natural and Conventional Meaning; an Examination of the Distinction* (Approaches to Semiotics) (The Hague: Mouton, 1976).

Roulet, E., *F. de Saussure: Cours de Linguistique Générale* (Paris: Hatier, 1975).

Rumbaugh, D., 'The emergence and state of ape language research', in Bourne, G. (ed.) (1977).

Rumbaugh, D. (ed.), *Language Learning by a Chimpanzee: the Lana Project* (New York: Academic Press, 1977).

Russell, B., *An Inquiry into Meaning and Truth* (London: Allen & Unwin, 1940).

Saussure, F. de, *Cours de Linguistique Générale* (Paris: Payot, 1916).

Savan, D., 'Questions concerning certain classifications claimed for signs', *Semiotica*, vol. 19, nos. 3/4 (1977).

Searle, J. R., 'Austin on locutionary and illocutionary acts', *Philosophical Review*, vol. 77 (1968).

Searle, J. R., *Speech Acts: An Essay in the Philosophy of Language* (London: Cambridge University Press, 1969).

Searle, J. R., 'A taxonomy of illocutionary acts', in Gunderson, K. (ed.), *Language, Mind and Knowledge* (reprinted in Searle, 1979) (Minneapolis (Minn.): University of Minnesota, 1975).

Searle, J. R., 'Literal meaning', *Erkenntnis*, vol. 13 (reprinted in Searle, 1979) (1978).

Searle, J. R., *Expression and Meaning* (London: Cambridge University Press, 1979).

Searle, J. R. *et al.* (eds), *Speech Act Theory and Pragmatics* (Dordrecht: Reidel, 1980).

Sebeok, T. (ed.), *Animal Communication* (Bloomington (Ind.): Indiana University Press, 1968).

Sebeok, T. (ed.), *Perspectives in Zoosemiotics* (Janua Linguarum Series Minor) (The Hague: Mouton, 1972).

Sebeok, T., *Contributions to the Doctrine of Signs* (Studies in Semiotics, vol. 5) (Bloomington (Ind.): Indiana University Press, 1976).

Thody, P., *Roland Barthes: a Conservative Estimate* (Atlantic Highlands (New Jersey): Humanities Press, 1977).

Thorpe, W. H., 'The process of song learning in the chaffinch as studied by means of the sound spectrograph', *Nature*, vol. 173 (1954).

Thorpe, W. H., 'The learning of song patterns by birds with especial reference to the song of the chaffinch, *Fringilla cœlebs*', *Ibis*, vol. 100 (1958).

Thorpe, W. H., *Bird-song; The Biology of Vocal Communication and Expression in Birds* (Cambridge: CUP, 1961).

Todorov, T., *Littérature et Signification* (Paris: Larousse, 1967).

Todorov, T., *The Fantastic; a Structural Approach to the Literary* (Cleveland (Ohio): Press of Case Western Reserve University, 1973.)

Todorov, T., *Poetics of Prose* (Ithaca (NY): Cornell University Press, 1977).

Toussaint, B., *Qu'est-ce que la Sémiologie* (Toulouse: Privat, 1978).

Ullmann, S., *The Principles of Semantics* (Glasgow: Jackson, 1957).

Ullmann, S., *Semantics* (Oxford: Blackwell, 1962).

Ullmann, S., *Meaning and Style* (Oxford: Blackwell, 1973).

Vachek, J., *The Linguistic School of Prague* (Bloomington (Ind.): Indiana University Press, 1966).

Watson, J. B., *Behaviourism* (New York: Norton, 1924).

Index